THE EUROPEAN UNFAIR COMMERCIAL PRACTICES DIRECTIVE

As the Unfair Commercial Practices Directive has had a profound impact on consumer law across Europe, a stock-taking of its effects is urgently needed. Such an assessment is offered by this book. It contains a convincing analysis of key issues like vulnerability, the relationship to other regimes and enforcement.

Thomas Wilhelmsson, Chancellor of the University of Helsinki, Finland

This book does an excellent job in picking out the principal tensions, challenges and evolving practices associated with Directive 2005/29 on unfair commercial practices, an intriguing measure which seeks to establish a common European understanding of 'unfairness' while also closing off the possibility of EU Member States choosing to apply stricter standards.

Stephen Weatherill, Oxford University, UK

The 2005 Unfair Commercial Practices Directive is a watershed in EU regulation of consumer markets. This book, written by experts in EU consumer law, provides insightful and incisive analyses of the emerging policy questions, issues of interpretation and debates on enforcement encountered in the implementation of the Directive throughout the EU.

Iain Ramsay, University of Kent, UK

This volume offers a timely analysis of the experience with the Unfair Commercial Practices and its full harmonisation character several years after it has come into force. It provides a welcome scholarly discussion of many of the post-implementation challenges which have been identified and provides interesting observations for the future development of this area of law.

Christian Twigg-Flesner, University of Hull, UK

Markets and the Law

Markets and the Law is concerned with the way the law interacts with the market through regulation, self-regulation and the impact of private law regimes. It looks at the impact of regional and international organizations (e.g. EC and WTO) and many of the works adopt a comparative approach and/or appeal to an international audience. Examples of subjects covered include trade laws, intellectual property, sales law, insurance, consumer law, banking, financial markets, labour law, environmental law and social regulation affecting the market as well as competition law. The series includes texts covering a broad area, monographs on focused issues, and collections of essays dealing with particular themes.

Other titles in the series

The Law and Economics of Enforcing European Consumer Law
A Comparative Analysis of Package Travel and Misleading Advertising
Franziska Weber
ISBN 978 1 4724 1704 6

The Organizational Contract
From Exchange to Long-Term Network Cooperation in European Contract Law
Edited by Stefan Grundmann, Fabrizio Cafaggi and Giuseppe Vettori
ISBN 978 1 4724 2124 1

International Insolvency Law
Reforms and Challenges
Edited by Paul Omar
ISBN 978 07546 7482 5

The European Unfair Commercial Practices Directive

Impact, Enforcement Strategies and National Legal Systems

Edited by

WILLEM VAN BOOM
Leiden University, the Netherlands

AMANDINE GARDE
University of Liverpool, UK

ORKUN AKSELI
Durham University, UK

Routledge
Taylor & Francis Group
LONDON AND NEW YORK

First published 2014 by Ashgate Publishing

Published 2016 by Routledge
2 Park Square, Milton Park, Abingdon, Oxon OX14 4RN
711 Third Avenue, New York, NY 10017, USA

Routledge is an imprint of the Taylor & Francis Group, an informa business

British Library Cataloguing in Publication Data
A catalogue record for this book is available from the British Library

The Library of Congress has cataloged the printed edition as follows:
The European Unfair Commercial Practices Directive: Impact, Enforcement Strategies and National Legal Systems / By Willem van Boom, Amandine Garde and Orkun Akseli.
p. cm.—(Markets and the Law)
Includes bibliographical references and index.
ISBN 978-1-4724-2340-5 (hardback: alk. paper)
1. Competition, Unfair—Law and legislation—European Union countries. 2. Consumer protection—Law and legislation—European Union countries. I. Boom, W. H. van, editor of compilation. II. Garde, Amandine, author editor of compilation. III. Akseli, N. Orkun (Nazim Orkun) editor of compilation.
KJE6536.E97 2014
343.2407'23—dc23

2014004136

ISBN 9781472423405 (hbk)

Contents

List of Abbreviations *vii*
Notes on Contributors *ix*
Acknowledgements *xii*

Introduction 1
Willem H. van Boom, Amandine Garde and Orkun Akseli

PART I IMPLEMENTATION, APPROXIMATION AND HARMONIZATION

1 UK Implementation of the Unfair Commercial Practices Directive 21
Marios Koutsias and Chris Willett

2 Pre-emption of National Prohibitions of Sale Below Cost: Some Reflections on EU Law between the Past and the Future 45
Bert Keirsbilck

3 The Blacklist of Unfair Commercial Practices: The Black Sheep, Red Herring or White Elephant of the Unfair Commercial Practices Directive? 65
Monika Namysłowska

PART II VULNERABILITY

4 The Vulnerable Consumer in the UCPD and Other Provisions of EU Law 89
Marine Friant-Perrot

PART III THE UCP DIRECTIVE AND OTHER REGIMES

5 Can the UCP Directive Really Be a Vector of Legal Certainty? 109
Amandine Garde

6 The Interaction between the Unfair Commercial Practices Directive and Self-Regulation: The Case of Codes of Conduct 137
Charlotte Pavillon

7 A Common Approach to the Enforcement of Unfair Commercial Practices and Unfair Contract Terms 173
Hans-W. Micklitz

PART IV ENFORCEMENT

8 Law and Economics of Enforcing Misleading Advertising Laws: Incentives of Bona and Mala Fide Traders Assessed 203
Franziska Weber

9 Private or Public Enforcement of the UCP Directive? Sanctions and Remedies to Prevent Unfair Commercial Practices 235
Dörte Poelzig

Index *267*

List of Abbreviations

ACM	Authority Consumer and Market (the Netherlands)
ADR	Alternative Dispute Resolution
AJA	Administration of Justice Act
ASA	Advertising Standards Authority (UK)
CA	Consumer Authority (the Netherlands)
CADR	Consumer Alternative Dispute Resolution
DGCCRF	Direction Générale de la Concurrence, de la Consommation et de la Répression des Fraudes (France)
EASA	European Advertising Standards Alliance
FCA	Financial Conduct Authority
FSA	Financial Services Authority
OFT	Office of Fair Trading (UK)*
TCF	Treating Customers Fairly
TDA	Trade Descriptions Act

*N.B. From 31 March 2014, the powers of the Office of Fair Trading (OFT) were transferred to a number of other bodies, including, most importantly, to the Competition and Markets Authority and, in the case of financial services, to the Financial Conduct Authority.

Notes on Contributors

Orkun Akseli is Senior Lecturer in Commercial Law at Durham University Law School, UK. Dr Akseli teaches Company Law, Commercial Law, International Banking Law and International Commercial Dispute Resolution. He is also the Co-Director of the Institute of Commercial and Corporate Law at Durham University. He has law degrees from Turkey, the United States and the United Kingdom. His monograph, *International Secured Transactions Law: Facilitation of Credit, International Conventions and Instruments*, was published by Routledge in 2011. He is the co-editor of *Financial Regulation in Crisis? The Role of Law and the Failure of Northern Rock* (Edward Elgar, 2011) and editor of *Availability of Credit and Secured Transactions in a Time of Crisis*, which was published in November 2013 by Cambridge University Press. He has published on secured transactions and harmonization of law, financial regulation, arbitration and sale of goods. He is a member of the Turkish Bar.

Marine Friant-Perrot is Director of the Master's Program on economic law at the University of Nantes, France–UMR-CNRS-6297–Droit et changement social. Her research interests and publications cover various aspects of consumer law and food law.

Amandine Garde is Professor of Law at the University of Liverpool, UK. Professor Garde previously lectured at King's College London, at the Faculty of Law in Cambridge where she was also a Fellow of Selwyn College, at the University of Exeter and at the University of Durham. Her research interests lie in the fields of EU Trade, Consumer, Advertising, Food and Public Health Law. She specializes more specifically on the role that legal instruments can play in promoting healthier lifestyles and the well-being of children as a group of particularly vulnerable consumers. She spent a year as a postdoctoral Jean Monnet Fellow at the European University Institute in Florence in 2005–2006 and is a qualified solicitor.

Bert Keirsbilck is Assistant Professor at the Law Faculty of the KU Leuven in Brussels, Belgium, and co-director of Consumer, Competition and Market. Professor Keirsbilck (1980, Oostende) studied law and philosophy at the KU Leuven (lic.iur. 2003; lic.phil. 2004). In 2010, he defended his PhD thesis ('The New European Law of Unfair Commercial Practices and Competition Law', Oxford, Hart Publishing, 2011, lxiv + 702 p.). From May until July 2013, he was a visiting fellow at the Law Department of the London School of Economics of Political Science.

Marios Koutsias is Lecturer in EU Commercial Law at the University of Essex, UK, after having been employed as a research assistant at the Centre for Commercial Law Studies, Queen Mary London. His research and teaching is mainly in the area of Company Law, European Union Law, European Union Company Law and Comparative Law.

Hans-W. Micklitz is Professor of Economic Law since 2007 at the European University Institute, Florence, Italy and Jean Monnet Chair of Private Law and European Economic Law at the University of Bamberg, Germany, on leave. He is head of the Institute of European and Consumer Law (VIEW) in Bamberg. Professor Micklitz studied law and sociology in Mainz, Lausanne/Geneva (Switzerland), Giessen and Hamburg. He has run consultancies for OECD in Paris, UNEP Geneva Switzerland/Nairobi Kenya and CI (Consumers International) Den Haag Netherlands/Penang Malaysia; completed study visits at the University of Michigan, Ann Arbor; been Jean Monnet Fellow at the European University Institute, Florence, Italy; been visiting professor at the Somerville College at the University of Oxford; and is co-founder of the Centre of Excellence at the University of Helsinki. He is holder of an ERC Grant 2011–2016 on European Regulatory Private Law. He has provided consultancies for ministries in Austria, Germany, the United Kingdom, the European Commission, OECD, UNEP, GIZ, and non-governmental organizations. His main fields of activities are European Law, European Private and Consumer Law.

Monika Namysłowska is Assistant Professor in the Chair of European Economic Law, in the Faculty of Law and Administration at the University of Lodz, Poland. She has been a visiting professor in Germany at the University in Regensburg, the Georg-August-University in Göttingen and the Humboldt-University in Berlin. Her research and publications focus on European, Polish and German Economic Law, and particularly unfair commercial practices and consumer law, advertising law and IT law.

Charlotte Pavillon is Assistant Professor of Private Law at Leiden University, the Netherlands. Dr Pavillon studied international relations (MA, 2004) and law (LLM, 2005 cum laude) at the University of Groningen (the Netherlands), where she also read for her PhD. She defended her thesis titled 'Open normen in het Europees consumentenrecht' (Open Norms in European Consumer Law) in 2011. She was appointed a postdoctoral researcher at the Groningen Centre for Law and Governance in 2011. After lecturing in international relations and private law at the University of Groningen from 2002 to 2012, she joined the University of Leiden (the Netherlands) as an assistant professor in January 2013. Her research interests lie in the field of European private law and European consumer law.

Dörte Poelzig is holder of the Chair for Civil Law, German and International Economic Law at the University of Passau in Germany since 2011. Professor Poelzig studied law in Dresden, Konstanz and Heidelberg, Germany, and at the University of Oxford. Her research focuses on Financial Regulation Law, Company Law, Competition Law and Unfair Commercial Practices Law. She has a keen interest in the role and effects of private enforcement.

Willem van Boom is Professor of Law at Leiden University, the Netherlands since 2014, and teaches private law. Formerly, he was professor at Durham Law School and at Erasmus School of Law, Rotterdam, the Netherlands. Van Boom has published widely on various topics in such areas as obligations, property, insolvency and insurance as well as in methodology of private law. He has a keen interest in multidisciplinary legal research; that is why he regularly works with experts in law and economics, empirical legal studies and jurisprudence. His current research focus lies in contracts, torts and insurance, consumer law and civil procedure.

Franziska Weber is Junior Professor for Civil Law and Law and Economics at the University of Hamburg, Germany and Research Fellow at the Erasmus University Rotterdam, the Netherlands. Her main fields of interest concern the law and economics of German and European consumer law enforcement. She successfully defended her European Doctorate in Law and Economics (EDLE) PhD thesis regarding the optimal mix of public and private law enforcement in consumer law in 2012. More generally, she engages in the economic analysis of European law. Her work has a strong focus on comparative law. Since 2011 she is admitted to the bar in Madrid as a Spanish lawyer.

Chris Willett is Professor of Commercial Law, University of Essex, UK, having previously taught at the Universities of De Montfort, Warwick, Brunel and Oxford Brookes. His work is mainly in the broad area of UK, EU and global consumer and contract law, encompassing in particular the law relating to supply of goods and services, food, digital content, financial services, services of general interest and unfair terms and practices.

Acknowledgements

This volume brings together essays on one of the most important consumer protection EU Directives of the past decade, the 2005 *Unfair Commercial Practices Directive*. We wholeheartedly thank the authors for their contributions. The papers were presented at a Durham Law School workshop held in December 2012. The papers were completed in January 2014. We gratefully acknowledge assistance by Durham Law School administrative staff in organising the workshop and to both Erasmus School of Law and Durham Law School for financial support.

The Editors

Introduction

Willem H. van Boom, Amandine Garde and Orkun Akseli

1. The UCP Directive

In 2005, the EU Directive on Unfair Commercial Practices (referred to as the UCP Directive or the Directive) was adopted.[1] The UCP Directive, which evolved from its precursor, the Misleading and Comparative Advertising Directive,[2] has the ambitious aim of addressing unfair commercial practices directly related to distorting consumers' economic behaviour concerning transactional decisions.[3] Here, we give a brief overview of the scope of application and framework of the UCP Directive for the benefit of readers who are new to the subject; those readers well familiar with the UCP Directive may choose to move to Part 2.

The UCP Directive is a horizontal framework directive of a maximum harmonization nature. It has a very broad scope of application as it covers all business-to-consumer commercial practices in all sectors of economic activity.[4] Any business-to-consumer commercial practice before, during and after a

---

1 Directive 2005/29 Directive 2005/29/EC of the European Parliament and of the Council of 11 May 2005 concerning unfair business-to-consumer commercial practices in the internal market and amending Council Directive 84/450/EEC, Directives 97/7/EC, 98/27/EC and 2002/65/EC of the European Parliament and of the Council and Regulation (EC) No 2006/2004 of the European Parliament and of the Council (Text with EEA relevance), *OJ* 2005 L 149/22 (hereafter: UCP directive).

2 Council Directive 84/450/EEC of 10 September 1984 relating to the approximation of the laws, regulations and administrative provisions of the Member States concerning misleading advertising, *OJ* 1984 L250/17, as amended by Directive 97/55/EC of the European Parliament and of the Council of 6 October 1997 amending Directive 84/450/EEC concerning misleading advertising to include comparative advertising, *OJ* 1997 L290/18. Further on the historical background of the UCP Directive, see J Stuyck, E Terryn and T Van Dyck, 'Confidence through Fairness? The New Directive on Unfair Business-to-Consumer Commercial Practices in the Internal Market' (2006) 43 *Common Market L.Rev*. 107, 109 ff.

3 According to art 2(k) UPC Directive, 'transactional decision' denotes 'any decision taken by a consumer concerning whether, how and on what terms to purchase, make payment in whole or in part for, retain or dispose of a product or to exercise a contractual right in relation to the product, whether the consumer decides to act or to refrain from acting'.

4 Cf. H Collins, 'The Unfair Commercial Practices Directive' (2005) *ECLR* 417, 418.

transaction is covered by the Directive, thus including marketing, advertising, sales practices and after-sales conduct.[5]

It contains core provisions on unfair commercial practices, a black list of practices deemed unfair, and dedicated rules on various topics such as Codes of Conduct and the relationship with various information duties in other EU legislation. Moreover, the Directive contains provisions on enforcement.

The core of the Directive lies in the prohibition of practices contrary to the requirements of professional diligence which materially distort or are likely to materially distort the economic behaviour of the average consumer with regard to a product or a service.[6] Thus, unfair commercial practices consist of two elements: the (potential for) material distortion of consumers' transactional decision-making and the normative yardstick of professional diligence.[7] The notion of 'material distortion' is further defined as the impairment of the ability to make an informed decision, thereby causing the (average) consumer to take a transactional decision that he would not have taken otherwise.[8] The open-textured concept of 'professional diligence' refers to 'the standard of special skill and care which a trader may reasonably be expected to exercise towards consumers, commensurate with honest market practice and/or the general principle of good faith in the trader's field of activity'.[9]

In practice, however, the main general clause prohibiting unfair commercial practices may be less important than the two more concrete subcategories of *misleading* and *aggressive* practices. If a particular practice fits the description

5 Art 2(d); art 3(1) UCP Directive.

6 Art 5 UCP Directive. Generally on the unfairness concept in the UCP Directive, see, e.g., B Keirsbilck, *The New European Law of Unfair Commercial Practices and Competition Law* (Oxford/Portland: Hart Publishing, 2011) 271 ff.; S Weatherill and U Bernitz (eds), *The Regulation of Unfair Commercial Practices under EC Directive 2005/29. New Rules and New Techniques* (Studies of the Oxford Institute of European and Comparative Law, Oxford: Hart Publishing, 2006) 1 ff.; H-W Micklitz, 'The General Clause on Unfair Practices' in GG Howells, H-W Micklitz and T Wilhelmsson (eds), *European Fair Trading Law. The Unfair Commercial Practices Directive* (Aldershot: Ashgate, 2006) 83 ff.

7 In light of arts 6 and 9 UCP Directive, art 5 UCP Directive serves as a stand-alone 'safety net'. See European Commission, 'First Report on the Application of Directive 2005/29/EC of the European Parliament and of the Council of 11 May 2005 Concerning Unfair Business-to-Consumer Commercial Practices in the Internal Market and Amending Council Directive 84/450/EEC, Directives 97/7/EC, 98/27/EC and 2002/65/EC of the European Parliament and of the Council and Regulation (EC) No 2006/2004 of the European Parliament and of the Council ("Unfair Commercial Practices Directive")' (COM (2013) 139 final) (Brussels: European Commission, 2013) 12.

8 Art 2(e) UCP Directive.

9 Art 2(h) UCP Directive. On 'professional diligence', see, e.g., H Collins, 'Harmonisation by Example: European Laws against Unfair Commercial Practices' (2010) 73 *Modern Law Review* 98 ff.

of either of these two, there is no need to further test whether the practice is also unfair according to the main general clause of unfairness.[10]

Misleading practices are divided into two categories: misleading information and misleading omissions. *Misleading information* consists of those utterances which contain incorrect information and are therefore untruthful or which in any way deceive or are likely to deceive the average consumer, even if the information is factually correct. Such practices cause distortion of the transactional decision-making process of the average consumer in relation to aspects such as the existence or nature of the product, fitness for purpose, usage, quantity, specification, the price or the manner in which the price is calculated, or the need for a service, part, replacement or repair.[11]

Misleading omissions concern the practice of omitting or hiding material information – including the provision of such information in an unclear, unintelligible, ambiguous or untimely manner – which the average consumer needs, according to the context, to take an informed transactional decision and thus causing distortion of the transactional decision-making process of this average consumer.[12]

Aggressive practices involve actual harassment, coercion, the use of physical force, or the use of more subtle techniques involving undue influence such as exploitation of vulnerability or the use of obstacles discouraging consumers from asserting their rights.[13] For example, artificially raising barriers to exit from a contract or to the exercise of contractual rights may constitute an unfair commercial practice.[14]

Apart from these open-textured standards on 'unfair', 'misleading' and 'aggressive' practices, the UCP Directive also imposes specific prohibitions. Annex I to the Directive consists of a 'black list' of certain practices deemed unfair under any circumstances.[15] For example, a commercial practice 'describing a product as "gratis", "free", "without charge" or similar, if the consumer has to pay anything other than the unavoidable cost of responding to the commercial practice and collecting or paying for delivery of the item'.[16] The same single list applies

---

10 ECJ 19 September 2013, Case C-435/11 (*CHS Tour Services GmbH v Team4 Travel GmbH*).

11 Art 6(1) UCP Directive.

12 Art 7 UCP Directive.

13 Art 8 and 9 UCP Directive.

14 European Commission, 'Commission Staff Working Document – Guidance on the Implementation/Application of Directive 2005/29/EC on Unfair Commercial Practices' (SEC (2009) 1666) (Brussels: European Commission, 2009) 11.

15 See art 5(5) in conjunction with Annex I of the UCP Directive. The blacklisted practices are deemed unfair in the sense that no further evidence of unfairness, misleading or aggressive nature is required. On the relationship between the different categories, see, e.g., Stuyck, Terryn and Van Dyck, 132 ff.

16 See Annex I, no 20 of the UCP Directive. Cf. ECJ 18 October 2012, Case C-428/11 (*Purely Creative Ltd and Ors v Office of Fair Trading*).

in all Member States and may only be modified by revision of this Directive. If a practice is listed, there is no need to assess whether it is contrary to the rules of professional diligence and whether it has materially distorted or would have been likely to materially distort the economic behaviour of the average consumer. If this list is not exhaustive of all unfair commercial practices,[17] it nonetheless lists exhaustively all the commercial practices presumed to be unfair.[18]

Apart from prohibitions of unfair commercial practices, the UCP Directive covers two further subjects aimed at introducing positive obligations and promoting fair commercial practices in the European Union. As far as the first aspect is concerned, the UCP Directive includes an obligation on traders to positively disclose certain information at a certain stage of the marketing and sales process. This obligation is incurred whenever traders make an 'invitation to purchase' to consumers.[19] The Directive lists a number of items on which traders need to positively disclose information when 'inviting' consumers to enter a commercial transaction, such as main characteristics and price.[20] As concerns the second aspect, the UCP Directive encourages the use of Codes of Conduct to support the dissemination of *fair* commercial practices. It does so, for example, by designating as misleading the practice of falsely claiming to be a signatory to a code of conduct as well as the practice of undertaking and publicly signalling to be bound by, while at the same time not complying with, firm commitments contained in a code of conduct.[21]

As mentioned, the UCP Directive follows the maximum harmonization principle. However, the Directive contains significant exceptions. Article 3(2) provides that the Directive is without prejudice to contract law and, in particular, to the rules on the validity, formation or effect of a contract (e.g., rules on fraud, mistake and misrepresentation). This is usually understood to be an exception in favour of national private law. Article 3(9) allows more restrictive national rules

17 Art 5(5) read in conjunction with Recital 17.

18 A Garde, 'The Unfair Commercial Practices Directive: A Successful Example of Legislative Harmonisation?', in P Syrpis (ed.), *The Judiciary, the Legislature and the Internal Market* (Cambridge University Press, 2012) 118.

19 According to art 2(i) UCP Directive, an 'invitation to purchase' means a commercial communication which indicates characteristics of the product and the price in a way appropriate to the means of the commercial communication used and thereby enables the consumer to make a purchase. Judging from ECJ 12 May 2011, C-122/10 (*Konsumentombudsmannen / Ving Sverige AB*), traders who advertise their products and services are well advised not to include a price reference in their advertisements since this may lead to the conclusion that they have made an 'invitation'. Cf. *Commission Staff Working Document – Guidance on the Implementation/Application of Directive 2005/29/EC on Unfair Commercial Practices (SEC (2009) 1666)* 47 f.

20 See art 7(4) UCP Directive.

21 See Annex I(1) and art 6(2) (b) UCP Directive. See also art 10 UCP Directive which allows Member States to encourage code owners to exercise control on unfair commercial practices.

in the area of financial services. Thus, as far as financial services are concerned, the Directive is an instrument of minimum harmonization. Furthermore, in case of conflict between the provisions of this Directive and other Community rules regulating specific aspects of unfair commercial practices, the latter shall prevail and apply to those specific aspects (article 3[4]).

Finally, as far as enforcement is concerned, Member States are to implement the Directive and to choose adequate and effective means of combatting unfair commercial practices in the interest of consumers.[22] It is left to Member States to choose the exact form enforcement will take on their territories, as long as it offers persons and organizations having legitimate interest (including competitors) recourse to an administrative or judicial procedure.[23] Such procedures should at least offer the possibility of ordering the prohibition of imminent unfair practices and cessation of on-going practices.[24] Moreover, Member States shall lay down and enforce effective, proportionate and dissuasive penalties for infringements.[25]

2. Three Recurring Themes

The key issues that stand out include: the problematic nature of maximum harmonization by means of general clauses in an area as broad as that of commercial practices; the unpredictable influence on national private law doctrines such as contract, tort and even the practice of self-regulation; and the relative open-endedness of the Directive in relation to both other forms of market regulation and the frameworks of enforcement at Member State level. Three topical and related issues deserve further analysis and have been given a prominent place throughout this volume. First, there is the tension between autonomy, empowerment and protection which can be sensed throughout the UCP Directive. Secondly, there is the problematic nature of the maximum harmonization principle. Thirdly, the ways in which the Directive is enforced at Member State level have given rise to a plethora of questions.

2.1 Tension between Autonomy, Empowerment and Protection

The core of the UCP Directive lies in the *information paradigm*: by assuring a flow of correct and meaningful information, transactional decisions of consumers are undistorted and can therefore be assumed to be taken in accordance with consumer preferences.[26] From this perspective, the UCP Directive is part and parcel of the

22 Art 11(1) UCP Directive.

23 Art 11(1) UCP Directive.

24 Art 11(1) and (2) UCP Directive.

25 Art 13 UCP Directive.

26 The information paradigm is also apparent from the requirement under art 7(4) UCP Directive to provide certain material information prior to contracting. For additional and overlapping 'material information' requirements see art 5(1) of the Consumer Rights

classical economic framework of EU consumer policy. The UCP Directive, like so many rules of EU consumer law, is modelled around the average consumer. This elusive 'average consumer' is a non-existent model of human being, not a statistical average, which serves as a normative yardstick.[27] The framework thus assumes that consumers are rational choice actors who are 'reasonably well informed and reasonably observant and circumspect'.[28]

That said, the UCP Directive does bear witness of the tension between the information paradigm aimed at bolstering autonomy and emphasizing individual responsibility on the one hand and protection of consumers generally and vulnerable groups in particular against repeat-players with superior knowledge on how consumers respond to certain commercial practices and how they can be encouraged, persuaded, seduced, bedazzled, pestered, overloaded and discouraged. The Directive aims at protecting consumers against unfair practices while on the other it underlines the individual's responsibility by reference to the average consumer. According to the Court's case law, the 'reasonably well informed and reasonably observant and circumspect' consumer can be expected to make a serious effort at collecting and understanding all available information on essential aspects of a contract.[29] So, the 'average consumer' is neither credulous, nor easily impressed nor quickly deceived. National courts applying this standard may find themselves offering less protection to consumers than they were used to under pre-existing national protective frameworks.[30]

On the other hand, the 'model consumer' who is confident and proactive in gathering and processing information before making transactional decisions is supplemented by the consumer who is particularly vulnerable 'to the practice or the underlying product because of their mental or physical infirmity, age or credulity'.[31] Obviously, the question is what makes these groups vulnerable in connection with commercial practices. And are they the only ones prone to succumb to certain unfair practices? Given the human model of 'homo heuristicus' developed by behavioural economics, one could even argue that all consumers

---

Directive 2011/83/EU. Obviously, the UCP Directive is also concerned with aggressive commercial practices.

27 *Commission Staff Working Document – Guidance on the Implementation/ Application of Directive 2005/29/EC on Unfair Commercial Practices (SEC (2009) 1666)* 28.

28 ECJ 16 July 1998, C-210/96 (*Gut Springenheide*).

29 ECJ 16 July 1998, C-210/96 (*Gut Springenheide*); ECJ 19 September 2006, C-356/04 (*Lidl and Colruyt*); cf. ECJ 6 July 1995, C-470/93, Jur. 1995 p. I-01923 (*Mars*).

30 On the damping effect of the UCP Directive on more protective legal systems, see eg., Stuyck, Terryn and Van Dyck, 134 ff.

31 Art 5(3). Cf. S Weatherill, 'Who Is the "Average Consumer"?', in S Weatherill and U Bernitz (eds), *The Regulation of Unfair Commercial Practices under EC Directive 2005/29. New Rules and New Techniques* (Oxford: Hart Publishing, 2006) 115 ff.; R Incardona and C Poncibò, 'The Average Consumer, the Unfair Commercial Practices Directive, and the Cognitive Revolution' (2007) 30 *Journal of Consumer Policy* 21, 21 ff.

are vulnerable individuals who merit some form of protection against traders who have superior knowledge on consumer behaviour and on how to make clever use of human deficiencies.[32]

It is sometimes said that consumers should take more responsibility for their decisions. For example, in discharging its duties, the Financial Conduct Authority (FCA), is under a duty to apply a number of principles including the principle 'that consumers should take responsibility for their decisions' (s. 3B FSMA 2000). This sounds stern; but what does that actually mean in markets where products are difficult to comprehend to begin with, are deliberately made even more complex, and where consumers are short-sighted, inert and/or literally or figuratively illiterate? The consequence of all this may be that national courts may feel restrained in offering redress to consumers according to the rather stern 'homo economicus' model underlying the UCP Directive. They may instead resort to national private law to provide fitting remedies when the UCP Directive turns out to be too 'trader friendly'. A prime example of this is offered by a Dutch case. A retail bank who had designed and marketed inherently dangerous investment products to the general public was held liable on the basis of the (precursor to the) UCP Directive for producing a misleading prospectus. The Supreme Court held, in a nutshell, that in this case the EU Directive did not offer any solace. In essence, it ruled that the 'homo economicus' consumer should have been more cautious when reading the material:[33] '[...] it may be expected from a reasonably observant and circumspect consumer that he makes reasonable efforts in advance to comprehend the implications of the contract and its ensuing obligations and risks, and that he prudently considers endorsements, praise and examples.' So, the Dutch Supreme Court did not consider this to be a case of misleading omission under EU rules. Yet, that was not the end of the case. The Court then switched to protection of the 'homo heuristicus' on the basis of national tort law. It ruled that the bank had neglected a duty to explicitly warn for inherent risks of the investment and to check suitability and affordability.[34]

So, the outcome apparently is that national private law may offer better protection for consumers than the UCP framework. Since the UCP Directive is

---

32 The literature is abundant. We merely refer by means of example to CR Sunstein (ed.), *Behavioral Law and Economics* (Cambridge Series on Judgment and Decision Making, Cambridge: Cambridge University Press, 2000); RH Thaler and CR Sunstein, *Nudge – Improving Decisions About Health, Wealth, and Happiness* (New Haven: Yale University Press, 2008); RB Korobkin and TS Ulen, 'Law and Behavioral Science: Removing the Rationality Assumption from Law and Economics' (2000) 88 *Cal. L. Rev.* 1051 ff. For a similar argument, see Stuyck, Terryn and Van Dyck, 121 f.

33 Dutch Supreme Court 5 June 2009, ECLI:NL:HR:2009:BH2815. Cf. WH van Boom, 'The Netherlands' in Civic Consulting (ed.), *Study on the Application of Directive 2005/29/EC on Unfair Commercial Practices in the EU / Part 2 – Country Reports* (Civic Consulting, Berlin, 2011) 7.1 ff.

34 Dutch Supreme Court 5 June 2009, ECLI:NL:HR:2009:BH2815.

without prejudice to contract law[35] – or perhaps even broader: private law? – at the Member State level there may be more than one track for disappointed consumers to follow.

2.2 Maximum Harmonization Principle

Subject to limited exceptions the UCP Directive is subject to the maximum harmonization principle.[36] The underlying rationale is that this guarantees a fair balance between traders' duties and consumers' rights, and creates legal certainty and a pan-European level playing field. However, the generic horizontal character of the Directive, combined with a broad-brushed scope, causes issues of demarcation. It is not entirely clear where the Directive begins and ends. Arguably, this is a problematic feature when combined with the maximum harmonization principle.

There are notable exceptions to the maximum harmonization principle which merit a brief overview. Moreover, the scope of the Directive is defined in such a way that in some respects or for some economic activities, the Directive does not stand in the way of more protective legislation at Member State level:

- *The UCP Directive is an instrument of minimum harmonization in the domains of financial services and immovable property.* By way of exception the UCP Directive is of a minimum harmonization character in these areas.[37] It was thought that the complexity and inherent serious risks surrounding these products and markets may require more detailed and tailored rulemaking at Member State level.[38] In its recent evaluation of the UCP Directive, the European Commission addresses the question whether article 3(9) UCP Directive merits repealing.[39] The Commission concludes that the exceptions to the maximum harmonization principle will be left unchanged.[40] Therefore, Member States will continue to be allowed to apply more stringent rules on commercial practices in the financial services domain.

---

35 Art 3(2) UCP Directive provides that it is 'without prejudice to contract law and, in particular, to the rules on the validity, formation or effect of a contract'.

36 Cf. Recital 14, 15, 5 UCP Directive.

37 Art 3(9) UCP Directive.

38 Recital (9).

39 Art 18 UCP Directive charges the EC with submitting a review of the experiences with the UCP Directive by 12 June 2011. The review was submitted in March 2013.

40 European Commission, 'First Report on the Application of Directive 2005/29/EC of the European Parliament and of the Council of 11 May 2005 Concerning Unfair Business-to-Consumer Commercial Practices in the Internal Market and Amending Council Directive 84/450/EEC, Directives 97/7/EC, 98/27/EC and 2002/65/EC of the European Parliament and of the Council and Regulation (EC) No 2006/2004 of the European Parliament and of the Council ("Unfair Commercial Practices Directive")' (COM (2013) 139 final), Brussels 2013.

- *The UCP Directive does not harmonize contract law.* The Directive explicitly states that it 'is without prejudice to contract law and, in particular, to the rules on the validity, formation or effect of a contract'.[41] One may ask whether 'contract law' should not be read as 'private law' since some jurisdictions categorize pre-contractual duties or defectiveness of consent as part of tort law rather than contract law.[42]
- *Health and safety aspects.* The Directive itself more or less excludes rules relating to 'the health and safety aspects of products' from its scope by stating that the Directive is 'without prejudice' to such rules.[43] This seems to be a rather enigmatic exception since the Directive concerns the protection of informed and unintimidated transactional decision-making. If the exclusion of health and safety aspects of products is to be justified by the fact that such rules relate to the quality of products or by some motive to protect consumers against specific risks or against themselves, then surely more rules can be deemed excluded. For instance, should commercial practices concerning gambling not be explicitly excluded as well?[44]
- *Rules pertaining to regulated professions are outside the scope of the Directive.* So, national authorization regimes and establishment restrictions remain unaffected by the Directive.[45] Also, national requirements related to 'taste and decency' are considered to be outside the scope of the Directive.[46]
- *Scope of consumer protection.* The Directive aims at protecting consumers. This raises the question whether more restrictive national rules which may have a bearing on business-to-consumer relationships but in fact have a different goal (for instance, the protection of competitors) are affected by the Directive. One can think of restrictions of retail shops opening hours for the protection of employees and prohibition of Sunday trading for religious reasons. In *Pelckmans Turnhout*, the ECJ ruled that national provisions genuinely pursuing other objectives than consumer protection are outside the scope of the Directive.[47]

---

41 Art 3(2) UCP Directive.

42 Cf. the German notion of liability for 'culpa in contrahendo' (§§ 311 [2] Bürgerliches Gesetzbuch) or the French liability for 'fautes' in precontractual dealings (art 1382 Code Civil).

43 Art 3(3) UCP Directive.

44 Note that Recital (9) of the Preamble to the UCP Directive suggests that regulation concerning gambling services remain unaffected by the Directive. This probably only follows if one underwrites to a broad interpretation of art 3(8) UCP Directive so as to include any regulatory regime setting quality standards or prohibiting certain practices. Admittedly, if one accepts such a broad construction of 'any conditions of establishment or of authorisation regimes imposed on professionals' then the UCP Directive as a whole is effectively neutralized by regulatory regimes at Member State level.

45 Art 3(8) UCP Directive.

46 See Recital 7 Preamble UCP Directive.

47 ECJ 4 October 2012, C-559/11, *Pelckmans Turnhout NV v Walter Van Gastel Balen et al.* Note that the ECJ queries whether the objectives are 'related' to consumer

- *Collisions with other EU rules.* In case of conflicting rules, the Directive gives way to those specific rules.[48] For instance, where a dedicated EU regulation sets particular rules on information disclosure in the online sales of airline tickets which are more specific and stricter than the UCP Directive rules on pre-contractual information duties, these special rules have priority. This is also the case where these specific EU rules are of a minimum harmonization character.

Leaving these exceptions aside, the scope of the maximum harmonization nature of the Directive is contested. The dominant position seems to be that the Directive does not allow categorical prohibitions of certain practices if and to the extent that such national prohibitions aim at consumer protection. This would interfere with the Directive's all-encompassing scope of maximum harmonization, or so the ECJ holds. In fact, the ECJ has ruled that a national regime generally prohibiting combined offers is incompatible with the UCP Directive. Likewise, a general prohibition of practices making the participation in a prize competition or lottery conditional on the purchase of goods is incompatible with the UCP Directive.[49] The same applies to general prohibitions of sales with bonuses,[50] general prohibitions of advertising upcoming sales in a particular period[51] or without authorization.[52] Note that while general prohibitions are not allowed, there can be good reasons to intervene in particular cases where a promotional offer or other marketing technique contravenes the standards for misleading, aggressive or otherwise unfair commercial practices. This would, however, require individual assessment in light of the given circumstances, which is significantly different from an unconditional and general ban on certain practices.

The upshot of all this is that Member States cannot administer their own national 'black lists'. The Annex is exhaustive. The basic idea of an exhaustive black list was justified with the argument that 'it was essential to overcome the

---

protection, which may a broader and more factual test than the mere enquiry into the aims of the national provisions. See also recital (6) of preamble to the UCP Directive, which states that the Directive "[…] neither covers nor affects the national laws on unfair commercial practices which harm *only* competitors' economic interests or which relate to a transaction between traders" (emphasis added, eds).

48 ECJ 23 April 2009, C-261/07 and C-299/07 (*VTB–VAB NV v Total Belgium NV* and *Galatea BVBA v Sanoma Magazines Belgium NV*). In a similar vein ECJ 11 March 2010, C-522/08 (*Telekomunikacja Polska*).

49 ECJ 14 January 2010, C-304/08 (*Zentrale zur Bekämpfung unlauteren Wettbewerbs eV v Plus Warenhandelsgesellschaft mbH*).

50 ECJ 9 November 2010, Case C-540/08 (*Mediaprint Zeitungs– und Zeitschriftenverlag GmbH & Co KG v 'Österreich'–Zeitungsverlag GmbH*).

51 ECJ 15 December 2011, C-288/10 (*Wamo BVBA v JBC NV and Modemakers Fashion NV*) and ECJ 11 December 2011, C-126/11 (*Inno NV v Unizo and others*).

52 ECJ 17 January 2013, C-206/11 (*Köck v Schutzverband gegen unlauteren Wettbewerb*).

specific legal barriers caused by the fragmented regulation of unfair commercial practices, which gave rise to cost, complexity and uncertainty for both businesses and consumers.'[53] However, it is debatable whether having a fixed list at the EU level without any room for considering 'local practices' that may merit similar outright banning is the most efficient way of dealing with unfair commercial practices in Europe. Responding to national incidents by amending rules and thus prohibiting certain unfair practices at a national level to curb excesses can be part of a rational, devolved policy-making process. By pre-empting legislative intervention at the Member State level, national 'black lists' have been rendered impossible and so have the national legislative policies targeting 'local' unfair practices. What remains, is the aspiration of maximum harmonization by means of a combination of a European black list and general clauses on misleading, aggressive and unfair commercial practices broadly defined. As will be shown throughout this volume, it remains to be seen whether this aspiration, supported by the EU 'mantra' of increasing legal certainty for both consumers and businesses through maximum harmonization,[54] is realistically attainable in this area.[55]

2.3 Enforcement

Member States are supposed to have implemented the UCP Directive by 12 June 2007.[56] The range of techniques applied by Member States in implementing the UCP Directive differs vastly.[57] In the United Kingdom, the Directive was implemented through the Consumer Protection from Unfair Trading Regulations 2008 (SI 2008/1277).[58] The legal embedding of the Directive in the United

53 (COM (2013) 139 final) 4.

54 See, e.g., Recital (12).

55 Cf. Stuyck, Terryn and Van Dyck, 148; B Keirsbilck, 'Towards A Single Regulatory Framework on Unfair Commercial Practices?' (2009) *EBLR* 507, 509.

56 Art 19 UCP Directive. The measures shall be applied by 12 December 2007. Until 12 June 2013, Member States are allowed under specific conditions to continue to apply 'national provisions within the field approximated by this Directive which are more restrictive or prescriptive than this Directive and which implement directives containing minimum harmonisation clauses' (art 3(5) UCP Directive).

57 Generally on the differences in enforcement style and culture in consumer law, see the contributions to WH van Boom and MBM Loos (eds), *Collective Enforcement of Consumer Law – Securing Compliance in Europe through Private Group Action and Public Authority Intervention* (European Studies in Private Law, Groningen: Europa Law Publishing, 2007) .

58 In the United Kingdom, administrative enforcement powers are assigned to the Competition and Markets Authority (CMA; formerly: OFT) and the local Trading Standards authorities. See Consumer Protection from Unfair Trading Regulations 2008 as amended by the Public Bodies (The Office of Fair Trading Transfer of Consumer Advice Scheme Function and Modification of Enforcement Functions) Order 2013. Enforcement in the financial services domain is the responsibility of the FCA. See S. 213 Enterprise Act 2002 as amended by s. 95 Financial Services Act 2012.

Kingdom is such that originally individual consumers were not entitled to redress on the basis of the Regulations, nor are their contracts directly affected. Instead, enforcement is largely achieved by administrative enforcement orders and criminal law sanctions.[59] However, the amendment of the Consumer Protection from Unfair Trading Regulations 2008, which is currently underway, will introduce under specified conditions individual rights of redress for consumers (i.e., the right to unwind, the right to a discount and a right to damages).[60]

In Germany, where there is a rich legislative tradition of prohibiting unfair commercial practices as part of competition law, the UCP Directive was implemented by means of amendment of the pre-existing framework of the Act against Unfair Competition (Gesetz gegen den unlauteren Wettbewerb; UWG). The German enforcement model traditionally relies on private actions for injunction initiated by representative organizations although recently a public authority was assigned the task to address cross-border unfair commercial practices.[61] Essentially, the German enforcement model relies on private law rather than criminal law remedies.[62]

By contrast, in the Netherlands implementation measures include implementing a tort of unfair commercial practices in the Civil Code supplemented by administrative law fining powers and enforcement orders. Here, the emphasis is on a two-track system of individual and representative civil litigation on the one hand and administrative law enforcement on the other. In Dutch practice, however, the role of sophisticated self-regulation to distinguish reputable traders from rogue traders plays an important 'soft-law enforcement role' as well.[63]

These few examples show some of the differences in enforcement culture at Member State level. In particular, the Member States are left to decide whether the concept of unfair commercial practices is introduced in private law and consequentially whether private law remedies are available to individual consumers.[64]

---

59 *McGuffick v Royal Bank of Scotland plc* (2009) EWHC 2386 (Comm). Cf. Enterprise Act 2002, Part 8 (Enforcement of certain consumer legislation). See also L Fox O'Mahony, *Home Equity and Ageing Owners – Between Risk and Regulation* (Oxford: Hart Publishing, 2012) 259; Collins, 111 ff.

60 Consumer Protection from Unfair Trading (Amendment) Regulations 2013 (draft regulations).

61 See the Consumer Protection and Food Safety Authority Act 2002 (Gesetz über die Errichtung eines Bundesamtes für Verbraucherschutz und Lebensmittelsicherheit [BVL-Gesetz-BVLG]).

62 Yet, the UWG does penalize certain infringements; see §16–19 UWG.

63 See further van Boom para 7.1 ff.

64 See G De Cristofaro, 'Die zivilrechtlichen Folgen des Verstoszes gegen das Verbot unlauterer Geschäftspraktiken: eine vergleichende Analyse der Lösungen der EU-Mitgliedstaaten' (2010) *Gewerblicher Rechtsschutz und Urheberrecht Internationaler Teil* (GRUR Int) 1017, for an overview of choices made by Member States.

The lack of uniformity in the choice of enforcement framework is obviously the result of the leeway left by the Directive to Member States. As long as the national framework sanctions infringements effectively, proportionately and dissuasively,[65] and offers individuals, businesses and interested organizations recourse to an administrative or judicial procedure concerning prohibition and stopping orders,[66] the obligations under the UCP Directive are satisfied. Understandably, the result of this application of the principle of national procedural autonomy is the continued existence of differences in enforcement framework, style and culture across the Member States. Hence, it may not come as a surprise that in its recent report on the application of the UCP Directive, the European Commission mainly considers pathways towards strengthening enforcement activities at member state level and for cross-border practices.[67]

3. The Contributions Gathered in This Collection

Having briefly introduced the three themes that are woven into the fabric of the contributions to this book, we can now summarize the various chapters and see how they interrelate. The book is roughly divided into four parts.

3.1 Implementation, Approximation and Harmonization

Part I deals with issues of implementation, approximation and harmonization. As noted earlier, the maximum harmonization nature of the UCP Directive and the exceptions to its scope raise particular issues of convergence and divergence of national legal systems. For instance, in what areas does the UCP Directive leave room for manoeuvring? In what ways does the UCP Directive cause frictions with domestic law? Does it conflict with other areas of EU and domestic consumer law?

In their contribution 'UK Implementation of the Unfair Commercial Practices Directive', Marios Koutsias and Chris Willett take some of these issues as a starting point to discuss the UK experience with the UCP Directive. Their analysis shows that while the traditional UK approach was one of criminal enforcement, the developments surrounding the implementation of the UCP Directive have prompted a blending of this traditional approach with a seemingly more European enforcement approach which stresses preventive techniques. In other respects, the authors argue, the process of 'Europeanization' through the UCP Directive has started to influence fairness concepts in the domestic regulatory landscape and perhaps even in private law. As concerns the substantive reach of the Directive, Koutsias and Willett also predict that the regulation of commercial practices in the financial services industry will largely remain outside the maximum harmonization

65 Art 13 UCP Directive.
66 Art 11(1) and (2) UCP Directive.
67 COM (2013) 139 final.

principle and hence within the national legislative realm. The 'home grown' financial services regime is likely to remain dominant, they convincingly argue.

Bert Keirsbilck devotes his contribution 'Pre-emption of National Prohibitions of Sale Below Cost: Some Reflections on EU Law Between Past and Future' to the troublesome pre-emptive effect of the maximum harmonization principle underlying the Directive. As mentioned earlier, the fact that the Directive moves well into border territories of generic market regulation raises numerous issues of demarcation. For instance, national prohibitions of sales below cost obviously affect consumers but are usually also aimed – or even primarily or exclusively aimed – at some sort of protected competition. To what extent do such market design rules clash with the UCP Directive? Keirsbilck focuses on the viability of national prohibitions of sales below cost in light of European law. He argues that the maximum harmonization principle underlying the Directive forbids national prohibitions of business-to-consumer sales below cost in so far as such prohibitions pursue consumer protection objectives.

In her contribution 'The Blacklist of Unfair Commercial Practices: The Black Sheep, Red Herring or White Elephant of the Unfair Commercial Practices Directive?', Monika Namysłowska focuses specifically on the Black List in Annex I to the UCP Directive, which bans 31 particular commercial practices. Although the introduction of a Black List was aimed at increasing legal certainty and consumer confidence, one may wonder whether this aim has been achieved. Some of the prohibitions encapsulated in the List are difficult to apply; others are in fact rather vague and open-textured creating uncertainty instead. Moreover, given the maximum harmonization principle the Black Lists pre-empts any legislative attempts at the Member State level to introduce, amend or extend the listed practices. Namysłowska argues that the various national methods of implementation of Annex I and the dissimilar notions and legal definitions at the Member State level add to the complexity of the UCP Directive regime, render uniform interpretation difficult and may even hinder effective enforcement.

3.2 Vulnerability

Part II of this volume deals with vulnerability issues. The UCP Directive is slightly ambiguous as concerns vulnerability due to age, mental or physical condition. On the one hand, the Directive assumes consumers to be 'reasonably well informed and reasonably observant and circumspect'.[68] Therefore, the 'model consumer' is considered to be confident and proactive in gathering and processing information before making transactional decisions. On the other hand, however, the Directive seems to offer specific protection to old, young, disabled and challenged consumers. Obviously, the question is what makes these groups vulnerable in connection with commercial practices. And are they the only ones prone to succumb to certain unfair practices? Given the human model of 'homo heuristicus' developed by

68 Cf. art 5(2) UCP Directive.

behavioural economics, one could even argue that all consumers are vulnerable individuals.

Against this background Marine Friant-Perrot discusses 'The Vulnerable Consumer in the UCPD and Other Provisions of EU Law'. She argues that the concept of vulnerability is multi-facetted and in fact covers different realities. Vulnerability may even consist of the lack of opportunities to access certain – essential or non-essential – services and goods. As Friant-Perrot shows, consumer vulnerability is widespread and as such needs to be taken into account when judging both the unfairness of commercial practices and the hazardous nature or suitability of certain goods and services.

3.3 The UCP Directive and Other Regimes

In Part III, the interaction between the UCP Directive regime with other forms of regulation of traders' behaviour is discussed. How does the UCP Directive relate to other EU rules of consumer protection? Does it complement or interfere with other regimes – be they legislative, regulatory or self-regulatory?

In her contribution, 'Can the UCP Directive Really Be a Vector of Legal Certainty?', Amandine Garde focuses on the extent to which the objective of legal certainty, which is strongly enshrined in the UCP Directive, can realistically be attained. She argues that if the UCP Directive may inject a degree of certainty into the EU regulatory framework, largely through its Annex of black-listed practices, the use of extremely broad, loosely defined concepts in the Directive's general clauses is unlikely to promote the level-playing field promised by the Commission to traders, consumers and Member States alike. The second part of the contribution focuses more specifically on the uneasy relationship existing between the UCP Directive and other provisions of EU law. In particular, it evaluates how the horizontal provisions of the UCP Directive relate to more specific provisions intended to refine the notions of misleading and unfair practices in specific sectors of the EU economy or in relation to specific business-to-consumer commercial practices. Overall, this contribution concludes that fine lines will have to be drawn to determine which practices fall within and which practices fall outside the scope of the UCP Directive and that difficult questions remain regarding the extent to which Member States still benefit, notwithstanding the maximum harmonization clause contained in the Directive, from a margin of autonomy to protect consumers from unfair commercial practices on their territories.

The contribution 'The Interaction between the Unfair Commercial Practices Directive and Self-Regulation: The Case of Codes of Conduct' by Charlotte Pavillon offers an in-depth analysis of the relationship between the UCP Directive and self-regulatory quality enhancement through voluntary codes of conduct. Pavillon shows that although the Directive seems to encourage the use of such codes, in practice such codes seldom extend or build on the Directive's general fairness clause and neither do they advance the Directive's pan-European harmonization aspirations. Pavillon therefore argues that ideally the Directive is to be amended so as to strengthen the contribution of codes of conduct to the standards laid down in the Directive while preserving the right balance between consumers' and traders' interests.

In his contribution 'A Common Approach to the Enforcement of Unfair Commercial Practices and Unfair Contract Terms', Hans Micklitz proposes that a more coordinated approach is taken in relation to unfair commercial practices and unfair contract terms. EU Member States tend to consider these two phenomena separate and distinct. Traditionally, the framework for tackling unfair commercial practices is primarily geared towards the regulation of markets and competition whereas unfair terms legislation is mostly concerned with substantive standards of protection in contract law. However, Micklitz shows that the worlds of unfair commercial practices and unfair contract terms are not as far apart as one might think and that in line with recent trends in ECJ case law a convergent approach to both fields of law is appropriate. If one looks at the UCP Directive, however, one will notice its wide scope. Thus, the assessment of the fairness of contract terms may quickly turn out to overlap with the UCP regime. Using unfair terms may mystify the consumer's legal position and may thus become misleading as a practice rather than as a term.

3.4 Enforcement Issues

Finally, in Part IV various issues of enforcement come to the fore. In principle, The UCP Directive leaves it to Member States to decide on the enforcement architecture. The result is a plethora of instruments across the European Union, each with their advantages and drawbacks. What lessons can be learned from the various choices made by Member States? Recently, the European Commission communicated its first report on the application of the Directive. The gist of the report is that the UCP Directive itself is adequate as it stands but that enforcement efforts need to be intensified.[69] This is all the more reason to delve deeper into the enforcement issues.

Franziska Weber writes on 'Law and Economics of Enforcing Misleading Advertising Laws: Incentives of Bona and Mala Fide Traders Assessed'. As the title suggests, this is a law and economics analysis of misleading advertising. The harm caused to society by such unfair commercial practices is exacerbated by the fact that enforcement efforts are non-existent, slow or ineffective. Weber argues that the law should try to distinguish between *bona fide* traders and *mala fide* traders. While the latter inadvertently breach the law, rogue traders' interests lie in the short-term profit generated by their illegal activities. Since the UCP Directive leaves national legislatures with considerable discretion regarding the choice of enforcement tools and the national configuration of the various institutions and enforcers differs, the question is how Member States may design an efficient enforcement framework. Weber tries to answer why no one-size-fits-all solution is

69 (COM (2013) 139 final).

available for all European Member States and how national legislatures may take certain design requirements into account when devising their national frameworks.

In the final contribution to this section, Dörte Poelzig poses the question 'Private or Public Enforcement of the UCP Directive? Sanctions and Remedies to Prevent Unfair Commercial Practices'. The various national enforcement strategies are reviewed. Poelzig surveys the main divide between Member States relying on public enforcement – using criminal law or administrative law – and those taking private law enforcement as a starting point. Given the need to ensure the full effectiveness of the UCP Directive, Poelzig argues that it is essential to establish a level playing field of effective enforcement and to identify the comparative strengths and weaknesses of the various available instruments.

4. Outlook

This volume addresses some of the practical concerns which have arisen since the UCP Directive entered into force. It assesses whether the difficulties which were anticipated in earlier academic writings have in fact materialized and what unexpected issues have arisen since. In doing so, it takes stock of the various policy developments, the growing body of case law developed both by the CJEU and by national courts, the decisions of relevant national enforcement authorities, as well as the legislative debates which have surrounded the implementation of the UCP Directive in Member States. If anything, the contributions to this book bear witness of the complexity of the field of commercial practices and the multitude of issues that deserve further research.

Bibliography

Collins H, 'The Unfair Commercial Practices Directive' (2005) *ECLR* 417.

———, 'Harmonisation by Example: European Laws against Unfair Commercial Practices' (2010) 73 *Modern Law Review* 89–118.

De Cristofaro G, 'Die zivilrechtlichen Folgen des Verstoszes gegen das Verbot unlauterer Geschäftspraktiken: eine vergleichende Analyse der Lösungen der EU-Mitgliedstaaten' (2010) *Gewerblicher Rechtsschutz und Urheberrecht Internationaler Teil* (GRUR Int) 1017.

European Commission, 'Commission Staff Working Document – Guidance on the Implementation/Application of Directive 2005/29/EC on Unfair Commercial Practices' (SEC (2009) 1666) (European Commission, Brussels, 2009).

———, 'First Report on the Application of Directive 2005/29/EC of the European Parliament and of the Council of 11 May 2005 Concerning Unfair Business-to-Consumer Commercial Practices in the Internal Market and Amending Council Directive 84/450/EEC, Directives 97/7/EC, 98/27/EC and 2002/65/EC of the European Parliament and of the Council and Regulation (EC) No 2006/2004 of the European Parliament and of the Council ("Unfair Commercial Practices Directive")' (COM (2013) 139 final) (European Commission, Brussels, 2013).

Fox O'Mahony L, *Home Equity and Ageing Owners – Between Risk and Regulation* (Oxford: Hart Publishing, 2012).

Garde A, 'The Unfair Commercial Practices Directive: A Successful Example of Legislative Harmonisation?', in P Syrpis (ed.), *The Judiciary, the Legislature and the Internal Market* (Cambridge: Cambridge University Press, 2012) 118.

Handig C, 'The Unfair Commercial Practices Directive – A Milestone in the European Unfair Competition Law?' (2005) *EBLR* 1117.

Incardona R and C Poncibò, 'The Average Consumer, the Unfair Commercial Practices Directive, and the Cognitive Revolution' (2007) 30 *Journal of Consumer Policy* 21.

Keirsbilck B, 'Towards A Single Regulatory Framework on Unfair Commercial Practices?' (2009) *EBLR* 507.

———, *The New European Law of Unfair Commercial Practices and Competition Law* (Oxford/Portland: Hart Publishing, 2011).

Korobkin RB and TS Ulen, 'Law and Behavioral Science: Removing the Rationality Assumption from Law and Economics' (2000) 88 *Cal. L. Rev.* 1051–1144.

Micklitz H-W, 'The General Clause on Unfair Practices', in GG Howells et al. (eds), *European Fair Trading Law. The Unfair Commercial Practices Directive* (Aldershot: Ashgate, 2006) 83–122.

Stuyck J, E Terryn and T Van Dyck, 'Confidence Through Fairness? The New Directive on Unfair Business-to-Consumer Commercial Practices in the Internal Market' (2006) 43 *Common Market L. Rev.* 107.

Sunstein CR (ed.), *Behavioral Law and Economics* (Cambridge Series on Judgment and Decision Making, Cambridge: Cambridge University Press, 2000).

Thaler RH and CR Sunstein, *Nudge – Improving Decisions About Health, Wealth, and Happiness* (New Haven: Yale University Press, 2008).

van Boom WH, 'The Netherlands in Civic Consulting', in WH van Boom (ed.), *Study on the Application of Directive 2005/29/EC on Unfair Commercial Practices in the EU / Part 2 – Country Reports* (Berlin: Civic Consulting, 2011) 7.1.

van Boom WH and MBM Loos (eds), *Collective Enforcement of Consumer Law – Securing Compliance in Europe through Private Group Action and Public Authority Intervention* (European Studies in Private Law, Groningen: Europa Law Publishing, 2007).

Weatherill S, 'Who Is the "Average Consumer"?', in S Weatherill and U Bernitz (eds), *The Regulation of Unfair Commercial Practices under EC Directive 2005/29. New Rules and New Techniques* (Oxford: Hart Publishing, 2006) 115–138.

Weatherill S and U Bernitz (eds), *The Regulation of Unfair Commercial Practices under EC Directive 2005/29. New Rules and New Techniques* (Studies of the Oxford Institute of European and Comparative Law, Oxford: Hart Publishing, 2006).

PART I
Implementation, Approximation and Harmonization

Chapter 1
UK Implementation of the Unfair Commercial Practices Directive[1]

Marios Koutsias and Chris Willett

1. Introduction

This chapter considers how the Unfair Commercial Practices Directive[2] (UCPD) has been implemented in the United Kingdom. We show that the United Kingdom has used a blend of preventive and traditional UK criminal enforcement techniques, while these techniques have been 'Europeanized' by the open-textured nature and breadth of application of the UCPD unfairness concepts. In addition, although the UCPD does not require Member States to grant private law enforcement rights, we also argue that UK *private* law may nevertheless be Europeanized by the UCPD in more 'spontaneous' ways, as a result of the planned introduction of private law remedies for some violations of the (distinctly European) UCPD concepts of fairness.

Nevertheless, we also show that there are limits to this Europeanizing effect. First of all, in the important area of financial services, the 'home grown' regime is likely to remain dominant; because it operates within a well-established institutional structure and may well set higher standards of protection than those in the UCPD (permitted by article 3[9] of the UCPD, which exempts financial services from the full harmonization principle that applies generally under the UCPD).

Secondly, there is a possibility that *judges* may limit the extent of Europeanization. In contrast to the particular position in relation to financial services, the UCPD's European concepts of fairness often have the potential to increase standards of protection relative to pre-existing UK law. However, these European concepts are sufficiently open textured as to run the risk of being interpreted in non-protective ways, based on underlying UK judicial ethics of self-interest and self-reliance that have shown themselves in the past. So far,

1 Subject to some amendments and updating, this chapter has already been published in (2012) *Erasmus Law Review* (5)4.

2 2005/29/EC; G Howells, H-W Micklitz and T Wilhelmsson, *European Fair Trading Law* (Ashgate, 2006); S Weatherill and U Bernitz, *The Regulation of Unfair Commercial Practices under EC Directive 2005/29* (Hart, 2007); C Willett, 'Fairness and Consumer Decision Making under the Unfair Commercial Practices Directive' (2010) 33 *JCP* 247.

courts have taken a relatively protective approach to interpretation of the UCPD concepts. However, we will only really have a clear picture as to the impact of European fairness standards in the United Kingdom when we hear the views of the Supreme Court; and, in particular, see what the response is to the recent, and any future, ECJ interpretation of the unfairness concept.

2. UK Implementation: Techniques and Europeanization

2.1 UCPD Unfairness Concepts and Requirements

As is well known, the UCPD contains general clauses on 'misleading practices' (divided into 'misleading actions' and 'misleading omissions') and 'aggressive practices' (the main operative provisions in practice); as well as an overriding general clause, catching practices that are 'contrary to the requirements of professional diligence'.[3] It seems that this 'professional diligence' clause is intended to encapsulate, but possibly sometimes extend beyond, what would be caught by the general clauses on misleading practices and on aggressive practices.[4] There is also a list of 31 practices that are in all circumstances considered to be unfair, i.e., without application of the above general clauses on misleading and aggressive practices.[5]

The UCPD requires Member States to ensure that there are adequate and effective means to combat the use of practices that are unfair in one of the above ways; including means by which persons or organizations regarded under national law as having a legitimate interest in combating unfair commercial practices may take legal or administrative action against such practices.[6]

2.2 Preventive Control

The UCPD was implemented by the Consumer Protection from Unfair Trading Regulations (CPUTR) 2008.[7] These introduce an injunctive or 'cease and desist'

3 Arts 5–9.

4 See Micklitz, in G Howells, H-W Micklitz and T Wilhelmsson, *European Fair Trading Law*, above, n 2 at 121.

5 UCPD, Annex 1.

6 UCPD art 11.

7 2008/SI/1277. For the full background to implementation of the Directive see http://www.berr.gov.uk/consultations/page39674.html. See also G Howells, 'The End of an Era – Implementing the Unfair Commercial Practices Directive in the United Kingdom: Punctual Criminal Law Gives Way to a General Criminal/Civil Law Standard' (2009) *Journal of Business Law* 183; H Collins, 'Harmonisation by Example: European Laws Against Unfair Commercial Practices' (2010) 73(1) *MLR* 89; C Willett, 'Unfairness under the Consumer Protection from Unfair Trading Regulations', in J Devenney, L Fox O'Mahony and M Kenny (eds), *Unconscionability in European Private Financial Transactions* (Cambridge University Press, 2010) 350; J Williams, C Hare 'Early Experiences of the Enforcement of

form of preventive control known as an 'enforcement order'. They provide that where a practice is unfair (following the definitions in the UCPD itself), it amounts to a 'Community infringement' under the Enterprise Act (EA) 2002; thereby allowing enforcement authorities to ask a court to issue an 'enforcement order' against the continued use of the practice.

Enforcement orders can be obtained against a trader carrying out the practice or likely to carry out the practice.[8] Under EA, s. 213, enforcement orders can be sought by the Office of Fair Trading (OFT), local trading standards authorities and the Department of Enterprise, Trade and Investment in Northern Ireland (all deemed 'general enforcers'). They can also be sought by those designated as enforcers by the Secretary of State (thus far the Civil Aviation Authority, the Information Commissioner, the Rail Regulator, the Gas and Electricity Markets Authority and the Director Generals of Telecommunications, Water, Gas and Electricity for Northern Ireland).[9] Enforcement orders can also be sought by those 'Community enforcers' listed in the Official Journal under Article 4.3 of the Injunctions Directive.[10] Finally, they can be sought by Consumer Protection Co-operation Enforcers, such as the Civil Aviation Authority, the Financial Conduct Authority, Ofcom, ICSTIS and the general enforcers mentioned above.[11]

Enforcement is coordinated by the OFT. The enforcer must consult the trader and the OFT to seek to ensure cessation of the practice.[12] Normally this consultation period is 14 days, but 7 days is sufficient for an interim order; and, if the OFT considers it necessary, consultation can be dispensed with altogether. An enforcer may accept an 'undertaking' that the practice will cease (and, therefore, not proceed to seek an enforcement order).[13]

The OFT issued guidance on the new concepts of unfairness when the law was first passed.[14] Of course, it must be emphasized that this guidance represents

---

the Unfair Commercial Practices Directive in Scotland' (2010) 33 *JCP* 377; P Cartwright, 'Under Pressure: Regulating Aggressive Practices in the UK' (2011) *LMCLQ* 123; and C Willett and M Morgan-Taylor, 'Consumer Protection', in J Chuah and M Furmston (eds), *Commercial and Consumer Law* (Longman, 2nd edn, 2013), 7.8.

8 The relevant courts are the High Court or county court in England, Wales or Northern Ireland or the Court of Session or Sheriff Court in Scotland. See EA, s. 212 and 217 and CPUTR, reg. 26; and C Willett and M Morgan-Taylor, 'Consumer Protection'.

9 SI 2003/1399.

10 98/27/EC. 'Community enforcers' refers to bodies from other Member States, this being intended to facilitate cross-border co-operation in enforcement.

11 EA, s. 215(5A), added by the Enterprise Act 2002 (Amendment) Regulations 2006 (SI2006/3363) in order to implement the EC Regulation on Consumer Protection Cooperation (Reg. [EC] No 2006/2004, as amended by the UCPD). Note also that the Financial Services Act 2012 introduced the new Financial Conduct Authority, replacing the old Financial Services Authority.

12 EA, s. 214.

13 EA, s. 219(4)

14 OFT/BERR (2008) *Guidance on the Consumer Protection from Unfair Trading regulations*, London, OFT/BERR, available at http://www.oft.gov.uk/shared_oft/business_leaflets/cpregs/oft1008.pdf.

the OFT view as to how the concepts of unfairness should be understood; it being open to the courts (when cases come before them) to take a different view.

This 'enforcement order' regime for UCPD-based unfair practices fits within a broader regime of preventive control in UK consumer protection. Enforcement orders can also be obtained against other 'Community infringements', that is, actions that represent breaches of standards contained in various other EU directives.[15] This would cover, for example, failure to abide by the various information obligations and cancellation rights that are provided for in doorstep and distance selling directives and the replacement provisions in the new Consumer Rights Directive.[16] It also covers selling goods that do not meet the conformity standards in the Consumer Sales Directive (or failing to provide the remedies in the Consumer Sales Directive);[17] the use of terms that are unfair under the Unfair Contract Terms Directive;[18] and breaches of the provisions of the Timeshare, Electronic Commerce and Television Broadcasting Directives.[19]

Enforcement orders can also be obtained against so called 'domestic infringements'. Essentially, 'domestic infringement' covers a variety of actions that represent breaches of contract, statutory duties, criminal offences and torts that harm 'the collective interests of consumers'.[20] The label 'domestic' infringement is used to indicate that the actions in question represent breaches of standards that have been set by domestic law, that is, they have not come from EU law. So, it would cover, for example, practices that amount to the criminal offence of harassment of debtors under the Administration of Justice Act (AJA), section 40; and breaking contracts by not delivering promised goods or services.[21] So, quite apart from harassment representing a criminal offence and failure to deliver goods or services giving consumers the right to seek private law remedies for breach of contract, an enforcement order can be issued requiring such conduct to cease in future.

2.3 Europeanization of Preventive Enforcement through the 'General Clause'

So, we can see that tools for preventive control of unfairness as defined by the UCPD have been 'slotted in' to a pre-existing national regime of preventive

---

15 EA, s. 212, Sch. 13.

16 Directives 85/577/EEC, 97/7/EC and 2011/83/EU respectively.

17 99/44/EC.

18 93/13/EEC.

19 Directives 94/47/EC, 2000/31/EC and 89/552/EEC (as amended by 97/36/EC) respectively.

20 EA, s. 211, 213(1)–(2) and 217(6); and C Willett and M Morgan-Taylor, 'Consumer Protection', above, n 7.

21 See EA, s. 211(a)–(b) and see the Enterprise Act 2002 (Domestic Infringements) Order 2003, SI 1593; and note that the Protection from Harassment Act is also solely of domestic origin, as is the general common law rule that failure to deliver goods or services promised under a contract represents a breach of contract.

consumer protection. However, it is our contention that this is more than a mere technical extension of such preventive consumer protection powers. The pre-existing 'domestic' and 'Community' infringements all tend to involve relatively narrow and specific issues (often only in particular sectors): e.g., failure to provide specific types of information in doorstep and distance sales; supply of defective goods; use of unfair contract terms; harassment of debtors etc.

In contrast, the UCPD concepts of unfairness, which can now form the basis of preventive action, are much broader in their scope. The various 'general clauses' – 'misleading actions', 'misleading omissions', 'aggressive practices', violation of 'professional diligence' – are 'general' partly because they are themselves very open textured.[22] In addition, they can be called 'general' because they cover such vast ground. They cover practices[23] 'before, during or after' any 'commercial transaction'[24] (there being no restriction to particular types of transaction or sector). So, in relation to almost all conceivable goods or services, there is a 'cradle-to-grave' regime covering practices such as advertising, persuasion and negotiation at the pre-contractual stage; post-contractual alterations or variations; performance, delivery etc. by the trader; performance, payment etc. by the consumer; complaint handling; after sales service; and enforcement by either party.

In short, UCPD implementation has brought a very significant expansion of the use of the 'general clause', a very significant 'Europeanization' of the UK preventive consumer protection regime.[25] (It is worth emphasizing that use of an open-textured general clause that covers considerable ground is not only 'European' in the sense that it comes from a European Union directive. It is also 'European' – and here, 'continental' European is the more precisely accurate term – in that this tradition of open-textured, broadly applicable general clauses is a

22 See, on this, C Willett, 'General Clauses and the Competing Ethics of European Consumer Law in the UK' (2012) 71(2) *CLJ* 412; and C Willett, 'Fairness and Consumer Decision Making', above, n 2.

23 Any 'act, omission, course of conduct or representation' (UCPD art 2[d]/CPUTR, reg 2 [1]).

24 UCPD, art 3(1)/CPUTR, reg 2(1).

25 On Europeanization see C Twigg-Flesner, *The Europeanisation of Contract Law* (Routledge, 2008); C Twigg-Flesner (ed.), *The Cambridge Companion to European Union Private Law* (Cambridge University Press, 2010); R Brownsword, H-W Micklitz, L Niglia and S Weatherill, *The Foundations of European Private Law* (Hart, 2011); and C Willett, 'General Clauses and the Competing Ethics of European Consumer Law in the UK', above n 22. Of course, 'Europeanization' more generally covers more than the use of concepts such as general clauses that derive from continental, civil law traditions than the common law tradition. It also covers, e.g., the way in these and other concepts are interpreted in an 'autonomous' European manner by the European Court of Justice; the 'spillover' or 'spontaneous' Europeanization that may take place in areas not directly covered by a Directive (e.g., in private law, on which see below); and, indeed, the impact of barrier to trade rules on national contract and trade law (see C Twigg-Flesner, *The Europeanisation of Contract Law*, ch. 3).

tradition that is deeply embedded in the civil law legal tradition of continental Europe, and not the common law UK tradition.)[26]

2.4 Criminal Sanctions: Tradition, Rationales, Policies and Operation

Criminal sanctions have been a core part of public enforcement of consumer law in the United Kingdom for centuries. There is plenty of scope for debate as to the rationales for using the criminal law in the consumer protection sphere.[27] Certainly, criminal sanctions can be viewed as having important deterrent effects that might be missing in the case of the preventive sanctions discussed above. More generally, the OFT have said that criminal enforcement should be used where:

> civil enforcement is unlikely to be effective in achieving a change in behaviour and/or the breach is sufficiently serious that the conviction and punishment of offenders ought to be pursued, for example to protect the public and to provide wider deterrence.[28]

The OFT elaborate on this by saying that they are likely to consider beginning a criminal investigation:

- where traders deliberately or recklessly use deceptive, misleading or fraudulent practices;
- where traders deliberately or recklessly use aggressive, intimidating or coercive practices;
- where flagrant and/or persistent offending by a trader or group of associated traders has occurred or is occurring;
- where a particular unlawful practice is widespread, or there is a risk determined that criminal enforcement is likely to be the most effective means by which to set a precedent for future action; or
- where false statements are made or false documents provided in the course of dealings with the OFT or another enforcement body or where the investigation is otherwise obstructed.[29]

---

26 Generally see G Howells, 'General Clauses in European Consumer Law', in HW Micklitz (ed.), *Verbraucherrecht in Deutschland* (Nomos, 2005); and S Grundman and D Mazeaud, *General Clauses and Standards in European Contract Law* (Kluwer International, 2005).

27 For an excellent and exhaustive review of rationales, see P Cartwright, *Consumer Protection and the Criminal Law* (Cambridge University Press, 2001).

28 OFT, Criminal Enforcement of the Consumer Protection from Unfair Trading Regulations, OFT, London, 2010, para 2.1, available at http://www.oft.gov.uk/shared_oft/policy/OFT1273.pdf.

29 Ibid, at 2.2

Criminal sanctions have been, and continue to be used, for instance, in relation to food labelling, quality and safety;[30] and general product safety.[31] They were used against 'false trade descriptions' (Trade Descriptions Act [TDA] 1968) (covering basically misleading statements about goods and services) and 'misleading pricing' (Consumer Protection Act 1987 Part III) until the implementation of the UCPD. These provisions were repealed by the CPUTR[32] and replaced by offences based on the UCPD concepts. So, a trader now commits an offence if he carries out a misleading act or omission or an aggressive practice (the definitions reflecting those in the UCPD).[33] These are all strict liability offences, there being no *mens rea* requirement (i.e., no need to prove that the trader acted intentionally, recklessly or negligently). A trader also commits an offence if he contravenes the requirement of professional diligence.[34] However, for the trader to be criminally liable for violation of the professional diligence standard, there *is* a *mens rea* requirement. The trader is only guilty of an offence if he '*knowingly or recklessly* [engages] in conduct that is contrary to professional diligence and materially distorts or is likely to materially distort consumer behaviour'.[35] It is important to stress here that the trader need only be 'knowing or reckless' as to his own behaviour. There is no need for him to know of (or be reckless as to) its actual or likely effects on consumers.

Finally, a trader also commits an offence if he engages in any practice set out in paras 1–10, 12–27 and 29–31 of the Schedule of practices that are always regarded as unfair.[36]

In the case of the misleading action and omission offences, the aggressive practice offence and the practices in Sch. 1, there are defences available.[37] The defences are those that have long been used for 'consumer protection' offences in the United Kingdom, so that earlier case law under the TDA and other legislation may still prove helpful.

One set of defences are those available under s. 17. Here the defendant must first prove that the commission of the offence is due to:

- a mistake; which must be a mistake by the person charged, rather than one of their employees;[38] or

---

30 B Atwood, K Thompson and C Willett, *Food Law* (Tottel, 2009).

31 G Howells, 'The End of an Era – Implementing the Unfair Commercial Practices Directive in the United Kingdom', above, n 7.

32 CPUTR, Schedule 4.

33 Regulations 9–11; and see regs 13 and 14 on penalties and time limits respectively.

34 Regulation 8.

35 Regulation 8(1)(a).

36 Regulation 12.

37 The defences are not available in the case of the 'violation of professional diligence' offence: if the trader has been 'knowing or reckless' (the required *mens rea*) then it is hard to see how he can have exercised 'reasonable precautions/due diligence' (s. 17 defence) or 'innocently' published an advertisement (s. 18 defence).

38 *Birkenhead Co-operative Society v Roberts* [1970] 1 WLR 1497.

- reliance on information supplied to him by another person (who the defendant must identify to the prosecution),[39] for example, information as to mileage from previous owners of a vehicle[40] or information on a product label placed there by the producer (and relied on by the retailer);[41] or
- the act or default of another person (who the defendant must identify to the prosecution)[42] who can be a party such as a sub-contractor or other party that is responsible for the activity in question, but can even be an employee,[43] for example, as in *Tesco v Nattrass*[44] where a supermarket manager who wrongly labelled washing powder counted as 'another person' for the purposes of the supermarket's defence; or
- an accident or another cause beyond his control, which may cover computer errors.[45]

Having established one of the above criteria, the defendant must then establish that he took all reasonable precautions *and* exercised all due diligence to avoid the commission of the offence by himself or any person under his control. Whether there have been 'reasonable precautions' is a question of fact which will be affected by the circumstances of each particular case. Different precautions may be necessary according to whether the defendant is a manufacturer, a retailer or a supplier of services; and what is required may well also vary according to whether the defendant is a large enterprise or a small corner shop.[46] In general, the key is that an appropriate system must be in place to prevent the practice taking place, for example, devising an adequate training programme for employees;[47] testing products (for example, to see if they comply with information on labels);[48] or (in the case of false mileage readings on cars), checking the history, for example, through the registration document and obtaining statements from previous owners.[49]

---

39 Regulation 17(2).

40 See *Simmons v Potter* [1975] RTR 347 and *Ealing LBC v Taylor* [1995] CLR 156.

41 *Hurley v Martinez* [1991] CCLR 1.

42 Regulation 17(2).

43 So long as they are not so senior as to be an 'alter ego' of the company (e.g., members of the Board of Directors, managing director and other senior officers) (see *Tesco v Nattrass* [1971] 2 All ER 127).

44 Ibid.

45 See *Berkshire CC v Olympic Holidays Ltd* (1994) 13 Trading LR 251.

46 See *Garrett v Boots the Chemist* (1980).

47 See *Tesco v Nattrass*, above n 43.

48 *Amos v Melcom (Frozen Foods)* (1985) 149 JP 712, DC (insufficient evidence of sampling to check if meat labelled 'rump steak' was actually thus).

49 See *Richmond upon Thames LBC v Motor Sales (Hounslow) Ltd* [1971] RTR 116; *Wandsworth LBC v Bentley* [1980] RTR 429 DC; and *Ealing LBC v Taylor* [1995] above, n 40. Even with some such checks, it has also been held that not enough had been done, and that a statement disclaiming knowledge as to whether the mileage was correct

Whether there has been 'due diligence' turns on whether the system of reasonable precautions has actually been used in practice. If it has not, then there will be no due diligence and the defence will fail.[50]

A further defence is provided by reg. 18. There is a defence if the defendant can establish that it is his business to publish (or arrange for publication) of advertisements; he received the advertisement for publication in the ordinary course of business; and he did not know, and had no reason to suspect, that its publication would amount to an offence. This covers those (such as newspapers and magazines) who publish advertisements, as well as those (such as advertising agencies) who arrange for publication.

These defences are available partly because the offences are strict liability and it is thought that some form of escape route from strict *criminal* liability should be available where blame is minimal. The 'reasonable precautions and due diligence' requirement can also be viewed as a way of incentivizing traders to manage their affairs so as to avoid the behaviour in question. We would suggest that this is why, as we saw above, it is key to successful use of this defence to establish that an effective system was in place to prevent the practice taking place; and that this system was operating properly in the circumstances in question.

2.5 Europeanization of Criminal Enforcement Through the 'General Clause'

So, we can see that the United Kingdom has chosen to back up preventive control of (UCPD-defined) unfair practices with traditional UK criminal sanctions. However, again, although the United Kingdom may be using traditional, 'home-grown' enforcement tools to enforce the European standards of fairness; we would suggest that these standards of fairness are, themselves, Europeanizing the home-grown enforcement tools. The point, again, is the general clause, and the very broad application of fairness that it has introduced to UK criminal law.

To take one example, the pre-existing criminal rules tended not to cover statements made during the performance or enforcement of a contract. The TDA, for instance, was focused on statements about the goods or services themselves; tending to mean that the focus was on statements made at or around when the contract is first made.[51] However, statements made in the context of performance or enforcement *are* covered by the new (Europeanized) regime. We noted above that the UCPD concept applies to practices 'before, during or after' any 'commercial transaction.[52] So the reach of criminal consumer protection law

---

was required as a 'reasonable precaution' against customers being misled (*Simmons v Potter* above, n 40 .

50 See *Turtington v United Co-operative Ltd* [1993] Crim LR 376; and see the judgment of Lord Diplock in the *Tesco v Nattrass* case (above n 43) for guidance on due diligence.

51 See TDA, ss 1–5 and 14; and C Willett and M Morgan-Taylor, 'Consumer Protection', above, n 7, at 7.8.3.1.

52 UCPD, art 3(1)/CPUTR, reg 2(1).

has been significantly extended by this European general clause. It will cover, for example, statements as to the rights of consumers, which might influence their decisions as to whether 'to exercise a contractual right'[53] (possibly covering statements that deceive consumers as to their rights and which are therefore being likely to cause them to make the decision not to enforce these rights).

3. Spontaneous Europeanization of Private Law

The consumer contract laws of England and Scotland have certainly been significantly Europeanized over the past two or three decades.[54] Most notably, we can speak of:

- the European information and cancellation rights from the doorstep and distance selling directives;[55]
- the European concept of fairness and preventive enforcement that applies to most standard terms;[56]
- the European conformity standard applicable to sale and supply of consumer goods and the European 'cure' remedies of repair and replacement from the Consumer Sales Directive.[57]

The UCPD 's general clauses on practices do not apply in private law as such. As is well known, UCPD Article 3(2) provides that the directive is 'without prejudice to contract law and, in particular, to the rules on the validity, formation or effect of a contract'. In other words, there is no direct obligation on Member States to provide consumers with private law remedies where contracts are negotiated, concluded, performed or enforced in ways that are unfair within the meaning of the general clauses on misleading actions or omissions; aggressive practices; or professional diligence.

---

53 For a misleading practice under the CPUTR/UCPD, the information must be false or be likely to deceive the average consumer and it must cause or be likely to cause the average consumer to take a transactional decision he would not have taken otherwise (UCPD, art 6[1]/CPUTR, Reg. 5[2] [a]–[b]); and 'transactional decision' includes a decision as to whether to exercise a contractual right (UCPD, art 2[k]/CPUTR, Reg. 2 [1]).

54 See C Twigg-Flesner, *The Europeanisation of Contract Law*, above, n 25.

55 Above, n 16; implemented in the United Kingdom by the Consumer Protection (Distance Selling) Regulations 2000, SI 2000/2334; and Package Travel, Package Holidays and Package Tours Regulations 1992, SI 1992/3288. See now the expansion of European information obligations contained in the Consumer Rights Directive (2011/83/EU).

56 Above, n 18; implemented in the United Kingdom by Unfair Terms in Consumer Contracts Regulations 1999, SI 1999/2083; and see C Willett, *Fairness in Consumer Contracts: The Case of Unfair Terms* (Ashgate, 2007).

57 Above, n 17, implemented by Sale and Supply of Goods to Consumers Regulations 2002, SI 2002/3045.

Of course, there are pre-existing private law remedies in the United Kingdom for practices such as misrepresentation (rescission and damages); and duress and undue influence (rescission). (It should be emphasized here that action to rescind the contract must be taken by the party – here the consumer – affected by the practice, i.e., the contract is voidable, not void). These concepts obviously cover a fair amount of the same ground as is covered by the misleading and aggressive practice concepts from the UCPD. At the same time, they are not necessarily always as protective as the UCPD concepts.[58] Nevertheless, when the Directive was first implemented, the United Kingdom chose not to extend the availability of private law remedies to cover cases of unfairness as defined by the UCPD general clauses.[59]

However, it was always likely that private law would be Europeanized in less direct ways by the UCPD concepts of fairness. Such 'spontaneous' or 'spillover' Europeanization might occur in the following ways.[60] First of all, even if compliance with the standards set by the general clauses cannot be enforced through private law action as such, these standards inevitably affect contracting *practice*. As we have noted above, the UCPD general clauses apply 'before, during or after' any 'commercial transaction'.[61] So the European standards of fairness set by these general clauses determine how traders must behave towards consumers while seeking to persuade them to enter *contracts*; negotiating *contracts*; and during the performance and enforcement of *contracts*.

Second, there is always the possibility that the courts may develop pre-existing domestic concepts (e.g., misrepresentation, duress, undue influence) incrementally in ways that reflect the UCPD general clauses.

Finally, based on work by the Law Commissions, the Draft Consumer Protection from Unfair Trading (Amendment) Regulations 2013 contain some

---

58 See generally C Willett, 'Fairness and Consumer Decision Making', above, n 2; and C Willett, 'General Clauses and the Competing Ethics of European Consumer Law in the UK', above, n 22.

59 The idea was that the Law Commissions should investigate more fully the way in which the UCPD concepts could interact with the traditional UK concepts. See now Law Commission, *A Private Right of Redress for Commercial Practices* (2008); Law Commission, *Consumer Redress for Misleading and Aggressive Practices* (2011) LCCP 199; and Law Commissions, *Consumer Redress for Misleading and Aggressive Practices* (2012) Law Com 332, Scot Law Com 226.

60 Generally on such forms of harmonization, see W. van Gerven, 'A Common Law for Europe: The Future Meeting the Past?' (2001) 4 *ERPL* 485 and MBM Loos, 'The Influence of European Consumer Law on General Contract Law and the Need for Spontaneous Harmonization' (2007) 4 *ERPL* 515. For an excellent early analysis of the issue in relation to the UCPD see S. Whittaker, 'The Relationship of the Unfair Commercial Practices Directive to European and National Contract Laws', in S Weatherill and U Bernitz (eds), *The Regulation of Unfair Commercial Practices*, above, n 2. Also, see C Willett, 'Fairness and Consumer Decision Making', above, n 2; and C Willett, 'General Clauses and the Competing Ethics of European Consumer Law in the UK', above, n 22.

61 UCPD, art 3(1)/CPUTR, reg 2(1).

statutory private law remedies for at least certain violations of the UCPD general clauses.[62] In brief, the idea is that there would be rescission and price reduction remedies on a 'strict liability' basis; while traders would be able to avoid damages liability by establishing that they had exercised 'due diligence' in seeking to avoid carrying out the practice in question. The remedies would not be available for misleading omissions or violation of professional diligence. This does mark a serious restriction on the degree of Europeanization; given that these are two key 'European' concepts that have not played a significant role in UK private law before now.

Nevertheless, the new remedies *would* be available for misleading actions and aggressive practices. The misleading action concept is perhaps not sufficiently different from domestic misrepresentation for us to say that the introduction of private law remedies in relation to it involves a significant Europeanization.[63] However, the aggressive practice concept has the potential to be understood in a significantly different and more protective way than the domestic duress and undue influence concepts.[64] As such, introducing private law remedies for breach of this might significantly Europeanize this branch of consumer private law. Further, this is a potentially important area in practice; as it is where consumers must look for private law remedies against high-pressure selling and debt collection by traders.

4. Full Harmonization, Minimum Harmonization and Limits to Europeanization: Financial Services

4.1 Full Harmonization

We have already seen that the CPUTR repealed key generally applicable rules on trade descriptions and misleading pricing. It also repealed a very large number of rules dealing with more specific types of practice.[65] One reason for all of these repeals was to foster simplicity, i.e., to avoid having complicated overlap and duplication as between the main piece of legislation (the CPUTR) and large numbers of pre-existing rules. However, another key reason for repealing as much as possible of the old law was the full harmonization clause in Article 4, which provides that 'Member States shall neither restrict the freedom to provide

62 See above, n 59; Department of Business, Innovation and Skill, BIS/13/1112; available at https://www.gov.uk/government/publications/misleading-and-aggressive-commercial-practices-the-draft-consumer-protection-from-unfair-trading-amendment-regulations-2013.

63 Although the price reduction remedy (referred to as a 'discount' in the draft law) would be a useful one that does not exist currently for common law misrepresentation.

64 See C Willett, 'Fairness and Consumer Decision Making', above, n 2; C Willett, 'General Clauses and the Competing Ethics of European Consumer Law in the UK', above, n 22; and see further below at notes 85–88 and related text.

65 CPUTR, Schedule 4.

services nor restrict the free movement of goods for reasons falling within the field approximated by this Directive.'

The final section (below) will suggest that the UCPD concepts often offer the potential to provide greater protection than was provided by pre-existing law. Nevertheless, the more pre-existing law remaining on the statute book, the greater the risk that some of it might, in some or other way, exceed the level of protection offered by the UCPD concepts. So, in order to avoid this risk of offending against the full harmonization principle in Article 4, vast swathes of pre-existing law were repealed; this further reinforces the Europeanization process that has been the key narrative of this article so far.

4.2 Minimum Harmonization and the Limits of Europeanization: The Case of Financial Services

Notwithstanding the significant Europeanizing effect of the UCPD explained above, 'home grown' UK rules may continue to play the main regulatory role in the areas of financial services and immovable property; which are exempted by Article 3(9) from the full harmonization principle that applies generally under the UCPD. In these sectors, there is, in effect, the *minimum* harmonization that has generally applied in the past to consumer protection directives.[66]

We will focus here on financial services as it is such an important element of the consumer economy. The 'home grown' regime here operates within a well-established institutional structure and (and, as is permitted by Article 3[9]) may well set higher standards of protection than those in the UCPD.[67]

We will concentrate on the regime regulating *secured* credit.[68] Secured credit and other financial services are regulated by the new Financial Conduct Authority (FCA), replacing the old Financial Services Authority (FSA).[69] This is done under the rules in the FCA Handbook (specific and detailed rules dealing with specific

66 E.g., the Doorstep and Distance Selling Directives (above n 16), the Consumer Sales Directive (above n 17) and the Unfair Contract Terms Directive (above n 18).

67 For similar conclusions in relation to immovable property, see Civic Consulting/EU Commission, DG Justice (F Alleweldt, S Kara, P Rott, C Willett and H Gamper), *Study on the Application of Directive 2005/29/EC on Unfair Commercial Practices in the EU*, 2013, Synthesis and Country Reports, available at http://ec.europa.eu/justice/consumer-marketing/files/ucpd_final_report_part_1_synthesis.pdf and http://ec.europa.eu/justice/consumer-marketing/files/ucpd_study_country_reports.pdf.

68 For similar conclusions in relation to unsecured credit, see Civic Consulting, ibid.

69 See Financial Services Act 2012, amending the Financial Services and Markets Act (FSMA) 2000. Credit (secured and unsecured) is also regulated in overlapping ways by the Consumer Credit Act 1974.

practices);[70] the general principles for business;[71] the Treating Customers Fairly (TCF) Outcomes;[72] and the CPUTR (the regime implementing the UCPD).[73]

Certainly it is difficult to make definitive comparisons between the very open-textured general principles for business, the TCF Outcomes and the similarly open-textured (but differently worded) definitions of 'unfair' practices from the UCPD. Comparison is further complicated by the huge volume of more specific rules (contained in the FCA Handbook), which support and complement the more general FCA principles of fairness.[74] The problem here is to say whether (as well as reflecting the broad FCA principles), these Handbook rules can be said to represent a natural 'unpacking' of the broader UCPD standards of fairness; or whether they go beyond this and provide greater protection.

Nevertheless, we would suggest that the FCA principles may often set higher standards than the UCPD. First of all, let us consider the rules on misleading actions. Violation of the UCPD 'misleading action' provision must involve information as to one of the matters on the list contained in Article 6(1) (a)–(g). This could be considered to be an exhaustive list; and, although it is very broad in scope, it does not necessarily cover every potential type of information. However, a practice might certainly be considered to be misleading, and therefore unfair, under the FCA regime despite involving information by the list in Article 6(1). FCA general principle 7 refers to the obligation to 'communicate information to [consumers] in a way which is clear, fair and not misleading'; and this applies whatever the subject matter of the information.

Also, under the UCPD, it is not sufficient to establish that the practice would mislead the average consumer. It must, in addition, be shown that the impact of the practice is or is likely to be such that the average consumer would take a

70 Available at http://www.fsa.gov.uk/Pages/handbook/index.shtml.

71 FCA, *Full Handbook*, Principle 2.1, available at https://fsahandbook.info/FSA/html/handbook/PRIN/2/1.

72 FCA, *Treating Customers Fairly*, available at http://www.fsa.gov.uk/Pages/Doing/Regulated/tcf/index.shtml; and see J Black, M Hopper and C Band, 'Making a Success of Principles Based Regulation' (2007) *Law and Financial Markets Review* 191; T. Williams, 'Open the Box: An Exploration of the Financial Service Authority's Model of Fairness in Consumer Financial Transactions', in J Devenney et al., above n 7, at 227; and P Cartwright, 'Conceptualising and Understanding Fairness: Lessons from and for Financial Services', in J Devenney et al., above n 7, at 205.

73 On the approach of the FSA (now FCA) to the UCPD/CPRs generally see http://www.fsa.gov.uk/Pages/About/What/International/ucp/index.shtml. Note also that the OFT is the main enforcer under the CPRs, but there is an agreement between the OFT and the old FSA (which will presumably carry over to the new FCA) on division of responsibilities for financial services matters – see Concordat between the OFT and FSA, November 2009, available at https://webmail.dmu.ac.uk/exchweb/bin/redir.asp?URL=http://www.fsa.gov.uk/pubs/other/concordat_fsa_oft_08.pdf.

74 The Handbook subdivides into separate 'sub'-books containing hundreds of rules on such issues as mortgages and home finance; insurance; banking; client assets; building societies; collective investment; credit unions; and dispute resolution.

'transactional decision' different from that which they would take otherwise.[75] This requirement can make a difference to whether a practice is unfair or not. For instance, a price or other charge that is understated by a few pence arguably still misleads the average consumer; but may be unlikely to cause him or her to contract for a service or product that they would not have bought in any case. If not, the understated price or charge will not be misleading under the UCPD. However, it would arguably be misleading under the FCA regime; which contains no 'transactional decision' requirement.

Turning to 'misleading omissions', first of all, the UCPD test turns on whether the information is 'material' and is 'needed' by the 'average consumer'. The TCF Principles say simply that consumers should be provided with 'clear information and [...] kept appropriately informed. Secondly, as with misleading actions, there is only a misleading omission under the UCPD where the omission is likely to cause the average consumer would take a 'transactional decision' different from that which they would take otherwise.[76] As indicated above, there is no such requirement in the FCA general principles. Third, the old FSA wrote to the payment protection insurance industry to remind them of typically unacceptable practices at the point of sale which had come to the FSA's attention. One of these was that 'The firm did not take reasonable steps to ensure the customer only bought a policy for which he was eligible to claim benefits.'[77] There is at least room for debate as to whether information as to eligibility would necessarily be 'needed' or 'material' under the UCPD test.

Now turning to aggressive practices, there are a number of requirements that are specific to the UCPD 'aggressive practices' clause that do not need to be established for there to be unfairness under the FCA regime. These requirements may mean that the FCA regime provides a higher level of protection than the UCPD regime. So, under the UCPD, one route to establishing an aggressive practice is to show that there is 'coercion or harassment' leading to an actual or likely 'significant restriction' on the average consumer's 'freedom of choice or conduct'.[78] Otherwise, it must be shown that there is 'undue influence'; for which there must be 'exploitation' of a 'position of power' through 'pressure', which 'significantly' impairs (or is likely to so impair) the average consumer's 'freedom of choice or conduct'; specifically, here, by 'significantly' limiting the ability of this average consumer to take an 'informed decision'.[79] None of these criteria are mentioned in discussing fairness/unfairness in general under the FCA regime. So, it is plausible that practices (pressure selling, aggressive enforcement etc.) might

75 See above, n 53.

76 Art 7(1).

77 FSA, Consultation Paper 10/6, *The Assessment and Redress of Payment Protection Insurance Complaints Feedback on CP09/23 and Further Consultation*, Appendix 3, Point 6.

78 Art 8.

79 Arts 8 and 2(j).

fail to meet these particular UCPD criteria but still be sufficient to amount to unfairness under the more open-textured FCA regime.

Then, as with misleading practices, there is the requirement of 'transactional decision making' which applies to all UCPD concepts. In the case of any practice claimed to be aggressive under the UCPD provisions, it must be shown that the result of the coercion, harassment or undue influence would be (or be likely to be) that consumers would take a transactional decision different to the one they would have taken otherwise.[80] As we have seen, the concepts of fairness under the FCA regime do not contain such a requirement. So, there could be aggressive behaviour that is of a more one-sided, unilateral nature, where the business simply imposes a detrimental outcome on a consumer or withdraws a service from a consumer. This has the potential to be viewed as unfair under the general FCA concepts of fairness; but it would be more difficult to show that it affects consumer transactional decision making as such (as required under the UCPD).[81]

What is clear from the above discussion is that regulation of secured credit operates within a well-established domestic institutional structure and may well set higher standards of protection than those in the UCPD. For these reasons, along with the minimum harmonization allowed by Article 3(9), this homegrown regime is likely to remain the dominant force in financial services regulation;[82] with the European UCPD norms being unlikely to play a major role.

5. Judicial Approaches to Europeanization

5.1 The Potential to Increase Standards of Protection Relative to Pre-existing UK Law

In contrast to the position just described in relation to financial services, the UCPD generally has the potential to increase standards of protection relative to pre-existing UK law. This is something that has been demonstrated at length elsewhere,[83] and there is no space here to provide a systematic comparison between the UCPD and pre-existing UK standards. However, it is worthwhile providing some key examples.

80 UCPD art 5.

81 See discussion in C Willett, 'Fairness and Consumer Decision Making under the Unfair Commercial Practices Directive', above, n 2 on possible ways around this problem.

82 The FSA regime appears to be very much the first 'port of call' for the FSA, the UCPD regime being viewed as a relatively residual 'back up'.

83 See C Willett, 'Fairness and Consumer Decision Making under the Unfair Commercial Practices Directive', above, n 2; and C Willett, 'Unfairness under the Consumer Protection from Unfair Trading Regulations', above, n 7.

To begin with, there is the UCPD 'misleading omissions' concept.[84] It is well known that there has never been such a general rule against omissions in UK domestic law; so there is clearly now potential for a higher level of protection. Next, one might cite the 'undue influence' limb of the *aggressive practices* general clause.[85] This, as outlined above, covers exploitation of a 'position of power' through 'pressure', which 'significantly impairs' (or is likely to so impair) the average consumer's 'freedom of choice or conduct'; specifically by significantly limiting the ability of this average consumer to take an 'informed decision'.[86] Pre-existing UK domestic criminal and preventive rules focused mainly on the specific problem of harassment of debtors.[87] The UCPD undue influence concept seems to have the potential to cover much more than this. For example, greater trader knowledge/skill might be considered to create a 'power relationship' and the potential for 'pressure' at the sales stage. In this context, some high-pressure selling might well amount to undue influence; where, for instance, consumers are put on the spot to make quick decisions (the decision may, then, not be 'informed', as there was insufficient time to think it through). *Post*-contractually, the power relationship and pressure might come, for instance, from vulnerability when struggling with commitments. This might enable traders to pressure consumers into new commitments, refinancing etc. Clearly, these examples go well beyond what is covered by rules on harassment of debtors. They also extend beyond the traditional scope of domestic private law undue influence. Inter alia, this requires a special relationship of trust and confidence (rather than just a 'relationship of power'); and has, in practice in modern times, been restricted to the 'bank guarantee' scenario.[88]

In summary, then, the point is that (outside the financial services sphere) the UCPD's European concepts of fairness contain the potential to increase levels of consumer protection in the United Kingdom. In this sense, the 'Europeanizing' effect of the UCPD could be said to be all the more significant. Not only does the UCPD Europeanize the preventive, criminal and private law *tools* (as shown in the first part of this article); it also Europeanizes the *substantive level of protection* provided.

84 UCPD, art 7/CPUTR, regs 6.

85 Generally, see C Willett, 'Fairness and Consumer Decision Making under the Unfair Commercial Practices Directive', above, n 2; C Willett 'Unfairness under the Consumer Protection from Unfair Trading Regulations', above, n 7; and P Cartwright, 'Under Pressure: Regulating Aggressive Practices in the UK', above n 7.

86 And thereby causes him to take or be likely to take a transactional decision he would not take otherwise: UCPD, art arts 8 and 2(j)/CPUTR, regs 7(1) & (3) (b).

87 Administration of Justice Act 1970, s. 40.

88 *RBOS v Etridge (No 2)* [2002] 2 AC 773 for a summary of the cases and a re-statement of the rules.

5.2 Some Illustrative Cases[89]

So far, the evidence suggests that judges have taken a relatively protective approach to interpretation of the UCPD concepts. For example, from a consumer protection perspective, one perennial risk with concepts of 'fairness' or 'good faith' is that they will be understood to require subjective dishonesty by the trader. Now we have noted above that, in the case of the 'professional diligence' concept, there is only *criminal* liability under the UK regime where there is indeed *mens rea* in the form of intention or recklessness by the trader.[90] There is no mention of trader intention or recklessness where preventive control measures (enforcement orders) are concerned. At the same time, professional diligence is defined for all purposes, by reference, inter alia, to 'honest market practice'.[91] Nevertheless, the High Court has resisted any temptation to read this in a non-protective way. It was made clear in *Tiscali UK Ltd v. British Telecommunications Plc* that there was an 'objective' test of dishonesty, in that it was not necessary to demonstrate that at the time of the offending statement, its maker knew it to be false or had no honest belief in its truth.[92]

Another encouraging decision from a consumer protection perspective is *OFT v Purely Creative.*[93] This case dealt with whether various 'scratch card' promotions violated the general clauses on misleading actions and omissions. On the facts, it was held that some did and some did not. However, the key point for our purposes is that the High Court understood the 'average consumer' concept by reference to a relatively protective ethic, recognizing that such a consumer will not necessarily read all information provided.[94]

---

89 Aside from the cases discussed here, for examples of cases decided under the CPUTR, see also *McGuffick v Royal Bank of Scotland Plc* [2009] EWHC 2386; *Kingspan Group Plc v Rockwool Ltd* [2011] EWHC 250(Ch); and *OFT v Peter Hall*, available at http://www.oft.gov.uk/news-and-updates/press/2010/38–10.

90 See n 33 and related text.

91 Art 2(h)/CPUTR, reg 2(1).

92 [2008] EWHC 3129(QB).

93 [2011] EWHC 106(Ch). For a discussion see M Morgan-Taylor, 'Preventing Distribution of Promotions to Consumers Involving Unfair Practices – OFT Application for Order Under Enterprise Act 2002: *OFT v Purely Creative Ltd et al*' (2011) 16(3) *Communications Law* 115–117. The case also involved analysis of the proper interpretation of Paragraph 31 of Annex 1 to the Directive (i.e., the list of practices that are always to be considered unfair, without the need to apply one of the general test of unfairness). This is because there was also a question as to whether the promotions in question were in breach of paragraph 31. This issue was appealed to the Court of Appeal, whose decision was stayed pending a reference to the ECJ to determine the scope of Paragraph 31 ([2011] EWCA Civ 920). On the ECJ decision see below notes 97–98 and related text.

94 This 'average consumer' concept (who is deemed to be 'reasonably well informed and reasonably circumspect' is, of course the core benchmark for assessing practices under the regime (UCPD, arts 5–9, Preamble, recital 18/CPUTR, reg. 2 [2]). Of course, this standard can be varied to the average member of targeted or vulnerable groups of

This case is obviously significant in the context of the misleading action and omission concepts. It suggests that courts should focus on the main information provided (or *not* provided, where omissions are concerned) in deciding whether the average consumer is likely to be misled and caused to take a transactional decision that would not otherwise be taken. This core information (or lack of it) is what should determine whether there has been a misleading action or omission, rather than information provided in supplementary form, small print etc.

The most recent case was *Ashbourne Management Services Limited*.[95] The plaintiff in this case was the Office of Fair Trading, while the defendant was a company which specialized in recruiting gym members for fitness clubs across the country. The case concerned, inter alia, threats to report consumers to credit reference agencies for non-payment of sums allegedly due under the agreements with the gyms. For our purposes the important point is that the High Court decided that such threats amounted to aggressive practices where the sums in question were legitimately in dispute and where the sums were no more than claims for unliquidated damages. This seems to approach the aggressive practices concept in a relatively protective manner. It takes account of the very significant detrimental impact on consumers of being reported to a credit reference agency and therefore having a poor credit record that will affect future attempts to borrow money. Importantly, also, it seems to recognize that traders should not simply be viewed as having a legitimate interest in taking any otherwise legal action to protect their interests. They should be expected to take seriously any genuine dispute as to the validity of their claim.

In summary, UK judges have been relatively sensitive to consumer protection needs in the way in which they have interpreted these UCPD concepts. On the trader side, subjective dishonesty is not required. So, the fairness of practices is to be judged objectively – a practice deemed unfair by these criteria does not become acceptable based on a 'pure heart and empty head' defence. On the consumer side of the equation, there is recognition of the information-processing limits of consumers. There also appears to be recognition that the fairness of practices (at least under the aggressive practices concept) should be understood by reference to the detrimental substantive impact of the practice on the consumer.

---

consumers (UCPD, arts 5[2] [b] and 5[3]/CPUTR, regs 2[4] and 2[5]). There is no space here to discuss these alternative benchmarks. However, see discussion in C Willett, 'Unfairness under the Consumer Protection from Unfair Trading Regulations', above, n 7; and see, for example, the OFT work on mental capacity: OFT, Mental Capacity consultation (OFT 1293con), available at http://www.oft.gov.uk/news-and-updates/press/2010/127–10.

95 *Office of Fair Trading v Ashbourne Management Services Limited, John Clayton-Wright and Dawne Clayton-Wright* [2011] EWHC 1237(Ch).

6. The Future

This paper has demonstrated that the United Kingdom has implemented the UCPD via a mixture of preventive and criminal enforcement techniques, but that these techniques have been 'Europeanized' by the open-textured nature and significant breadth of application of the UCPD concepts. It has also shown that the UCPD may also lead to a more spontaneous (less direct) Europeanization of UK private law, in particular by moving towards introducing remedies for certain violations of the UCPD concepts of fairness.

At the same time, we have demonstrated an important limit to the Europeanization brought about by the UCPD. In the hugely important financial services sector, Article 3(9) of the UCPD, inter alia, is likely to mean that the pre-existing domestic regime will not be significantly Europeanized by the UCPD concepts.

In the latter part of the paper, we focused on the role of judges when it comes to the reception of the UCPD in the United Kingdom. It was argued that the UCPD's European concepts of fairness often have the potential to increase consumer protection in the United Kingdom, and that, so far, UK judges have been relatively protective in the way in which they have interpreted these UCPD concepts.

Of course, as we have noted many times throughout this paper, the UCPD unfairness concepts are of a rather 'open-textured' nature. This means that, while they *can* (and have so far) been interpreted in relatively protective ways, they might also be interpreted in ways that are rather more grounded in values of trader self-interest and consumer self-reliance. For instance, for the purposes of the misleading action concept, it might be taken that consumers can be expected to read not only the 'headline' information, but also less-prominent information that in some way qualifies or negates a misleading impression that has been given by the headline information.

The point is that we have yet to hear the views of the Supreme Court on such matters.[96] So we cannot be sure as yet as to what ethic of fairness will ultimately take hold in the United Kingdom. However, it will be interesting to see how the UK courts, in particular the Supreme Court, respond in the longer term to the decision of the ECJ in response to the reference made by the Court of Appeal in the *Purely Creative* case.[97] The ECJ decided that when para. 31 refers to a 'false impression' in relation to winning a prize (when in fact this is subject to some

---

96 See Willett, above n 22, where one of the present authors argues that (i) the Supreme Court has chosen to unpack and apply the similarly open-textured general clause on unfair contract terms (and associated provisions) (from Directive 93/13/EEC) by reference to an ethic of trader *self-interest* and consumer *self-reliance*, rather than by reference to an ethic of protection; and (ii) that this is in contrast to the more protective approaches taken by the OFT and the Court of Appeal. This may be one reason why the Court of Appeal chose to make a reference to the ECJ in the *Purely Creative* case (above, n 93).

97 See above, n 93.

action or cost for the consumer), this, inter alia, includes cases where any one of the optional ways in which to claim the prize requires the consumer to incur any cost whatsoever. The Court explained that para. 31 aims to address the aggressive practice of exploiting the psychological effect of being told a prize has been won, this being likely to induce consumers to take the irrational choice of choosing the more expensive (but quicker) route (e.g., a premium rate call) to discover the nature of the prize.[98]

Of course, this reference went specifically to the interpretation of paragraph 31 of Annex 1 to the Directive and not to interpretation of the general tests of unfairness (i.e., the clauses on misleading and aggressive practices and on professional diligence). However, paragraph 31 is supposed to be a concrete example of the general aggressive practices concept. This concept is concerned with practices which significantly impair consumer freedom of choice.[99] It might then be argued that the ECJ decision in *Purely Creative* indicates an ECJ view as to how this freedom of choice concept might be understood under the general clause on aggressive practices. It could indicate that the ECJ is sensitive to the potential for consumer freedom of choice to be readily compromised when 'put on the spot' by attractive offers that tend to induce speedy and economically detrimental decisions.

We must now wait to see whether the UK courts (in particular the Supreme Court) decide to take such a protective approach to the aggressive practices concept; whether the UK courts make references under the aggressive practices (or the other) general clauses; and whether the ECJ does indeed choose to take to carry over the protective approach taken under para. 31 to the aggressive practices (and the other) general clauses.

Addendum

From 31 March 2014, the powers of the Office of Fair Trading (OFT) were transferred to a number of other bodies, including, most importantly, to the Competition and Markets Authority and, in the case of financial services, to the Financial Conduct Authority.

Bibliography

Atwood B, K Thompson and C Willett, *Food Law* (Tottel, 2009).

Black J, M Hopper and C Band, 'Making a Success of Principles Based Regulation' (2007) *Law and Financial Markets Review* 191.

Brownsword R, H-W Micklitz, L Niglia and S Weatherill, *The Foundations of European Private Law* (Hart Publishing, 2011).

98 C-428/11.

99 See n 78 above.

Cartwright P, *Consumer Protection and the Criminal Law* (Cambridge University Press, 2001).

———, 'Conceptualising and Understanding Fairness: Lessons from and for Financial Services', in J Devenney, L Fox O'Mahony and M Kenny (eds), *Unconscionability in European Private Financial Transactions* (Cambridge University Press, 2010) 205.

———, 'Under Pressure: Regulating Aggressive Practices in the UK' (2011) *Lloyds Maritime and Commercial Law Quarterly* 123.

Civic Consulting/EU Commission, DG Justice (F Alleweldt, S Kara, P Rott, C Willett and H Gamper), *Study on the Application of Directive 2005/29/EC on Unfair Commercial Practices in the EU*, 2013, Synthesis and Country Reports, available at http://ec.europa.eu/justice/consumer-marketing/files/ucpd_final_report_part_1_synthesis.pdf and http://ec.europa.eu/justice/consumer-marketing/files/ucpd_study_country_reports.pdf.

Collins H, 'Harmonisation by Example: European Laws against Unfair Commercial Practices' (2010) 73(1) *Modern Law Review* 89.

FCA, *Full Handbook*, available at http://www.fsa.gov.uk/Pages/handbook/index.shtml.

———, *Treating Customers Fairly*, available at http://www.fsa.gov.uk/Pages/Doing/Regulated/tcf/index.shtml.

FSA, Consultation Paper 10/6, *The Assessment and Redress of Payment Protection Insurance Complaints Feedback on CP09/23 and Further Consultation*, FSA/OFT Concordat, November 2009, available at http://www.fsa.gov.uk/pubs/other/concordat_fsa_oft_08.pdf.

Grundman S and D Mazeaud, *General Clauses and Standards in European Contract Law* (Kluwer International, 2005).

Howells G, 'General Clauses in European Consumer Law', in H-W Micklitz (ed.), *Verbraucherrecht in Deutschland* (Nomos, 2005).

———, 'The End of an Era – Implementing the Unfair Commercial Practices Directive in the United Kingdom: Punctual Criminal Law Gives Way to a General Criminal/Civil Law Standard' (2009) *Journal of Business Law* 183.

Howells G, H-W Micklitz and T Wilhelmsson, *European Fair Trading Law* (Ashgate, 2006).

Law Commission, *A Private Right of Redress for Commercial Practices* (2008).

———, *Consumer Redress for Misleading and Aggressive Practices* (LCCP, 2011) 199.

Law Commissions, *Consumer Redress for Misleading and Aggressive Practices* (2012) Law Com 332, Scot Law Com 226.

Loos MBM, 'The Influence of European Consumer Law on General Contract Law and the Need for Spontaneous Harmonization' (2007) 4 *European Review of Private Law* 515.

Morgan-Taylor M, 'Preventing Distribution of Promotions to Consumers Involving Unfair Practices – OFT Application for Order Under Enterprise Act 2002: *OFT v Purely Creative Ltd et al*' (2011) 16(3) *Communications Law* 115.

OFT, *Criminal Enforcement of the Consumer Protection from Unfair Trading Regulations* (OFT, 2010), para 2.1, available at http://www.oft.gov.uk/shared_oft/policy/OFT1273.pdf.

———, *Mental Capacity Consultation* (OFT, 2010) (OFT 1293con), available at http://www.oft.gov.uk/news-and-updates/press/2010/127–10.

OFT/BERR, *Guidance on the Consumer Protection from Unfair Trading Regulations* (OFT/BERR 2008), available at http://www.oft.gov.uk/shared_oft/business_leaflets/cpregs/oft1008.pdf.

Twigg-Flesner C, *The Europeanisation of Contract Law* (Routledge, 2008).

——— (ed.), *The Cambridge Companion to European Union Private Law* (Cambridge University Press, 2010).

van Gerven W, 'A Common Law for Europe: The Future Meeting the Past?' (2001) 4 *ERPL* 485.

Weatherill S and U Bernitz, *The Regulation of Unfair Commercial Practices under EC Directive 2005/29* (Hart, 2007).

Whittaker S, 'The Relationship of the Unfair Commercial Practices Directive to European and National Contract Laws', in S Weatherill and U Bernitz (eds), *The Regulation of Unfair Commercial Practices under EC Directive 2005/29* (Hart, 2007).

Willett C, *Fairness in Consumer Contracts: The Case of Unfair Terms* (Ashgate, 2007).

———, 'Fairness and Consumer Decision Making under the Unfair Commercial Practices Directive' (2010) 33 *JCP* 247.

———, 'Unfairness under the Consumer Protection from Unfair Trading Regulations', in J Devenney, L Fox O'Mahony and M Kenny (eds), *Unconscionability in European Private Financial Transactions* (Cambridge University Press, 2010) 350.

———, 'General Clauses and the Competing Ethics of European Consumer Law in the UK' (2012) 71(2) *Cambridge Law Journal* 412–440.

Willett C and M Morgan-Taylor, 'Consumer Protection', in J Chuah and M Furmston (eds), *Commercial and Consumer Law* (2nd edn, Longman, 2013, 7.8).

Williams J and C Hare, 'Early Experiences of the Enforcement of the Unfair Commercial Practices Directive in Scotland' (2010) 33(4) *Journal of Consumer Policy* 377–401.

Williams T, 'Open the Box: An Exploration of the Financial Service Authority's Model of Fairness in Consumer Financial Transactions', in J Devenney, L Fox O'Mahony and M Kenny (eds), *Unconscionability in European Private Financial Transactions* (Cambridge University Press, 2010).

Chapter 2
Pre-emption of National Prohibitions of Sale Below Cost: Some Reflections on EU Law between the Past and the Future[1]

Bert Keirsbilck

1. Introduction

In some Member States, sales below costs are prohibited. These national prohibitions aim to establish a certain threshold price under which undertakings are not allowed to sell except in a limited set of circumstances. However, the nature and scope of these national prohibitions vary widely (e.g., application of the prohibition to all retail sectors or only to certain firms or products; circumstances under which a sale below cost would be allowed even if the practice is generally prohibited; elements included in the calculation of 'costs', etc.).

In France, for example, Article L. 420–5 of the Commercial Code prohibits abusively low pricing as an 'anticompetitive practice', where the object or effect of such offers or practices is to exclude an undertaking from the market. The conditions of application of this prohibition are similar to those concerning predatory pricing under competition law, but its scope is limited to sales to final consumers, and it does not require proof of a dominant position. In addition, Article L. 442–2 of the Commercial Code, as amended by the 2008 *Loi Chatel*, prohibits resale below cost as a 'practice restricting competition'. The threshold was lowered in 2008 in order to allow deeper discounting by resellers without breaching Article L. 420–5 (abusively low pricing).[2] In Belgium, Article 101 of the 2010 Market Practices and Consumer Protection Act contains a *per se* prohibition of sales below cost (retaking ex Article 41 of the 1991 Commercial Practices and

---

1 This chapter is an amended, extended and updated version of a paper which was published in the online journal *Erasmus Law Review* in 2012. See B Keirsbilck, 'Does EU Economic Law Preclude National Prohibitions of Sales Below Cost?' (2012) *Erasmus Law Review* 253–266. The *Erasmus Law Review* kindly accepted the publication of the new version of this paper in this edited volume.

2 The Attali report called for the removal of the prohibition of resale at loss (as amended by the 1996 'Loi Galland'). See 'Rapport de la Commission pour la libération de la croissance française, sous la présidence de Jacques Attali', 23 January 2008, 245, available at http://lesrapports.ladocumentationfrancaise.fr/BRP/084000041/0000.pdf.

Consumer Protection Act). Likewise, Spain and Portugal have certain unfair trade rules prohibiting sales below cost. However, several Member States, including Ireland, Italy and the United Kingdom, have removed their rules concerning resale below cost in recent years.

The purpose of this chapter is to discuss whether EU law precludes national prohibitions of sales below cost. In the first section, the focus will be on the *Keck and Mithouard* judgment of the European Court of Justice (ECJ) and on the withdrawn Amended Commission Proposal for a Sales Promotions Regulation. In the second section, it will be argued that the Unfair Commercial Practices Directive 2005/29 has a pre-emptive effect on national prohibitions of business-to-consumer sales below cost that pursue consumer protection objectives. Subsequently, the chapter will discuss whether EU antitrust law, which has recently been interpreted as 'living apart together' with the Unfair Commercial Practices Directive 2005/29,[3] precludes the application of national prohibitions of sales below cost to practices which are not incompatible with EU antitrust law. Finally, this chapter will open up new avenues for further research on whether EU law *should* preclude national prohibitions of sales below cost. In any case, there is an urgent need for the Union to take an unequivocal position on this matter.

2. Past Answers

2.1 The 1993 Keck and Mithouard Judgment

It is well known that the ECJ ruled in *Oosthoek* that

> legislation which restricts or prohibits certain forms of advertising and certain means of sales promotion may, although it does not directly affect imports, be such as to restrict their volume because it affects marketing opportunities for the imported products. The possibility cannot be ruled out that to compel a producer either to adopt advertising or sales promotion schemes which differ from one Member State to another or to discontinue a scheme which he considers to be particularly effective may constitute an obstacle to imports even if the legislation in question applies to domestic products and imported products without distinction.[4]

The *Oosthoek* criterion led to a flood of litigation where traders invoked the illegality of any (unfair) trade rules even where such rules did not have any greater impact on imported than on domestic products and merely reduced the overall volume of sales. This led to the possible subjection of any (unfair) trade rules to supervision under EU law and started to damage the image and legitimacy of the

3 B Keirsbilck, *The New European Law of Unfair Commercial Practices and Competition Law* (Oxford: Hart Publishing, 2011).

4 ECJ 15 December 1982, Case C–286/81, Criminal proceeding against Oosthoek's Uitgeversmaatschappij BV, (1982) ECR I–4575, para 15.

ECJ. Moreover, the ECJ's approach was not always consistent and when dealing with national rules restricting the circumstances in which goods may be marketed, Article 34 TFEU was sometimes interpreted narrowly, other times broadly.[5]

In *Keck and Mithouard*, the ECJ considered it necessary, in view of 'the increasing tendency of traders to invoke [Article 34 TFEU] as a means of challenging any rules whose effect is to limit their commercial freedom even where such rules are not aimed at products from other Member States', to 're-examine and clarify its case law on this matter'.[6] In this case, the ECJ examined the compatibility with Article 34 TFEU of the French general prohibition on resale below cost. Keck and Mithouard, managers of two French supermarkets in Mundolsheim (close to the German border), were prosecuted in criminal proceedings for reselling beer and coffee in an unaltered state to consumers, at prices lower than their actual purchase price. Advocate General van Gerven presented two opinions with opposite results.[7] The ECJ first observed that a general prohibition on resale below cost is not designed to regulate trade in goods between the Member States, but may, admittedly, be considered as 'legislation which restricts certain means of sales promotion and which restricts their volume' (*Oosthoek*). But the question remained whether such a possibility was sufficient to characterize the French

5 See, with regard to this pre-*Keck* case law and different possible tests for Article 34 TFEU, W Wils, 'The Search for the Rule in Article 30 EEC: Much Ado About Nothing?' (1993) *EL Rev.* 475–492.

6 Para 14.

7 See Opinion of Advocate General van Gerven of 18 November 1992 (before the 2nd Chamber), Joined Cases C–267/91 and C–268/91, Criminal proceeding against Bernard Keck and Daniel Mithouard, (1993) ECR I–6097, stating that the French prohibition was basically suitable to ensure fair trading and consumer protection (para 8) but did not satisfy the proportionality test (para 9): 'The problem with a ban framed in general terms [...] is, however, that use of the sales promotion method which it prohibits is also banned in trading situations which cannot be regarded as unfair, anti-competitive or detrimental to the consumer. [...] In so far as it also covers those situations, a prohibition of sale at a loss framed in general terms therefore goes further than is necessary to achieve the aims allowed by Community law.'

See Opinion of Advocate General van Gerven of 28 April 1993 (before the full Court, to which the case was referred due to its importance), Joined Cases C–267/91 and C–268/91, Criminal proceeding against Bernard Keck and Daniel Mithouard, (1993) ECR I–6097, focusing on the question whether the French prohibition worked as an obstacle to intra–Union trade in the specific factual setting before the national court. He concluded (para 13) that 'a statutory prohibition of resale at a loss is not incompatible with Article [34] of the EEC Treaty since it appears that the events at issue in the main proceedings occurred at the retail level, that is to say at a level in respect of which a recognised ground of justification may be invoked for the rules in question and that at that level there is no more than a purely hypothetical effect on trade between Member States and certainly no more than an hypothetical hindering of trade flows'. However, he added (para 14) that 'that is not to say [...] that France would not do well to amend its legislation to bring it more into conformity with Community law'.

prohibition in question as a measure having equivalent effect to a quantitative restriction.[8] The ECJ argued that

> in the absence of harmonization of legislation, obstacles to free movement of goods which are the consequence of applying, to goods coming from other Member States where they are lawfully manufactured and marketed, rules that lay down requirements to be met by such goods (such as those relating to designation, form, size, weight, composition, presentation, labelling, packaging) constitute measures of equivalent effect prohibited by Article [34]. This is so even if those rules apply without distinction to all products unless their application can be justified by a public-interest objective taking precedence over the free movement of goods.[9]
>
> By contrast, contrary to what has previously been decided, the application to products from other Member States of national provisions restricting or prohibiting certain selling arrangements is not such as to hinder directly or indirectly, actually or potentially, trade between Member States within the meaning of the Dassonville judgment, so long as those provisions apply to all relevant traders operating within the national territory and so long as they affect in the same manner, in law and in fact, the marketing of domestic products and of those from other Member States.[10]

The *Keck* proviso is actually a double discrimination test. Rules concerning selling arrangements are excluded so long as they are not discriminatory (i) with regard to their application and (ii) with regard to their legal or factual effect. The ECJ indicated that the basic idea underlying the discrimination test is that of *equal market access*:

> Provided that those conditions are fulfilled, the application of such rules to the sale of products from another Member State meeting the requirements laid down by that State is not by nature such as to prevent their access to the market or to impede access any more than it impedes the access of domestic products. Such rules therefore fall outside the scope of Article [34] of the Treaty.[11]

Whereas Advocate General van Gerven in his two Opinions argued that the French prohibition of resale at a loss could, in some cases, impede access to the French market of imported products more than access of domestic products, the ECJ simply held that Article 34 TFEU 'is to be interpreted as not applying to legislation of a Member State imposing a general prohibition of resale at a loss'.[12]

---

8 ECJ 24 November 1993, Joined Cases C–267/91 and C–268/91, Criminal proceeding against Bernard Keck and Daniel Mithouard, (1993) ECR I–6097, paras 12–13.

9 Para 15.

10 Para 16.

11 Para 17.

12 Para 18.

According to the ECJ, national requirements relating to 'selling arrangements', such as sales below cost, are by nature, as far as imported products are concerned, not 'such as to prevent their access to the market or to impede access more than they impede the access of domestic products'. Such requirements do not require the intrinsic or extrinsic characteristics of imported products to be adapted. The producer/supplier faces no additional costs, which would have the effect of impeding the imported product's access to the market or even, where those costs are prohibitive, of making access impossible.[13]

By contrast, product requirements are by nature, as far as imported products are concerned, 'such as to prevent their access to the market or to impede access more than they impede the access of domestic products'. As a result, products lawfully manufactured and marketed in the Member State of origin must be adapted in order to suit the product requirements of the Member States of destination and to be lawfully marketed in that Member State. Hence, they must satisfy the requirements of two different sets of legislation (contrary to the *Cassis de Dijon* principle of mutual recognition).

In opting for an overall assessment, the ECJ diverged from the *Cassis de Dijon* test. Indeed, at least as regards 'national provisions restricting or prohibiting certain sales arrangements', the ECJ no longer presumes that every national rule 'capable of hindering, directly or indirectly, actually or potentially, intra-[Union] trade' falls within the scope of Article 34 TFEU.[14]

Pursuant to *Keck and Mithouard*, national prohibitions of sales below cost are not precluded by EU law, as long as they are not discriminatory with regard to their application and with regard to their legal or factual effect.[15]

2.2 The 2002 Amended Commission Proposal for a Sales Promotions Regulation

In 2001, the Commission adopted a first *Proposal for a Regulation on Sales Promotions in the Internal Market*.[16] Drawing on the outcome of the assessment of the internal market barriers resulting from significant differences in national rules concerning commercial communications, the Commission was not in favour of a

13 Opinion of Advocate General van Gerven of 16 March 1994, Joined Cases C–401/92 and C–402/92, Criminal proceedings against Tankstation 't Heukske vof and J.B.E. Boermans, (1994) ECR I–2199, para 20.

14 Para 24.

15 The ECJ confirmed the *Keck* judgment on the French prohibition of sales below cost in relation to the Belgian prohibition of sales yielding only a very low profit margin. See ECJ 11 August 1995, Case C–63/94, Groupement national des négociants en pomme de terre de Belgique v ITM Belgium SA and Vocarex SA, (1995) ECR I–02476. This is also settled Belgian case law: see e.g., President of the Antwerp Commercial Court 19 June 2003 (2003) *Jb. Hand. Med.* 380.

16 Original Commission Proposal for a European Parliament and Council Regulation on Sales Promotions in the Internal Market, 2 October 2001, COM (2001) 546 final, 37 p.

harmonized European ban on 'sales below cost' (defined as 'discounts consisting of a sale of a product or service by a retailer below the retailer's net invoice price inclusive of carriage, insurance and other delivery costs as well as tax'[17]). According to the Commission, the proportionality analysis suggested that the objective of preventing market destabilization, abuse of dominance and consumer deception could be realized by less-restrictive measures such as harmonized transparency provisions. The protection against unfair competition and consumer protection could be achieved in a more effective and proportionate manner through specific information requirements than through prohibitions of sales below cost, which are in addition difficult to enforce. Therefore, the Commission proposed that suppliers would have to be informed *ex ante* by their resellers, in conformity with contractual terms, of the possibility that their goods or services are to be resold at a loss. The Commission also proposed that consumers would have to be made aware of the real value of the good or service in order to ensure that they would be able to properly compare the real economic value of competing goods and services. Promoters would have to indicate in the relevant commercial communication whether a sale represents a sale below cost.

The European Parliament opposed the idea that the Sales Promotions Regulation would preclude national 'measures which, in the interests of protecting consumers, supplier companies and competition, partially restrict the use and commercial communication of particular sales promotions such as sales below cost'.[18] Therefore, the European Parliament proposed that the Regulation would be

---

17 Art 2, n. See also Explanatory Memorandum: 'This definition is based on existing national definitions and is also consistent with jurisprudence of the Court in the field of competition rules (predatory pricing). A sales below cost is defined as a sale where the price at which the product or service is sold is lower than the net invoice price at which that retailer or wholesaler purchased the product or service from the relevant supplier. The net invoice price is the unit price on the invoice from the supplier or the wholesaler to the promoter including carriage, insurance or other costs and value added tax. The invoice and other costs used for the calculation should be dated the same day of the sales promotion or its commercial communication. Where no such invoice exists, the net invoice price should be based on the most recent invoice supplied to that promoter for such goods or services that are subject to the sales promotion'.

18 European Parliament legislative resolution of 4 September 2002 on the proposal for a European Parliament and Council regulation on sales promotions in the Internal Market, A5–0253/2002, P5_TA(2002)0400, amendments 28 and 32, with the following justifications: 'In the report accompanying its proposal for a regulation the Commission confirms that sales below cost are legitimate. The legitimacy of sales promotions of this kind is not in question, but we feel that, in addition to specific conditions on transparency (requirement that the organisers of the promotion state clearly that the offer of a product or a service with a major reduction represents a sale below cost) to protect the consumer or the company supplying the products or services, consideration should be given to a further and no less damaging aspect of sales below cost, namely that they distort the conditions of competition to the detriment of other commercial companies, particularly small ones, as well as consumers. It is therefore proposed to amend the provisions of Article 3(2), first

made explicitly without prejudice to national prohibitions of sales below cost. The Commission accepted the amendments of the European Parliament as they would contribute to 'a constructive compromise on the treatment of sales below costs'.[19] The Commission's 2002 *Amended Proposal for a Sales Promotions Regulation* provided in Article 3(3) that the Regulation is without prejudice to national provisions governing sales below cost. This meant that national legislators would remain free to introduce or maintain prohibitions of sales below cost.[20]

Ultimately, however, the legislative work on the Amended Commission Proposal was slowed down and finally stopped, awaiting the outcome of the work on the 2003 Commission Proposal for a Directive Concerning Unfair Business–to–Consumer Commercial Practices.[21] The Amended Commission Proposal for a Sales Promotions Regulation was withdrawn in 2006.

3. Present Answers

3.1 The 2005 Unfair Commercial Practices Directive (2005/29)

In 2005, the European legislator adopted *Directive 2005/29 Concerning Unfair Business-to-Consumer Commercial Practices* ('UCPD').[22] This Directive establishes a single regulatory framework concerning unfair business-to-consumer

---

indent, of the proposal for a regulation, preventing Member States from imposing a general prohibition on the use or commercial communication of sales promotions, so that rules can be adopted at national level to regulate sales below cost in order to safeguard competition and protect supplier companies and consumers. [...] Sales below cost should not be governed by Community law, but by national law in accordance with local circumstances. The subsidiarity principle should apply here.' See also Report of the Committee on Legal Affairs and the Internal Market of 10 July 2002 on the Proposal for a European Parliament and Council Regulation Concerning Sales Promotions in the Internal Market – Committee on Legal Affairs and the Internal Market, A5–0253/2002, PE 312.784.

19 Amended Commission Proposal for a Regulation on Sales Promotions in the Internal Market, 25 October 2002, COM (2002) 585 final, 17 p.

20 Interestingly, the revision clause of art 7 provided that the comprehensive report on the application of the Regulation and of the impact of sales promotions law on both consumers and businesses would also have to contain 'a detailed evaluation of the Internal Market effects on the differing national prohibitions on sales below cost and an assessment of the impact of a potential liberalisation of such sales'.

21 Commission Proposal for a Directive of the European Parliament and of the Council Concerning Unfair 'Business-to-Consumer' Commercial Practices in the Internal Market and amending directives 84/450/EEC, 97/7/EC and 98/27/EC (the Unfair Commercial Practices Directive), 18 June 2003, COM (2003) 356 final, 41 p.

22 Directive 2005/29/EC of the European Parliament and of the Council of 11 May 2005 Concerning Unfair Business-to-Consumer Commercial Practices in the Internal Market and Amending Council Directive 84/450/EEC, Directives 97/7/EC, 98/27/EC and 2002/65/EC of the European Parliament and of the Council and Regulation (EC) No 2006/2004 of the European Parliament and of the Council, OJ L 149, 11.06.2005, 22–39.

commercial practices and is based on maximum harmonization.[23] It will be argued that the Directive must be interpreted as meaning that it precludes a national prohibition of sales below cost such as Article 101 of the Belgian Market Practices and Consumer Protection Act. On 7 March 2013, the European Court of Justice ordered in the *Euronics Belgium* case that a national provision, such as Article 101 of the Belgian Act, which provides for a general prohibition of offering for sale or selling at a loss is precluded by the UCPD in so far as that provision pursues objectives relating to consumer protection.[24]

Step 1 – Do sales below cost constitute 'B2C commercial practices'?

The first thing to assess is of course whether sales below cost constitute 'commercial practices' within the meaning of Article 2(d) UCPD. It is well known that the Directive gives a particularly wide definition to the concept of 'business-to-consumer commercial practices', namely: 'any act, omission, course of conduct or representation, commercial communication including advertising and marketing, by a trader, directly connected with the promotion, sale or supply of a product to consumers'. It seems that Member States such as Belgium and France, while agreeing on the Directive and slowing down the project for a Sales Promotions Regulation, were or even still are not fully aware of the fact that both the use and the commercial communication of B2C sales promotions are clearly covered by the Directive.

In the *VTB–VAB* proceedings concerning the compatibility of the Belgian prohibition of joined offers to consumers, the Belgian and French Governments basically developed two arguments for the opposite view. They argued, principally, that neither the use nor the commercial communication of B2C sales promotions constitute 'commercial practices' within the meaning of the UCPD as they were subject to the Amended Proposal for a Sales Promotions Regulation, and that the withdrawal of that Proposal (in 2006 only, one year after the adoption of the Directive) did not permit the inference that the Directive would now cover the use and commercial communication of B2C sales promotions previously covered by the Amended Proposal for a Sales Promotions Regulation. Belgium and France argued, in the alternative, that the use and commercial communication of B2C

23 The maximum harmonization character of the Directive has been confirmed in various ECJ judgments: ECJ 23 April 2009, Joined Cases C–261/07 and C–299/07, *VTB–VAB NV v Total Belgium NV* and *Galatea BVBA v Sanoma Magazines Belgium NV*, (2009) ECR I–02949, paras 51–52; ECJ 14 January 2010, Case C–304/08, *Zentrale zur Bekämpfung unlauteren Wettbewerbs eV v Plus Warenhandelsgesellschaft mbH*, (2010) ECR I–00217, para 41; ECJ 9 November 2010, Case C–540/08, *Mediaprint Zeitungs- und Zeitschriftenverlag GmbH & Co KG v 'Österreich'-Zeitungsverlag GmbH*, (2010) ECR 2010, I–10909, para 30; ECJ Order of 30 June 2011, Case C–288/10, *Wamo BVBA v JBC NV and Modemakers Fashion NV*, nyr, para 33.

24 ECJ Order of 7 March 2013, Case C–343/12, *Euronics Belgium CVBA v Kamera Express BV & Kamera Express Belgium BVBA*, nyr.

sales promotions only fall within the scope of application of the Directive, where, additionally, they are unfair within the meaning of its grand general clause.

However, the Advocate General Trstenjak and the ECJ rightly rejected these two arguments in the following manner. First, it was argued that both the commercial communication and the use of B2C sales promotions constitute 'commercial practices' within the meaning of the Directive, as they 'clearly form part of an operator's commercial strategy and relate directly to the promotion thereof and its sales development'[25]; by no later than the date of withdrawal of the Amended Proposal for a Sales Promotions Regulation (in 2006, at a time when the period for the transposition of the Directive was still running), the national legislators should have examined, if necessary, to what extent the scope of the Directive would also apply to fields previously covered by the Amended Proposal for a Sales Promotions Regulation. In my view, business-to-consumer sales below cost undeniably constitute 'business-to-consumer commercial practices' within the meaning of the Directive and the *VTB–VAB* judgment. Moreover, the fact that the Amended Proposal for a Sales Promotions Regulation is without prejudice to national prohibitions of sales below cost is irrelevant, since it was repealed in 2006, well before the end of the transposition deadline of the Directive. Second, the argument that only *unfair* business-to-consumer commercial practices fall within the scope of application of the Directive was rightly disqualified in *VTB–VAB* as circular reasoning, stemming from an equation of the Directive's scope of application with the conditions of application of its general clause.[26]

It is worth noting that the Belgian legislator developed an additional argument for the view that the Belgian prohibition of B2C sales below cost falls outside the scope of the Directive. When transposing the Directive in 2007, the Belgian legislator argued, in the further alternative, that the Directive covers only commercial communications of sales below cost, not the use of sales below cost as such. The Directive was said to be without prejudice to national prohibitions on the use of sales below cost or to any 'fundamental requirements' to be met by such sales, such as Article 41 of the 1991 Commercial Practices and Consumer Protection Act. When drafting the new Market Practices and Consumer Protection Act in 2010, the Belgian legislator argued again that price setting below cost, as prohibited by Article 101 of that Act, is not a 'commercial practice' within the meaning of the Directive on the ground that price setting as such, whether below

---

25 ECJ 23 April 2009, Joined Cases C–261/07 and C–299/07, *VTB–VAB NV v Total Belgium NV* and *Galatea BVBA v Sanoma Magazines Belgium NV*, (2009) ECR I–02949, paras 49–50; ECJ 14 January 2010, Case C–304/08, *Zentrale zur Bekämpfung unlauteren Wettbewerbs eV v Plus Warenhandelsgesellschaft mbH*, (2010) ECR I–00217, paras 36–37; ECJ 9 November 2010, Case C–540/08, *Mediaprint Zeitungs- und Zeitschriftenverlag GmbH & Co KG v 'Österreich'-Zeitungsverlag GmbH*, (2010) ECR 2010, I–10909, paras 17–18; ECJ Order of 30 June 2011, Case C–288/10, *Wamo BVBA v JBC NV and Modemakers Fashion NV*, nyr, paras 30–31.

26 See B Keirsbilck, *The New European Law of Unfair Commercial Practices and Competition Law* (Oxford: Hart Publishing, 2011) 231 e.s.

cost or not, represents nothing but an internal business decision. The Belgian legislator seemed to argue that commercial communications (to the public) that prices of particular goods are below cost, constitute commercial practices, while sales below cost as such do not.

Yet, it is evident that the distinction between the prohibition of certain commercial communications on business practices on the one hand and the prohibition of the use of certain business practices, or the regulation of their 'basic conditions', is artificial and in line neither with the Directive nor with Belgian unfair trade law itself. As mentioned, the Directive's definition of 'commercial practices' includes not only 'commercial communication including advertising and marketing' but also 'any act, omission, course of conduct or representation, by a trader, directly connected with the promotion, sale or supply of a product to consumers'. Similarly, the Commission Proposals for a Sales Promotions Regulation deliberately covered both the use and the commercial communication of sales promotions, as use and communication cannot be isolated from each other. Likewise, Belgian unfair trade law traditionally simultaneously regulates the use and the commercial communication of 'market practices'.

Furthermore, the Belgian legislator argued that the Belgian prohibition of sales below cost must be considered as a national contract law rule to which the Directive is, pursuant to Article 3(2), without prejudice.[27] From this perspective, a retail price is primarily seen as the individually negotiated consideration for the transfer of the property of the good from the business to the consumer. Under this reading, the Belgian prohibition is seen as a contract law rule prohibiting the conclusion of below cost B2C sales contracts and it is stressed that, according to Belgian case law, infringements of that prohibition may result in the invalidity of the contract at issue. Hence, the prohibition is said to fall outside the scope of the Directive.

However, retail prices (whether below cost or not) are very often not individually negotiated but rather offered on a take-it-or-leave-it basis. Unfair trade law extensively regulates pricing practices, as they may have a *substantial* impact on the market by addressing or reaching a (large) number of consumers and influencing if not materially distorting their economic behaviour.[28] The Belgian prohibition of B2C sales below cost has a similar *collective* dimension and prohibits the use and commercial communication of below-cost pricing practices directly connected with the promotion of goods to consumers. In my view, the Belgian prohibition thus pertains to a commercial practice falling within the scope of the Directive. This conclusion cannot be called into question by the fact that infringements of that prohibition may result in the invalidity of the contract at

27 See also H De Bauw, 'De impact van de richtlijn oneerlijke handelspraktijken op de regeling van de verkooppromoties onder de WHPC' (2006) *DCCR* 19.

28 See also J Glöckner, 'The Scope of Application of the UCPD – I Know What You Did Last Summer' (2010) *IIC* 589, who regrets that the *collective* protective purpose of the Directive has not been adequately expressed in the definition of commercial practice.

issue. Article 3(2) of Directive 2005/29 must be interpreted as merely seeking to ensure that undesirable overlapping of the Directive and European or national contract law instruments does not occur at the level of legal consequences.[29]

Hence, national prohibitions of sales below cost fall within the scope of the Directive, in so far as they apply to B2C relationships, and they fall outside the scope of the Directive, in so far as they apply to B2B relationships. This was clearly confirmed by the ECJ in the *Euronics* order:

> The practice of selling at a loss, at issue in the main proceedings, which is used, as the referring court observes, as bait, serves the purpose of attracting consumers to the business premises of a trader and encouraging them to make purchases. It clearly forms part of an operator's commercial strategy and relates directly to its promotion and sales development. It follows that it constitutes a commercial practice within the meaning of Article 2(d) of the Unfair Commercial Practices Directive and, consequently, comes within its material scope.[30]

Step 1*bis *– Do prohibitions of sales below cost pursue objectives related to consumer protection?

Upon finding that a national measure concerns a 'commercial practice' within the meaning of the Directive, the next step is to determine whether that measure pursues objectives relating to consumer protection. A measure concerning a 'commercial practice' falls outside the scope of the Directive if it does not pursue consumer protection objectives. It is settled case law since the ECJ judgments in *Plus*[31] and *Mediaprint*[32] that the statement in recitals 6 and 8 that the UCPD 'neither covers nor affects the national laws on unfair commercial practices which harm only competitors' economic interests' should be interpreted as meaning that the Directive is without prejudice to any national measure concerning a 'commercial practice' that only has competitor protection objectives.[33] A national measure regulating or prohibiting a commercial practice with the dual aim of protecting

---

29 See Opinion of Advocate General Trstenjak, Case C–453/10, *Jana Pereničová, Vladislav Perenič v SOS financ spol. s r. o.*, nyr, paras 89–90.

30 ECJ Order of 7 March 2013, Case C–343/12, *Euronics Belgium CVBA v Kamera Express BV & Kamera Express Belgium BVBA*, nyr, para 22.

31 ECJ 14 January 2010, Case C–304/08, *Zentrale zur Bekämpfung unlauteren Wettbewerbs eV v Plus Warenhandelsgesellschaft mbH*, (2010) ECR I–00217, paras 38–39.

32 ECJ 9 November 2010, Case C–540/08, *Mediaprint Zeitungs- und Zeitschriftenverlag GmbH & Co KG v 'Österreich'-Zeitungsverlag GmbH*, (2010) ECR 2010, I–10909, paras 21–22.

33 According to an alternative interpretation of recitals 6 and 8, the UCPD would neither cover nor affect national provisions regulating or prohibiting a commercial practice without actually having any consumer protection effect. See on this alternative interpretation in relation to the Belgian prohibition of discounts preceding seasonal sales B Keirsbilck, 'De invloed van het Europees recht op het Belgisch handelspraktijken- en belendende verbintenissenrecht', in I Samoy, E Terryn and V Sagaert (eds), *De invloed van het Europese recht op het Belgische privaatrecht* (Antwerp: Intersentia, 2012)

competitors and consumers falls within the scope of the UCPD. This is also the view promoted by the Commission in its UCP Guidance.[34] In order to establish whether a national provision (also) aims at protecting consumers, the general purpose of the law, the background and genesis of the measures in question, the preparatory works and academic comments should be taken into account.[35] In the *Wamo* and *Inno* orders concerning the incompatibility of the Belgian prohibition of discounts preceding seasonal sales, the ECJ confirmed, upon finding that the national prohibition pertains to a 'commercial practice' within the meaning of the directive, that the relevant question is whether 'the national provision [...] pursues objectives relating to consumer protection so that it comes within the scope of the Unfair Commercial Practices Directive'.[36]

According to the European Commission, national prohibitions of selling below cost fall outside the scope of the UCPD if the sole rationale is to ensure fair competition in the market space. Such national prohibitions fall within the scope of the Directive (and are precluded by that Directive) insofar as they pursue objectives relating to consumer protection (e.g., protection against bait practices).[37]

In this respect, a close examination of the legislative proceedings leading to the adoption of the Belgian prohibition of sales below cost demonstrates that the prohibition of ex Article 41 of the Commercial Practices and Consumer Protection

591–634; H De Wulf, B Keirsbilck and E Terryn, 'Overzicht van rechtspraak – Algemeen handelsrecht en handelspraktijken'(2012) *TPR* 1117–1123.

34 Commission Staff Working Document, Guidance on the Implementation/ Application of Directive 2005/29/EC on Unfair Commercial Practices, SEC (2009) 1666, 3 December 2009, 14: 'National rules regulating commercial practices [...] for which the sole rationale is to ensure fair competition in the market space, do not fall within the scope of the Directive. [...] Where consumers' and competitors' interests coincide and national measures regulate a practice with the dual aim of protecting consumers and competitors, such national measures are covered by the Directive [...]'.

35 See Commission Staff Working Document, Guidance on the Implementation and Application of Directive 2005/29/EC Concerning Unfair Commercial Practices, SEC (2009) 1666, 3 December 2009, 15 and 16, clearly drawing inspiration from the Opinion of Advocate General Trstenjak of 3 September 2009, Case C–304/08, *Zentrale zur Bekämpfung unlauteren Wettbewerbs eV v Plus Warenhandelsgesellschaft mbH*, (2010) ECR I–00217, para 66 and from her Opinion of 24 March 2010, Case C–540/08, *Mediaprint Zeitungs- und Zeitschriftenverlag GmbH & Co KG v 'Österreich'-Zeitungsverlag GmbH*, (2010) ECR 2010, I–10909, paras 55–58.

36 ECJ Order of 30 June 2011, Case C–288/10, *Wamo BVBA v JBC NV and Modemakers Fashion NV*, nyr, para 20; ECJ Order of 15 December 2011, Case C–126/11, *INNO NV v Unie van Zelfstandige Ondernemers VZW (UNIZO), Organisatie voor de Zelfstandige Modedetailhandel VZW (Mode Unie), Couture Albert BVBA*, nyr, para 22. See also J Vannerom, 'Case Wamo: And the Question Remains ... Who Is (Actually) Protected?' (2012) *REDC* 151–162.

37 Commission Staff Working Document, Guidance on the Implementation/ Application of Directive 2005/29/EC on Unfair Commercial Practices, SEC (2009) 1666, 3 December 2009, 14.

Act was introduced in order to protect both the economic interests of competitors and of consumers. Undoubtedly, the main objective was to protect small retailers against big chain stores, who have sufficient lines of products to cross-subsidize sales below cost systematically, and to ensure fair competition. However, the legislator also sought to protect consumers against businesses selling selected goods below cost, thereby attracting consumers who will make up for the losses on highlighted products with additional purchases of profitable goods.[38]

As mentioned, Article 101 of the 2010 Market Practices and Consumer Protection Act re-enacts Article 41 of the repealed 1991 Commercial Practices and Consumer Protection Act. Not unsurprisingly, the proponents of the Belgian prohibition of sales below cost may now argue that from 2010 the Belgian prohibition no longer seeks to protect the economic interests of consumers. However, this argument is not very convincing,[39] as there are no indications that in 2010 the Belgian legislator has renounced the consumer protection objectives when deciding to re-enact the prohibition. Even if the Belgian prohibition of sales below cost was introduced first and foremost with a view to protect the economic interests of small retailers, it falls within the scope of the Directive, as it does not exclusively seek to protect those interests and also pursues objectives related to consumer protection.[40]

In the *Euronics* order, the ECJ confirmed, upon finding that a national prohibition pertains to a 'commercial practice' within the meaning of the directive, that the relevant question is whether it pursues objectives relating to consumer protection so that it comes within the scope of the Directive. However, the ECJ was not willing to endorse the view of the referring court that the Belgian prohibition of sales below cost pursues (also) consumer protection objectives and to conclude that it falls within the scope of the UCPD.[41] The ECJ simply noted that the referring court has identified consumer protection as one of the objectives of the Belgian prohibition of sales below cost and, precisely on account of these objectives, has asked the ECJ whether the UCPD precludes such a provision.[42] This is to be regretted.

It is worth noting that not all national prohibitions of sales below cost may fall outside the scope of the Directive. For each and every national prohibition of sales

---

38 See e.g., President of the Liège Commercial Court 17 July 2008 (2008) *Jb.Hand. Med.* 250.

39 Compare Brussels Court of Appeal 17 January 2012, *not publ.*, arguing that that prohibition of discounts preceding seasonal sales was maintained in art 32 of the 2010 Market Practices and Consumer Protection Act with the double aim of consumer protection and competitor protection, which inspired the introduction of that prohibition in 1985 in art 53 of the Commercial Practices and Consumer Protection Act.

40 See also B Keirsbilck and J Stuyck, 'Een kritische analyse van de Wet Marktpraktijken en Consumentenbescherming' (2010) *TBH* 739.

41 ECJ Order 7 March 2013, Case C–343/12, *Euronics Belgium CVBA v Kamera Express BV & Kamera Express Belgium BVBA*, nyr, para 17.

42 Paras 18–19.

below cost one should examine whether the *national* protective purpose of the measure includes consumer protection or not. This means that similar prohibitions may fall outside the scope of the Directive in one Member State and inside the scope of the Directive in another. Thus, it may seem a mission impossible to autonomously define the (pre-emptive) scope of the Directive: in determining whether a national measure on business-to-consumer commercial practices falls within the pre-emptive scope of the UCPD, the ECJ will take into account the national legislator's intent. Evidently, this may jeopardize the Directive's goal of market integration. This is an evident drawback from the interpretative choice first made by the ECJ in the *Plus* judgment and recently confirmed in a judgment in relation to an Austrian prohibition of unauthorized liquidation sales.[43]

Step 2 – Sales below cost have not been prohibited per se by the UCPD

As selling below cost does not appear in Annex I to the UCPD, it cannot be prohibited in all circumstances, but can be prohibited only following a specific assessment allowing the unfairness of those practices to be established.[44] In light of the content and the general scheme of the provisions of the Directive, the UCPD precludes any national provision which establishes a presumption of unlawfulness of sales below cost and prohibits, generally and pre-emptively, sales below cost, without any verification of their unlawfulness in the light of the criteria laid down in Articles 5 to 9.

Besides, the Directive provides for adequate and sufficient consumer protection against bait advertising. In addition, competition law provides for adequate and sufficient protection against predatory pricing.[45]

Hence, national consumer protection rules prohibiting business-to-consumer sales below cost are contrary to the Directive, in so far as they generally outlaw sales below cost, whereas the Directive does not blacklist such sales practices.

The ECJ ordered in the *Euronics* case that the practices of offering for sale or selling goods at a loss does not appear in Annex I to the UCPD and, therefore,

43 ECJ Judgment of 17 January 2013, Case C-206/11, *Georg Köck v Schutzverband gegen unlauteren Wettbewerb*, nyr.

44 ECJ 23 April 2009, Joined Cases C–261/07 and C–299/07, *VTB–VAB NV v Total Belgium NV* and *Galatea BVBA v Sanoma Magazines Belgium NV*, (2009) ECR I–02949, paras 53 e.s.; ECJ 14 January 2010, Case C–304/08, *Zentrale zur Bekämpfung unlauteren Wettbewerbs eV v Plus Warenhandelsgesellschaft mbH*, (2010) ECR I–00217, paras 42 e.s.; ECJ 9 November 2010, Case C–540/08, *Mediaprint Zeitungs- und Zeitschriftenverlag GmbH & Co KG v 'Österreich'-Zeitungsverlag GmbH*, (2010) ECR 2010, I–10909, paras 31 e.s.; ECJ Order of 30 June 2011; Case C–288/10, *Wamo BVBA v JBC NV and Modemakers Fashion NV*, nyr, paras 34 e.s.

45 See B Keirsbilck and J Stuyck, 'Een kritische analyse van de Wet Marktpraktijken en Consumentenbescherming' (2010) *TBH* 739.

cannot be prohibited in all circumstances (in so far as the prohibition in dispute pursues consumer protection objectives).[46]

Thus, the answer of the UCPD is yes: EU law precludes national prohibitions of sales below cost insofar as the particular national prohibition pursues objectives related to consumer protection. Strangely enough, the positive integration wave of the UCPD goes further than the negative integration wave of *Keck and Mithouard*: the UCPD precludes certain national rules relating to selling arrangements for goods (commercial practices), where they do not exclusively seek to protect the economic interests of competitors; yet, under the *Keck* conditions, they used to fall outside the scope of Article 34 TFEU. The presumption of the Directive is the opposite to that in *Keck*: illegality of national rules restricting or prohibiting certain commercial practices and a presumption in favour of free trade.[47] In my view, the UCPD has considerably improved consumer protection in and across the Member States, while better protecting legitimate businesses from competitors who do not play by the rules. Being based on maximum harmonization, the Directive has certainly simplified the regulatory environment and helped to remove obstacles to cross-border commerce, by replacing the divergent regulations of the Member States on unfair commercial practices with one set of rules.

3.2 The 2003 Antitrust Regulation (1/2003)

Whereas the new European law of unfair commercial practices predominantly seeks to safeguard undistorted economic behaviour of consumers, and indirectly, seeks to protect the public interest in undistorted competition, EU antitrust law predominantly seeks to safeguard undistorted competition on the market, and indirectly, seeks to protect undistorted economic behaviour of all market participants.

Does EU antitrust law preclude the application of national prohibitions of sales below cost to practices which are not incompatible with EU antitrust law? Article 3(2), first sentence, of Regulation 1/2003 on the Implementation of the Rules on Competition Laid Down in Articles 101 and 102 TFEU[48] states:

> The application of national competition law may not lead to the prohibition of agreements, decisions by associations of undertakings or concerted practices

46 ECJ Order of 7 March 2013, Case C–343/12, *Euronics Belgium CVBA v Kamera Express BV & Kamera Express Belgium BVBA*, nyr, para 29.

47 See also A Pliakos and G Anagnostaras, 'Harmonising National Laws on Commercial Practices: Sales Promotions and the Impact on Business-to-Business Relations' (2010) *EL Rev.* 429–430; G Anagnostaras, 'The Unfair Commercial Practices Directive in Perspective: From Legal Disparity to Legal Complexity?' (2010) *CML Rev* 156; B Keirsbilck, *The New European Law of Unfair Commercial Practices and Competition Law* (Oxford: Hart Publishing, 2011) 232.

48 Regulation (EC) No 1/2003 of 16 December 2002 on the Implementation of the Rules on Competition Laid Down in arts 81 and 82 of the Treaty, *OJ* L 1, 4.1.2003, 1–25.

> which may affect trade between Member States but which do not restrict competition within the meaning of Article 81(1) of the Treaty, or which fulfil the conditions of Article 81(3) of the Treaty or which are covered by a Regulation for the application of Article 81(3) of the Treaty. [...][49]

This 'convergence rule' means that the application of national competition laws to agreements, decisions or concerted practices may not lead to the prohibition of such agreements, decisions and concerted practices if they are not also prohibited under Article 101 TFEU. Application of Article 101 TFEU to a particular case precludes inconsistent application of national competition law to that case. Stricter national competition laws can be applied only to local or regional cases which do not affect trade between Member States.[50] The convergence rule seeks to create a level playing field by providing for a single standard of assessment which allows undertakings to design EU-wide business strategies without having to check them against all the relevant national sets of competition rules. It is a directly applicable rule that can be relied on before national courts, which implies that any measure adopted in breach of that rule would be inapplicable and unenforceable.[51]

In its current wording, the obligation of convergence covers only the application of national competition law to agreements, concerted practices and decisions by associations of undertakings within the meaning of Article 101 TFEU. Member States remain free to adopt or maintain stricter national competition laws than Article 102 TFEU in order to prohibit or sanction unilateral conduct.[52] Article 3(2), second sentence, Regulation 1/2003 states,

> Member States shall not under this Regulation be precluded from adopting and applying on their territory stricter national laws which prohibit or sanction unilateral conduct engaged in by undertakings.[53]

This exception from the level playing field implies that undertakings doing cross-border business in the internal market may be subjected to a variety of standards as to their unilateral behaviour. According to the Commission, 'the prohibition rule of Article [102], in so far as it applies to unilateral conduct, constitutes only a minimum standard that must be applied throughout the Community.'[54] The Commission identified certain categories of national provisions of the type referred to in Article 3(2), second sentence, including national prohibitions of 'resale below cost' or 'resale at loss', typically based on a similar economic rationale as the prohibition of predatory pricing (abuse of dominance) but not requiring

49 See also Recital 8 Regulation 1/2003.

50 Communication Report of 29 April 2009 on the Functioning of Regulation 1/2003, COM (2009) 206 final, 6.

51 Commission Staff Working Paper of 29 April 2009 accompanying the Report on Regulation 1/2003, SEC (2009) 574 final, at 48–49.

52 Report on Regulation 1/2003, 6.

53 See also Recital 8 Regulation 1/2003.

54 Staff Working Paper on Article 3 Proposal 1/2003, 19.

proof of dominance.[55] A study commissioned by the European Commission is in the pipeline (COMP/2009/A4/021). This study will inter alia (i) provide an exhaustive overview of stricter national provisions on unilateral conduct in the 27 Member States, based on an assessment of the aim and the contents of the national provisions and, therefore, being independent of whether these provisions are included in national competition laws and (ii) give a clear explanation of the impact which stricter national competition law provisions on unilateral conduct have on undertakings.

4. Future Answers?

In the 2009 Report on the Functioning of Regulation 1/2003, the Commission stated that the exclusion of unilateral conduct from the scope of the convergence rule is a matter which should be further examined.[56] The divergence of standards regarding unilateral conduct has been criticized by the business and legal communities, considering that diverging standards fragment business strategies that are typically formulated on a pan-European or global basis.[57] The Commission also stated that such per se prohibitions may result in price increases and loss of consumer welfare.[58] In my view, the Commission should consider to extend the convergence rule to national laws covering unilateral conduct.[59] National prohibitions of resale below cost would then be precluded by EU antitrust law.

Article 18 UCPD required the Commission to submit a Report on the UCPD to the European Parliament and the Council on 12 June 2011 at the latest. With a consultation concluded on 15 October 2011, the Commission gathered suggestions and opinions of the Member States and selected stakeholders in relation to the Directive.[60] The questionnaire for stakeholders contained the following question:

---

55 Staff Working Paper accompanying the Report on Regulation 1/2003, 52–53.

56 Report on Regulation 1/2003, 6–7.

57 See also E Morgan De Rivery and F Amato, 'The System of Interplay between EC and National Laws as Laid Down in Article 3', in M Merola and D Waelbroeck (eds), *Towards an Optimal Enforcement of Competition Law in Europe* (Brussels: Bruylant, 2010) 143.

58 Staff Working Paper accompanying the Report on Regulation 1/2003, 54–55, referring to inter alia U.K. Office of Fair Trading, 'Supermarkets: The Code of Practice and Other Competition Issues, Conclusions' (August 2005); OECD Roundtable on Resale Below Cost Laws and Regulations, Note by the Secretariat, Directorate for Financial and Enterprise Affairs, Competition Committee, 22 September 2005.

59 The above-mentioned study on the impact of national rules on unilateral conduct that diverge from art 102 TFEU will also give an explanation and quantification of the impact of a possible extension of the convergence rule to national competition laws concerning unilateral conduct on undertakings.

60 Questionnaires currently not available on the website of the European Commission. The deadline for the Member States questionnaire was 30 September 2012. The first part focused on general issues concerning the implementation of the Directive in the Member States; the second on the main UCP provisions; the third on the application

> Do you consider that there are any legislative gaps in certain areas (e.g. sales promotions) which have affected the effective enforcement against certain unfair commercial practices? Should specific commercial practices be excluded from the scope of the Directive? In reply to this question, please provide a detailed description of the problems encountered and motivate your response as extensively as possible.[61]

The questionnaire for the Member States contained the following questions:

> a) Do you have any national rules restricting the use of specific commercial practices (such as in the field of sales promotions, price reductions, advertising to children, doorstep selling [...]) In reply to this question, please provide a short description of these provisions (e.g. the obligation of displaying a reference price when announcing sales/promotions and the associated requirements).
>
> b) How did the Directive impact this legislation? Do you consider that the full harmonisation character of the UCPD has created legislative gaps in certain areas (e.g. sales promotions) which have affected the effective enforcement against certain unfair commercial practices? In reply to this question, please provide a detailed description of the problems encountered.
>
> c) Would there be a need, in your opinion, to further regulate any of these practices in the Directive?
>
> d) Would a clarification in the Guidance on the implementation/application of the UCPD be an adequate mean to address these issues?
>
> e) Should specific commercial practices be excluded from the scope of the Directive? In reply to this question, please motivate the reasons as extensively as possible.[62]

In its UCPD Report of 14 March 2013, the Commission considered that it would be inappropriate to amend the Directive at this stage, not least because the enforcement experience in the Member States is still too limited in time for such an encompassing body of legislation. The Commission will now focus its attention on the coherence of the implementation of the Directive, taking concrete actions to make enforcement work better in key areas to the benefit of consumer confidence and growth.[63] According to the Commission, the unpublished responses to the

---

to specific areas. The deadline for the stakeholders questionnaire – a light version of the Member States questionnaire – was 14 October 2012.

61 UCPD questionnaire for stakeholders, Question 11 (under the heading of 'scope of application of the Directive').

62 UCPD questionnaire for the Member States, question 8 (under the heading of 'Full harmonisation character [Art. 4]').

63 Commission Communication of 14 March 2013 on the application of the Unfair Commercial Practices Directive, 'Achieving a High Level of Consumer Protection – Building Trust in the Internal Market', COM (2013) 138 final, at 9.

consultation showed that some Member States and stakeholders would be in favour of making legislative changes to the UCPD in the area of sales promotions, either in the form of further regulation or by excluding sales promotions from the scope of the Directive. The remainder of the Member States and stakeholders would explicitly reject the possibility of any further regulation of this area, while some others would welcome more guidance from the Commission on the topic. The Commission believed that most of the concerns raised by Member States and stakeholders can be addressed through measures aiming at increasing legal certainty and uniform application of the Directive in this field.[64]

Bibliography

Anagnostaras G, 'The Unfair Commercial Practices Directive in Perspective: From Legal Disparity to Legal Complexity?' (2010) *CML Rev* 147–171.

De Bauw H, 'De impact van de richtlijn oneerlijke handelspraktijken op de regeling van de verkooppromoties onder de WHPC' (2006) *DCCR* 3–30.

De Wulf H, B Keirsbilck and E Terryn, 'Overzicht van rechtspraak – Algemeen handelsrecht en handelspraktijken' (2012) *TPR* 921–1320.

Glöckner J, 'The Scope of Application of the UCPD – I Know What You Did Last Summer' (2010) *IIC* 570–592.

Keirsbilck B, 'De invloed van het Europees recht op het Belgisch handelspraktijken- en belendende verbintenissenrecht', in I Samoy, E Terryn and V Sagaert (eds), *De invloed van het Europese recht op het Belgische privaatrecht* (Antwerp: Intersentia, 2012) 591–634.

———, 'Does EU Economic Law Preclude National Prohibitions of Sales Below Cost?' (2012) *Erasmus Law Review* 253–266.

———, *The New European Law of Unfair Commercial Practices and Competition Law* (Oxford: Hart Publishing, 2011).

Keirsbilck B and J Stuyck, 'Een kritische analyse van de Wet Marktpraktijken en Consumentenbescherming' (2010) *TBH* 703–744.

Morgan De Rivery E and F Amato, 'The System of Interplay between EC and National Laws as Laid Down in Article 3', in M Merola and D Waelbroeck (eds), *Towards an Optimal Enforcement of Competition Law in Europe* (Brussels: Bruylant, 2010) 131–155.

Pliakos A and G Anagnostaras, 'Harmonising National Laws on Commercial Practices: Sales Promotions and the Impact on Business-to-Business Relations' (2010) *EL Rev.* 425–435.

Vannerom J, 'Case Wamo: And the Question Remains … Who Is (Actually) Protected?' (2012) *REDC* 151–162.

---

64 Commission Report of 14 March 2013 on the application of the Unfair Commercial Practices Directive, COM (2013) 139 final, at 10.

Chapter 3
The Blacklist of Unfair Commercial Practices: The Black Sheep, Red Herring or White Elephant of the Unfair Commercial Practices Directive?[1]

Monika Namysłowska

1. Introduction: Buy a Pig in a Poke

The Unfair Commercial Practices Directive (UCP Directive),[2] which aims at the full harmonization of the Member States' regulations prohibiting business-to-consumer (B2C) unfair commercial practices, was structured to comprise a general clause and specific provisions on misleading and aggressive commercial practices. Following the prohibitions in the core text of the UCP Directive and therefore almost inconspicuously, the European legislator has additionally attached as Annex I a list of commercial practices which are in all circumstances considered unfair. Due to the per se character of the prohibitions, Annex I is called, also by the Commission itself,[3] the blacklist of unfair commercial practices. It is known as such in all the languages of the Member States, e.g., as *Schwarze Liste der unlauteren Geschäftspraktiken* in German or *czarna lista nieuczciwych praktyk handlowych* in Polish.

Meanwhile, notwithstanding its seemingly supplementary character, it is Annex I that has proved to be the key item of the UCP Directive. Despite having the strongest impact on the national laws on unfair competition and being the

---

1 The research leading, inter alia, to this article has been financed by the National Science Centre (*Narodowe Centrum Nauki*) in Poland on the basis of decision No DEC-2011/01/B/HS5/00509.

2 Directive 2005/29/EC of the European Parliament and of the Council of 11 May 2005 Concerning Unfair Business-to-Consumer Commercial Practices in the Internal Market and Amending Council Directive 84/450/EEC, Directives 97/7/EC, 98/27/EC and 2002/65/EC of the European Parliament and of the Council and Regulation (EC) No 2006/2004 of the European Parliament and of the Council ('Unfair Commercial Practices Directive') (2005) OJ L149/22.

3 Commission, 'Guidance on the Implementation/Application of Directive 2005/29/EC on Unfair Commercial Practices' (2009) *SEC* 1666, 51.

subject of 11 from 20 ECJ preliminary rulings[4] concerning the UCP Directive, among which nine rulings highlight the consequences of the blacklist and only two in which the ECJ interprets a particular provision of Annex I, the blacklist remains enigmatic and misunderstood.

2. The European Blacklist: Dark Horse or Wolf in Sheep's Clothing

The blacklist is not a legislative surprise at the European level, although its concept has significantly evolved. The idea of a list of unfair commercial practices was introduced in the Green Paper on European Union Consumer Protection (2001).[5] The Commission suggested a non-binding practical guidance in the form of recommendations or an indicative list. According to the Green Paper, such guidance, even if not legally binding, could, ensuring the common approach, enhance certainty and reduce the risk of fragmentation caused by the divergent interpretation by national courts. It was, moreover, praised for establishing a more formal link to the underlying legislation than this of the similar list used in the Unfair Contract Terms Directive.[6] The Commission and the Member States were supposed to update that list by means of a regulatory committee.[7]

The respondents to the Green Paper showed little enthusiasm for these plans. Whereas 61 participants were in favour of such guidance, 19 were against and 89 either did not express their opinion or requested further information. Of the then 15 Member States, 10 supported the use of the guidance. Even the consumer groups were divided (15 in favour, 1 against, 17 no view), and business associations even more (19 in favour, 17 against, 52 no view). The opponents feared that the guidance would not solve the problem of fragmentation and expressed concerns about how it would work in practice. Nevertheless, when formulating the elements

4 Rulings concerning Annex I: Joined cases C-261/07 and C-299/07 *VTB-VAB* and *Galatea* [2009] ECR I-2949; case C-304/08 *Plus Warenhandelsgesellschaft* [2010] ECR I-217; case C-522/08 *Telekomunikacja Polska* [2010] ECR I-2079; case C-540/08 *Mediaprint Zeitungs- und Zeitschriftenverlag* [2010] ECR I-10909; case C-288/10 *Wamo* (ECJ, 30 June 2011); case C-126/11 *Inno* (ECJ, 15 December 2011); case C-428/11 *Purely Creative* (ECJ, 18 October 2012); case C-206/11 *Köck* (ECJ, 17 January 2013); case C-343/12 *Euronics Belgium* (ECJ, 7 March 2013); case C-391/12 *RLvS* (ECJ, 17 October 2013); case C-515/12 *4finance* (ECJ, 3 April 2014). See for more on the rulings concerning Annex I Monika Namysłowska, 'Trifft die Schwarze Liste der unlauteren Geschäftspraktiken ins Schwarze? Bewertung im Lichte der EuGH-Rechtsprechung' (2010) *GRUR Int.* 1033.

5 Commission, Green Paper on European Union Consumer Protection. COM (2001) 531 final.

6 Council Directive 93/13/EEC of 5 April 1993 on unfair terms in consumer contracts [1993] OJ L95/29.

7 COM (2001), 531 final, point 4.5.

of a potential directive, the Commission still emphasized the illustrative, non-exhaustive, but also non-binding character of the list.[8]

Unexpectedly, the proposal for the UCP Directive (2003) did not contain a non-binding list of commercial practices, but an annexed blacklist, imposing an *ex ante* prohibition on some specific commercial practices which should be deemed to be unfair in all Member States. This solution was meant to contribute to legal certainty and consumer confidence.[9]

The nature of the list as well as the form of an annex were maintained by recital 17 of the Preamble and Article 5(5) of the UCP Directive, according to which: 'Annex I contains the list of those commercial practices which shall in all circumstances be regarded as unfair. The same single list shall apply in all Member States and may only be modified by revision of this Directive.'

Both the principles of the blacklist and its formal expression seem to be relatively clear and simple. Firstly, all commercial practices from Annex I are considered to be unfair and are therefore prohibited without a case-by-case assessment against the provisions of Articles 5 to 9 of the UCP Directive. It is thus precluded to analyse the unfairness of a blacklisted commercial practice, in particular as regards its contrariness to the requirements of professional diligence and the existence of a material distortion of the economic behaviour of consumers, i.e., identifying whether it constitutes a misleading or aggressive practice. The duty to prohibit a blacklisted commercial practice irrespective of its influence on consumer decision is the most visible characteristic of Annex I. Its aim is to clear the market from 31 types of commercial practices even if they do not distort the behaviours of the addressed public. Secondly, the same blacklist shall apply in all Member States. Hence, national laws are to impose a prohibition on all of the 31 blacklisted commercial practices, but only and exactly the ones appearing on the blacklist. Thirdly, Annex I is meant to be a complete list of commercial practices banned per se. The exhaustive character of the blacklist is strengthened by the fact that it can be modified only through a revision of the UCP Directive. Consequently, the Member States are not empowered to amend Annex I by themselves and to apply the blacklist to similar, but not identical cases.[10] And fourthly, any assessment will, in the first place, have to be made against the blacklisted prohibitions. Only

8 Commission, 'Follow-up Communication to the Green Paper on EU Consumer Protection' COM (2002) 289 final, point 18, Annex I points II and IV, Annex II.

9 Commission, 'Proposal for a Directive of the European Parliament and of the Council Concerning Unfair Business-to-Consumer Commercial Practices' COM (2003) 356 final, 9.

10 See e.g., Thomas Wilhelmsson, 'Misleading Practices', in Geraint Howells, Hans-Wolfgang Micklitz, Thomas Wilhelmsson, *European Fair Trading Law: The Unfair Commercial Practices Directive* (Ashgate, 2006) 159; Frauke Henning-Bodewig, 'Die Richtlinie 2005/29/EG über unlautere Geschäftspraktiken' (2005) *GRUR Int.* 629, 631. Compare with the ruling of the German Supreme Court (Bundesgerichtshof) I ZR 134/10 – Auftragsbestätigung (17 August 2011); Inge Scherer, 'Zum Anwendungsbereich von Nr. 29 des UWG-Anhangs ("Schwarze Liste")' (2012) *WRP* 139.

if an evaluated commercial practice is not on the list, it may be examined with regard to its compliance with the small general clauses in Articles 6 to 9 of the UCP Directive. Should the analysed commercial practice be assessed neither as misleading nor as aggressive, it may finally be evaluated on the basis of the big general clause set out in Article 5 of the UCP Directive.[11]

As regards the formal concept of the blacklist, its specific nature is reasonably expressed in its being a separate piece only annexed to the UCP Directive. Originally proposed as a short[12] blacklist of 19 prohibitions, Annex I has expanded during the legislative process. The Member States have managed to blacklist a remarkable number: 31 commercial practices.[13] Yet, the long Annex I is divided into two parts covering 23 misleading and 8 aggressive practices. The distinction between misleading and aggressive practices is an evident consequence of the structure of the UCP Directive – only these forms are prohibited by the specific provisions of Articles 6 to 7 and Articles 8 to 9 of the UCP Directive, respectively. The uniform character of Annex I has, however, not been disturbed by this division due to the uniform and continuous numbering of the practices from 1 to 31.

Thus, the simplicity of the blacklist of unfair B2C commercial practices is deceptive. Annex I has revealed diverse confusing features and consequences.

The presumption that the blacklisted commercial practices always materially distort the decision making of average consumers and are contrary to the requirements of professional diligence[14] means that protection is in fact provided to each consumer, not to the average one. Yet, it is the standard of the average consumer, derived from the judgments of the ECJ, which was meant to serve as a benchmark for the UCP Directive.[15] Subsequently, protecting all consumers in general might not be in line with the principle of proportionality, and does not necessarily guarantee an effective application of the law. Surely, some commercial practices would not have been prohibited if the material distortion test was applied. It means that some practices would have remained fair if an assessment was possible. Some room is, however, left for the application of a case-by-case assessment as it was moved from the evaluation of unfairness to the appraisal of the facts of the case.[16]

Furthermore, the idea of a single and exhaustive list can easily lead to focusing the attention only on the method of modifying Annex I. There is, however, the other side of the coin. The legislative competences of the Member States have been notably limited in the area covered by the UCP Directive. The rule that Annex I may be changed only in the same way as the rest of the UCP Directive not

---

11 SEC (2009) 1666, 62.

12 COM (2003) 356 final, point 30, 9.

13 Hugh Collins, 'Harmonisation by Example: European Laws against Unfair Commercial Practices' (2010) 73 *Modern Law Review* 89, 96.

14 SEC (2009) 1666, 9.

15 Recital 18 of the Preamble of the UCP Directive.

16 Jochen Glöckner, Frauke Henning-Bodewig, 'EG-Richtlinie über unlautere Geschäftspraktiken: Was wird aus dem "neuen" UWG?' (2005) *WRP* 1311, 1323.

only precludes the adoption of new blacklisted practices or the modification of the existing ones by the Member States, but also has a strong impact on other national regulations, even those that seem to be far removed from the law on unfair B2C commercial practices. To prove the importance thereof it is sufficient to mention that almost all of the ECJ judgments following the preliminary questions of national courts were dealing with exactly this effect of the UCP Directive and its Annex I. The ECJ has repeatedly confirmed that the blacklist precludes Member States from applying national regulations which prohibit a commercial practice without a case-by-case assessment against the provisions of Articles 5 to 9 of the UCP Directive, except for the blacklisted ones.[17] Moreover, such regulation will be seen as contrary to the UCP Directive, irrespective of the exceptions contained therein, as they do not eliminate the necessity of conducting an unfairness test in a particular case.[18] The national court also may not order the cessation of a commercial practice not listed in Annex I only on the grounds that the practice has not been the subject of prior authorization by the competent administrative authority.[19] Additionally, it has to be noticed that a national regulation falls within the scope of that rule even if it aims at protecting the interest of consumers from unfair B2C practices only partly, in parallel with other aims. The problem requires serious consideration as all national provisions that the ECJ found to be non-compliant with the UCP Directive imposed per se prohibitions on various forms of combined offers or announcements about price reductions and sales, not necessarily for reasons limited to consumer protection. The Member States claimed that they wanted to protect competitors[20] or even to maintain the pluralism of the press.[21] It is evident both from the similarity of the national regulations and the frequency of the appearance of such provisions that the problem cannot be simply put down to a country-specific attitude to unfairness.

In light of the above, the doubts concerning the formal aspect of the blacklist may seem to be relatively unimportant. Yet, their impact on everyday practice should not be underestimated.

The choice to include the blacklist in the form of an annex cannot be excessively criticized, even though this way it is easy to simply overlook it at first. However,

---

17 Joined cases C-261/07 and C-299/07 *VTB-VAB* and *Galatea*, paras 61–62; case C-304/08 *Plus Warenhandelsgesellschaft*, paras 49–51; case C-522/08 *Telekomunikacja Polska*, para 31; case C-540/08 *Mediaprint Zeitungs- und Zeitschriftenverlag*, para 35; case C-288/10 *Wamo*, para 38; case C-126/11 *Inno*, para 31; case C-206/11 *Köck*, para 35; case C-343/12 *Euronics Belgium*, para 29.

18 Joined cases C-261/07 and C-299/07 *VTB-VAB* and *Galatea*, paras 64–65; case C-304/08 *Plus Warenhandelsgesellschaft*, paras 53–54; case C-540/08 *Mediaprint Zeitungs- und Zeitschriftenverlag*, paras 39–40.

19 Case C-206/11 *Köck*, para 50.

20 Case C-304/08 *Plus Warenhandelsgesellschaft*, para 38.

21 Case C-540/08 *Mediaprint Zeitungs- und Zeitschriftenverlag*, para 39.

the rather lengthy[22] list in Annex I which covers 31 per se prohibitions brings back the question whether the B2C unfairness has not been overregulated[23] and whether all of the practices mentioned there deserve to be blacklisted. The question why per se prohibitions were imposed on these particular commercial practices also raises doubts. One could argue that the EU legislator wanted to prohibit the most important, the most common or the most unfair B2C commercial practices. Some blacklisted practices occur very frequently indeed, e.g., describing a product as 'gratis', 'free', 'without charge' or similar if the consumer has to pay anything other than the unavoidable cost of responding to the commercial practice, which is prohibited by point[24] 20 of Annex I.[25] But then again, no comparable importance can be attributed to some types of commercial practices,[26] like those related to the language of the after-sales service, prohibited under point 8, or those concerning the presentation of rights given to consumers in law as a distinctive feature of the trader's offer, which are banned under point 10 of the blacklist.[27]

Misleading and aggressive practices, as distinguished in the blacklist, are not the only forms of unfair commercial practices. It is the purpose of the general clause to identify and prohibit commercial practices, which irrespective of being non-misleading and non-aggressive may still be considered unfair. The blacklist neglects this problem and by prohibiting only misleading and aggressive practices creates the impression that those are the only unfair forms of unfair competition. Moreover, although all blacklisted commercial practices must be considered unfair without a case-by-case assessment, the classification of a given commercial practice as being either misleading or aggressive is not irrelevant, at least from the point of view of the ECJ. The misleading character of the commercial practice prohibited under point 31 was strongly contested in an extensive reasoning of the ECJ.[28]

---

22 Jules Stuyck, Evelyne Terryn and Tom Van Dyck, 'Confidence through Fairness? The New Directive on Unfair Business-to-Consumer Commercial Practices in the Internal Market' (2006) 43 *CMLRev.* 107, 130.

23 Bert Keirsbilck, *The New European Law of Unfair Commercial Practices and Competition Law* (Hart Publishing, 2011) 387.

24 Particular prohibitions of Annex I are named "paragraph" in English (e.g., judgment in case C-428/11 *Purely Creative and Others*), "number" (e.g., SEC (2009) 1666) or "item" (e.g., Database https://webgate.ec.europa.eu/ucp). At present, however, the notion "point" prevails.

25 See https://webgate.ec.europa.eu/ucp for numerous decisions of national courts and authorities on e.g., point 20 of Annex I.

26 Stuyck, Terryn, Van Dyck (n 22) 132; Rogier W. de Vrey, *Towards a European Unfair Competition Law. A Clash Between Legal Families* (Martinus Nijhoff Publishers, 2006) 70; Fernando Gomez, 'The Unfair Commercial Practices Directive: A Law and Economics Perspective' (2006) 2 *ERCL* 4, 23.

27 Keirsbilck (n 23) 397–398.

28 See more in point 4.

Furthermore, the impression that the obligation to implement a uniform list of prohibitions automatically leads to a uniform application of Annex I is of illusory nature. The minutely detailed[29] prohibitions contain many unclear and undefined notions.[30] The problem is strengthened by the fact that national blacklists implement Annex I in various ways. Not only does it cause uncertainties in applying a blacklisted prohibition to a particular case but it also creates difficulties in determining the factual limits of the per se prohibitions. A wide interpretation would expand the blacklist to other commercial practices, which it is not allowed at the national level. Moreover, the wording used in Annex I does not preclude the need to assess a case in accordance with the understanding of an average consumer, even though, as stated above, the blacklist theoretically protects each consumer. Although the material distortion test is not a relevant precondition to ban a blacklisted commercial practice, the use of the average consumer's standard is necessary to determine whether a prohibited practice has actually taken place,[31] i.e., whether an impression has been created.[32] Because of the dissimilar application of the average consumer test, the same commercial practice might be banned by some national enforcers and at the same time be permitted by others.

The concept of Annex I to the UCP Directive has, thus, resulted in the creation of an exceptionally strong and, at the same time, extremely equivocal legal instrument that serves both as a starting and a reference point for the national blacklists.

3. The National Blacklists: Take the Bull by the Horns

The implementation of the UCP Directive was a challenging and time-consuming task because of its structure,[33] vague notions or its deceptive simplicity.[34] Due to the non-transposition of the UCP Directive within the prescribed period the

29 Christopher Wadlow, 'The Emergent European Law of Unfair Competition and Its Consumer Law Origins' (2012) *IPQ* 1, 5.

30 See more in point 4.

31 For example, when assessing an advertisement as compliant or not with point 17 of Annex I, which prohibits the practice of falsely claiming that a product is able to cure illnesses, dysfunction or malformations, the Competition Council of the Republic of Lithuania has stated that an average consumer links a doctor's recommendation with the use of medicines rather than cosmetics. See the decision of the Competition Council of the Republic of Lithuania (11 February 2010) National ID: 2S-5, https://webgate.ec.europa.eu/ucp.

32 E.g., points 9, 21, 22 of Annex I to the UCP Directive.

33 Jules Stuyck, 'The Unfair Commercial Practices Directive and Its Consequences for the Regulation of Sales Promotion and the Law of Unfair Competition', in Stephen Weatherill and Ulf Bernitz (eds), *The Regulation of Unfair Commercial Practices under EC Directive 2005/29. New Rules and New Techniques* (Hart Publishing, 2007) 168.

34 For more see Stuyck, Terryn, Van Dyck (n 22) 148–151.

Commission launched infringement proceedings against Germany,[35] Hungary,[36] the Netherlands,[37] the United Kingdom,[38] Luxembourg[39] and Spain.[40] In two judgments the ECJ confirmed the failure of a Member State to fulfil its obligations.[41] One new infringement proceeding is pending at present.[42]

The implementation of the UCP Directive was even more difficult for Member States in which, before the UCP Directive, the protection of consumers and competitors from unfair commercial practices had been regulated under one act.[43] This was the case for Germany and Poland – the Member States I have chosen as illustrations of the functioning of national blacklists. The legal system of Poland and that of Germany constitute a perfect mix of differences and similarities which demonstrate the consequences of the European blacklist. On the one hand, a comparison will be drawn between the legislative solutions of an old Member State, which already since 1896 has had a long legal tradition of protection against unfair competition on the basis of a single regulation and could boast of an impressive body of both judicial and doctrinal interpretations, with the legal solutions devised by a new Member State, where the original law on combating unfair competition of 1926 was not in force during the long period of socialist planned economy, and where the later implementation of the UCP Directive has led to the introduction of two parallel regulations,[44] and where the expertise of courts and the depth of scholarly research are moderate in juxtaposition with their German counterparts. On the other hand, both legal systems share many similarities in the field of combating unfair competition because Poland drew inspiration from German solutions, and, more recently, because currently the two countries, being Member States of the European Union, are obliged to approximate their legal systems to the European standard. Furthermore, both the German and Polish laws have been the subject of interpretations by the ECJ with regard to the blacklist.

In Germany the blacklist was introduced at the end of 2008[45] by means of the one-and-a-half-year late transposition of the new rules into the existing, but still

35 Case C-326/08 *Commission v Germany*, OJ C272/37.

36 Case C-270/08 *Commission v Hungary*, OJ C209/35.

37 Case C-283/08 *Commission v the Netherlands*, OJ C223/32.

38 Case C-284/08 *Commission v United Kingdom*, OJ C223/32.

39 Case C-282/08 *Commission v Luxembourg*, OJ C209/36.

40 Case C-321/08 *Commission v Spain*, OJ C223/38.

41 Case C-282/08 *Commission v Luxembourg*, ECR (2009) I-00013; C-321/08 *Commission v Spain*, ECR [2009] I-00063.

42 Case C-421/12 *Commission v Belgium*, OJ C355/11.

43 Stuyck, 'The Unfair Commercial Practices Directive and Its Consequences for the Regulation of Sales Promotion and the Law of Unfair Competition' (n 33) 174.

44 For more see Igor B Nestoruk, 'Country Report. Poland' in Frauke Henning-Bodewig (ed.), *International Handbook on Unfair Competition* (C.H. Beck, 2013), paras 1–8.

45 First Act Amending the Act against Unfair Competition (Erstes Gesetz zur Änderung des Gesetzes gegen den unlauteren Wettbewerb), 22 December 2008, BGBl. I, 2949.

relatively recent, Act against Unfair Competition (Gesetz gegen den unlauteren Wettbewerb; UWG) of 2004[46] which had been adopted only one year before the UCP Directive was passed. It was, however, Annex I to the UCP Directive that from the very beginning raised significant doubts. Even the necessity of implementing Annex I was questioned because of the existence of various specific provisions similar to the prohibitions contained therein.[47] The supporters of the transposition proposed a reference to Annex I to the UCP Directive be made in the UWG[48] or at least a presentation thereof in the explanatory memorandum to the act modifying the UWG of 2004.[49] Eventually, in order to secure the legal certainty,[50] the European blacklist was implemented as Annex to § 3(3) of the UWG. Contrary to the other provisions of the UWG, which cover both the B2B and B2C relations, the German blacklist applies only to B2C commercial practices.

It is necessary to point out three characteristics of the German blacklist. The Annex to § 3(3) of the UWG is a single list without headings indicating which of the practices are either misleading or aggressive. The ECJ has stated, however, that the exclusion of the headings appearing in Annex I does not have any bearing on the interpretation of the UCP Directive, as the national court must interpret national law as far as possible in the light of the wording and the purpose of the UCP Directive in order to achieve the objectives pursued by that directive and thereby comply with the third paragraph of Article 288 TFEU.[51] Furthermore, the German blacklist prohibits only 30 unfair commercial practices. The per se prohibition mentioned in point 26 of Annex I to the UCP Directive was claimed to be covered by provision § 7(2)(1) of the UWG.[52] This solution impedes the application of the German blacklist and necessitates a proper interpretation or even the modification of the UWG.[53] Finally, the German blacklist changes the sequence of the original prohibitions. Point 31 of Annex I has been transposed as point 17 of the Annex to § 3(3) of the UWG. Despite the already mentioned lack of headings, point 17 is

46 Act against Unfair Competition (Gesetz gegen den unlauteren Wettbewerb), 3 July 2004, BGBl. I, 1414.

47 Helmut Gamerith, 'Der Richtlinienvorschlag über unlautere Geschäftspraktiken – Möglichkeiten einer harmonischen Umsetzung' (2005) *WRP* 391, 432.

48 Helmut Köhler and Tobias Lettl, 'Das geltende europäische Lauterkeitsrecht, der Vorschlag für eine EG-Richtlinie über unlautere Geschäftspraktiken und die UWG-Reform' (2003) *WRP* 1019, 1048.

49 Anja Steinbeck, 'Richtlinie über unlautere Geschäftspraktiken: Irreführende Geschäftspraktiken – Umsetzung in das deutsche Recht' (2006) *WRP* 632, 633.

50 Explanatory Memorandum to the First Act Amending the Act against Unfair Competition, 20 August 2008, BT-Drs. 16/10145, 30.

51 Case C-428/11 *Purely Creative and Others*, para 41.

52 Explanatory Memorandum to the First Act Amending the Act against Unfair Competition, 20 August 2008, BT-Drs. 16/10145, 27.

53 Helmut Köhler, 'Die Umsetzung der Richtlinie über unlautere Geschäftspraktiken in Deutschland – eine kritische Analyse' (2012) *GRUR* 1079, 1081.

placed among the other per se prohibitions on misleading commercial practices,[54] and not as the last aggressive commercial practice as foreseen in Annex I to the UCP Directive. The transfer of point 31 to point 17 changes the numbering of subsequent prohibitions. A re-import of point 17 of the Annex to § 3(3) of the UWG to the aggressive practices should not be excluded considering the recent judgment of the ECJ in the *Purely Creative and Others* case, in which the Court denied the misleading character of this practice.[55]

Concerns about the correct transposition of the UCP Directive led to a reference for a preliminary ruling from the Supreme Court (*Bundesgerichtshof*) in the *Plus Warenhandelsgesellschaft* case. In the main proceeding the *Bundesgerichtshof* was to assess the potential unfairness of a commercial practice of a trader who had launched a promotional campaign which was meant to encourage consumers to buy in his shops. Points were offered to clients in return for their purchases, which then entitled them to take part in the lotteries. The referring court has asked whether Article 5(2) of Directive 2005/29/EC

> precludes a national provision which states that a commercial practice whereby the participation of consumers in a prize competition or lottery is made conditional on the purchase of goods or the use of services is in principle unlawful, irrespective of whether, in any particular case, the advertising in question affects consumers' interests.

Thus, it is not the general clause that influenced the reasoning of the ECJ, but the blacklist itself. The ECJ recalled the threefold structure of the UCP Directive which differentiates between the general clause in Article 5, the specific provisions of Articles 6 and 7 as well as Articles 8 and 9 prohibiting misleading practices and aggressive practices respectively, and Annex I which establishes the exhaustive list of commercial practices banned in all circumstances. As these are the only admissible per se prohibitions concerning commercial practices, the UCP Directive precludes similar forms of national legislation, i.e., one which introduces a prohibition in principle which does not take account of the specific circumstances of an individual case. This rule cannot be called into question on the basis of the fact that a national provision, unlike the UCP Directive, actually aims at protecting the competitors against unfair commercial practices, if the provision is also in any way related to the protection of consumers. Exceptions to such a prohibition cannot restrict either the scope or the necessity of an analysis of the 'unfairness' of a commercial practice in accordance with the criteria set out in Articles 5 to 9.[56] Of little importance is the fact that the *Bundesgerichtshof* made the reference to the ECJ before the implementation of the UCP Directive. The § 4(6) of the UWG in question has not been modified and remains unchanged till now.

---

54 Explanatory Memorandum to the First Act Amending the Act against Unfair Competition, 20 August 2008, BT-Drs. 16/10145, 30.

55 See more in point 4.

56 C-304/08 *Plus Warenhandelsgesellschaft*, paras 42–54.

As regards Poland, the Polish blacklist has been adopted in August 2007 as part of the new Act on the Prevention of Unfair Market Practices.[57] Although the Polish legislator has applied a technically simple copy-paste method of implementation, introducing only small adjustments, the differences between the European and Polish blacklists are immediately apparent. The Polish blacklist is not annexed to the regulation, and neither does it constitute a single list of commercial practices considered unfair in all circumstances. Annex I to the UCP Directive has been included directly in the Act on the Prevention of Unfair Market Practices itself in Article 7 and Article 9 which follow the provisions on misleading and aggressive commercial practices, respectively. Additionally, the blacklist has been divided into two separate pieces, leading de facto to the establishment of two blacklists. The transparency of the threefold structure of the regulation has thus been slightly impaired. The particular per se provisions resemble the specific provisions, despite the fact that Article 7 and Article 9 explicitly state that the commercial practices are prohibited in all circumstances. This in turn leads to a non-negligible risk of falsely applying the blacklisted prohibitions.

The substance of the particular per se prohibitions in Polish law is generally similar to that of the European blacklist as the Polish legislator intentionally went for a literal transposition of Annex I.[58] Therefore, the meaning of the Polish per se prohibitions raises similar doubts. The Polish judicial practice is additionally limited due to the specificities of procedural provisions. It is solely the consumer who has the individual right to make a claim against a trader who is acting unfairly.[59] This solution is highly inconvenient. The Polish consumer may not be characterized by proficiency in law or willingness to take legal action even against e.g., an advertisement promoting his favourite good-value coffee in a way which suggests an exquisite German coffee which might be prohibited under point 13 of Annex I. Unsurprisingly, the claims are rare. The situation is not significantly improved by the fact that the right to take legal action has also been granted to the Ombudsman, the Insurance Ombudsman, the national or regional organizations for consumer protection, and the district (municipal) consumer ombudsman.[60] More often, claims are filed by the President of the Office of Competition and Consumer Protection (Urząd Ochrony Konkurencji i Konsumentów; UOKiK) who protects the collective interests of consumers[61] by assessing whether a given

57 Act on the Prevention of Unfair Market Practices (Ustawa o przeciwdziałaniu nieuczciwym praktykom rynkowym), 23 August 2007, Dz.U. 2007 Nr. 171, poz. 1206.

58 Explanatory Memorandum to the proposal for the Act on the Prevention of Unfair Market Practices (Uzasadnienie rządowego projektu ustawy o przeciwdziałaniu nieuczciwym praktykom rynkowym), 27 April 2007, part II, point 3, 33.

59 Act on the Prevention of Unfair Market Practices, art 12(1).

60 Act on the Prevention of Unfair Market Practices, art 12(2).

61 Act on the Protection of Competition and Consumers (Ustawa o ochronie konkurencji i konsumentów), 16 February 2007, Dz. U. 2007 Nr 50, poz. 331, art 24(2)(3).

practice constitutes an infringement of the Polish provisions implementing Annex I to the UCP Directive.[62]

What runs counter to the Polish legal tradition is the current lack of the provisions that would enable the competitor to take legal action while having a legitimate interest in combating an unfair commercial practice. Until the implementation of the UCP Directive both the B2C and B2B unfair commercial practices were prohibited under one regulation – the Act on Combating Unfair Competition of 1993.[63] This regulation used to provide the competitor with the right to file a claim against an unfair trader, and gave such a right to national or regional organizations protecting the interests of traders. Since 2002 the consumer was deprived of any possibility of pursuing enforcement, contrary to the legislation presently in force. The Act on the Prevention of Unfair Market Practices implementing the UCP Directive, as stated above, focuses on the consumer's claim. In effect, the new act does not provide the competitor of a trader violating the blacklisted prohibitions of B2C commercial practices with a right to make a claim. Something to consider is the application of the old act which has still been left in force theoretically for B2B commercial practices. In practice, the distinction between B2C and B2B regulations is understood as a procedural one – the enforcement of regulations combating unfair competition for consumers will be based on the new Act on the Prevention of Unfair Market Practices, while for traders it will follow the rules of the Act on Combating Unfair Competition. Technically it is, therefore, possible for traders to file a claim against a commercial practice of his competitor blacklisted under the new regulation on the basis of its inconsistency with *bonos mores* from the old regulation. This way the aggrieved competitor may make use of his right to make a claim in accordance with the rules established in the old regulation. Regrettably, the issue of the questionable compliance of such a legislative solution and practice with the UCP Directive is not given consideration in Poland.

The Polish judicial practice pertaining to the application of the blacklist may be assessed as poor when compared with German case law. Still, the most far-reaching judgment of the ECJ concerning the effects of Annex I to the UCP Directive, even if partly incidental and needing further clarification, is the answer to the questions referred for a preliminary ruling by the Polish Supreme Administrative Court (Naczelny Sąd Administracyjny) in proceedings between the Polish Telecom Provider – Telekomunikacja Polska – and the President of the Office for Electronic Communications (Urząd Komunikacji Elektronicznej; UKE). The President of UKE prohibited Telekomunikacja Polska from concluding a contract for the provision of services dependent on the conclusion by the end-user of a contract for the provision of other services. As the prohibition was imposed under the

62 E.g., Decision RLU 21/ 2012 of 5. 10. 2012 (point 5), decision RPZ 2/2012 of 13. 3. 2012 (point 17), decision DDK 18/2011 of 30. 12. 2011 (point 26), decision DDK 6/2011 of 2. 11. 2011 (point 29), decision RBG 37/2012 of 31. 12. 2012 (point 31).

63 Act on Combating Unfair Competition (Ustawa o zwalczaniu nieuczciwej konkurencji), 16 April 1993, Dz.U. 1993 Nr 47, poz. 211.

rules of the Polish Law on Telecommunications, the Polish court asked the ECJ in particular about the compliance of such a provision with the directives contained in the telecommunications package. But the broadly formulated question allowed the ECJ to assess the prohibition in the light of EU law in general. A detailed analysis of the aforementioned directives led the ECJ to declare that the Polish provision did in fact comply with the relevant legislative acts. Then, however, the ECJ made a reference to the UCP Directive and cited a judgment in the joined cases *VTB-VAB* and *Galatea*, according to which 'the Directive 2005/29 is to be interpreted as precluding national legislation which, with certain exceptions, and without taking account of the specific circumstances, imposes a general prohibition of combined offers made by a vendor to a consumer.'[64] No further argumentation was presented. The ECJ also did not address the fact that the preliminary questions pertained to the assessment of the Law on Telecommunications and not the Act on the Prevention of Unfair Market Practices. The fact that the ECJ made reference only to one paragraph of a previous judgment without assessing the different legal basis of the case at hand, or that it did not engage in an analysis of the relations between the UCP Directive and specific provisions does not lessen the importance of the *Telekomunikacja Polska* case. The judgment broadens the impact of the blacklist on national legislations. Even though the ECJ did not dedicate a single line to clarify this question, the *Telekomunikacja Polska* judgment means that the per se prohibitions of unfair commercial practices contained in the blacklist are the only possible ones, regardless of the fact whether an analogous prohibition would be part of a regulation directly transposing the UCP Directive, as was the case in *Plus Warenhandelsgesellschaft*, or not. Consequently, all national legal systems should be scrutinized for hidden per se prohibitions on B2C commercial practices other than the ones listed in Annex I. As for Germany, the *Bundesgerichtshof* referred to the ECJ with a similar issue, asking about the relations between point 11 of Annex I and a provision of the Law Governing the Press of the Land of Baden-Württemberg. Once again the ruling of the ECJ concerned the scope and the consequences of the full harmonization set by the UCPD.[65]

Only a short analysis of the national blacklists provided as examples is sufficient to reveal the problematic and complex consequences caused by Annex I to the UCP Directive with regard to its implementation and its impact on national legislation. Further questions spring to mind when reading through the particular prohibitions of the blacklists.

4. The Interpretation of the Blacklisted Prohibitions: The Work Is Going at a Snail's Pace

According to the Commission, the blacklist in Annex I was drawn up to enable enforcers, traders, marketing professionals and customers to identify commercial

64 Case C-522/08 *Telekomunikacja Polska*, para 31.
65 Case C-391/12 *RLvS*, para 50.

practices which are to be considered unfair in all circumstances and are therefore prohibited.[66] Eight years after the adoption of the UCP Directive it is justified to ask whether it is at all feasible to identify such blacklisted practices.

Annex I to the UCP Directive was intended to be written in user-friendly language for the benefit of consumers, businesses, judges and enforcement officials.[67] Yet, it becomes evident already at first glance that this plan has failed. The prohibitions are dubious because of the use of unclear, imprecise and undefined notions such as 'reasonable period' (point 5), 'reasonable quantities' (point 5), 'normal market conditions' (point 18) or 'failing systematically to respond' (point 27). The blacklist unnecessarily employs different synonymous expressions – e.g., 'create impression' (point 9), 'create false impression' (point 23) or 'give impression' (point 21), 'passing on information' (point 18) or 'informing' (point 30), 'stating' (point 7) or 'claiming' (point 1). This in turn raises questions regarding their uniformity and coherence. Some superficially comprehensible prohibitions later turn out to be problematic because of the undefined scope of the notions used therein, such as 'children' (point 28) or 'the ability to cure illnesses' (point 17).

All complications caused by an imperfect legislative technique are multiplied by the existence of the diverse translations of the UCP Directive, each of which is equally binding. In the Polish version of Annex I, for example, the notion 'claiming' (*twierdzenie*) is used in those points of the blacklist[68] where the English version uses both 'claiming'[69] and 'stating'.[70] However, 'claiming' is used in the English version also in point 1, where the Polish version uses a different term (*podawanie się*). All the points where the Polish version uses a single notion for the English 'claiming' and 'stating', are handled similarly in the German version (*Behauptung*) which, then, additionally uses this term in point 1, but not in point 19.

Last but not least, there are not only disparities to be noticed in relation to Annex I as such, or between its different translations. Significant are also differences between Annex I and the national blacklists. The Polish act uses, for example, the term 'contrary to the truth' (*niezgodne z prawdą*) while the Polish version of Annex I uses in the same prohibitions the notion 'contrary to reality' (*niezgodne z rzeczywistością*). The German UWG chose the notion 'goods and services' (*Waren und Dienstleistungen*) in lieu of the notion 'product' (*Produkt*) used in the German version of Annex I. The superficiality of such modifications is, however, not always the rule. For example, the German UWG prohibits promoting goods and services similar to a product made by a particular competitor (*Mitbewerber*), while the blacklist in Annex I bans promoting goods and services similar to a product

66 SEC (2009) 1666, 53.

67 Green Paper on COM (2001), 531 final, 15.

68 Points 3, 4, 7, 9, 15, 16, 17, 19, 22 of the Polish version of Annex I to the UCP Directive.

69 Points 3, 4, 15, 16, 17, 19, 22 of the English version of Annex I to the UCP Directive.

70 Points 7 and 9 of the English version of Annex I to the UCP Directive.

made by a particular manufacturer (point 13). Such a small linguistic change made in the national regulation considerably changes the scope of a prohibition and, consequently, the scope of a national blacklist. As a solution, an appropriate interpretation[71] or even a modification[72] of point 13 of the Annex to the § 3(3) of the UWG is called for.

The results of a linguistic analysis go beyond simple academic discourse. Numerous unclear notions used in Annex I increase the risk of false implementation.[73] The diverse interpretations of the national blacklists create the possibility of an incoherent application and enforcement of the per se prohibitions. A commercial practice might thus be assessed as falling within the scope of Annex I in one Member State, while the same might not hold true in another. Even if this effect may be seen as inevitable for any directive transposed into national legislation, it is certainly contrary to the aim of the full harmonization and the blacklist as its ultimate expression. If the blacklist is meant to clear the market from 31 unfair commercial practices, a uniform application of the national blacklists should be considered.

The notions of the blacklists should only to a limited extent be interpreted in the light of the rulings and doctrinal interpretations dating back to the time before the UCP Directive was adopted, even though the national prohibitions might have previously covered similar commercial practices. Such a tendency, however, is visible both in Poland[74] and in Germany.[75] The national terms of Annex I should develop into autonomous European notions. Even if it were easier for the national

---

71 Hendrik Schöttle, 'Die Schwarze Liste – Übersicht über die neuen Spezialtatbestände des Anhangs zu § 3 Abs. 3 UWG' (2009) *WRP* 673, 678; Olaf Sosnitza, 'Anhang zu § 3 Abs. 3 UWG', in Henning Piper, Ansgar Ohly and Olaf Sosnitza, *Gesetz gegen den unlauteren Wettbewerb. Kommentar* (5th edn, C.H. Beck, 2010), para 33.

72 Helmut Köhler, 'Nr. 13 des Anhangs zu § 3 Abs. 3 UWG', in Helmut Köhler and Joachim Bornkamm, *Gesetz gegen den unlauteren Wettbewerb* (30th edn, C.H. Beck, 2012), para 13.2; Gunda Dreyer, 'Nr. 13 des Anhangs zu § 3 Abs. 3 UWG', in Henning Harte-Bavendamm and Frauke Henning-Bodewig (eds), *Gesetz gegen den unlauteren Wettbewerb (UWG). Kommentar* (2nd edn, C.H. Beck, 2009), para 8.

73 Aleksandra Kunkiel-Kryńska, *Metody harmonizacji prawa konsumenckiego w Unii Europejskiej i ich wpływ na procesy implementacyjne w państwach członkowskich* (*Methods of Harmonization of Consumer Law in the European Union and Their Impact on the Implementation Processes in the Member States*) (Wolters Kluwer Polska SA, 2013) 356.

74 E.g., Robert Stefanicki, *Ustawa o przeciwdziałaniu nieuczciwym praktykom rynkowym. Komentarz* (*Act on the Prevention of Unfair Market Practices. Commentary*) (LexisNexis, 2009) 416–418; Małgorzata Sieradzka, *Ustawa o przeciwdziałaniu nieuczciwym praktykom rynkowym. Komentarz* (*Act on the Prevention of Unfair Market Practices. Commentary*) (Wolters Kluwer, 2008) 199.

75 E.g., Stefan Völker, 'Nr. 21 des Anhangs zu § 3 Abs. 3 UWG', in Harte-Bavendamm and Henning-Bodewig (n 72), paras 6–9.

enforcer to use only the national regulation,[76] one has to bear in mind that the terms devised at the supra-national level are meant to facilitate the uniform application of the per se prohibitions in all Member States.

In the light of the above, it seems more than surprising that only two ECJ judgments so far dealt with the interpretation of a prohibition from Annex I itself and, remarkably, the first ruling was handed down more than 7 years (!) after the adoption of the UCP Directive.

The ECJ in the *Purely Creative and Others* judgment deals with point 31 of Annex I which prohibits in all circumstances an aggressive commercial practice consisting of

> creating the false impression that the consumer has already won, will win, or will on doing a particular act win, a prize or other equivalent benefit, when in fact either there is no prize or other equivalent benefit, or taking any action in relation to claiming the prize or other equivalent benefit is subject to the consumer paying money or incurring a cost.

Without going into details as regards the interpretation of point 31,[77] it has to be emphasized that the *Purely Creative and Others* case reveals some general rules on how Annex I should be interpreted. Noteworthy is that the literal interpretation of a prohibition, which seems to be the basic method to be applied, may be combined with an analysis of the context of the ban.[78] The ECJ also applied a historical interpretation[79] as well as a teleological one, which was far removed from the literal one, since as a result the ECJ reduced the notion 'false impression' to 'impression'.[80] Additionally, as mentioned before, the ECJ has stated that national law must be interpreted in the light of the wording and the purpose of the UCP Directive.[81]

The recent ECJ judgment in case *4finance* deals with point 14 of Annex I which prohibits per se an misleading commercial practice consisting of

> Establishing, operating or promoting a pyramid promotional scheme where a consumer gives consideration for the opportunity to receive compensation that is derived primarily from the introduction of other consumers into the scheme rather than from the sale or consumption of products.

---

76 Karl-Heinz Fezer, 'Plädoyer für eine offensive Umsetzung der Richtlinie über unlautere Geschäftspraktiken in das deutsche UWG' (2006) *WRP* 781, 782.

77 See Helmut Köhler, '"Gratuliere, Sie haben gewonnen!" – neue Kontrollmaßstäbe für Gewinnmitteilungen' (2012) *GRUR* 1211; Christian Alexander, 'Die Rechtsprechung des EuGH zur Richtlinie 2005/29/EG bis zum Jahr 2012' (2013) *WRP* 17, 23–24; Inge Scherer, 'Massiver Irrtum bei Nr. 17 der "Schwarzen Liste" des UWG-Anhangs?' (2013) *WRP* 143–146.

78 Case C-428/11 *Purely Creative and Others*, para 35.

79 Case C-428/11 *Purely Creative and Others*, para 28.

80 Case C-428/11 *Purely Creative and Others*, para 29.

81 Case C-428/11 *Purely Creative and Others*, para 41.

The doubts raised by the Lithuanian court were based on the inconsistent translations of point 14 of Annex I in different official versions of the UCP Directive. In a short judgment the ECJ confirmed that a pyramid promotional scheme constitutes an unfair commercial practice only where such a scheme requires the consumer to give financial consideration, regardless of its amount, for the opportunity to receive compensation that is derived primarily from the introduction of other consumers into the scheme rather than from the sale or consumption of products.[82]

In the *Purely Creative and Others* judgment the ECJ made no reference to the Guidance from the Commission on the implementation and application of the UCP Directive, which deals with point 31 of Annex I. Such reference could have served as an indication of the usefulness of the Guidance. Although the Guidance cannot provide a formal interpretation of law, it offers numerous examples of the scope of the UCP Directive. It is, however, disappointing that an explicit interpretation is presented only in relation to points 9, 17, 20 and 31 of Annex I. As for the other per se prohibitions, the Guidance gives only examples of selected commercial practices covered by the blacklist.

Furthermore, to facilitate an analysis of national legislation and judicial practice with regard to the UCP Directive the Commission has developed a webgate (https://webgate.ec.europa.eu/ucp). This website was designed to gather and publicize information relating to the UCP Directive and the national laws transposing the UCP Directive, European as well as national jurisprudence, administrative decisions and references to relevant legal literature.[83] The website also offers a database compiling all implementations of the UCP Directive and all relevant national rulings summarized in English. However, some reservations have to be expressed with regard to how up-to-date and reliable the data collected for the project actually is. At the end of May 2014 only 97 national rulings were found to be related to Annex I, the newest one dates back to 25 January 2013. The way the database classifies the rulings by assigning them to one of the prohibitions in Annex I is also more than questionable as e.g., all rulings linked to point 1 of Annex I deal exclusively with other prohibitions. Nevertheless, the database enables a simplified comparative analysis of the national blacklists by giving enforcers and academics[84] various examples of specific situations in which the blacklists may be applied as well as by illustrating how the specific rules of the blacklist are understood or misunderstood by national courts and administrative bodies.

European activities towards achieving a better understanding and more efficient application of the blacklist are noteworthy, but they progress very slowly. The forthcoming legislative actions at the EU level may, however, decrease their applicability and importance.

---

82 Case C-515/12 *4finance*, para 34.

83 http://ec.europa.eu/justice/consumer-marketing/unfair-trade/unfair-practices/index_en.htm.

84 See Hans-Wolfgang Micklitz, 'Anhang I', in *Münchener Kommentar zum Lauterkeitsrecht* (C.H. Beck, 2014), paras 3–8.

5. The Future of the Blacklist: Change Horses in Midstream?

The blacklist may only be modified by revision of the UCP Directive.[85] Any modifications at the national level are not allowed. Although a Member State might have another vision of what should always be considered unfair, it may not extend or shorten the list of 31 commercial practices prohibited per se.

The modification of Annex I by revision of the UCP Directive is currently unlikely. On 14 March 2013 the Commission submitted a report on the application of the UCP Directive,[86] which was expected by 12 June 2011.[87] According to the Commission there is no need to amend the blacklist as no new practices, which are not covered by the UCP Directive, have been identified. However, the report emphasized the importance of a uniform interpretation of the criteria and concepts contained in Annex I which is supposed to be achieved by enhancing the Guidance and the database on UCP Directive.[88]

The other legislative actions prove that the blacklist of unfair commercial practices is clearly a favourite of the Commission. In November 2012, the concept of a blacklist for B2B relations was introduced in a Communication[89] issued following public consultations on Directive 2006/114/EC concerning misleading and comparative advertising (MCA Directive).[90] The Commission pointed at the inefficiency of testing whether a B2B commercial practice is misleading on the basis of a general clause, as it was broad, general and open to different interpretations and case-by-case assessment. Contrarily, an additional level of protection granted by a blacklist would strengthen legal certainty, the level of protection, without unduly affecting the contractual freedom in B2B relations and would facilitate clearer enforcement. According to the Commission, the blacklist of misleading marketing practices could cover such practices as e.g., concealing the commercial intent of a communication, the identity of a trader or material

85 UCP Directive, art 5(5).

86 Commission, 'First Report on the Application of Directive 2005/29/EC of the European Parliament and of the Council of 11 May 2005 Concerning Unfair Business-to-Consumer Commercial Practices in the Internal Market and Amending Council Directive 84/450/EEC, Directives 97/7/EC, 98/27/EC and 2002/65/EC of the European Parliament and of the Council and Regulation (EC) No 2006/2004 of the European Parliament and of the Council ('Unfair Commercial Practices Directive')' COM (2013) 139 final.

87 UCP Directive, art 18.

88 COM (2013) 139 final, 20.

89 Commission, 'Protecting Businesses against Misleading Marketing Practices and Ensuring Effective Enforcement. Review of Directive 2006/114/EC Concerning Misleading and Comparative Advertising' COM (2012) 702 final.

90 Directive 2006/114/EC of the European Parliament and of the Council of 12 December 2006 Concerning Misleading and Comparative Advertising (codified version) [2006] OJ L376/21.

information on the consequences of a reply to a communication, and practices of misleading directory companies.[91]

In this respect, the planned B2B blacklist opens up the opportunity to reconsider the future shape of European unfair competition law. One example given by the Commission of a commercial B2B practice, which consists of disguising a commercial communication as an invoice or obligatory payment, clearly shows the identity between some B2C and B2B commercial practices and the per se prohibitions thereof.[92] Even in the present B2C blacklist some prohibitions are a typical example of the protection of competitors (e.g., point 13, point 17 of Annex I to the UCP Directive).[93] It is therefore possible to cover, as the Austrian example proves, in one blacklist both B2C and B2B commercial practices, even though this is not an unproblematic solution.[94] Hence, the similarity of structure, content and wording of a future B2B and the old B2C blacklists, irrespective of the fact whether they will be included in separate B2C and B2B regulations or linked together under one legislative act, will result in the necessity to confront problems similar to the present ones.

6. Conclusions: Hit the Bull's-Eye

Since the general clause is called the heart[95] of the UCP Directive, the blacklist may be described as the brain that coordinates and takes control of the functioning of the UCP Directive in national legal systems.

The blacklist of unfair commercial practices has been devised to enable the creation of a more coherent, transparent and predictable legal system. The market participants and the enforcement bodies were expected by this means to gain the legal certainty with regard to commercial behaviour that would always be considered unfair. The idea of a blacklist of unfair commercial practices is, therefore, praiseworthy. This makes it all the more unfortunate that the blacklist may only actually work in a simplified theory. Eight years after the adoption of the UCP Directive it may be asserted that the aimed objectives have ultimately failed. The implementation of the rules contained in Annex I has resulted in unforeseen or

91 COM (2012) 702 final, 10 and 12.

92 Point 21 of Annex I to the UCP Directive prohibits as unfair in all circumstances including in marketing material an invoice or similar document seeking payment which gives the consumer the impression that he has already ordered the marketed product when he has not.

93 De Vrey (n 26) 71.

94 See Hans-Georg Koppensteiner, 'Das UWG nach der Novelle 2007', in Susanne Augenhofer (ed.), *Die Europäisierung des Kartell- und Lauterkeitsrechts* (Mohr Siebeck, 2009) 93–94.

95 Stephanie Jungheim and Markus Haberkamm, 'Probleme der UWG-Novelle zur Umsetzung der Richtlinie über unlautere Geschäftspraktiken' (2009) *VuR* 250, 253; Henning-Bodewig, 'Die Richtlinie 2005/29/EG über unlautere Geschäftspraktiken' (n 9) 631.

even unforeseeable consequences. Neither the impact of the blacklist on national legislation nor the prohibitions themselves have turned out to be applicable in an acceptable and predictable manner.

Annex I combined with the full harmonization clause excluded the freedom of Member States to regulate commercial practices more restrictively or in a different way than prescribed in the UCP Directive. The Member States' innovation in consumer protection is thereby significantly restricted and not welcome.

Moreover, the domination of Annex I over the provisions of the UCP Directive is obvious, just by considering the number and results of preliminary rulings dealing with the blacklist. Unsurprisingly, the Member States are able neither to correctly apply the rules of the blacklist and its particular prohibitions nor to accept the loss of their legislative power in relation to setting or modifying the per se prohibitions on unfair commercial practices. But the national courts also seem to have finally noticed the complexity of particular prohibitions on the blacklist which can be observed in the example of the recent cases.

Still, one may not expect the ECJ to solve all the problems. National enforcers themselves have to apply the blacklist, which is a challenging task. It is again worth noticing that the different methods of transposition and the resulting disparities, no matter how small, in 28 national blacklists create a snowball effect, which is, then, only further aggravated by the poor legislative technique employed both at European and national level. The presented examples show no real solution that would help in approaching the correct application of the blacklist. Both implementations – the Polish blacklist included in a separate act transposing the UCP Directive yet in the form of two non-consecutive provisions, as well as the German transposition of Annex I into a regulation covering both B2C and B2B relations that is at the same time very dissimilar to the original European blacklist – constitute a threat to the coherent application of domestic law. A uniform application of the blacklist seems to be nothing but a daydream.

Annex I is the most powerful and, at the same time, the most controversial feature of the UCP Directive. Because of the enormous problems it is causing for practitioners, courts, academics, as well as for consumers, the blacklist cannot be expected capable of performing legal miracles for the protection of consumers from unfair commercial practices.

It would be an exaggeration to describe the blacklist of unfair commercial practices as the black sheep or the red herring of the UCP Directive. Hopefully, the future will not prove the opposite to be true. At present, the blacklist is a white elephant as it is a valuable yet burdensome instrument, the costs of which are out of proportion to its usefulness.

Bibliography

Alexander Ch, 'Die Rechtsprechung des EuGH zur Richtlinie 2005/29/EG bis zum Jahr 2012' (2013) *WRP* 17.

Collins H, 'Harmonisation by Example: European Laws against Unfair Commercial Practices' (2010) 73 *Modern Law Review* 89.

Commission, 'Green Paper on European Union Consumer Protection' COM (2001) 531 final.

———, 'Follow-up Communication to the Green Paper on EU Consumer Protection' COM (2002) 289 final.

———, 'Guidance on the Implementation/Application of Directive 2005/29/EC on Unfair Commercial Practices' SEC (2009) 1666, 51.

———, 'First Report on the Application of Directive 2005/29/EC of the European Parliament and of the Council of 11 May 2005 Concerning Unfair Business-to-Consumer Commercial Practices in the Internal Market and Amending Council Directive 84/450/EEC, Directives 97/7/EC, 98/27/EC and 2002/65/EC of the European Parliament and of the Council and Regulation (EC) No 2006/2004 of the European Parliament and of the Council ("Unfair Commercial Practices Directive")' COM (2013) 139 final.

Fezer K-H, 'Plädoyer für eine offensive Umsetzung der Richtlinie über unlautere Geschäftspraktiken in das deutsche UWG' (2006) *WRP* 781.

Gamerith H, 'Der Richtlinienvorschlag über unlautere Geschäftspraktiken – Möglichkeiten einer harmonischen Umsetzung' (2005) *WRP* 391.

Glöckner J and F Henning-Bodewig, 'EG-Richtlinie über unlautere Geschäftspraktiken: Was wird aus dem "neuen" UWG?' (2005) *WRP* 1311.

Gomez F, 'The Unfair Commercial Practices Directive: A Law and Economics Perspective' (2006) 2 *ERCL* 4.

Harte-Bavendamm H and F Henning-Bodewig (eds), *Gesetz gegen den unlauteren Wettbewerb (UWG). Kommentar* (2nd edn, C.H. Beck, 2009).

Henning-Bodewig F, 'Die Richtlinie 2005/29/EG über unlautere Geschäftspraktiken' (2005) *GRUR Int.* 629.

Howells G, H-W Micklitz and T Wilhelmsson, *European Fair Trading Law: The Unfair Commercial Practices Directive* (Ashgate, 2006).

Jungheim S and M Haberkamm, 'Probleme der UWG-Novelle zur Umsetzung der Richtlinie über unlautere Geschäftspraktiken' (2009) *VuR* 250.

Keirsbilck B, *The New European Law of Unfair Commercial Practices and Competition Law* (Hart Publishing, 2011) 387.

Köhler H, 'Die Umsetzung der Richtlinie über unlautere Geschäftspraktiken in Deutschland – eine kritische Analyse' (2012) *GRUR* 1079.

———, '"Gratuliere, Sie haben gewonnen!" – neue Kontrollmaßstäbe für Gewinnmitteilungen' (2012) *GRUR* 1211.

Köhler H and J Bornkamm, *Gesetz gegen den unlauteren Wettbewerb* (30th edn, C.H. Beck, 2012).

Köhler H and T Lettl, 'Das geltende europäische Lauterkeitsrecht, der Vorschlag für eine EG- Richtlinie über unlautere Geschäftspraktiken und die UWG-Reform' (2003) *WRP* 1019.

Koppensteiner H-G , 'Das UWG nach der Novelle 2007', in S Augenhofer (ed.), *Die Europäisierung des Kartell- und Lauterkeitsrechts* (Mohr Siebeck, 2009).

Kunkiel-Kryńska A, *Metody harmonizacji prawa konsumenckiego w Unii Europejskiej i ich wpływ na procesy implementacyjne w państwach członkowskich* (*Methods of Harmonization of Consumer Law in the European Union and Their Impact on the Implementation Processes in the Member States*) (Wolters Kluwer Polska SA, 2013).

Micklitz H-W, 'Anhang I', in *Münchener Kommentar zum Lauterkeitsrecht* (C.H. Beck, 2014).

Namysłowska M, 'Trifft die Schwarze Liste der unlauteren Geschäftspraktiken ins Schwarze? Bewertung im Lichte der EuGH-Rechtsprechung' (2010) *GRUR Int.* 1033.

Nestoruk IB, 'Country Report. Poland', in F Henning-Bodewig (ed.), *International Handbook on Unfair Competition* (C.H. Beck, 2013).

Piper P, A Ohly and O Sosnitza, *Gesetz gegen den unlauteren Wettbewerb. Kommentar* (5th edn, C.H. Beck, 2010).

Scherer I, 'Zum Anwendungsbereich von Nr. 29 des UWG-Anhangs ("Schwarze Liste")' (2012) *WRP* 139.

———, 'Massiver Irrtum bei Nr. 17 der „Schwarzen Liste" des UWG-Anhangs?' (2013) *WRP* 143.

Schöttle H, 'Die Schwarze Liste – Übersicht über die neuen Spezialtatbestände des Anhangs zu § 3 Abs. 3 UWG' (2009) *WRP* 673.

Sieradzka M, *Ustawa o przeciwdziałaniu nieuczciwym praktykom rynkowym. Komentarz* (*Act on the Prevention of Unfair Market Practices. Commentary*) (Wolters Kluwer, 2008).

Stefanicki R, *Ustawa o przeciwdziałaniu nieuczciwym praktykom rynkowym. Komentarz* (*Act on the Prevention of Unfair Market Practices. Commentary*) (LexisNexis, 2009).

Steinbeck A, 'Richtlinie über unlautere Geschäftspraktiken: Irreführende Geschäftspraktiken – Umsetzung in das deutsche Recht' (2006) *WRP* 632.

Stuyck J, 'The Unfair Commercial Practices Directive and Its Consequences for the Regulation of Sales Promotion and the Law of Unfair Competition', in S Weatherill and U Ulf Bernitz (eds), *The Regulation of Unfair Commercial Practices under EC Directive 2005/29. New Rules and New Techniques* (Hart Publishing, 2007).

Stuyck J, E Terryn and T Van Dyck, 'Confidence through Fairness? The New Directive on Unfair Business-to-Consumer Commercial Practices in the Internal Market' (2006) 43 *CMLRev.* 107.

de Vrey RW, *Towards a European Unfair Competition Law. A Clash Between Legal Families* (Martinus Nijhoff Publishers, 2006).

Wadlow Ch, 'The Emergent European Law of Unfair Competition and Its Consumer Law Origins' (2012) *IPQ* 1.

PART II
Vulnerability

Chapter 4
The Vulnerable Consumer in the UCPD and Other Provisions of EU Law

Marine Friant-Perrot

1. Introduction

The concept of 'vulnerable consumer' is relatively new in European Consumer law.[1] It is part of the evolution of consumer policy that focuses on enhancing consumers' confidence in the internal market. This approach considers the consumer as an economic agent whose interests are mainly protected by the benefits of the single market's proper functioning.[2] Although this neo-liberal approach aims to benefit the average consumer, it may leave on the side the vulnerable consumer. Indeed, his discernment – altered by age, infirmity or excessive credulity – could prevent him from acting as the abstract model of *homo economicus*.

This vulnerability that affects a certain category of consumers is highlighted in other fields of Law. The concept of 'vulnerability' has indeed become 'in fashion' in legal thought.[3] From the Latin '*vulnerare*' (to injure), vulnerability means 'likely to be injured, to be attacked', and characterizes the person in a position of weakness. This weakness covers a variety of situations. Thus, Professor J. Hauser lists a broad range of vulnerabilities to build a general theory about the protection of vulnerable subjects: 'medical vulnerabilities, social vulnerabilities, those of the minor person, those of the medically targeted major person, but also subjects in an unfair economic or psychological position, consumers, users of health services, citizens against government etc.'. Vulnerability aggregates multiple situations in which a person's autonomy should be restored in the name of the principle

1 See nevertheless, CJEC, 9 July 1997, *Konsumentombudsmannen (KO) v De Agostini (Svenska) Förlag AB*, 34/95, Rec. 1997, CCL AG Jacobs, pt. 102 ('It is settled law that the fairness of commercial transactions and consumer protection in general figure among the objectives which can justify restrictions on the free movement of goods. (62) The protection of a particularly vulnerable sector of consumers such as children must a fortiori also constitute an overriding public-interest ground capable of justifying such restrictions').

2 G Howells and S Weatherill, *Consumer Protection Law* (Ashgate, 2005) 1.

3 J Hauser, 'Une théorie générale de la protection du sujet vulnérable?' (2011) *Revue Lamy Droit Civil* 83; Cour de cassation, Les personnes vulnérables dans la jurisprudence de la Cour de cassation, Annual report 2009, http://www.courdecassation.fr/publications_cour_26/rapport_annuel_36/rapport_2009_3408.

of dignity. Built as a provider of rights, it is 'less the personal characteristic of an individual than the possible qualification of its relationships with others.'[4] Therefore, civil law (especially for 'dys-capables') and economic law are likely to create links around the concept of vulnerability. Indeed, according to Fossier:

> 'Dys-capables' – who apply their will like all of us but against their own interest –, and 'Para-capables' – misfits who do not understand the ins and outs of the social stream – are aggregated to the tutelary protection. Thus, the former and hated category of 'incapacitated' has lost its meaning and the word vulnerability has begun its career.[5]

The bridge between civil law and consumer law is particularly obvious concerning the field of prevention and treatment of over-indebtedness in France. Measures of social[6] and legal[7] support under the French Dyscapables Act (2007)[8] allow preventing over-indebtedness in helping protected people to find autonomy in managing their resources. Some forms of social maladjustment place the person in a state of vulnerability. This weakness deprives the person of the autonomy which could allow him to make choices more favourable to his interests and enjoy the benefits of the market.

This variety of figures of the vulnerable person in private law and especially in consumer law makes it difficult to grasp the concept of vulnerability. In a very pragmatic way, provisions of EU consumer law and other provisions of EU law reflecting the emergence of the concept should therefore be identified (1) in order to analyse the effects of the vulnerability regarding the protection afforded to consumers (2).

2. The Emergence of the Notion of the Vulnerable Consumer

European consumer law has been built following the liberal approach of the law, where the market is the appropriate regulatory tool. This conception considers the consumer as a rational economic agent who, when properly informed, can optimize his interest and reap benefits from the internal market realization. The reference model is therefore the one of the 'average consumer' i.e., a consumer 'reasonably well informed and reasonably observant and circumspect'[9], as defined

---

4 Th Fossier, 'Peut-on légiférer sur la vulnérabilité?' (2011) *Dr. Famille* dossier 2.

5 Th Fossier, 'Peut-on légiférer sur la vulnérabilité?' (2011) *Dr. Famille* dossier 2.

6 Art L. 271–1 French Code of the social and family action.

7 Art 495 al 1 French Civil Code.

8 Dyscapables Act (2007) of 5 March 2007 (*LOI* n° 2007 308 *du 5 mars 2007* portant réforme de la protection juridique des majeurs, JORF n° 56 du 7 mars 2007 page 4325).

9 Art 5.2 of Directive 2005/29/EC of the European Parliament and of the Council of 11 May 2005 Concerning Unfair Business-to-Consumer Commercial Practices in the Internal Market and Amending Council Directive 84/450/EEC, Directives 97/7/EC, 98/27/

by the European Court of Justice (ECJ).[10] However, to protect consumers who are particularly exposed to unfair commercial practices, Directive 2005/29 has set out, next to the model of the 'average consumer', the new category of 'vulnerable consumers'.[11] This innovation[12] was not really followed by a general theory surrounding this new concept that embraces diverse realities (A). For this reason, it could be concluded that there is only a fragmented consideration of the vulnerable consumer (B).

2.1 A Plurality of Vulnerable Consumers in EU Consumer Law

Directive 2005/29 pays particular attention to vulnerable consumers. Thus, Recital 18 states that the Directive 'contains provisions aimed at preventing the exploitation of consumers whose characteristics make them particularly vulnerable to unfair commercial practices'. Recital 19 states that

> where certain characteristics such as age, physical or mental infirmity or credulity make consumers particularly susceptible to a commercial practice or to the underlying product and the economic behaviour only of such consumers is likely to be distorted by the practice in a way that the trader can reasonably foresee, it is appropriate to ensure that they are adequately protected by assessing the practice from the perspective of the average member of that group.

As a result, when business practices are targeting a particular category of vulnerable consumers, the unfairness is assessed in terms of the average capacity of discernment of the category in question.[13]

EC and 2002/65/EC of the European Parliament and of the Council and Regulation (EC) No 2006/2004 of the European Parliament and of the Council (Text with EEA Relevance), OJ L 149, 11.6.2005, p. 22–39 (UCP Directive).

10 ECJ Case law C-210/96, *Gut Springenheide and Tusky*, Rec. 1998, p. I-4657, point 31; see also for Community Trade Marks, ECJ, 6 September 2012, *August Storck KG v Office for Harmonisation in the Internal Market (Trade Marks and Designs) (OHIM)*, Case C-96/11 P., ECR 2012, pt 39.

11 S Weatherill, 'Who Is the "Average Consumer"?', in S Weatherill and U Bernitz (eds), *The Regulation of Unfair Commercial Practices under EC Directive 2005/29 – New Rules and New Techniques* (Oxford: Hart Publishing, 2007) 115.

12 Concern for the possible exploitation of the economically weaker party is visible in some directives (e.g., misleading advertising is prohibited by Directive 84/450), but these directives do not refer to the 'vulnerable consumer'; S Weatherill, 'Who Is the "Average Consumer?"' 122.

13 Report from the Commission to the European Parliament, the Council and the European Economic and Social Committee, First Report on the Application of Directive 2005/29/EC of the European Parliament and of the Council of 11 May 2005 Concerning Unfair Business-to-Consumer Commercial Practices in the Internal Market and Amending Council Directive 84/450/EEC, Directives 97/7/EC, 98/27/EC and 2002/65/EC of the European Parliament and of the Council and Regulation (EC) No 2006/2004 of

But when the criteria are analysed for identifying persons likely to be classified as 'vulnerable', it should be noted that this category is eclectic. Article 5.3 of Directive 2005/29 refers to consumers who are particularly vulnerable 'to the practice or the underlying product because of their mental or physical infirmity, age or credulity'.[14] Natural deficiencies due to a mental or physical disability, cognitive deficiencies and situations of weakness due to youth or old age,[15] are thus considered at the same level. In this respect, the real cause of disability does not matter. Indeed, the cause could be endogenous, exogenous, natural or the result of social maladjustment, or it could be permanent or temporary. What matters is its manifestation, i.e., the loss or lack of autonomy in consumption choices – thus, according to Xavier Lagarde, 'persons in a pathological situation or out of the ordinary, who are not able to properly exercise their rights and freedoms, are thus vulnerable ones'.[16] But being considered as an easy prey is not enough to qualify a business practice as unfair. A requirement of 'foreseeability' must be added.

All business practices misleading vulnerable consumers are not de facto unfair: the negative impact of an unfair business practice on a category of vulnerable consumers must be predictable by professionals[17] within the meaning of Article 5.3 of Directive 2005/29. The caution expected from the professional has to remain within a reasonable frame and should not integrate irrational consumers' reactions of extreme naivety or ignorance.[18]

---

the European Parliament and of the Council ('Unfair Commercial Practices Directive'), Brussels, 14.3.2013, COM (2013) 139 final.

14 The list in art 5(3) has been described as 'quite arbitrary' in its restrictive approach: S Weatherill, 'Who Is the "Average Consumer"?', in S Weatherill and U Bernitz (eds), *The Regulation of Unfair Commercial Practices under EC Directive 2005/29 – New Rules and New Techniques* (Oxford: Hart Publishing, 2007) 115 (136) ('What of educational attainment? Income? Ethnicity?'); R Incardona and C Poncibo, 'The Average Consumer, the Unfair Commercial Practices Directive, and the Cognitive Revolution' (2007) 30 *J.Consum Policy* 21–38 (n 38) ('It lacks practical and logical foundations'); J Stuyck, E Terryn and T Van Dyck, 'Confidence through Fairness ? The New Directive on Unfair Business-to-Consumer Commercial Practices in the Internal Market' (2006) 43 *CMLRev* 107, at 121–122 ('It would have been – and still is – recommended to conduct sound empirical research, at EC level, about correlation between the characteristics of certain groups of consumers and the likelihood of being specifically vulnerable for certain commercial practices').

15 Merlyn A Griffiths and Tracy R Harmon, 'Aging Consumer Vulnerabilities Influencing Factors of Acquiescence to Informed Consent' (2011) 25(3) *Journal of Consumer Affairs* 445–466; George P Moschis, Jill Mosteller and Choong Kwai Fatt, 'Research Frontiers on Older Consumers' Vulnerability' (2011) 25(3) *Journal of Consumer Affairs* 467–491.

16 X Lagarde, foreword in the *Cour de cassation* 2009 annual report, http://www.courdecassation.fr/publications_cour_26/rapport_annuel_36/rapport_2009_3408.

17 Art 5.3 of the UCP Directive.

18 Commission Staff Working Document, Guidance on the Implementation/Application of the Directive 2005/29 on Unfair Commercial Practices, SEC (2009) 1666, 30.

Since the adoption of Directive 2005/29, the notion of vulnerable consumers has become widespread and appears as a counterpoint to the notion of the average consumer in the texts defining the contours of EU consumer policy.[19] Thus, the Communication of the Commission 'A European Consumer Agenda' of May 2012[20] reports the economic and social evolution, emphasizing the increased risk of social exclusion in times of economic crisis in the context of digital revolution. The Commission states that this risk is amplified by the aging of the population. Decreasing the division between vulnerable consumers and others appears as a necessity.[21] This requirement is also highlighted in the future Consumer Programme for the period 2014–2020.[22] Thus, the Council adopted without debate on 18 June 2012 a general approach on the proposal for a regulation and in particular the fourth objective, aimed to improve the education and information of consumers, while

---

19 See also Directive 2011/83/EU of the European Parliament and of the Council of 25 October 2011 on Consumer Rights, Amending Council Directive 93/13/EEC and Directive 1999/44/EC of the European Parliament and of the Council and repealing Council Directive 85/577/EEC and Directive 97/7/EC of the European Parliament and of the Council Text with EEA Relevance, OJ, L 304 , 22/11/2011 P. 0064 – 0088 (Recital (34) 'The trader should give the consumer clear and comprehensible information before the consumer is bound by a distance or off-premises contract, a contract other than a distance or an off-premises contract, or any corresponding offer. In providing that information, the trader should take into account the specific needs of consumers who are particularly vulnerable because of their mental, physical or psychological infirmity, age or credulity in a way which the trader could reasonably be expected to foresee. However, taking into account such specific needs should not lead to different levels of consumer protection'); V Mak, 'Standards of Protection: In Research of the "Average Consumer" of EU Law in the Proposal for a Consumer Rights Directive' (2011) 19(1) *European Review of Private Law* 25–42.

20 Communication from the Commission to the European Parliament, the Council, the Economic and Social Committee and the Committee of the Regions A European Consumer Agenda – Boosting Confidence and Growth.

21 Communication from the Commission to the European Parliament, the Council, the Economic and Social Committee and the Committee of the Regions A European Consumer Agenda – Boosting Confidence and Growth, 6: 'Social exclusion, vulnerable consumers and accessibility – Wherever the economic and sovereign debt crisis has struck, it has dented consumer confidence and, for some consumers, led to a very significant fall in income or purchasing power, thus increasing the risk of social exclusion and the risk that citizens are unable to afford essential goods and services. These risks are heightened by the fact that our population is ageing, markets are becoming increasingly complex and some people may neither have the opportunity nor the ability to master the digital environment. The question of accessibility is key to reaping the benefits of digital change in the physical, digital and economic senses. The current context may also exacerbate the disadvantaged situation of vulnerable consumers, such as people with disabilities or with reduced mobility, who face difficulties in accessing and understanding information and in finding appropriate products and services on the market.'

22 Proposal for a Regulation of the European Parliament and of the Council on a Consumer Program 2014–2020 {SEC (2011) 1320 final} {SEC (2011) 1321 final}.

adding a reference to the specific needs of 'young consumers, old consumers and vulnerable consumers'. The attention consistently given to vulnerable consumers shows the rooting of the concept in European consumer law.

However, this recognition is not accompanied by a homogenization of the concept of vulnerability. As underlined by European Parliament Resolution of 22 May 2012 on a strategy for strengthening the rights of vulnerable consumers,[23]

> the diversity of vulnerable situations, both when consumers are placed under statutory protection and when they are in a specific situation of sectoral or temporary vulnerability, hinders a uniform approach and the adoption of a comprehensive legislative instrument, which has thus led the existing legislation and policies in place to address the problem of vulnerability on a case-by-case basis; stresses, therefore, that European legislation must address the problem of vulnerability among consumers as a horizontal task, taking into account consumers' various needs, abilities and circumstances.

Therefore, this diversity of causes of vulnerability corresponds to a variety of texts protecting vulnerable consumers.

2.2 The Fragmented Consideration of the Vulnerable Consumer in Other Provisions of EU Law

The issue of vulnerability is acknowledged across all different provisions of EU law. Texts that give special attention to vulnerable consumers are disseminated, and provide a pragmatic response to the heterogeneity of the concept of vulnerability.

Considering the sectors qualified as particularly problematic by the European Parliament Resolution of 8 May 2012, there are protective provisions under different EU policies (transport policy, energy policy, food policy). These texts have in common to contribute to the restoration of consumers' autonomy, by giving effective content to certain fundamental rights.[24] Certain rights such as the right to food, the right to housing or the right to health express the human dignity[25] and must be guaranteed, in order to extract some vulnerable consumers from situations of exclusion.

Regarding food, the vulnerability of young consumers is put forward in the fight against advertisements for food that are particularly fatty, sugary and salty (like junk food) in Directive 2010/13 'Audiovisual Media Services'.[26] Similarly,

---

23 European Parliament resolution of 22 May 2012 on a strategy for strengthening the rights of vulnerable consumers (2011/2272[INI]).

24 L Dutheil-Warolin, 'La notion de vulnérabilité de la personne physique en droit privé', PhD diss., Université de Limoges, 2004, 259.

25 B Maurer, *Le principe du respect de la dignité humaine et la Convention européenne des droits de l'homme* (Paris, Coll. Monde européen et international, Jacques Bourrinet (Sous-dir.), La documentation française, 1999) 267.

26 Directive 2010/13/EU of the European Parliament and of the Council of 10 March 2010 on the Coordination of Certain Provisions Laid Down by Law, Regulation

Regulation 178/2002 on Food Law takes into account 'the particular health sensitivities of a specific category of consumers where the food is intended for that category of consumers' to determine whether a food is prejudicial to health[27] (e.g., baby food and food for seniors).[28]

To fight against energy poverty, and to avoid disrupting connection to gas or electricity to such customers in critical times, the protection of vulnerable consumers is included as an objective in the directives of the third energy package. In order to assure decent housing conditions to consumers, the access to energy should be possible for the poorest people.[29] In this context, the European Directives 2009/72/EC[30] and 2009/73/EC[31] laying down common rules for the internal market in electricity and natural gas require that

---

or Administrative Action in Member States Concerning the Provision of Audiovisual Media Services ('Audiovisual Media Services Directive') (Text with EEA relevance), OJ L 95, 15.4.2010, 1–24; A Garde, 'Freedom of Commercial Expression and Public Health Protection: The Principle of Proportionality as a Tool to Strike the Balance', in L Gormley and N Nic Shuibhne (eds), *From Single Market to Economic Union – Essays in Honour of John A. Usher* (Oxford University Press, 2012) 117–133; A Garde, 'The Best Interests of the Child and EU Consumer Law and Policy: A Major Gap between Theory and Practice?', in J Devenney and M Kenny (eds), *European Consumer Protection: Theory and Practice* (Cambridge University Press, 2012) 164–201; M Friant-Perrot and A Garde, 'La publicité alimentaire et la lutte contre l'obésité infantile en droit français et en droit anglais', in *Actualités de droit économique: aspects de droit de la concurrence et de la consommation et de droit de l'agroalimentaire*, co-organised by the Lascaux Programme and the UMR–Droit et changement social, Faculty of Law and Political Science, Nantes, 17 September 2010 (*Petites Affiches*, Numéro spécial – *Actes de colloque*, 6 Octobre 2011) 199, 27–39.

27 Art 14 of Regulation n° 178/2002 of the European Parliament and the Council of 28 January 2002 Laying Down the General Principles and Requirements of Food law, Establishing the European Food Safety Authority and Laying Down Procedures in Matters of Food Safety, OJ L 31, 1.2.2002, 1–24; see also recital (15) of Regulation n°1924/2006 of 20 dec 2006 *on nutrition and health claims made on foods*: 'It is important that claims on foods can be understood by the consumer and it is appropriate to protect all consumers from misleading claims […] . *Where a claim is specifically aimed at a particular group of consumers, such as children, it is desirable that the impact of the claim be assessed from the perspective of the average member of that group.* The average consumer test is not a statistical test. National courts and authorities will have to exercise their own faculty of judgment, having regard to the case-law of the Court of Justice, to determine the typical reaction of the average consumer in a given case.'

28 For example, margarines fortified with plant sterols to improve cardiovascular functioning.

29 M Bartl, 'The Affordability of Energy: How Much Protection for the Vulnerable Consumers?' (2010) 33 *J Consum Policy* 225–245.

30 Art 3.7 of Directive 2009/72/EC of the European Parliament and of the Council of 13 July 2009 Concerning Common Rules for the Internal Market in Electricity and Repealing Directive 2003/54/EC (Text with EEA Relevance) OJ L211 of 14.8.2009.

31 Art 3.3 of Directive 2009/73/EC of the European Parliament and of the Council of 13 July 2009 Concerning Common Rules for the Internal Market in Natural Gas and Repealing Directive 2003/55/EC (Text with EEA Relevance), OJ L 211, 14.8.2009, 94–136.

> Member States shall take appropriate measures, such as formulating national energy action plans, providing benefits in social security systems to ensure the necessary electricity supply to vulnerable customers, or providing for support for energy efficiency improvements, to address energy poverty where identified, including in the broader context of poverty.

However, it is clear that the concept of 'vulnerable customers' and 'appropriate measures' shall be defined by each State.[32] In France, the category of vulnerable consumers is determined by taking into account income levels, and measures leading to a reduction in price compared to the regulated tariff, which could vary according to the number of persons in the household.

On mobility, which is a key element in the fight against social exclusion, the action plan on urban mobility adopted in 2009[33] proposes concrete actions on specific aspects of urban mobility. The Commission offers a partnership to local, regional and national authorities based on their voluntary commitment to co-operate in selected areas of mutual concern. It invites also other stakeholders in the Member States, citizens and industry, to closely co-operate, 'paying particular attention to the mobility needs of vulnerable groups such as elderly, low-income groups and persons with disabilities, whose mobility is reduced due to a physical, intellectual or sensory disability or impairment, or as a result of age'.[34]

The European Union is also committed to reducing what has become known as the 'digital divide'.[35] Internet access is becoming a necessity to feed social links and prevent the exclusion of the most vulnerable people. Thus, in its Communication of May 2012 on 'a European Consumer Agenda',[36] the Commission noted that 'some people may neither have the opportunity nor the ability to master the digital environment' and adds that 'The question of accessibility is key to reaping the benefits of digital change in the physical, digital and economic senses.' Indeed, in France for example, a quarter of the population has no access to the internet. Of the younger population, almost all are equipped with internet, only a quarter

---

32 *Warm Home Discount* in Great Britain; the "tarif de première nécessité" (TPN) for electricity and the "tarif spécial de solidarité du gaz naturel" for natural gas (TSS) in France.

33 Communication from the Commission to the European Parliament, the Council, the European Economic and Social Committee and the Committee of the Regions – Action Plan on Urban Mobility [COM (2009) 490 final – Not published in the Official Journal].

34 Communication from the Commission to the European Parliament, the Council, the European Economic and Social Committee and the Committee of the Regions – Action Plan on Urban Mobility [COM (2009) 490 final – Not published in the Official Journal], 3 (below).

35 See J Attali, *Rapport de la Commission pour la libération de la croissance française: 300 décisions pour changer la France* (La documentation française, 2008).

36 Communication from the Commission, to the European Parliament, the Council, the Economic and Social Committee and the Committee of the Regions – A European Consumer Agenda - Boosting Confidence and Growth, {SWD (2012) 132 final}, COM 2012 (225) final, 3.

of the population over 70 years are in this case. Disparities remain also strong considering the standard of living: less than half of those earning less than 900 euros monthly have access to the internet. To curb this, the European Commission has adopted on 11 January 2012, the Communication on e-commerce and online services[37] with special attention to 'Vulnerable people (the elderly, those with reduced mobility, those isolated in rural areas, those with low purchasing power) (which) will particularly benefit.' France is committed to this fight by encouraging operators to implement a social tariff internet on a voluntary basis.

Finally, to fight against debt, it is important that the most vulnerable consumers have access to credit.[38] In this regard, credits are essentially excluded from the people who have limited resources,[39] even if the debt also affects the most gullible who are not fully aware of the scope of their commitments. This segment of the population is very important in France where 40 per cent of people are excluded from consumer credit, knowing that among the 60 per cent who have access, only 30 per cent have access to the full range of credit products to consumers (affected, depreciable, renewable) and 15 per cent of them can only access revolving credit.[40] In developing countries, this phenomenon is known and the development of micro-credit has helped to facilitate access to credit for the poor.[41] An opinion of the Economic and Social Committee on 'Financial education and responsible consumption of financial products'[42] (own-initiative opinion) highlights the particular risks for vulnerable consumers. It therefore advocates that 'Measures for improving consumers' understanding of financial issues need to be targeted as a priority on the sections of the population that are least protected and are in danger of suffering from financial exclusion or of suffering as a result of certain speculative behavior.' Under current EU legislation, there

---

37 Communication from the Commission, to the European Parliament, the Council, the Economic and Social Committee and the Committee of the Regions – A Coherent Framework for Building Trust in the Digital Single Market for E-commerce and Online Services, {SEC (2011) 1640} {SEC (2011) 1641}, COM (2011) 942 final, 3.

38 OECD Report, Corporate Governance and the Financial Crisis: key Findings and Main Messages, June 2009.

39 For the United States, see Ch Mansfield, 'Predatory Lending: The Failure of Consumer Choice as a Regulatory Model in the United States', in *Risk and Choice in Consumer Society* (Bruyland, 2007) 299.

40 Report of the French Ombudsman, *Crédit, croissance et urgence sociale*, 10 February 2009, 4.

41 See Conference of Esther Duflo (Collège de France) on 'Pauvreté et développement dans le monde- Accès aux instruments financiers', first part, 8 July 2009, http://www.college-de-france.fr/site/esther-duflo/index.htm#|q=/site/esther-duflo//_audiovideos.jsp|p=http://www.college-de-france.fr/site/esther-duflo/acces_aux_instruments_financie.htm.

42 Opinion of the European Economic and Social Committee on 'Financial Education and Responsible Consumption of Financial Products' (own-initiative opinion) (2011/C 318/04); see also the Opinion of the European Economic and Social Committee on 'Accessing Consumer and Household Credit: Abusive Practices' (own-initiative opinion) (2011/C 18/05).

is no specific consideration of vulnerable consumers.[43] Certainly, the future revision of the Regulation of 26 May 2000, No. 1346/2000 on insolvency[44] could lead to the adoption of substantive rules applicable to particular difficulties. The public consultation ended 21 June 2012 plans to extend the scope of regulation to procedures for bankruptcies affecting individuals. But the goal is not to give a special protection to the most indebted consumers. This objective is nevertheless highlighted by the Commission in its Communication on the European Platform against Poverty and Social Exclusion which states:

> Access to financial services for the most vulnerable can be enhanced through internal market and consumer policies. Financial exclusion can prevent people from getting a job, creating a business and accessing to other services. Ensuring access to basic financial services is a responsibility of public authorities – both at national and European level.[45]

As to the various figures of the vulnerable consumer corresponds an abundance of scattered texts taking into account this particular weakness, it is necessary to consider the effects of vulnerability on protection.

3. The Effects of Vulnerability on Protection

What protection is given to vulnerable consumers? Is there a plurality of regimes or is a uniform treatment of situations of vulnerability emerging? (A) Even if the treatment of the vulnerability can gain consistency by standardizing the rules made by the European consumer law, penalties remain the responsibility of the Member States (B).

3.1 The Treatment of Vulnerability

Consumer vulnerability is taken into account in two ways. On the one hand, to ensure consumer access to basic goods and services, a tariff policy helps fight against social exclusion of the poorest (1). On the other hand, the vulnerability of a targeted group of consumers modifies the assessment of the rules in a more protective way (2).

---

43 For national laws in a selection of European countries, see, J Spooner, 'Fresh Start or Stalemate? European Consumer Insolvency Law Reform and the Politics of Household Debt' (2013) 21(3) *European Review of Private Law* 747–794.

44 Council Regulation (EC) No 1346/2000 of 29 May 2000 on Insolvency Proceedings, OJ L 160 , 30/06/2000 P. 0001 – 0018.

45 Communication from the Commission, to the European Parliament, the Council, the Economic and Social Committee and the Committee of the Regions – The European Platform against Poverty and Social Exclusion: A European Framework for Social and Territorial Cohesion, /* COM/2010/0758 final */, p 13.

3.1.1 The access to essential goods and services

For consumers, the services of general interest are those that:

> – are essential to life and health. For example, the lack of access to essential supplies such as water, electricity or gas, can be a cause not only of discomfort and inconvenience, but also a threat to health or life itself;
>
> – are essential to social participation, in the case of a vital service for social inclusion. This is the case, for example, of telecommunications services (which are a salvation for people in vulnerable situations) and some transport services (essential for people who live in remote areas and those who live, work and move in a community).[46]

Regarding affordability, the benefits of the liberalization of major supply markets are unequally distributed and certain categories of low-income consumers are excluded. Maintaining affordable access should allow all consumers to benefit from essential services (water, electricity, gas). The legal treatment of vulnerability occurs by the introduction of social tariffs.

Regarding physical accessibility, vulnerability may result from reduced mobility due to a disability or physical, intellectual, sensory or age deficiency. The protection of vulnerable persons in this case consists in adapting transports and commercial premises to the specific needs of disabled people.

Besides the rules concerning people with disabilities, there are codes of good conduct or private approaches recoverable by labels[47] that allow excluded consumers, particularly older, to move and effectively access shops if only to buy essential goods such as food.

Access to essential consumer goods and services does not belong to consumer policy and is focused on a single source of vulnerability (poverty, disability). However, the protective rules belong to a public order of protection that is also at work in the implementation of consumerist rules in favour of vulnerable people.

3.1.2 The specific implementation of protective rules

Vulnerability does not create new rights, it simply changes the legal standard to which we refer for judging the unfair practice or the hazardous nature of a product.

The authors who criticize French consumer law consider that the rules of consumer law place the consumer in a minority. Thus, they argue that 'consumer rights tend to make of him an incompetent adult or an eternal minor' contending that 'general Guardianship, the spirit of safety and risk aversion are the fatal disease of contemporary industrial societies' and that 'mothering stifles initiative'.[48]

---

46 EU Consumers Committee, Elaborating the Universal Service Concept in the Services of General Interest – A Draft Consumer Committee Position Paper, 1999.

47 See in France, Panorama des dispositifs locaux d'aide à la mise en accessibilité des commerces, 13 November 2012, http://www.developpement-durable.gouv.fr/Dispositifs-locaux-d-aide-a-la.html.

48 Ph Malaurie, L Aynès and Ph Stoffel-Munck, *Les obligations* (Defrénois, 2011).

It is not the purpose of entrenching the notion of vulnerable consumers. It does not aim to establish two categories of consumers: average consumers, who have full capacity and can enjoy the benefits of the proper functioning of the internal market and vulnerable consumers, considered as incapable.

In truth, consumer law is both an economic and social law[49] and the protection of the average consumer and the more vulnerable consumer differ more in their intensity than in their nature.

Concerning the protection of economic interests of consumers, the objective of Directive 2005/29 was to avoid that certain business practices are always considered unfair even though they do not alter the economic behaviour of most consumers. In reality, only the most vulnerable are affected by certain practices and Member States tended to place the cursor beyond the protection necessary to ensure that the weakest would be protected.

This resulted in a law that may unnecessarily impede intra-EU trade.[50] The European legislator did not choose the '"weak and vulnerable" consumer as the generally applicable standard,'[51] and opted for an abstract model, the 'average consumer reasonably well informed and reasonably circumspect'.[52]

As an exception, the assessment of a business practice will be by reference to a model, an average member of the group of consumers particularly vulnerable to the practice or the product to which it relates. According to the Commission, 'The aim of the provision is to capture cases of dishonest market practices which reach the majority of consumers, but in reality are devised to exploit the weaknesses of certain specific consumer groups.'[53]

---

49 D Mazeaud, 'Le droit de la consommation est-il un droit social ou un droit économique?' (2006) 9 *Revue Lamy de la Concurrence*.

50 See Court's case law under art 28 EC: S Weatherill, 'Who Is the "Average Consumer?"' 115.

51 Commission Staff Working Document Guidance on the Implementation/ Application of Directive 2005/29/EC on Unfair Commercial Practices, 2009 SEC (2009) 1666, 29.

52 Art 5 of Directive 2005/29. Social, Cultural or Linguistic Factors May Justify Special Appreciation of the National Courts (Recital (18) of Directive 2005/29) : See Case C- 220/98 Estee Lauder Cosmetics (2000) ECR I-117, n°29 ('In order to apply that test to the present case, several considerations must be borne in mind. In particular, it must be determined whether social, cultural or linguistic factors may justify the term "lifting" used in connection with a firming cream, meaning something different to the German consumer as opposed to consumers in other Member States, or whether the instructions for the use of the product are in themselves sufficient to make it quite clear that its effects are short-lived, thus neutralising any conclusion to the contrary that might be derived from the word "lifting"'.

53 Commission Staff Working Document Guidance on the Implementation/ Application of Directive 2005/29/EC on Unfair Commercial Practices, 2009 SEC (2009) 1666, p 31; H Collins, 'Harmonisation by Example: European Laws against Unfair Commercial Practices' (2010) 73(1) *Modern Law Review* 89–118 (99).

Apart from this differentiated test that is intended to apply to any commercial practice,[54] certain practices that are per se considered as misleading or aggressive are likely to affect especially vulnerable consumers. For example, the practice of 'Claiming that products are able to facilitate winning in games of chance'[55] is considered as misleading. This type of claim affects the most gullible. Taking into account specific people with a gambling addiction is also considered in a Commission Communication of October 2012 on online gambling.[56] The practice of 'Falsely claiming that a product is able to cure illnesses, dysfunction or malformations'[57] may affect particularly the infirm, elderly and gullible. Finally, among the aggressive practices, there is a reference to advertising that constitutes 'a direct exhortation to children to buy advertised products or persuade their parents or other adults to buy advertised products for them'.[58] The particular vulnerability of children is also taken into account by specific provisions such as those relating to food advertising in audiovisual media services to fight against growing rates of childhood obesity.[59]

Concerning the protection of the health and safety of consumers, the danger of a particular foodstuff and its harmful nature are evaluated differently if the product is intended for a specific category of consumers who present particular health sensitivities.[60] The analysis is the same as for unfair commercial practices. Particular caution is required from professionals that specifically target vulnerable consumers because, due to age or illness, their body is more sensitive to

54 See Case Law C-428/11 of 18 October 2012 – Purely Creative, §54 and 55.

55 Annex I n°16 of Directive 2005/29.

56 Communication from the Commission, to the European Parliament, the Council, the Economic and Social Committee and the Committee of the Regions – Towards a Comprehensive European Framework for Online Gambling, {SWD (2012) 345 final} COM (2012) 596 final.

57 Annex I n°17 of Directive 2005/29

58 Annex I n°28 of Directive 2005/29. The legal difficulty is to decide when and under what circumstances an advertising measure is directed at children, see. H-W Micklitz, J Stuyck and E Terryn (gen. eds) and D Droshout (coord. ed.), *Cases, Materials and Text on Consumer Law* (Oxford: Hart Publishing, 2010) 112.

59 Directive 2010/13/EU of the European Parliament and of the Council of 10 March 2010 on the Coordination of Certain Provisions Laid Down by Law, Regulation or Administrative Action in Member States Concerning the Provision of Audiovisual Media Services ('Audiovisual Media Services Directive') (Text with EEA Relevance), OJ L 95, 15.4.2010, p. 1–24; A Garde, 'The Best Interests of the Child and EU Consumer Law and Policy: A Major Gap between Theory and Practice?', in J Devenny and M Kenny (eds), *European Consumer Protection: Theory and Practice* (Cambridge University Press, 2012) 164–201.

60 Art 14 of Regulation No 178/2002 of the European Parliament and the Council of 28 January 2002 Laying Down the General Principles and Requirements of Food Law, Establishing the European Food Safety Authority and Laying Down Procedures in Matters of Food Safety.

contaminants or pathogens.[61] The requirement imposed is, however, lower than for unfair commercial practices because only the vulnerable consumer products trigger the change of the reference standard. In the framework of Directive 2005/29, it is sufficient that the practice has the effect (not necessarily the purpose) of affecting the economic behaviour of a class of vulnerable consumers and that this impact could be foreseen by the professional.

Thus, the legal treatment of the vulnerability gains in consistency even if large parts of consumer law do not take into account the specificity of particularly weak consumers. Regarding the sanctions, we find a mosaic of remedies that reflects national choices.

3.2 The Penalties for Exploiting Consumer Vulnerability

The penalties for exploiting consumer vulnerability largely fall within the competence of Member States.

Firstly, it shall be for each Member State to decide which of these facilities shall be available and whether to enable the courts or administrative authorities to require prior recourse to other established means of dealing with complaints.[62] These facilities shall be available regardless of whether the consumers affected are in the territory of the Member State where the trader is located or in another Member State.

Secondly, if Directive 2005/29 provides that 'penalties must be effective, proportionate and dissuasive', Member States still enjoy a broad margin of discretion in deciding how to protect vulnerable consumers.

If one focuses on the French example, the sanctions appear rather inadequate. For the consumers that are victims of the practice, the civil penalty for an aggressive practice consists of the nullity of the contract in the presence of an aggressive practice.[63]

By contrast, no specific penalty is provided for misleading practices, and the general law of contracts should apply. Thus the nullity is not automatically applied and it also appears to be difficult to obtain.[64]

---

61 V. also for toys, Directive 2009/48/EC of the European Parliament and of the Council of 18 June 2009 on the Safety of Toys (Text with EEA Relevance), OJ L 170, 30.6.2009, 1–37 (Recital (21): '(21) It is also necessary to adopt new essential safety requirements. In order to ensure a high level of protection of children against risks caused by chemical substances in toys, the use of dangerous substances, in particular substances that are classified as carcinogenic, mutagenic or toxic for reproduction (CMR), and allergenic substances and certain metals, should be subject to careful attention [...]. Those provisions should, however, also be adapted to the particular needs of children, who are a vulnerable group of consumers [...].'

62 ECJ, 17 January 2013. *Georg Köck v Schutzverband gegen unlauteren Wettbewerb.*, Case C-206/11, *ECR 2013.*

63 Art L.122–15 French Consumer Code.

64 The consumer has to prove a defect of consent.

It requires an individual lawsuit for the vulnerable consumer who has been led to contract because of the harassment, coercion or undue influence of the professional. The failure to take into account the vulnerability in procedural consumer law makes such an action very hypothetical. One author concludes that

> Basically, with respect to the initial victim of unfair commercial practice, the sanctions will not differ from those applied in common law. But precisely such sanctions do not seem necessarily suited to the definition of unfair commercial practices. Their restorative vocation rooted in the present does not fit with the only potential effect of practices.[65]

Criminal sanctions are provided by the Consumer Code,[66] but the doctrine states that 'it is feared that the weapon is more theoretical than practical'[67] in times of drastic restriction of resources allocated to government control. In reality, the competitors, indirect victims,[68] take legal action to denounce the unfair commercial practices that disrupt the normal competition. Their action allows the effective end of the practice, but damages allocated to the competitor in the field of unfair competition[69] divert the rule from its original purpose, which is the protection of consumers.

If we look at French case law, the most effective lawsuits are those initiated by consumer associations.[70] The defence of the collective interest of consumers makes it possible for approved associations to request the end of an unlawful practice and obtain damages for the prejudice suffered by the consumer group.[71] The fight led by the UFC (Union Fédérale des Consommateurs) about the sale of computers with pre-installed software is particularly topical in this respect.[72] It even led the operators to create new alternative commercial offers offering for sale bare

---

65 G Chantepie, 'La détermination de sanctions effectives, proportionnées et dissuasives des pratiques commerciales déloyales', in E Terryn and D Voinot (eds), *Droit européen des pratiques commerciales déloyales. Evolution et perspectives* (Larcier, 2012) 91.

66 Art L. 121–6 and art L. 213–1 French Consumer Code.

67 D Fenouillet, 'Loi du 3 janvier 2008, pratiques commerciales déloyales, trompeuses, agressives' (April 2008) 2 *Revue des contrats* 350.

68 Art 11.1 of Directive 2005/29: 'Such means shall include legal provisions under which persons or organisations regarded under national law as having a legitimate interest in combating unfair commercial practices, including competitors, may: (a) take legal action against such unfair commercial practices; and/or (b) bring such unfair commercial practices before an administrative authority competent either to decide on complaints or to initiate appropriate legal proceeding.'

69 Art 1382 French Civil Code.

70 See, the French consumer Bill of 2 May 2013 (Projet de loi relatif à la consommation, n° 1015, déposé le 2 mai 2013).

71 Arts L. 421–1 and 421–2, Code de la consommation.

72 See Cass.civ1, 6 oct 2011, D.2011, actu 2464, obs. Delpech ; Cass.Ci1, 12 July 2012, n°11.18807.

computers to avoid tying be considered as unfair. Note however that the sanctions have an effect especially for the future (end of practice) as compensation for the collective damage is symbolic[73] and is not collected by individual consumers harmed by unfair behaviour. Only the introduction of a collective redress would allow to overcome judicial inertia of vulnerable consumers and to effectively punish unfair commercial practices that affect them particularly.

Conclusion

If the concept of 'vulnerable consumer' covers different realities, its manifestations multiply themselves and highlight the legal mechanisms in existence to face the particular weaknesses of certain groups of consumers.

Even the access to consumption is sometimes lacking, which we remedy by making certain goods or services affordable for people that are excluded from the benefits expected from the market. More generally, consumer vulnerability is taken into account by judging the unfairness of a commercial practice or the hazardous nature of certain products.

But the marketing restrictions or the limitation of freedom of commercial expression cannot be sufficient to protect vulnerable consumers efficiently. Consumer education should still be improved to allow a real understanding of the transmitted information.

Cognitive biases identified by proponents of behavioural economics are particularly prevalent among vulnerable consumers, and informational mechanisms are not sufficient to reduce the existing fracture.[74]

The effective protection of vulnerable consumers therefore requires their 'empowerment' through the adjustment of the protective rules to reflect their actual capabilities. This would allow for the protection of consumers as components of humanity with their weaknesses beyond their role as economic agents.

In this regard, the emergence of the figure of the vulnerable consumer is in the thinking of Amartya Sen[75] that builds the idea of justice around the notion of 'capability', i.e., the real possibility that an individual could have to select various combinations of functioning. This equality of power for people, 'capability', is the cornerstone of the protection of vulnerable consumers.

---

73 Versailles, 5 May 2011, D. 2011, pan 82363 – UFC c/ Hewlett Packard France.

74 E Hanson and D Kysar, 'Taking Behavioralism Seriously' (1999) 112 *Harvard Law Review* 1420; C Sunstein, *Behavioral Law and Economics* (Cambridge University Press, 2000); R Incardona and C Poncibo, 'The Average Consumer, the Unfair Commercial Practices Directive, and the Cognitive Revolution' (2007) 30 *J Consum Policy* 21–38.

75 A Sen, *L'idée de justice* (Flammarion, 2010).

Bibliography

Attali J, *Rapport de la Commission pour la libération de la croissance française: 300 décisions pour changer la France* (La documentation française, 2008).

Bartl M, 'The Affordability of Energy: How Much Protection for the Vulnerable Consumers?' (2010) 33 *J Consum Policy* 225–245.

Chantepie G, 'La détermination de sanctions effectives, proportionnées et dissuasives des pratiques commerciales déloyales', in E Terryn and D Voinot (eds), *Droit européen des pratiques commerciales déloyales. Evolution et perspectives* (Larcier, 2012) 91.

Cour de cassation, Les personnes vulnérables dans la jurisprudence de la Cour de cassation, Annual report 2009, http://www.courdecassation.fr/publications_cour_26/rapport_annuel_36/rapport_2009_3408.

Dutheil-Warolin L, 'La notion de vulnérabilité de la personne physique en droit privé', PhD diss., Université de Limoges, 2004.

Fenouillet D, 'Loi du 3 janvier 2008, pratiques commerciales déloyales, trompeuses, agressives' (April 2008) 2 *Revue des contrats* 350.

Fossier Th, 'Peut-on légiférer sur la vulnérabilité?' (2011) *Dr. Famille* dossier 2.

Friant-Perrot M and A Garde, 'La publicité alimentaire et la lutte contre l'obésité infantile en droit français et en droit anglais', in *Actualités de droit économique: aspects de droit de la concurrence et de la consommation et de droit de l'agroalimentaire*, co-organized by the Lascaux Programme and the UMR-Droit et changement social, Faculty of Law and Political Science, Nantes, 17 September 2010 (Petites Affiches, Numéro spécial – Actes de colloque, 6 Octobre 2011) 199, 27–39.

Garde A, 'The Best Interests of the Child and EU Consumer Law and Policy: A Major Gap between Theory and Practice?', in J Devenny and M Kenny (eds), *European Consumer Protection: Theory and Practice* (Cambridge University Press, 2012) 164–201.

———, 'Freedom of Commercial Expression and Public Health Protection: The Principle of Proportionality as a Tool to Strike the Balance', in L Gormley and N Nic Shuibhne (eds), *From Single Market to Economic Union – Essays in Honour of John A. Usher* (Oxford University Press, 2012) 117–133.

Griffiths Merlyn A and Tracy R Harmon, 'Aging Consumer Vulnerabilities Influencing Factors of Acquiescence to Informed Consent' (2011) 25(3) *Journal of Consumer Affairs* 445–466.

Hanson E and D Kysar, 'Taking Behavioralism Seriously' (1999) 112 *Harvard Law Review* 1420.

Hauser J, 'Une théorie générale de la protection du sujet vulnérable?' (2011) 83 *Revue Lamy Droit Civil*.

Howells G and S Weatherill, *Consumer Protection Law* (Ashgate, 2005).

Incardona R and C Poncibo, 'The Average Consumer, the Unfair Commercial Practices Directive, and the Cognitive Revolution' (2007) 30 *J Consum Policy* 21–38 (n 38).

Mansfield Ch, 'Predatory Lending: The Failure of Consumer Choice as a Regulatory Model in the United States', in *Risk and Choice in Consumer Society* (Bruyland, 2007) 299.

Maurer B, *Le principe du respect de la dignité humaine et la Convention européenne des droits de l'homme*, Paris, Coll. Monde européen et international, Jacques Bourrinet (Sous-dir.) (La documentation française, 1999).

Mazeaud D, 'Le droit de la consommation est-il un droit social ou un droit économique?' (2006) 9 *Revue Lamy de la Concurrence.*

Micklitz H-W, J Stuyck and E Terryn (gen. eds) and D Droshout (coord. ed.), *Cases, Materials and Text on Consumer Law* (Oxford: Hart Publishing, 2010) 112.

Moschis George P, Jill Mosteller and Choong Kwai Fatt, 'Research Frontiers on Older Consumers' Vulnerability' (2011) 25(3) *Journal of Consumer Affairs* 467–491.

OECD Report, Corporate Governance and the Financial Crisis: Key Findings and Main Messages, June 2009.

Report of the French Ombudsman, Crédit, croissance et urgence sociale, 10 February 2009.

Sen A, *L'idée de justice* (Flammarion, 2010).

Stuyck J, E Terryn and T Van Dyck, 'Confidence through Fairness? The New Directive on Unfair Business-to-Consumer Commercial Practices in the Internal Market' (2006) 43 *CMLRev* 107, at 121–122.

Sunstein C, *Behavioral Law and Economics* (Cambridge University Press, 2000).

Weatherill S, 'Who Is the "Average Consumer"?', in S Weatherill and U Bernitz (eds), *The Regulation of Unfair Commercial Practices under EC Directive 2005/29 – New Rules and New Techniques* (Oxford: Hart Publishing, 2007) 115.

PART III
The UCP Directive and Other Regimes

Chapter 5
Can the UCP Directive Really Be a Vector of Legal Certainty?

Amandine Garde

1. Introduction

On 14 March 2013, the Commission published the first report on the application of Directive 2005/29/EC on unfair business-to-consumer commercial practices (the UCP Directive or the Directive), in which it confirmed the significance of the Directive for the EU economy.[1]

The UCP Directive clearly states its dual purpose: 'to contribute to the proper functioning of the internal market and achieve a high level of consumer protection'.[2] To this effect, it combines a broad prohibition on all unfair commercial practices harming consumers' economic interests, with a clause of maximum harmonization requiring that the national rules in place shall be replaced by a single, uniform EU framework, therefore departing from the minimum harmonization technique traditionally used in EU consumer law.[3] This combination was intended to promote legal certainty, increase business and consumer confidence in the internal market and, in turn, promote market integration.

The question whether the UCP Directive has contributed to ensuring a high level of consumer protection has been the focus of extensive academic debate: the Directive represents a trade-off between the two objectives it pursues in that it has required that some Member States lower the level of protection they traditionally provided to consumers in the name of internal market integration, whereas others

---

1 First Application Report on the Application of Directive 2005/29/EC on Unfair Business-to-Consumer Practices COM (2013) 139 final.

2 Art 1.

3 Examples of minimum harmonization directives in the area of consumer protection include: Council Directive 85/577/EEC of 20 December 1985 to Protect the Consumer in Respect of Contracts Negotiated Away from Business Premises (Doorstep Selling) [1985] OJ L372/31; Council Directive 90/314/EEC of 13 June 1990 on Package Travel, Package Holidays and Package Tours (Package Travel) [1990] OJ L158/59; Council Directive 93/13/EEC of 5 April 1993 on Unfair Terms in Consumer Contracts (Unfair Contract Terms) [1993] OJ L95/29; Directive 97/7/EC of the European Parliament and of the Council of 20May 1997 on the Protection of Consumers in Respect of Distance Contracts (Distance Selling) [1997] OJ L144/19; Directive 1999/44/EC of the European Parliament and of the Council of 25 May 1999 on Certain Aspects of the Sale of Consumer Goods and Associated Guarantees (Sales Guarantee) [1999] OJ L171/12.

have had to increase the level of protection applicable on their territories.[4] This contribution does not propose to focus on this question – though any assessment of the UCP Directive cannot avoid it. Rather, it proposes to assess the effectiveness of the UCP Directive in light of its other objective and attempts to answer the question of whether the Directive does promote legal certainty through market integration.

The question will be envisaged from two distinct angles. The discussion will first consider the extent to which the provisions of the UCP Directive themselves promote legal certainty, before scrutinizing the relationship of the UCP Directive with other EU legislative instruments whose objectives also include the protection of consumers.

2. Legal Certainty within the UCP Directive

The objective of legal certainty through market integration is strongly enshrined in the UCP Directive. This objective is even the key justification for the European Union's preference for maximum over minimum harmonization, as the Preamble of the Directive clearly confirms:

> The laws of the Member States relating to unfair commercial practices show marked differences which can generate appreciable distortions of competition and obstacles to the smooth functioning of the internal market. [...] These disparities cause *uncertainty* as to which national rules apply to unfair commercial practices harming consumers' economic interests and create many barriers affecting business and consumers. [...] These obstacles can only be eliminated by establishing uniform rules at Community level which establish a high level of consumer protection and by clarifying certain legal concepts at Community level to the extent necessary for the proper functioning of the internal market and to meet the requirement of legal certainty.[5]

Consequently, the unfairness standard laid down in the Directive is intended to replace all pre-existing national standards with a uniform EU standard in order to promote the security and predictability of business-to-consumer commercial transactions. It is in this sense that the multi-facetted notion of legal certainty is used throughout the UCP Directive. Article 3(5) confirms that Member States will only be able to maintain in force 'national provisions within the field approximated by this Directive which are more restrictive or prescriptive than this Directive and which implement directives containing minimum harmonization clauses' for a transition period of six years as of 12 June 2007 and provided that they

4 The case law of the Court is very clear in this respect. See in particular: Joined Cases C-261 and 299/07 *VTB-VAB* [2009] ECR I-2949; Case C-304/08 *Plus Warenhandelsgesellschaft* [2010] ECR I- 217; Case C-540/08 *Mediaprint* [2010] ECR I-10909; Case C-206/11 *Köck* [2013] ECR I-xxx, judgment of 17 January 2013.

5 Recitals 3 to 5. Emphasis added.

are 'essential to ensure that consumers are adequately protected against unfair commercial practices' and 'proportionate to the attainment of this objective'. The transition period expired on 12 June 2013. Furthermore, by virtue of the internal market clause contained in Article 4 of the UCP Directive, Member States cannot restrict the free movement of goods or services for reasons falling within the field it harmonizes.[6] There are only two areas explicitly identified in the Directive where Member States may impose requirements which are more restrictive or prescriptive: financial services and immoveable property.[7] How does the Directive fare in light of this rhetoric? The assessment will distinguish the general clauses of unfairness and the black list of unfair commercial practices.

2.1 The General Clauses of Unfairness as a Source of Fragmentation?

The Directive is extremely broad in scope in that it prohibits all business-to-consumer commercial practices before, during and after a commercial transaction.[8] It is 'horizontal in nature' and 'covers the totality of business-to-consumer transactions whether offline or online involving both goods and services'.[9] The ambition is clear: to establish a uniform level playing field.

Nevertheless, the general unfairness clause and the two sub-clauses remain open to interpretation: what should be the standard of special skill and care to be expected from a trader? What constitutes an honest market practice and conduct in good faith? The use of general clauses is not unheard of in EU consumer law,[10] and it should not necessarily be a cause for concern. It remains that the use of such loose concepts raises serious doubt as to whether the UCP Directive will suppress the fragmentation of consumer protection rules on unfair commercial practices in the European Union, irrespective of the fact that it is a measure of maximum harmonization. The degree of fragmentation may be reduced over

---

6 Art 4. The significance of this clause is difficult to define, as discussed by A Bakardjieva-Engelbrekt, *EU Marketing Practices Law in the Nordic Countries: Consequences of a Directive on Unfair Business-to-Consumer Commercial Practices* (Helsinki: Nordic Council of Ministers Committee on Consumer Affairs, January 2005) 14–23, and by H Micklitz, 'Minimum/Maximum Harmonisation and the Internal Market Clause', in G Howells, H Micklitz and T Wilhelmsson, *European Fair Trading Law: The Unfair Commercial Practices Directive* (Aldershot: Ashgate, 2006), 27.

7 Art 3(9). In its First Application Report, the Commission considered that there was 'no case for removing this limitation, whether in relation to financial services or in relation to immoveable property', see (n 1) 4.

8 Art 3(1).

9 First Application Report (n 1) 2.

10 For example, art 3(1) of Council Directive 93/13/EEC of 5 April 1993 on unfair terms in consumer contracts [1993] OJ L95/29, provides that 'a contractual term which has not been individually negotiated shall be regarded as unfair if, contrary to the requirement of good faith, it causes a significant imbalance in the parties' rights and obligations arising under the contract, to the detriment of the consumer'.

time if the Court is called upon to interpret key notions of the UCP Directive and provides the necessary guidance to national authorities. In theory, concepts such as unfairness, professional diligence or good faith could be interpreted in a way that would allow (and even oblige) national courts to apply them uniformly from one Member State to another. It is, however, unlikely to be so, first because of the decentralized application of EU law by national courts or other competent authorities[11] and secondly because of the reluctance the Court has shown to date to provide detailed guidance in preliminary rulings.

In effect, the Court's case law suggests that the interpretation of the general unfairness clause and the two sub-clauses on misleading and aggressive practices will continue to vary significantly from one Member State to another, depending on pre-existing rules and traditions in place at national level. For example, after holding in *Mediaprint* that Austrian law did not fit within the regulatory framework set up by the UCP Directive, the Court was called upon to determine whether the commercial practice under review could be regarded as unfair. The Court repeated that a practice could only be regarded as unfair after a specific assessment in light of the criteria set out in Articles 5 to 9 of the UCP Directive[12] and stated:

> The fact that, for at least part of the public concerned, the possibility of participating in a competition represents a determining factor in the purchase of the newspaper constitutes one of the factors which the national court may take into account when making such an assessment.
>
> That fact may lead the national court to consider that the commercial practice in question materially distorts or is likely to materially distort the economic behaviour of the consumer, within the meaning of Article 5(2) of the Directive.
>
> However, that fact does not in any way lead in itself to the conclusion that a sale with a bonus constitutes an unfair commercial practice within the meaning of the Directive. For that purpose, it must also be verified whether the practice in question is contrary to the requirements of professional diligence within the meaning of Article 5(2) of the Directive.[13]

The Court did not provide further guidance on the scope of the general unfairness clause in this case; it simply stated the obvious: to be held unfair, not only should a practice materially distort or be likely to materially distort the economic behaviour of the average consumer, but it should also be contrary to the requirements of professional diligence.

---

11 It is arguable that the risk of divergences is exacerbated in the Member States that have entrusted the implementation, the interpretation and the application of the UCP Directive in national law to a multitude of administrative authorities alongside national courts.

12 Case C-540/08 *Mediaprint* [2010] ECR I-10909.

13 At paragraphs 44 to 46.

More recent case law indicates similar trends. For example, in its ruling in *Köck*, which involved the Austrian legislation requiring that prior authorization be obtained before announcing a clearance sale, the Court ruled that the Directive must be interpreted as precluding a national court from ordering the cessation of a commercial practice not covered by Annex I to the Directive on the sole ground that the practice had not been the subject of prior authorization by the competent administrative authority, without itself carrying out an assessment of the unfairness of the practice in question against the criteria set out in Articles 5 to 9 of the Directive.[14] However, the Court did not engage at all with the extent to which requiring a prior authorization for clearance sales could constitute an unfair commercial practice, leaving the matter to be exclusively determined by the national referring court.

In its decisions involving what would constitute a misleading commercial practice more specifically, the Court has appeared slightly more forthcoming. In *Ving*, which involved the interpretation of Article 7 of the Directive on misleading omissions,[15] the Swedish Consumer Ombudsperson initiated court proceedings against the travel agency Ving on the ground that one of its commercial communications advertising a trip to New York was an invitation to purchase containing a misleading omission insofar as it did not provide sufficient information on the main characteristics of the trip, including the price. The national court referred seven questions to the Court, and asking in particular whether Article 7(4)(a) meant that it was sufficient or only certain of a product's main characteristics to be given and for the trader to refer in addition to its website, on condition that on that site there was essential information on the product's main characteristics, price and other terms in accordance with the requirements in Article 7(4). After noting that this Article referred to the main characteristics of the product without defining that notion or providing an exhaustive list, the Court stated that it was for the national court to assess, on a case-by-case basis, taking into consideration the context of the invitation to purchase, the medium of communication used and the nature and characteristics of the product, whether a reference only to certain main characteristics of the product enabled the consumer to take an informed transactional decision.[16] Even though the Court gave more guidance in *Ving* than it did in *Mediaprint*, it remains that its lack of *detailed* guidance is unlikely to foster a uniform application of the UCP Directive across the European Union.

In its recent *CHS Tour Services* judgment,[17] the Court has clarified that if a commercial practice satisfies all the criteria expressly set out in the provisions of the UCP Directive specifically governing misleading practices, it is not necessary to determine whether such a practice is also contrary to the requirements of

14 Case C-206/11 *Köck*, judgment of 17 January 2013, at paragraph 50.

15 Case C-122/10 *Ving* [2011] ECR I-3903.

16 At paragraphs 50 to 59.

17 Case C-435/11 *CHS Tour Services GmbH v Team4 Travel GmbH*, judgment of 19 September 2013.

professional diligence as referred to Article 5 of the Directive in order for it legitimately to be regarded as unfair and, therefore, prohibited. This is because the misleading nature of a commercial practice derives solely from the fact that it is untruthful inasmuch as it contains false information or that, generally, it is likely to deceive the average consumer in relation to, inter alia, the nature or main characteristics of a product or a service and that, therefore, it is likely to cause that consumer to take a transactional decision that he would not have taken if there had been no such practice. Thus, the constituent features of a misleading commercial practice are in essence expressed with reference to the consumer as the person to whom unfair commercial practices are applied. This judgment is helpful to determine the relationship between the general clause of unfairness and the two general sub-clauses on misleading and aggressive practices. However, it does not explain how notions such as unfair, misleading or aggressive should be interpreted and therefore only contributes to a limited extent to reducing the uncertainty stemming from the use of general clauses.[18]

One may ask whether this lack of certainty really matters. EU consumer policy has always been characterized by a certain degree of fragmentation. Fragmentation is not necessarily problematic in itself. One may even argue that such fragmentation may be seen as an expression of the principle of subsidiarity, that is, a way to strike a balance between national diversity and the demands of the internal market. An alternative way to look at the problem may be to argue that the application of the fairness criteria to specific cases is a question of fact, rather than a question of law. As De Vries has argued:

> it is unrealistic to assume that general clauses will be interpreted similarly in all Member States. However divergent national interpretations of a directive do not necessarily conflict with the aim for maximum harmonization. The statement that full harmonization cannot be established due to divergent national applications is [...] based on a misperception of what constitutes maximum harmonization. First, [...] the Commission's notion of maximum harmonization is highly a political statement, expressing an aspiration rather than a legal reality. Furthermore, it is posited that maximum harmonization establishes a legal framework that offers a uniform legal benchmark for all Member States but does not harmonize the content of this benchmark. The legal framework is uniform in the sense that it prescribes all relevant legal criteria. However, it is primarily up to the national courts to decide on the content of these criteria.[19]

18 The documents published by the Commission since the Directive was adopted leave no doubt as to how important it regards 'uniformity' for legal certainty and the functioning of the internal market. The publicly accessible EU database the Commission has developed may be useful in this quest, but it cannot compensate for the lack of detailed guidance from the Court: https://webgate.ec.europa.eu/ucp.

19 A De Vries, 'The Aim for Complete Uniformity in EU Private Law: An Obstacle to Further Harmonization' (2012) 20(4) *European Review of Private Law* 913, at 923.

This view may at first sight help resolve the question as to whether it is a contradiction in terms to harmonize fully the law of business-to-consumer unfair commercial practices through the use of general clauses. However, De Vries' argument brings a few comments to mind. Firstly, it is difficult to suggest that the Commission's explicit choice for maximum harmonization is a political aspiration rather than a legal reality, bearing in mind the changes that the UCP Directive has led to in national laws across the European Union. One only needs to read the Court's case law in cases such as *VTB*,[20] *Plus Warenhandelsgesellschaft*,[21] *Mediaprint*[22] or *Köck*[23] to grasp the very practical consequences for Member States' legal systems of the move from minimum to maximum harmonization. Secondly, and directly related to our argument, if the Court is not willing to engage more thoroughly with the interpretation of the general clauses and its two sub-clauses, the promises of the UCP Directive are bound to remain empty promises. The Directive was supposed to herald a new era, where different national rules would be replaced by a unique EU standard. One may therefore argue that the Court's reluctance to provide detailed guidance to national courts is somewhat at odds with the fact that it has otherwise embraced the intention of the EU legislature to reduce regulatory fragmentation. It is true that the mechanism of maximum harmonization is intended to constrain national authorities by preventing them from adopting more protective standards at national level, without necessarily constraining the Court itself. Moreover, one could argue that expecting the Court to determine how the general clauses should apply to specific cases could lead to an unmanageable multiplication of preliminary references. Nevertheless, if the objective of the UCP Directive to reduce market fragmentation and thereby increase business and consumer confidence is to be achieved, one may legitimately expect the Court to give far more detailed guidance to national courts entrusted with the application of its provisions than it would have done for a text of minimum harmonization.[24] This does not necessarily mean that the Court should engage in applying the legal concepts on which the uniform interpretation of the Directive rests to specific cases. This is the role of national courts. Rather, it is suggested that the Court should help delineate the scope of these overtly loose concepts and provide the

---

20 Joined Cases C-261 and 299/07 *VTB-VAB* [2009] ECR I-2949.

21 Case C-304/08 *Plus Warenhandelsgesellschaft* [2010] ECR I- 217.

22 Case C-540/08 *Mediaprint* [2010] ECR I-10909.

23 Case C-206/11 *Köck*, judgment of 17 January 2013.

24 For a similar argument, see I Otken Eriksson and U Oberg, 'The Unfair Commercial Practices Directive in Context', in S Weatherill and U Bernitz (eds), *The Regulation of Unfair Commercial Practices under EC Directive 2005/29: New Rules and New Techniques* (Oxford: Hart Publishing 2007) 100. One may therefore add the level of harmonization pursued by an EU harmonizing measure to the list of criteria very usefully identified by Tridimas to distinguish between what he calls 'deference cases', 'guidance cases' and 'outcome cases' in the context of preliminary rulings: T Tridimas, 'Constitutional Review of Member State Action: The Virtues and Vices of an Incomplete Jurisdiction' (2011) 9 *International Journal of Constitutional Law* 737.

interpretative guidance which national courts and other national authorities need to apply the Directive as consistently across Member States as possible. Member States, traders and consumers should know what the meaning of a specific rule is if maximum harmonization is to have any practical advantage (that is, cutting down on transaction and legal costs when engaging in cross-border transactions).[25] Clarity and predictability are two inherent components of legal certainty. The question of how likely it is that maximum harmonization may be achieved through the use of general clauses remains. Even though the general clauses of the UCP Directive only play a subsidiary role in the assessment of the compatibility of a national measure with its provisions, the Court's case law to date tends to confirm that they are likely to constitute an obstacle to the fulfilment of the Commission's expectations that:

> [h]armonisation will considerably increase legal certainty for both consumers and business. Both consumers and businesses will be able to rely on a single regulatory framework based on clearly defined legal concepts regulating all aspects of unfair commercial practices across the EU. The effect will be to eliminate the barriers stemming from the fragmentation of the rules on unfair commercial practices harming consumer economic interests and to enable the internal market to be achieved in this area.[26]

2.2 The Black List as a Source of Increased Certainty?

Article 5(5) of the Directive refers to Annex I as containing the list of those commercial practices which shall in all circumstances be regarded as unfair. The practices listed are grouped into misleading and aggressive practices, reflecting the two categories of commercial practices which the UCP Directive has identified as unfair in Articles 6 and 7 (misleading practices) and Articles 8 and 9 (aggressive practices). The same single list shall apply in all Member States and may only be modified by revision of this Directive. In other words, a practice falling within the scope of the 31 practices listed in Annex I are unfair without the need for national authorities to engage in any specific fact assessment. The list therefore reverses the burden of proof by laying down an irrefutable presumption of unfairness. If a practice is listed, there is no need to assess whether it is contrary to the rules of professional diligence and whether it has materially distorted or would have been likely to materially distort the economic behaviour of the average consumer. If this list is not exhaustive of all unfair commercial practices,[27] it nonetheless lists exhaustively all the commercial practices presumed to be unfair. Thus, if a claim is made that the economic behaviour of the average consumer has been distorted

---

25 See also to this effect S Whittaker, 'Unfair Contract Terms and Consumer Guarantees: The Proposal for a Directive on Consumer Rights and the Significance of Full Harmonisation' (2009) 5 *European Review of Contract Law* 244.

26 Recital 18, UCP Directive.

27 Art 5(5) read in conjunction with Recital 17.

as a result of a practice which is not listed, the claimant will need to establish that the practice is indeed unfair to succeed in its claim, and therefore that the criteria of either the general unfairness clause or the two sub-clauses have been fulfilled.[28]

It is undeniable that by defining the practices deemed unfair across the European Union in all circumstances, the Annex circumscribes the uncertainty of the general clauses. This is all the more as the Annex has been interpreted by the European Court of Justice and by the Commission in its guidance documents.

In its *Purely Creative* judgment,[29] the Court interpreted the scope of one of the practices listed for the first time, shedding light on the scope of Point 31 of Annex I which classifies as aggressive the fact of:

> creating the false impression that the consumer has already won, will win, or will on doing a particular act win, a prize or other equivalent benefit, when in fact either, there is no prize or other equivalent benefit, taking any action in relation to claiming the prize or other equivalent benefit is subject to the consumer paying money or incurring a cost.

In this case, the Court issued an unequivocal ruling that Point 31 must be interpreted as prohibiting aggressive practices by which traders give the false impression that the consumer has already won a prize, while the taking of any action in relation to claiming that prize, be it requesting information concerning the nature of that prize or taking possession of it, is subject to an obligation on the consumer to pay money or to incur any cost whatsoever. It is irrelevant that the cost imposed on the consumer, such as the cost of a stamp, is *de minimis* compared with the value of the prize or that it does not procure the trader any benefit, such as the cost of a stamp. It is also irrelevant that the trader offers the consumer a number of methods by which he may claim the prize, at least one of which is free of charge, if, according to one or more of the proposed methods, the consumer would incur a cost in order to obtain information on the prize or how to acquire it. As the Court stated:

> the practice referred to in [Point 31] is considered, pursuant to [the UCP Directive] to be aggressive because the reference to a prize seeks to exploit the psychological effect created in the mind of the consumer by the perspective of having won something and to cause him to take a decision which is not always rational and which he would not have taken otherwise. It is, therefore, in order to protect the consumer that the concept of a true 'prize' should be preserved, by interpreting [Point 31] as meaning that a prize in respect of which the consumer is obliged to make a payment of whatever kind cannot be regarded as a 'prize'.[30]

---

28 See in particular: Joined Cases C-261 and 299/07 *VTB-VAB* [2009] ECR I-2949; Case C-304/08 *Plus Warenhandelsgesellschaft* [2010] ECR I-217; Case C-540/08 *Mediaprint* [2010] ECR I-10909; Case C-206/11 *Köck* [2013] ECR I-xxx, judgment of 17 January 2013. For a more detailed discussion of Annex I, see Namysłowska in this volume.

29 Case C-428/11 *Purely Creative*, judgment of 18 October 2012.

30 At paragraph 49.

In other words, traders should not exploit the excitement consumers justifiably feel when told that they have won a prize. In particular, it is not acceptable for businesses to hide behind providing one route to claim a prize that is free, if the other ways of claiming the prize incur a cost.

This ruling suggests that the Court will provide guidance, and even detailed guidance, on the scope of the 31 practices listed in Annex I, thus contributing to the harmonization agenda of the EU legislature in this area. However, a broad range of difficult questions remain, and the guidance which both the Commission and the Court have provided fails to answer several of them. Once again, in light of the largely decentralized application of EU law by national courts and other competent authorities, one may wonder how far the European Union's explicit promises of a level playing field can ever be fulfilled.

One cannot help but mention the 'isitfair.eu' website which the Commission has set up to provide 'practical information for consumers on how to check if they have fallen victim to an unfair commercial practice, and how to get help'. However, the examples it uses to illustrate the types of practices falling within the scope of Annex I are all extremely obvious. What it does not contain is more contentious examples. As it fails to help draw boundaries, the contribution of this website to the provision of legal certainty is therefore extremely limited. For example, Point 28 of Annex I prohibits 'the inclusion in an advertisement of a direct exhortation to children to buy advertised products or persuade their parents or other adults to buy advertised products for them'. The example the 'isitfair.eu' website provides of such an aggressive practice provides very limited help in delineating the scope of this provision: 'Hey kids! Get your parents to buy the Golden Horrorscope Trilogy DVD and we'll enter your name to win a trip for four people to the Golden Hills Theme Park'. As one would have expected, this statement is automatically unfair, as it clearly is a direct exhortation to get parents to buy on children's behalf and therefore falls within Point 28 of the Annex. But where should the line be drawn between direct and indirect exhortations? For example, what about the many company-owned websites promoting their goods and services through a page specifically intended to attract children with advergames or give-aways, funny characters, bright attractive colours and graphics and whose purpose is to impact directly on their purchase requests and consumption patterns? The relevant question remains outstanding: how direct should an exhortation to buy be to fall within the scope of Annex I?

The question where the line should be drawn was recently put in sharp focus by the Office of Fair Trading (OFT) in the United Kingdom. In April 2013, it launched an investigation into whether children were being unfairly pressured or encouraged to pay for additional content in 'free' web and app-based games, including upgraded membership or virtual currency such as coins, gems or fruit. Typically, players can access only portions of these games for free, with new levels or features, such as faster game play, costing money. The OFT investigation is exploring whether these games are misleading, commercially aggressive or otherwise unfair. In particular, the OFT is looking into whether these games include 'direct exhortations' to children – a strong encouragement to make a purchase, or to do something that will necessitate making a purchase, or to persuade their parents or other adults to make a purchase for them, and would therefore fall as such within the scope of the UCP Directive and the UK implementing legislation. Following extensive consultation, the OFT has proposed a set of principles on online and app-based games. Comments are invited until 21 November 2013.[31] Looking at the proposed principles, however, it is clear that tough questions remain. For example, Principle 7 requires, in line with Point 28 of Annex to the UCP Directive, that 'a game should not include direct exhortations to children to make a purchase or persuade others to make purchases for them.' The examples illustrating how this principle could be implemented in practice distinguish the statement 'You have run out of cherries. Cherries are available to buy in the shop for real money or you can earn them by completing challenges' (fair because it does not constitute a direct exhortation) and the statement 'You have run out of cherries. BUY MORE NOW from the shop!' with a link that takes the consumer directly to the shop (unfair as a direct exhortation). However, the extent to which this distinction makes sense from a child psychology point of view remains arguable.

The Commission must engage with such questions, rather than infantilize consumers and suggest that all is clear-cut and obvious. It is not.[32] One is tempted to ask whether it is not somewhat paradoxical to expect a high level of consumer awareness through the rather demanding 'average consumer' benchmark, even if adapted to the average consumer of a particularly vulnerable group, whilst simultaneously oversimplifying inherently complex issues to the point of ridicule on the website which is intended to help these very consumers find their way around the scope of as complex a regulatory instrument as the UCP Directive.

Overall, the categorization of practices as automatically unfair across the European Union would suggest that more legal certainty has been injected into the EU legal order. This is all the more so as, if several terms leave scope for interpretation, the Court seems willing to provide clarification on the practices listed.[33] However, the black list is limited to 31 practices only, some of them being a safeguard against the most unfair, rogue commercial practices. Beyond the 31

31 The summary of the investigation, the proposed principles and all related documents are available at http://www.oft.gov.uk/OFTwork/consumer-enforcement/consumer-enforcement-current/childrens-online-games/#.UlJ9MBhwbMw.

32 On the inadequacy of the EU regulatory framework in protecting children from unfair commercial practices, and marketing techniques in particular, see European Parliament, Resolution of 22 May 2012 on a Strategy for Strengthening the Rights of Vulnerable Consumers (2011/2272(INI)). See also A Garde, 'Advertising Regulation and the Protection of Children-Consumers in the European Union: In the Best Interests of … Commercial Operators?' (2011) 19 *International Journal of Children's Rights* 149. The question of the protection of vulnerable consumers, including children, is discussed more thoroughly by Marine Friant-Perrot, in this volume.

33 This is not to suggest, however, that no interpretation questions remain. See also Namysłowska's contribution in this volume for further examples.

practices listed, it is difficult to argue that the UCPD has injected much certainty regarding the notion of 'unfairness', and it would seem to be a contradiction in terms to fully harmonize national laws on the basis of general clauses with such a broad scope as the general unfairness clause and the two sub-clauses contained in the UCP Directive. The analysis of the relationship existing between the UCPD and other provisions of EU law further reinforces the argument.

3. Legal Certainty beyond the UCP Directive: The Relationship between the Directive and Other Instruments of EU Law

In light of its broad scope, it is inevitable that the UCP Directive attempts to define how it interacts with other provisions of EU law. In order to address this question, it is necessary to assess the matter from two distinct perspectives. The first relates to the more specific provisions that have been adopted to add some flesh to the bones of the notions of 'unfair', 'misleading' and 'aggressive' practices. The second concerns the relationship between the UCP Directive and other instruments of EU law which are not intended to complement per se the unfairness test but which nonetheless interact with the UCP Directive.

3.1 Fleshing out the Provisions of the UCP Directive: From Horizontal to Sectoral Provisions

The UCP Directive is a framework directive which applies in the absence of more specific provisions: 'In the case of conflict between the provisions of this Directive and other Community rules regulating specific aspects of unfair commercial practices, the latter shall prevail and apply to those specific aspects.'[34]

The reference to more specific provisions acknowledges that the definition of broad concepts such as misleading, aggressive and unfair may have to be fleshed out in relation to certain categories of goods/services or certain commercial practice. Thus, the Directive must be read in light of more specific provisions which have been introduced to further improve legal certainty.

As the Commission explained in its First Application Report:

> The Directive is the general law governing unfair commercial practices in business-to-consumer transactions. [...] Where sectoral legislation conflicts with the Directive's general provisions, the corresponding provisions of the *lex specialis* will prevail. Often, such conflict occurs because the *lex specialis* contains more detailed pre-contractual information requirements, or stricter rules on the way information is presented to consumers (see Recital 10 of the Directive). However, the existence of specific EU rules in a given sector does not exclude the application of the Directive: in these cases and in relation to all the aspects not covered by the *lex specialis*, the UCP Directive complements these

34 Art 3(4).

> sectoral provisions and fills any remaining gaps in the protection of consumers against unfair commercial practices.[35]

In light of the importance that it attaches to consumer information as a tool of consumer protection, the European Union has adopted a broad range of sectoral measures on information disclosure. Commercial transactions are generally seen as fair if consumers have sufficient, clear and transparent information at their disposal. It is then up to them to process this information and make the most appropriate consumption choices for them and their families.

Examples abound. One of them is Regulation (EC) 1008/2008 on the operation of air services in the European Union.[36] It increases legal certainty regarding what constitutes a misleading price indication in that it requires that air carriers indicate the final price to consumers and provide a breakdown of this price:

> The final price to be paid shall at all times be indicated and shall include the applicable air fare or air rate as well as all applicable taxes, and charges, surcharges and fees which are unavoidable and foreseeable at the time of publication. In addition to the indication of the final price, at least the following shall be specified:
>
> (a) air fare or air rate;
> (b) taxes;
> (c) airport charges; and
> (d) other charges, surcharges or fees, such as those related to security or fuel;
>
> where the items listed under (b), (c) and (d) have been added to the air fare or air rate. Optional price supplements shall be communicated in a clear, transparent and unambiguous way at the start of any booking process and their acceptance by the customer shall be on an 'opt-in' basis.[37]

This provision does improve legal certainty in that it lays down clear, specific requirements on traders to enable consumers to understand more easily what they will have to pay to travel by air and thus compare prices more accurately.[38] The Court has further clarified its scope by holding that an 'optional price supplement' had to be interpreted as meaning that it covers costs, connected with the air travel, arising from services, such as the flight cancellation insurance at issue in the main proceedings, supplied by a party other than the air carrier and charged to the customer by the person selling that travel, together with the air fare, as part

---

35 At p. 5. The use of the word 'conflicts' is not representative of the situation: very often, rules do not conflict as such, in the sense that one goes against another; rather sectoral rules complement the general clauses.

36 [2008] OJ L 293/3. This directive complements Regulation (EC) 261/2004 on air passengers' rights in the event of denied boarding and of cancellation or long delay of flights [2004] OJ L 46/1.

37 Art 23(1). Paragraphs 18 and 19 of art 2 define 'air fare' and 'air rate' respectively.

38 Recital 16 of Regulation (EC) 1008/2008.

of a total price.[39] This provision is more specific regarding what the 'price' covers than the notion of 'price' in Article 7(4)(c) of the UCP Directive.[40] Even though the Air Services Regulation does not refer to the UCP Directive, the former will therefore supersede the latter in that it provides useful indication of what type of practice would be considered unfair across the European Union.[41] This is not to say, however, that the UCP Directive does not play an important role in relation to other potentially unfair commercial practices, such as bait advertising and marketing of air fares, which are not covered by Regulation (EC) 1008/2008.

Regrettably, however, provisions designed to apply to specific sectors do not always promote as much legal certainty as they should do. If this is somewhat counter-intuitive, the following example drawing on what would constitute misleading food information will attempt to demonstrate the point.

The principle that information should not be misleading is at the heart of EU food law,[42] and in the last few years, the European Union has invested a significant amount of energy to flesh out the notion of misleading food information. In particular, it has adopted Regulation (EC) 1924/2006 on nutrition and health claims made on foods which is intended to regulate the type of claims which food operators are entitled to use to promote their products,[43] as well as Regulation (EU) 1169/2011 on the provision of food information to consumers.[44]

Regulation (EC) 1924/2006 defines a claim as 'any message or representation, which is not mandatory under [Union] or national legislation, including pictorial, graphic or symbolic representation, in any form, which states, suggests or implies that a food has particular characteristics'.[45] The Regulation then divides food claims into two main sub-categories: nutrition claims and health claims. A nutrition claim 'suggests or implies that a food has particular nutrition properties due to the energy it provides (or does not provide) or the nutrients or other substances it contains

39 Case C-112/11 *ebookers.com Deutschland*, judgment of 19 July 2012.

40 'In the case of an invitation to purchase, the following information shall be regarded as material, if not already apparent from the context: [...] (c) the price inclusive of taxes, or where the nature of the product means that the price cannot reasonably be calculated in advance, the manner in which the price is calculated, as well as, where appropriate, all additional freight, delivery or postal charges or, where these charges cannot be reasonably be calculated in advance, the fact that such additional charges may be payable [...].'

41 The First Application Report explicitly refers to Regulation (EC) 1008/2008 to illustrate the relationship between the UCP Directive and EU sectoral legislation. See (n 1) 5, fn 21.

42 M Friant-Perrot and A Garde, 'From BSE to Obesity – EFSA's Growing Role in the EU's Nutrition Policy', in A Alemanno and S Gabbi (eds), *Foundations of EU Food Law and Policy – 10 Years of European Food Safety Authority* (Ashgate, 2014).

43 [2007] OJ L 12/3.

44 [2011] OJ L 304/18. Art 7 specifically defines what constitutes misleading food information.

45 Art 2(2).

or does not contain' (for example: 'low fat').[46] A health claim 'states, suggests or implies that a relationship exists between a food and health' (for example: 'reduces cholesterol').[47] As the definition clearly explains, claims are voluntarily provided by food operators and should therefore be distinguished from the information which must be disclosed as part of a legal requirement, such as the compulsory nutrition declaration provided for in Regulation (EU) 1169/2011.[48]

The increased reliance of consumers on nutrition and health claims may be seen as a positive evolution insofar as these claims can inform their purchasing decisions. It may also encourage food manufacturers to reformulate their products and place more nutritious foods on the market. It is therefore not surprising that the food industry has supported the harmonization of national rules on food claims at the EU level to reduce regulatory diversity and facilitate the free movement of food from one Member State to another. On the other hand, nutrition and health claims may also offer a powerful marketing tool to food industry operators. It is consequently imperative to ensure that the claims in question are reliable and do inform consumer choices rather than mislead them. Several public health and consumer associations have therefore supported the introduction at the EU level of the regulation of nutrition and health claims made on foods, on the ground that such claims aspire to be treated as objective truths capable of influencing the eating decisions of consumers and, ultimately, their health. This is particularly so as they are often made on branded foods which tend to be highly processed and as such contribute to unhealthy diets, overweight and obesity.

After more than three years of intense debate, the Council and the European Parliament adopted Regulation (EC) 1924/2006, which entered into force on 1 July 2007. It lays down the overriding principle that nutrition and health claims may only be used if they are not misleading[49] and if they are scientifically substantiated.[50] The European Food Safety Agency (EFSA) provides support to the Commission and assesses whether claims relating to the nutrition and health benefits of foods are substantiated by scientific evidence.[51] It is on the basis of this scientific evaluation that EU political institutions then decide whether or not such claims should be authorized at the EU level.

---

46 Art 2(4).

47 Art 2(5).

48 [2011] OJ L 304/18. See in particular the mandatory nutrition declaration provided for in art 9(l) and art 29 to 35.

49 Arts 3, 4 and 5.

50 Art 6.

51 See Regulation (EC) 1924/2006 read in light of Regulation (EC) 178/2002 laying down the general principles and requirements of food law, establishing the European Food Safety Authority and laying down procedures in matters of food safety [2002] OJ L 31/1: '[The EFSA] shall provide scientific advice and scientific and technical support for the Community's legislation and policies in all fields which have a direct or indirect impact on food and feed safety. It shall provide independent information on all matters within these fields and communicate on risks' (art 22[2]).

Nutrition claims are only permitted if they are listed in the Annex and if they respect precise and quantifiable values.[52] For example, a claim that a food is a 'source of fibre' may only be made 'where the product contains at least 3 grams of fibre per 100 grams or at least 1.5 grams of fibre per 100 kcal'.[53] The Commission may require that amendments to the Annex be made subject, where appropriate, to the consultation of the EFSA.[54] To date, five nutrition claims have been added to the original list of 24,[55] whereas two have been rejected.[56]

As far as health claims are concerned, a positive list of health claims other than those referring to the reduction of a disease risk will be drawn up by the Commission, on the basis of claims submitted by Member States. These health claims will then be allowed on labels, provided that the producer can verify the link between the claim and a given product. The EFSA is responsible for verifying the scientific substantiation of the submitted claims, some of which are currently in use, some of which are proposed by applicants.[57] The Commission has established an EU register of nutrition and health claims made on food which will be updated regularly to include the list of permitted nutrition and health claims together with the conditions applying to them, as well as a list of rejected health claims and the reasons for their rejection. A first list of health claims was published on 16 May 2012.[58] Overall, the amount of health claims the EFSA has had to assess has exceeded all expectations: out of the 4,637 claims (of a total of 44,000 health claims Member States had proposed) the Commission submitted to the EFSA between July 2008 and March 2010, the Commission asked the EFSA to evaluate 2,758 claims by June 2011, 331 claims were withdrawn and 1,548 claims on 'botanicals' have been placed on hold by the Commission pending further consideration on how to proceed with these.

To this extent, there is no doubt that Regulation 1924/2006 has injected far more certainty regarding the claims made on foods than a horizontal, non-sector-specific text such as the UCP Directive could ever have done. However, seven years after its adoption, the framework that this Regulation lays down still contains glaring gaps which necessarily limit the effectiveness of this instrument and the

---

52 Art 8(1).

53 Annex to Regulation (EC) 1924/2006.

54 Arts 8(2) and 25, which refer to Council Decision 1999/468/EC laying down the procedures for the exercise of implementing powers conferred on the Commission [1999] OJ L 184/23.

55 Commission Regulation (EU) 116/2010 [2010] OJ L 37/10.

56 These two rejections resulted from the objection of the European Parliament on 2 February 2012: P7_TA(2012)0022).

57 Four types of health claims are identified in Regulation (EC) 1924/2006: general function claims; new function claims; disease reduction claims; and child development or health claims. For more information on each type of claims, see arts 13 and 14 of the Regulation, as well as the EFSA's webpage on nutrition and health claims, available at http://www.efsa.europa.eu/en/topics/topic/nutrition.htm.

58 The EU Register is available at http://ec.europa.eu/nuhclaims.

certainty resulting from its provisions. It is all the more regrettable that these gaps could have been avoided with a bit more political courage from the Commission whose quest for uniformity and legal certainty has tended to give way before the opposition it has faced from the powerful food industry lobby. The question of nutrition profiling illustrates the point.

Article 4 of Regulation (EC) 1924/2006 provides that food must have appropriate nutrient profiles to bear nutrition or health claims.[59] The rationale for the establishment of nutrient profiles is that food containing high levels of nutrients whose excessive intakes as part of the overall diet is not recommended should not be able to be marketed as providing nutrition or health benefits if, ultimately, such consumption is not conducive to health. The EFSA was consulted and in preparing its scientific advice to the Commission, it concluded:

> When classifying food products as eligible to bear claims, the potential of the food to adversely affect the overall dietary balance is the main scientific consideration. This consideration relates in particular to nutrients for which there is evidence of a dietary imbalance in EU populations that might influence the development of overweight and obesity or diet-related diseases such as cardiovascular disease or other disorders; they include nutrients that might be consumed to excess, as well as those for which intake might be inadequate.[60]

However, in setting the nutrient profiles, the Commission is also required to 'carry out consultations with interested parties, in particular food business operators and consumer groups'. Thus, the Commission has conducted specific and extensive consultations of stakeholders on the setting of nutrient profiles, including two meetings of a working group on nutrient profiles.[61] Member State experts were also consulted within the Commission expert working group on nutrition and health claims, in which the EFSA also participated. Nevertheless, nearly four years after the deadline laid down in Regulation (EC) 1924/2006, nutrient profiles still remain to be published. The difficulties facing the Commission largely stem from the fact that the boundary between the scientific sphere and the policy decision sphere is particularly difficult to draw in this area.[62] Hopefully the next Commission has more political stamina than the current one and can reconcile sweeping statements on legal certainty (and the use of maximum harmonization and regulations to promote such certainty) with practical reality.

This example demonstrates that, even if some significant progress has been made to increase legal certainty, the Commission's rhetoric on uniformity fails to

---

59 The term 'nutrient profile' refers to the nutrient composition of a food or diet. 'Nutrient profiling' therefore is the classification of foods for specific purposes based on their nutrient composition. For more information on nutrient profiling, see the dedicated webpage of the WHO on this issue: http://www.who.int/nutrition/topics/profiling/en.

60 http://ec.europa.eu/food/food/labellingnutrition/claims/nut_profiles_en.htm.

61 http://ec.europa.eu/food/committees/advisory/sum_wg_11072008.pdf.

62 This point is discussed more fully in M Friant-Perrot and A Garde (n 42).

convince. Whilst the elephant remains in the room (in the absence, for example, of a robust nutrition profiling system), legal certainty will not improve as much as it should nor as much as the Commission promised when it proposed the Nutrition and Health Claims Regulation back in 2003. The intention of the European Union to regulate misleading claims is laudable, but in practice, these efforts will not deliver the promised outcomes until difficult decisions are made to confront the relevant industry lobbies at the EU level.

3.2 'Without Prejudice...' to Legal Certainty? Delineating the Scope of the UCP Directive and Its Relationship with Other Provisions of EU Law

In light of its broad scope, it is inevitable that the UCP Directive attempts to define how it interacts with other provisions of EU law. One therefore notes the phrase 'without prejudice to' in various places – a phrase which adds an extra layer of complexity to the existing and already particularly complex regulatory framework. Admittedly, complexity does not necessarily mean uncertainty. However, the case study discussed in this section, and which is by no means an isolated example,[63] shows that the relationship may render the regulatory landscape most uncertain for traders, consumers and Member States alike. It focuses on the relationship between the UCP Directive and Directive 89/552/EEC on television broadcasting (the TV Directive),[64] now replaced by Directive 2010/13/EU on audiovisual media services (the AVMS Directive).[65] More specifically, it attempts to untangle the extent to the European Union allows the use of product placement as a legitimate marketing technique.

The practice of product placement has given rise to a lot of controversies. When the UCP Directive was adopted, the Commission was firmly of the view that the practice should be allowed at the EU level. Thus, Recital 6 explicitly states:

> this Directive does not affect *accepted advertising and marketing practices, such as legitimate product placement*, brand differentiation or the offering of incentives which may legitimately affect consumers' perceptions of products

63 For a similar analysis focusing on the regulation of marketing to children, see A Garde, 'The Unfair Commercial Practices Directive: A Successful Example of Legislative Harmonisation?', in P Syrpis (ed.), *The Judiciary, the Legislature and the Internal Market* (Cambridge University Press, 2012) 118.

64 [1989] OJ L 298/23.

65 [2010] OJ L 95/1. For more information on the AVMS Directive (in English), see A Harcourt and S Weatherill (eds), 'Special Issue on the Consumer and EU Audiovisual Policy' (2008) 31 *Journal of Consumer Policy*; O Castendyk, E Dommering and A Scheuer, *European Media Law* (The Hague: Kluwer Law International, 2008); J Harrison and L Woods, *European Broadcasting Law and Policy* (Cambridge: Cambridge University Press, 2007); I Katsirea, *Public Broadcasting Standards and European Law* (The Hague: Kluwer Law International, 2008); M Burri-Nenova, 'The New Audiovisual Media Services Directive: Television Without Frontiers, Television Without Cultural Diversity' (2007) 44 *CMLRev.* 1689.

> and influence their behaviour without impairing the consumer's ability to make an informed decision.[66]

Similarly, in the first version of its proposal for an AVMS Directive,[67] the Commission took a clear stance in favour of liberalizing the practice of product placement across the European Union, subject to certain conditions being met.[68] During the consultation phase of the revision process of the TV Directive, the Commission argued that product placement should be allowed on two main grounds. Firstly, it claimed that the liberalization of product placement would allow European audiovisual media services to obtain an additional source of revenue by which to bolster diminishing revenue streams and which would facilitate the production of better quality programmes.[69] Secondly, the Commission argued that liberalizing product placement would render European audiovisual media services more competitive in that it would minimize the problems associated with dual regimes in which product placement would be allowed in programmes originating from outside the European Union but not in programmes originating from within the European Union.

Despite its clear position in favour of product placement, the Commission did meet some opposition not only from public health and consumer associations, but also from some Member States (not least northern countries and Germany). In particular, the argument was made that product placement was unfair to consumers: first, because it had a more insidious influence than traditional forms of advertising

---

66 Emphasis added.

67 COM (2005) 646 final. See in particular at Recital 40: 'product placement should be allowed under certain circumstances'; Recital 46: 'Product placement is a reality in cinematographic works and in audiovisual works made for television, but Member States regulate this practice differently. To ensure a level playing field, and thus enhance the competitiveness of the European media industry, it is necessary to adopt rules for product placement'; and art 3h laying down the conditions at which product placement should be allowed.

68 Even though there were controversies regarding whether the TV Directive should be interpreted as prohibiting product placement in television programmes produced in the European Union (the TV Directive does not mention product placement), the general view seemed to be that product placement was banned as a result of the separation principle enshrined in the directive that 'television advertising shall be readily recognisable as such and kept quite separate from other parts of the programme service by optical and/or acoustic means' (art 10(1) of the TV Directive).

69 The Commission estimated that 'product placement, in particular, could generate substantial additional resources for the audiovisual value-chain, starting from linear service providers. On the grounds of data referring to the US market and statistics from the European Audiovisual Observatory, estimations indicate that such resources could amount to EUR 500 million': Impact Assessment of the Commission's Proposal of December 2005, COM (2005) 646 final, at paragraph 3.2.4. One cannot help but notice, however, the lack of precision of the figures put forward, both in terms of their geographical scope and the time period they cover.

insofar as viewers were not always aware of brand presence in the programmes they watched; and secondly, because it related the product to the situation in which it was used and arguably constituted a more aggressive marketing technique as a result.[70]

This did not affect the wording of the UCP Directive but it did affect the wording of the AVMS Directive when it was finally adopted in December 2007.[71] Indeed, Article 11 – which is exclusively devoted to product placement[72] – departs significantly from the original position expressed by the Commission in that it lays down a statement of principle prohibiting product placement: 'Product placement shall be prohibited.'[73] Immediately afterwards, however, it provides for derogations: product placement is allowed in a range of programmes, on the conditions that certain requirements are respected and unless Member States decide otherwise.[74] The AVMS Directive therefore allows Member States to liberalize product placement in certain programmes, whilst they have the option of opting out and maintaining a prohibition of product placement in all programmes. Nevertheless, the AVMS Directive contains exceptions: irrespective of the programme genres concerned, no product placement is allowed either in children's programmes or for tobacco products and medicines or medical treatments available only on prescription. Article 11 thus lays down a prohibition on product placement, followed by an exception to the prohibition, followed by an exception to the exception to the prohibition.[75] Only Denmark has maintained a prohibition of principle against product placement.[76] Other Member States have liberalized it, but they have often exercised their discretion and added more conditions for such liberalization than the ones laid down in the AVMS Directive. For example, the United Kingdom has extended the list of products that cannot be placed on television to include alcoholic drinks; foods or drinks high in fat,

70 The consultation documents are available at ec.europa.eu/avpolicy/reg/history/consult/index_en.htm. The European Parliament argued in favour of prohibiting unduly prominent placement as well as informing viewers of the presence of product placement in programmes. For the legislative history of the AVMS Directive, see: ec.europa.eu/avpolicy/reg/history/codecision/index_en.htm.

71 Directive 2007/65/EC [2007] OJ L332/27. The Commission then proposed to codify the AVMS Directive, and a new directive was adopted to this effect in March 2010: Directive 2010/13/EU [2010] OJ L95/1. The AVMS Directive expands the scope of the TV Directive to all audiovisual media services, including the internet and on-demand services.

72 Art 11 must be read in light of art 9 which contains the rules applying to all forms of audiovisual commercial communications.

73 Art 11(2).

74 Art 11(3) provides a list of programmes in which product placement may be used (except if Member States decide otherwise), as well as a list of the minimum requirements any programme containing product placement shall meet.

75 O Castendyk, E Dommering and A Scheuer (n 65) 912.

76 For an overview of the implementation of art 11 in the Member States, see *Product Placement* (European Audiovisual Observatory, 2010).

salt or sugar; gambling services; infant formula (baby milk), including follow-on formula; all medicinal products; electronic or smokeless cigarettes, cigarettes lighters, cigarette papers, or pipes intended for smoking; and any product, service or trade mark that is not allowed to be advertised on television (including guns, weapons and escort agencies).[77]

If assessed from the point of view of legal certainty, the regulatory situation is most peculiar. Looking at the Preamble of the UCP Directive, there is no doubt that product placement is a lawful marketing practice, provided that it is 'legitimate'. However, the Directive offers no guidance on what distinguishes 'legitimate' from 'illegitimate' product placement beyond the general unfairness clause and the two sub-clauses on misleading and aggressive commercial practices. By analogy with the AVMS Directive, one may argue that surreptitious advertising, which is defined as 'the representation in words or pictures of goods, services, the name, the trade mark or the activities of a producer of goods or a provider of services in programmes when such representation is intended by the media service provider to serve as advertising and might mislead the public as to its nature'[78] and which remains prohibited under the AVMS Directive,[79] would constitute an illegitimate marketing technique, as it would omit material information and may as a result significantly distort the economic behaviour of the average consumer. By contrast, product placement which is disclosed to the consumer via notices, logos or other means should perhaps not be considered unfair insofar as it would not satisfy the requirements of the general clause in Article 5 or those of the sub-clause defining a misleading practice.[80]

---

77 See Rule 9.13 of Ofcom Broadcasting Code on commercial references featuring within television programming, which entered into force on 28 February 2011 and which should be read in light of paragraphs 1.109 to 1.116 of Ofcom's interpretative (non-binding) guidance. For a discussion of the relationship between the UK rules on product placement and the AVMS Directive, see A Garde, 'Towards the Liberalisation of Product Placement on UK Television?' (2011) 16 *Communications Law* 93. More generally, on the regulation of product placement across the EU Member States, see C Angelopoulos, 'Product Placement in European Audiovisual Productions', in *Product Placement* (European Audiovisual Observatory, 2010).

78 Art 1(1)(j) of the AVMS Directive.

79 Art 9(1) of the AVMS Directive provides that 'audiovisual commercial communications shall be readily recognisable as such. Surreptitious audiovisual commercial communication shall be prohibited.' On surreptitious advertising, see also the Court's decision in Case C-52/10 *Eleftheri tileorasi and Giannikos* [2011] ECR I-3239.

80 Recital 90 of the AVMS Directive provides that 'surreptitious audiovisual commercial communication is a practice prohibited by this Directive because of its negative effect on consumers. The prohibition of surreptitious audiovisual commercial communication should not cover legitimate product placement within the framework of this Directive, where the viewer is adequately informed of the existence of product placement. This can be done by signalling the fact that product placement is taking place in a given programme, for example by means of a neutral logo.'

The boundary is all the more difficult to draw if the question is considered in light of the different starting point which the AVMS Directive takes that 'product placement shall be prohibited'. It is only if it is expressly authorized by a Member State and that it fulfils the conditions which the AVMS Directive lays down that product placement becomes 'legitimate'. However, such reasoning cannot apply to the UCP Directive which relies on a maximum harmonization clause, as opposed to Article 11 of the AVMS Directive which is an instrument simultaneously of optional, minimum and partial harmonization: optional in the sense that Member States can decide whether or not to liberalize product placement; minimum in the sense that Member States can decide to exceed the minimum level of protection provided in the AVMS Directive and extend the list of programmes where no product placement can take place or the list of products which cannot be placed;[81] and partial in the sense it leaves certain fields uncoordinated at the EU level, as discussed below.

One should also establish the scope of both instruments to determine the extent to which product placement is allowed at the EU level. The AVMS Directive deals specifically with audiovisual commercial communications, defined as

> images with or without sound which are designed to promote, directly or indirectly, the goods, services, or images of a natural or legal entity pursuing an economic activity. Such images accompany or are included in a programme in return for payment or for similar consideration or for self-promotional purposes. Forms of audiovisual commercial communication include, inter alia, television advertising, sponsorship, teleshopping and product placement.[82]

Thus, if a communication is not offered in return for remuneration or self-promotional purposes, and does not accompany a programme, then it falls outside the scope of the AVMS Directive. It is therefore arguable that communications which do not accompany a programme may fall within the scope of the UCP Directive, which is more broadly defined,[83] and similarly for media which are not

---

81 Art 4 provides that 'Member States shall remain free to require media service providers under their jurisdiction to comply with more detailed or stricter rules in the fields coordinated by this Directive provided that such rules are in compliance with Union law.' However, the freedom of Member States to exceed the minimum standard of protection is subject to two limits: the State of Establishment principle and the general Treaty provisions and more specifically arts 34 and 56 TFEU on the free movement of goods and services respectively. This mechanism set up is illustrated by the Court's decision in Case C-34/95 *De Agostini* [1997] ECR I-3875. See also O Bartlett and A Garde, 'Time to Seize the (Red) Bull by the Horns: The EU's Failure to Protect Children from Alcohol and Unhealthy Food Marketing' (2013) 38, no 4 *EL Rev* 498.

82 Art 1(h).

83 This would be the case, for example, of advergames which contain a lot of in-game advertising and therefore constitute a form of product placement. On advergames, see A Nairn and H Hang, *Advergames, It's Not Child Play* (Family and Parenting Institute, London, 2012).

covered by the AVMS Directive but may nonetheless contain product placement. As already stated above, it is all the more important to determine the respective scopes of application of the UCP and the AVMS Directives, as these two directives do not rely on the same harmonization techniques and, consequently, do not leave the same margin of regulatory discretion to Member States. The AVMS Directive is a measure of minimum harmonization which allows Member States to adopt more protective measures in the fields it coordinates, while the UCP Directive is not. One is therefore led to conclude that the objective of legal certainty pursued by the UCP Directive is significantly eroded as a result of a poor definition of its scope and its relationship with other provisions of EU law which also pursue consumer protection objectives.

Another way to look at the problem may be to consider the interests that the UCP Directive and the AVMS Directive respectively purport to protect. Whilst the UCP Directive focuses exclusively on the economic interests of consumers,[84] the TV and now the AVMS Directives are intended to ensure the protection of other concerns, including health and safety.[85] Article 9(1) of the AVMS Directive prohibits audiovisual commercial communications which encourage 'behaviour prejudicial to health or safety', and in particular those which cause 'physical or moral detriment to minors', for tobacco products, as well as for medicinal products and medical treatments available only on prescription. The AVMS Directive also requires that 'audiovisual commercial communications for alcoholic beverages shall not be aimed specifically at minors and shall not encourage immoderate consumption of such beverages.'[86] Furthermore, it provides that 'Member States and the Commission shall encourage media service providers to develop codes of conduct regarding inappropriate audiovisual commercial communications, accompanying or included in children's programmes, of [unhealthy] foods and beverages.'[87] Such concerns are explicitly excluded from the scope of the UCP Directive, which is 'without prejudice to [EU] or national rules relating to the health and safety aspects of products'.[88] Member States are therefore able to 'retain or introduce restrictions on grounds of the protection of the health and safety of consumers in their territory wherever the trader is based, for example in relation

84 Recital 8 of the Preamble provides that the Directive 'directly protects consumer economic interests from unfair business-to-consumer commercial practices' and ensures, as stated in particular in art 1 of the Directive, 'a high level of consumer protection by approximating the laws, regulations and administrative provisions of the Member States on unfair commercial practices harming consumers' economic interests'. See also the Court's case law: e.g., Order of 4 October 2012 in Case C-559/11 *Pelckmans Turnhout*, at paragraph 19 (and the case-law cited), and Case C-206/11 *Köck* judgment of 17 January 2013, at paragraph 29.

85 See also A Bakardjieva-Engelbrekt (n 6), 58.

86 Art 9(1)(e).

87 Art 9(2).

88 Art 3(3).

to alcohol, tobacco or pharmaceuticals'.[89] The UK rules, which have extended the ban on product placement to a range of products and services whose consumption should be limited, clearly rest on a public health rationale. Consequently, even under the UCP Directive regime, a Member State should not be prevented from adopting rules banning the placement of products whose consumption is detrimental to the health and safety of consumers.

The issue is further complicated by the fact that the AVMS Directive is (as was the TV Directive) a measure of partial harmonization. As such, it does not cover all matters relating to the regulation of audiovisual media commercial communications but leaves certain areas either unregulated or subject to other EU law provisions, including the UCP Directive. Thus, when called upon to assess the relationship between the TV Directive and the Misleading Advertising Directive (the predecessor to the UCP Directive),[90] the Court held in its *De Agostini* judgment:

> The TV Directive does not preclude a Member State from taking, pursuant to general legislation on the protection of consumers against misleading advertising, measures against an advertiser in relation to television advertising broadcast from another Member State, provided that those measures do not prevent the retransmission, as such, in its territory of television broadcasts coming from that other Member State.[91]

The Court therefore confirmed that the Misleading Advertising Directive rather than the TV Directive applied to misleading commercial practices. This judgment remains relevant to the relationship between the AVMS and UCP Directives. Thus, in the event that the form of marketing under consideration raises concerns because it may be a commercial practice likely to materially distort consumer behaviour, then it seems that Member States are prevented from introducing an outright ban on 'legitimate' forms of product placement, due to the explicit wording of Recital 6 of the UCP Directive. Furthermore, as the UCP Directive is a measure of maximum harmonization, Member States no longer have the freedom which they had under the Misleading Advertising Directive to adopt stricter national rules banning such a form of marketing: the Court's case law interpreting the scope of the UCP Directive is unequivocal in this respect. Nevertheless, the ambiguous wording of Recital 6 is likely to give rise to difficult questions of interpretation for both EU and national authorities when carrying out assessments on what kind of

89 Recital 9 of the Preamble. The list is not exhaustive and could extend to the marketing of food high in fat, salt or sugar, to gambling services, as well as to other goods and services whose excessive consumption is similarly detrimental to public health.

90 Council Directive 84/450/EEC of 10 September 1984 Relating to the Approximation of the Laws, Regulations and Administrative Provisions of the Member States Concerning Misleading Advertising [1984] OJ L250/17, as amended by Directive 97/55/EC of the European Parliament and of the Council of 6 October 1997 Amending Directive 84/450/EEC Concerning Misleading Advertising to Include Comparative Advertising [1997] OJ L290/18.

91 Case C-34/95 *De Agostini* [1997] ECR I-3875, at paragraph 38.

product placement is 'legitimate' and does not, as such, fulfil the requirements of unfairness laid down in Article 5 or Articles 6 to 9 of the UCP Directive.

This raises the question of how measures pursuing simultaneously the dual objective of protecting the economic interests of consumers and their health should be assessed. The two rationales will often co-exist. The wording of Article 11 itself is very revealing in this respect and clearly shows that the reasons for banning product placement may be several: the condition that the presence of product placement should be disclosed to the public illustrates that the economic interests of consumers should be protected, so that they are not led into making a transaction they would not have made otherwise; whilst the ban on the product placement for tobacco or medicines or medicinal treatments only available on prescriptions or any other good or service whose excessive consumption is detrimental to public health clearly shows that health considerations may be at the heart of the restrictions imposed. How should a measure pursuing both objectives be assessed? Should it fall within the scope of the UCP Directive, even though public health considerations may be paramount? Applying the *Mediaprint* case law by analogy,[92] the conclusion would seem to be that it does.[93] This would lead to the paradoxical situation that Member States wishing to protect the economic and health interests of their citizens simultaneously would be well advised to argue that any ban on product placement they would be minded to impose and which would exceed the scope of the AVMS Directive is based on public health grounds. This may have the disadvantage of limiting the scope of the ban to specific products whose consumption does impact negatively on public health. However, it would also have the advantage of falling within the public health exception of the UCP Directive, thus allowing the laws of the Member States to escape the scrutiny of the EU legislature and the argument that the measure is contrary to the UCP Directive. The fact remains that such a line of reasoning has a very strong potential to frustrate simultaneously both objectives pursued by the UCP Directive: firstly, it would be somewhat paradoxical to argue that consumer protection is better ensured if the measure adopted to protect consumers falls outside the very text of EU law which is intended to grant a high level of protection to consumers with a view to increasing their confidence in the internal market. Secondly, and very obviously, these tactics which Member States may, in time, be led to develop, cannot be conducive to legal certainty.[94]

---

92 Case C-540/08 *Mediaprint* [2010] ECR I-10909, in which the Court held that the Austrian government could not legitimately argue that its legislation fell outside the scope of the Directive because it essentially envisaged objectives relating to other goals than the protection of consumers (at paragraphs 25 to 28).

93 On this case law, see Keirsbilck in this volume.

94 However, the Commission considers in its First Application Report that 'the derogation should not be further extended. Whilst a few Member States signalled a need for such an extension, this need to apply certain rules at national level can be met by virtue of other EU legislation' (n 1) 5.

Conclusion

The regulatory framework is inherently complex, and it may be preferable to acknowledge this complexity, rather than pretend that the UCP Directive will create a uniform level playing field. Overall, one cannot but question the Commission's statement:

> The Internal Market clause has resulted in a major simplification of the rules on misleading advertising and unfair commercial practices in business-to-consumer transactions across the EU, by replacing the 28 national regimes with one set of rules, whilst maintaining a high level of consumer protection. It was essential to overcome the specific legal barriers caused by the fragmented regulation of unfair commercial practices, which gave rise to cost, complexity and uncertainty for both businesses and consumers.[95]

The question remains whether businesses feel confident that they can save on costs by dispensing from seeking legal advice on how the UCP Directive and its general clauses more specifically apply in different EU jurisdictions. Let us not dismiss altogether the potential contribution that the UCP Directive can make to the proper functioning of the internal market, but let us not pretend either that the all the 'legal barriers' identified by the Commission have been overcome and a uniform level playing established. Seven years after the UCP Directive entered into force, the question remains as vividly as ever whether the gains in terms of legal certainty really justify the loss of flexibility by some Member States to increase the level of consumer protection which they were traditionally able to provide.

Bibliography

Anagnostaras G, 'The Unfair Commercial Practices Directive in Context: From Legal Disparity to Legal Complexity?' (2010) 47 *Common Market Law Review* 147.

Angelopoulos C, 'Product Placement in European Audiovisual Productions', in *Product Placement* (European Audiovisual Observatory, 2010).

Bakardjieva-Engelbrekt A, *EU Marketing Practices Law in the Nordic Countries: Consequences of a Directive on Unfair Business-to-Consumer Commercial Practices* (Helsinki: Nordic Council of Ministers Committee on Consumer Affairs, January 2005).

Bartlett O and A Garde, 'Time to Seize the (Red) Bull by the Horns: The EU's Failure to Protect Children from Alcohol and Unhealthy Food Marketing' (2013) 38 *European Law Review* 498.

95 First Application Report (n 1) 4.

Burri-Nenova M, 'The New Audiovisual Media Services Directive: Television Without Frontiers, Television Without Cultural Diversity' (2007) 44 *Common Market Law Review* 1689.

Castendyk O, E Dommering and A Scheuer, *European Media Law* (The Hague: Kluwer Law International, 2008).

De Vries A, 'The Aim for Complete Uniformity in EU Private Law: An Obstacle to Further Harmonization' (2012) *European Review of Private Law* 913.

Friant-Perrot M and A Garde, 'From BSE to Obesity – EFSA's Growing Role in the EU's Nutrition Policy', in A Alemanno and S Gabbi (eds), *Foundations of EU Food Law and Policy – 10 Years of European Food Safety Authority* (Aldershot: Ashgate, 2014).

Garde A, 'Advertising Regulation and the Protection of Children-Consumers in the European Union: In the Best Interests of ... Commercial Operators?' (2011) 19 *International Journal of Children's Rights* 149.

———, 'Towards the Liberalisation of Product Placement on UK Television?' (2011) 16 *Communications Law* 93.

———, 'The Unfair Commercial Practices Directive: A Successful Example of Legislative Harmonisation?', in P Syrpis (ed.), *The Judiciary, the Legislature and the Internal Market* (Cambridge University Press, 2012).

Harcourt A and S Weatherill (eds), 'Special Issue on the Consumer and EU Audiovisual Policy' (2008) 31 *Journal of Consumer Policy*.

Harrison J and L Woods, *European Broadcasting Law and Policy* (Cambridge: Cambridge University Press, 2007).

Howells G, H Micklitz and T Wilhelmsson, *European Fair Trading Law: The Unfair Commercial Practices Directive* (Aldershot: Ashgate, 2006).

Katsirea I, *Public Broadcasting Standards and European Law* (The Hague: Kluwer Law International, 2008).

Keirsbilck B, *The New European Law of Unfair Commercial Practices and Competition Law* (Oxford: Hart Publishing, 2011).

Micklitz H, 'Minimum/Maximum Harmonisation and the Internal Market Clause', in G Howells, H Micklitz and T Wilhelmsson, *European Fair Trading Law: The Unfair Commercial Practices Directive* (Aldershot: Ashgate, 2006).

Micklitz H and N Reich, 'Crónica de una muerte anunciada: The Commission Proposal for a "Directive on Consumer Rights"' (2009) 46 *Common Market Law Review* 471.

Micklitz H, N Reich and P Rott, *Understanding EU Consumer Law* (Antwerp: Intersentia, 2008).

Nairn A and H Hang, *Advergames, It's Not Child Play* (Family and Parenting Institute, London, 2012).

Otken Eriksson I and U Öberg, 'The Unfair Commercial Practices Directive in Context', in S Weatherill and U Bernitz, *The Regulation of Unfair Commercial Practices under EC Directive 2005/29* (Oxford: Hart Publishing, 2007).

Raitio J, *The Principle of Legal Certainty in EC Law* (Kluwer Academic Publishers, 2003).

Stuyck J, E Terryn and T van Dyck, 'Confidence through Fairness? The New Directive on Unfair Business-to-Consumer Commercial Practices in the Internal Market' (2006) 43 *Common Market Law Review* 107.

Tridimas T, 'Constitutional Review of Member State Action: The Virtues and Vices of an Incomplete Jurisdiction' (2011) 9 *International Journal of Constitutional Law* 737.

Weatherill S and U Bernitz, *The Regulation of Unfair Commercial Practices under EC Directive 2005/29* (Oxford: Hart Publishing, 2007).

Whittaker S, 'Unfair Contract Terms and Consumer Guarantees: The Proposal for a Directive on Consumer Rights and the Significance of Full Harmonisation' (2009) 5 *European Review of Contract Law* 244.

Willett C, 'Fairness and Consumer Decision Making under the Unfair Commercial Practices Directive'(2010) 33 *Journal of Consumer Policy* 247.

Chapter 6
The Interaction between the Unfair Commercial Practices Directive and Self-Regulation: The Case of Codes of Conduct[1]

Charlotte Pavillon

1. Introduction

In their relations with consumers, businesses must abide by legal rules, which often originate from European directives such as the Unfair Commercial Practices Directive (UCPD).[2] In addition to legal rules, traders may also voluntarily subject themselves to rules and standards that are the product of self-regulation in the sector.[3] The Association of British Travel Agents (ABTA) has for instance launched a code of practice that safeguards and promotes consumer interests beyond the legal minimum. Likewise, the French FEVAD (Fédération du e-commerce et de la Vente à Distance) and several other trade organizations have issued a code governing their members' e-commerce and distant selling practices.[4]

This chapter revolves around the question of *whether the UCPD allows for self-regulation to help reach the directive's twofold goal of consumer protection and harmonization.* The UCPD aims at both a high and a common level of consumer protection in order to smoothen the functioning of the internal market.[5]

---

1 This chapter is an updated and amended version of an article that appeared under the title 'The Interplay between the Unfair Commercial Practices Directive and Codes of Conduct' in 5 *Erasmus Law Review* (2012) 267.

2 Directive 2005/29/EC on unfair business-to-consumer commercial practices in the internal market (OJ 2005 L 149/22), see art 18.

3 Self-regulation is 'defined as the possibility for economic operators, the social partners, non-governmental organizations or associations to adopt amongst themselves and for themselves common guidelines at European level (particularly codes of practice or sectoral agreements)': Inter-institutional Agreement on Better Law Making (OJ 2003 C 321/1), 22.

4 This code can be consulted at http://www.fevad.com/uploads/files/Publications/Guide_bonnes_pratiques_ecommerce_251011.pdf.

5 Recital 1 of the UCPD states that the European Community ought to contribute to the attainment of a high level of consumer protection. According to recital 5, obstacles to the free movement of services and goods across borders or the freedom of establishment

A high level of consumer protection enhances consumer confidence and a harmonized level of protection induces (small) businesses to participate in the internal market. As such, this chapter explores the interplay between the UCPD and codes of conduct regulating business-to-consumer (B2C) trade at the EU and at the national level. Codes of conduct can potentially add to advancing the consumer protection and harmonization goals of the directive by impacting both the interpretation and the enforcement of the directive's standards. This impact is, however, to some extent either constrained or stimulated by the UCPD itself and by how it is implemented, interpreted and enforced at the national level. The purpose of this paper is to examine how the interplay between private regulation and the UCPD could be optimized with a view to ensuring the interests of both consumers and traders.

Section 2 establishes how the foundation for this interplay was laid, that is, how codes were integrated into the UCPD. Section 3 delves into the influence codes of conduct exercise on the fairness assessment by public authorities and national courts, and section 4 takes a closer look at the enforcement of the UCPD standard by private bodies. Both sections 3 and 4 assess how codes of conduct add to a high level of consumer protection whereas section 5 determines their contribution to harmonization. In sum, sections 3, 4 and 5 investigate how the directive allows for those contributions to be made. This chapter focuses on three Member States in particular: the United Kingdom, the Netherlands and France. In the first two Member States, codes of conduct often serve as a complement to legislation. In various fields of activity, many codes of conduct in place in the United Kingdom and the Netherlands preceded the UCPD.[6] In France, codes of conduct are less common (except in the advertising industry). The differences and resemblances between Member States will help map both the increase and convergence in self-regulatory enterprise.

can only be eliminated by establishing uniform rules at European level, which establish a high level of consumer protection. Member States are not allowed to adopt more protective rules within the field approximated by the UCPD (art 4). A high level of consumer protection is therefore subordinate to the harmonization goal.

6 The Dutch process of self-regulation entails above all a dialogue between business and consumer organizations that gives rise to bipartisan general terms and conditions (GTC). In the Netherlands, the number of bilateral sets of GTC has increased over the years, but this development can hardly be linked to the enforcement of the UCPD. The bilateral GTC dictate commercial conduct and describe many commercial practices. Public enforcers see them as codes of conduct: CFI Rotterdam 19 January 2010, ECLI:NL:RBROT:2010:BK9796 and ECLI:NL:RBROT:2010:BK9798. They lack, however, a number of commitments that characterize codes of conduct such as standards of service and advertising guidelines.

2. The UCPD and Self-Regulation of Commercial Practices Directed to Consumers

2.1 The Commission's Initial Wish for European Codes of Conduct

In the Green Paper that lit up the path towards the UCPD, the Commission considered self-regulation to be a potentially effective complement to regulation and wondered whether it would be useful to include a basis for self-regulation in a framework directive. The Commission also observed that self-regulation remained severely constrained at the EU level because of the degree of national diversity.[7] Before the UCPD came into being, the Commission clearly expressed the wish that EU-wide codes of conduct would develop. In its Follow-up Communication to the Green Paper, the Commission uttered such codes should provide an 'implicit "presumption of conformity"' with the fairness standard.[8] It also announced it would consult further on whether there was a need to provide for endorsement of such codes. None of these wishes and intentions, however, have materialized in the UCPD. The potential role of self-regulation in tackling unfair commercial practices and overcoming national legal diversity has been strongly reduced during the negotiations on the UCPD. The next sections analyse what was left of the references to self-regulation[9] and codes of practice in the directive.

2.2 The Honest and Responsible Use of Codes of Conduct

2.2.1 Voluntary codes bind signatories

Concerning self-regulation, article 6(2)(b) UCPD is perhaps the farthest-reaching provision in the directive. The non-compliance by a trader with a code of conduct to which he has openly agreed to adhere constitutes a misleading practice and is therefore prohibited:

> A commercial practice shall also be regarded as misleading if, in its factual context, taking account of all its features and circumstances, it causes or is likely to cause the average consumer to take a transactional decision that he would not have taken otherwise, and it involves:
> (b) non-compliance by the trader with commitments contained in codes of conduct by which the trader has undertaken to be bound, where:
> (i) the commitment is not aspirational but is firm and is capable of being verified, and

7 European Commission, 'Green Paper on EU Consumer Protection' COM (2001) 531 final, 2, 5 and 15.

8 European Commission, 'Follow-up Communication to the Green Paper on EU Consumer Protection' (Communication) COM (2002) 289 final, 11.

9 The UCPD only implicitly favours the co-regulatory approach: F Cafaggi, 'Private Regulation in European Private Law', in AS Hartkamp et al. (eds), *Towards a European Civil Code* (Kluwer Law International, 2011) 119–120.

(ii) the trader indicates in a commercial practice that he is bound by the code.

The misleading claim to abide by a code requires the trader to have undertaken to be bound by this code. The trader does not need to have *actually* signed up to the code. The commitment the trader fails to live up to must be firm and capable of being verified afterwards. The distinction between a firm and an aspirational commitment is, however, a blurred one.[10] The infringement on an open-ended provision by a code member may assumingly be intercepted by the general clause.

In its Green Paper, the Commission stressed the benefits of article 6(2)(b).[11] From the consumers' point of view, the advantage of more rigorously enforced voluntary commitments is the increased confidence that public enforcement bodies would act as the 'enforcer of last resort'. By reinforcing the control exercised by the code owners themselves, this article could provide a stronger case for less substantive regulation, which is beneficial for traders. Effectively enforced codes of conduct would also provide an additional point of reference for courts and supervisory bodies in confronting traders outside self-regulatory agreements (the so-called free-riders who benefit a competitive advantage to traders adopting higher standards).

Article 6(2)(b) is concerned with striking a balance between the voluntary character of a code and the confidence it raises amid consumers. Consumers should be protected without traders being discouraged from adhering to a code.

This article has, however, principally been regarded as a disincentive for voluntary adhering to a code of conduct. It has been maintained that the article puts a signatory trader at risk since a 'challenge to its marketing practices could be successful on a technical non-compliance with some detailed provision of a code'.[12] This type of non-compliance may, however, not always bear a significant effect on the average consumer's economic behaviour, depending on the content of the obligation imposed by the provision in question. That being said, there is a risk that *unintended* non-compliance – a trader misjudging his obligations – would amount to a misleading practice, the article not being limited to situations where the trader *deliberately* breaches a code.

2.2.2 Forbidden false claims about codes and marks

The list of commercial practices that are under all circumstances deemed unfair provides further support for the honest use of codes of conduct and trust marks.

10 G Howells, 'Codes of Conduct', in G Howells, H-W Micklitz and T Wilhelmsson, *European Fair Trading Law: The Unfair Commercial Practices Directive* (Aldershot: Ashgate, 2006) 208.

11 COM (2001) 531 final (n 7), 14.

12 H Collins, 'EC Regulation of Unfair Commercial Practices', in H Collins (ed.), *The Forthcoming EC Directive on Unfair Commercial Practices* (Kluwer Law International 2004) 31.

The following practices are forbidden because of their flagrantly misleading nature (Annex 1):

1. Claiming to be a signatory to a code of conduct when the trader is not.

2. Displaying a trust mark, quality mark or equivalent without having obtained the necessary authorisation.

3. Claiming that a code of conduct has an endorsement from a public or other body which it does not have.

Those provisions ensure that traders make responsible use of codes of conduct in their marketing activities. The black list seems to have a deterrent effect. As follows from an analysis of online databases,[13] there are yet hardly any administrative and no court decisions at all regarding the black list provisions relating to self-regulation.[14]

2.3 Codes of Conduct as Benchmark of Fairness

2.3.1 Compliance with a code

The breach of a firm commitment in a code constitutes a misleading practice for it deceives the consumer and breaches his trust. The question is to what extent, according to the directive, codes also help define the (un-)fair content of a trade practice, irrespective of a trader's adherence to them. To what degree can codes flesh out the directive's general clauses?

The general fairness clause is built upon two concepts. According to article 5(2) an unfair commercial practice is

> contrary to the requirements of professional diligence [... and ...] materially distorts or is likely to materially distort the economic behaviour with regard to the product of the average consumer whom it reaches or to whom it is addressed, or of the average member of the group when a commercial practice is directed to a particular group of consumers.

The professional diligence requirement is defined in article 2(h) as 'the standard of special skill and care, which a trader may reasonably be expected to exercise towards consumers, commensurate with honest market practice and/or the general principle of good faith in the trader's field of activity'.

---

13 http://www.oft.gov.uk and http://www.bailii.org (United Kingdom), https://www.acm.nl/nl and http://www.rechtspraak.nl (the Netherlands), http://www.economie.gouv.fr/dgccrf and, http://www.legifrance.gouv.fr (France).

14 I have, however, found an example of a breach of point 1 of Annex 1 – a trader making false claims about its credentials (Anna Tillman) – and an example of a breach of point 2 – Displaying an unauthorized trustmark or equivalent (Bradley's Fine Jewellery Ltd) – being tackled by the trading standards in the United Kingdom.

The professional diligence requirement is founded on a combination of customary and normative criteria. The normative criteria ensure that the business community does not itself determine the minimum content of the honest market practice standard. In the build-up to the UCPD, the Commission relinquished the regulatory technique consisting of offering codes of conduct the status of 'safe harbour' (unlike the 'New Approach' to technical standards).[15] Under the directive, compliance with a code of conduct does not entail (virtual) immunity against the charge of unfair commercial practice. It does not even lead to a 'presumption of conformity' with the legal standard. It has been suggested that a presumption of conformity would not be feasible for codes of conduct anyway, since compliance with the open-textured standards of a code cannot easily be measured and controlled.[16]

Not even codes that have been devised in consultation with consumer organizations or approved by a relevant public authority are presumed to be fair. There are no provisions that lay down criteria 'fair' codes of conduct should meet. Neither are there any directive provisions that tackle unfair codes as such (whilst the trader subscribing to the code would himself be immune from legal challenge). The directive does not hold accountable a trade association that devises a code that promotes or contains unfair practices. It leaves it to each Member State to decide 'whether legal facilities may be directed against a code owner[17] where the relevant code promotes non-compliance with legal requirements' (article 11[1] 2nd section [b]). The Commission thereby meant to avoid the risk that trade associations would become reluctant to draft codes.[18]

Compliance with a code (and definitely with a publicly approved, widely established and reputable code) nevertheless provides strong evidence of compliance with the duty to trade fairly.[19] This is expressed in recital 20 of the preamble to the directive.[20] The Court of Justice of the European Union (CJEU)

15 Collins (n 12), 30.

16 H-W Micklitz, 'A General Framework Directive on Fair Trading', in H Collins (ed.), *The Forthcoming EC Directive on Unfair Commercial Practices* (Kluwer Law International, 2004) 83–84.

17 A code owner is any entity, including a trader or group of traders, which is responsible for the formulation and revision of a code of conduct and/or for monitoring compliance with the code by those who have undertaken to be bound by it (art 2[g]).

18 Collins (n 12), 31.

19 Ch Twigg-Flesner et al., *An Analysis of the Application and Scope of the Unfair Commercial Practices Directive. A Report for the Department of Trade and Industry* (2005), 8, http://www.dti.gov.uk/files/file32095.pdf.

20 Cf. European Commission, 'Explanatory Memorandum Proposal for a Directive Concerning Unfair Business-to-Consumer Commercial Practices in the Internal Market and Amending Directives 84/450/EEC, 97/7/EC and 98/27/EC', COM (2003) 356 final, s. 73. Recital 20 suggests that consumer organizations be involved in the drafting of codes of conduct. Arguably, the involvement of consumer organizations in the drafting of codes would confer legitimacy upon them.

has not yet provided for an autonomous interpretation of the professional diligence requirement but the Commission Guidance states that high standards, which are widely supported and largely complied with, 'may be a useful term of reference for national authorities and courts in assessing whether, in a concrete case, a commercial practice is unfair'.[21]

2.3.2 Non-compliance with a code

In 2006, Howells expected codes to prove more 'useful' in providing evidence that a practice is unfair than in establishing its fairness and clearing the trader whose practice is being investigated.[22] According to him, it is indeed more acceptable for code owners to set the 'minimum standards' consumers may reasonably expect than 'to set a cap on what the law accepts'.[23] Since under the directive, code owners may apply their own higher standards and are most likely to do so, codes will however generally entail everything but a low standard.[24] Compliance with a code of conduct may well not exonerate the trader, but non-compliance does inversely not automatically incriminate him. A trader failing to comply with a code of conduct *he has not undertaken and indicated to be bound to* will not necessarily breach the requirements of professional diligence. This trader might still behave in accordance with the legal standard. Codes are not subjected to full harmonization and may reflect more stringent views on what the fairness standard entails. The purpose of most codes of conduct is to set out good trading practices towards consumers that exceed legal requirements. Code owners are allowed and even spurred to raise the level of protection required by the UCPD.[25]

Although consumers and code-abiding traders would largely benefit from this approach, requiring traders to follow the most demanding private standards would have anti-competitive effects and bar new entrants from the market.[26] It

21 European Commission, 'Guidance on the Implementation/Application of Directive 2005/29/EC on Unfair Commercial Practices' SEC (2009) 1666, 20.

22 Howells, 'Codes of Conduct' (n 10), 213.

23 Howells, 'Codes of Conduct' (n 10), 213. For instance, the Dutch Financial Markets Authority (AFM) considers the standard laid down in the Code of Conduct of the Dutch Home Shopping Organization (NTO) as a reasonable basis for assessing whether the expenses of a consumer credit are responsible under section 4:34(2) of the Financial Supervision Act. 'In the case of consumer credit, the AFM considers the NTO's Code of Conduct as a minimum supplement to the open standards for prevention of excessive borrowing in accordance with the Wft': http://www.afm.nl/en/nieuws/2011/jan/boete-l-easy.aspx.

24 G Howells, 'Co-Regulation's Role in the Development of European Fair Trading Laws', in H Collins (ed.), *The Forthcoming EC Directive on Unfair Commercial Practices* (Kluwer Law International, 2004) 122.

25 The Office of Fair Trading (OFT) for example only approves and promotes codes that are shown to safeguard and promote consumers' interests beyond the basic requirements of the law. It has been empowered to endorse codes of conduct meeting core criteria since 2002.

26 Twigg-Flesner et al. (n 19), 8.

is therefore not allowed to hold uncommitted traders to a self-regulatory ban on certain practices, without testing their commercial practices against the UCPD clauses. Public supervisory bodies and courts using a code as a benchmark of fairness should, in light of the maximum harmonizing and exhaustive nature of the directive black list, always evaluate the level of protection granted by the code in comparison to the UCPD standard. This, admittedly, is a very difficult, nearly impossible assessment to make considering the openness of the directive standards and the lack of European guidance. This assessment may also have some drawbacks as regards self-regulation's appeal. The finding that a code is more restrictive or prescriptive than is required by the UCPD and hence not binding on a trader who has not publicly undertaken to be bound by it, may threaten the very existence of the self-regulatory rules instead of inciting traders to fill in the professional diligence clause. But this assessment is what it takes to strike the balance between fair competition and consumer protection.

2.4 The Recourse to Self-Regulatory Bodies

The legal regime of the UCPD is largely based on enforcement through courts and public supervisory bodies. Codes of conduct are voluntarily accepted rules and are supplementary to both legislation and case law. Articles 10 and 11(1) define the role of self-regulation in controlling unfair practices. Article 10 is 'not overly friendly towards codes'.[27] Although self-regulation cannot replace judicial or administrative recourse, Member States may encourage the recourse to self-regulatory bodies in addition to court or administrative proceedings. This provision does not oblige Member States to stimulate control of unfair commercial practices by code owners, nor does it require them to foster the development of codes (unlike the E-commerce or the Services Directive). Article 11(1) goes a little further in encouraging reliance on codes. It enables Member States to decide whether to enable the courts or administrative authorities to require prior recourse to 'other' established means of dealing with complaints, including those referred to in article 10.[28] Finally, article 17 asks Member States, where appropriate, to encourage traders and code owners to *inform* consumers of their codes of conduct.

2.5 The UCPD and Codes of Conduct: Incentive or Disincentive?

Codes were very cautiously brought into the UCPD, which places the emphasis on the honest use of codes of conduct rather than on their development and content. When it comes to stimulating the drafting and membership of codes, the UCPD

27 Howells, 'Codes of Conduct' (n 10), 211.

28 Established means are well-founded and effective systems of regulation (including self-regulation).

does not adopt a 'carrot approach'. No privileges were granted to those who voluntarily comply with a non-binding code. Codes, according to the directive's wording, are neither 'safe harbours' nor presumed to be in conformity with the UCPD, even if they have been publicly endorsed. The 'stimulating' effect of the UCPD as regards self-regulation will mainly reside in a 'stick approach': the public threat to start proceedings under the directive or to legislate in case traders do not draft, sign up to or abide by a code of conduct.

According to the European Association of Communication Agencies, the UCPD even expresses a bias against self-regulation, threatening self-regulatory regimes instead of stimulating them.[29] Because of article 11(1) 2nd section (b) trade associations may be disheartened from drafting codes and, having regard to article 6(2)(b), code membership increases the risk to be found guilty of a misleading practice. Furthermore, code membership could be discouraged by the fact that, in view of the full harmonization nature of the UCPD, 'free-riders' may not be held to code provisions outreaching the directive standards.

Is such a deterrent effect noticeable at the national level? Or has the national implementation of the UCPD had a positive impact on the codes' share in the achievement of the consumer protection and harmonization goals of the directive?[30] And does this impact result from either a carrot or a stick approach? The interplay between the UCPD and codes of conduct will be assessed through an analysis of Dutch, French and English case law and self-regulatory practice. The UCPD has been transposed in the Civil Code in the Netherlands,[31] in the Consumer Code in France[32] and in the Consumer Protection from Unfair Trading Regulations 2008 in the United Kingdom (CPR 2008).[33]

---

29 Position Paper of the European Association of Communication Agencies 15 November 2003.

30 It goes without saying that the increase of self-regulatory practice depends on more factors than the legal status of codes of conduct such as the need and the willingness to ban rogue traders from the market and to prefer 'fair' regulation above minimum standards which are cheaper to comply with: Collins (n 12), 32. This paper, however, focuses on the interplay between the law and self-regulation.

31 *Wet van 25 september 2008 tot aanpassing van de Boeken 3 en 6 van het Burgerlijk Wetboek en andere wetten aan de richtlijn betreffende oneerlijke handelspraktijken van ondernemingen jegens consumenten op de interne markt, Stb.* 2008, 397 and 398.

32 *Loi no 2008–3 du 3 janvier 2008 pour le développement de la concurrence au service des consommateurs* JORF n°0003 January 4th 2008 and *Loi no 2008–776 du 4 août 2008 de modernisation de l'économie*, JORF n°0181 August 5th 2008.

33 The Consumer Protection from Unfair Trading Regulations 2008 (2008 No 1277).

3. Codes of Conduct's Contribution to Consumer Protection as a Benchmark of Fairness

3.1 Codes of Conduct and the Professional Diligence-Test

As the Commission predicted,[34] administrative bodies and courts rarely need to resort to the general clause and the professional diligence requirement laid down in article 5(2) UCPD. This general clause operates as a safety net, the smaller general clauses covering most unfair commercial practices. However, even though the definitions of misleading and aggressive practices do not entail a separate reference to the professional diligence test,[35] codes of conduct may also be relevant to the assessment of such practices.[36] This section assesses whether codes serve as a benchmark of fairness binding all traders irrespective of their allegiance to a code and, if so, whether the level of protection granted by the code is being compared to the UCPD standard.

3.2 France

According to article 2(h) UCPD, the professional diligence requirement of the general fairness clause encompasses both customary ('standard of special skill and care', 'market practice') and normative criteria ('honest', 'good faith'). By failing to transpose this definition, French law keeps the normative dimension of the professional diligence requirement out of sight. The reason why the directive provision has been left aside is not clear as it was not explicitly motivated during the transposition process.[37] Although the lack of visibility of the normative bearing of the requirement could have led to a market-based interpretation of the criterion, it hasn't. As it turned out, French courts have shown a great willingness to interpret French law in conformity with the directive. The professional diligence criterion has been applied to the tied sales practice (which was banned before the UCPD was enacted). Doing so, French courts put normative criteria before current market practice.[38] Likewise, the French Direction Générale de la Concurrence, de la Consommation et de la Répression des Fraudes (DGCCRF) – the public body in charge of the enforcement of the UCPD – emphasizes the normative criteria. It explicitly acknowledges, however, that codes of ethics common to licensed

34 COM (2003) 356 final (n 20), s. 52 and 56.

35 Since 'Misleading a consumer or treating them aggressively are considered in themselves to be distortions of consumer behaviour rather than legitimate influence and, as such, contrary to the requirements of professional diligence': COM (2003) 356 final (n 20) s. 57.

36 Howells, 'Codes of Conduct' (n 10), 213.

37 *XIII° législature/Assemblée Nationale* (No 408), 14 November 2007, 55–56 mentions this choice but does not explain it.

38 JProx Lorient 27 August 2009, No 91–08–000276; C. Cass. 13 July 2010, No 09–15304 and 09–66970; C. Cass. 12 July 2012, No 11–18807.

(self-employed) professionals in the field of law and medicine and the codes of conduct drawn up by the Distant and Direct Selling Federations may help inform the content of the professional diligence requirement, alongside with trade usage.[39]

Apart from the field of advertising,[40] self-regulation of commercial practices is, however, not broadly developed in France and does not have much impact on the fairness assessment. As for the misleading clause, exceptions exist, an example being the case wherein a French price comparison website was accused of misleading and unfair commercial practices as it did not warn the consumer about its advertising nature.[41] Information duties laid down in the *Charte des sites Internet comparateurs* helped flesh out the misleading clause of article 6(1) UCPD.[42] Since the trader had adhered to the code, emphasis was also put on him breaching his commitment (article 6[2][b] has not been transposed into French law). The French Supreme Court eventually reversed this decision, finding that the Court of Appeal omitted to verify whether the omissions were likely to substantially distort the average consumer's economic behaviour.[43]

3.3 The Netherlands

The Dutch provision implementing the definition of the professional diligence requirement – article 193a(1)(f) of Book 6 of the Civil Code – initially lacked the normative criteria and it still does not comprise the explicit reference to the good faith principle. Besides, the legislator has, in his explanatory documents, underlined the relevance of codes of conduct to this requirement, especially when consumer associations have been involved into their drafting.[44] In the absence of alternative benchmarks, courts and supervisory bodies will assumingly often conclude that a code matches the level of protection aimed at by the UCPD. As it is, in the domain of public enforcement of the UCPD, codes of conduct largely set the professional diligence standard. One of the two Dutch public authorities in charge of the enforcement of the UCPD[45] – the Consumer Authority (CA), which has merged into the Authority Consumer and Market (ACM) on 1 April 2013 – fills in the professional diligence requirement by referring to codes of conduct.[46] In

39 DGCCRF note No 2009–07, 29 January 2009. See also INC Hebdo No 1497, 1 December 2008.

40 The advertising industry is regulated by its own professional association: the Professional Regulation Authority of Advertising (ARPP).

41 CA Grenoble 21 October 2010, No 08/03251.

42 See also CA Paris 8 November 2011, No 11/16050.

43 C. Cass. 29 November 2011, No 10–27402.

44 Dutch Parliamentary Papers 2006–07, 30928, No 3, 16–17.

45 The other supervisory authority being the AFM (cf. n 19).

46 *Celldorado* (case 510, 17 June 2010) s. 333ff followed by CFI Rotterdam 19 April 2012, ECLI:NL:RBROT:2012:BW3358 and *Nederlandse Energie Maatschappij* (case 527, 6 September 2010) s. 308ff followed by CFI Rotterdam 12 November 2010, ECLI:NL:RBROT:2010:BO3707, s. 2.3.2.

two separate cases, it considered the requirement was breached because the trader had failed to abide by the standard of conduct laid down in a code.

In its decision concerning the *Nederlandse Energie Maatschappij* (NLE), the breach of the requirement of professional diligence was not only assessed in reference to the Consumer and Energy Supplier Code the trader had signed up to, but also to the Currence Rules & Regulations. According to the CA, the NLE had violated a ban on cold callers asking new customers to set up a direct debit, which was contained in both sets of rules. The NLE defended itself by contradicting that the Consumer and Energy Supplier Code encompassed such a ban and by arguing that the Currence Rules & Regulations should not define the level of professional diligence it ought to attain.[47] In the appeal procedure, the court agreed that the CA's (extensive) interpretation of the Consumer and Energy Supplier Code was wrong. The Administrative Court declared, however, that the public body was right to found its decision on the Currence rules since the Telemarketing Code, which is part of the Consumer and Energy Supplier Code, states that telemarketers will abide by the self-regulatory rules in place. The Currence rules qualify as such rules. What is more, by making use of a service owned by Currence (direct debit), the NLE is contractually bound by the Currence rules (through its contract with the bank). Having regard to the concreteness of the rule, the question then arises why the CA did not base its decision to fine the NLE on article 6(2)(b). The most plausible explanation would be that the CA did not consider the NLE to have *indicated* in a commercial practice to have undertaken to operate in accordance with the Currence rules (as is required by this article). In this case, the Currence rules helped the CA kill two birds (an unfair practice and a violation of 'confidence inspiring'[48] self-regulatory rules that is not being caught by article 6[2][b]) with one stone (the professional diligence requirement).

The same goes for the *Celldorado* case concerning unfair SMS practices, where the general clause was used to tackle the infringement on an *open-ended* provision of the SMS Code of Conduct by a code signatory having publicly undertaken to be bound by this code (article 6[2][b] only deals with the breach of firm and verifiable commitments). The CA found that Celldorado, a SMS services provider, had acted in breach of an information duty that was deemed to equate to the expected level of professional diligence. Celldorado denied the breach of the code and appealed the decision. In its decision on appeal, the Administrative Court emphasized the factual and normative dimension of the professional diligence test and the necessity to test the trader's behaviour against the legal standard.[49] It stated that acting in compliance with a code did not automatically amount to fair conduct in the sense of the UCPD. However, from the CA's point of view, there was no

47 CFI Rotterdam 13 December 2012, ECLI:NL:RBROT:2012:BY6184, s. 15.3. See also CFI Rotterdam 12 November 2010, ECLI:NL:RBROT:2010:BO3707, s. 2.2.3.

48 CFI Rotterdam 13 December 2012, ECLI:NL:RBROT:2012:BY6184, s. 15.4.5.

49 CFI Rotterdam 19 April 2012, ECLI:NL:RBROT:2012:BW3358, s. 21.5 and s. 23.2–3.

compliance with the code. Hence Celldorado's and, allegedly,[50] the code owner's interpretation of the code diverged considerably from the interpretation conferred by the administrative authority on the open-textured commitments laid down in the SMS Code.

3.4 The United Kingdom

In the United Kingdom, the professional diligence requirement has been linked to the common law concepts of 'due diligence' and 'due care'[51] on which is based the 'standard of (reasonable) care'.[52] This standard is fixed by 'current market practice',[53] that is, a 'practice common to a reasonable body of opinion'.[54] During the transposition process, the UK government stated that in 'regulated sectors like financial services [the requirement of professional diligence was] likely to equate to compliance with existing regulation and conduct of business rules'.[55] Although compliance with a code does not constitute a formal guarantee for passing the professional diligence test, a market-based interpretation of the fairness clause laying the emphasis on the customary criteria is therefore likely to prevail. Such an interpretation may allow for codes of conduct to provide conclusive evidence as to the requirements of professional diligence in a specific sector.

As of today, the professional diligence requirement has not been applied very often and the 'standard of care/due diligence' has barely impacted the interpretation of the UCPD. The traditional inclination to self-regulation has not yet been reflected in the way the UCPD is being enforced by the Office of Fair Trading (OFT). Approved codes do for instance not give 'safe harbours' from potential OFT action.[56] The OFT has, however, not yet taken any action against a trader who has subscribed to an approved code. The judiciary has recently, for

---

50 Opinion of the Adviescommissie bezwaarschriften (BAC) of the Dutch authority in the *Celldorado* case (case 510, 7 December 2010), s. 5.20: http://www.acm.nl/nl/publicaties/publicatie/7436/Besluit-op-bezwaar-met-BAC-in-de-zaak-Celldorado/. The trader failed to substantiate this argument: CFI Rotterdam 19 April 2012, ECLI:NL:RBROT:2012:BW3358, s. 23.3.

51 GB Abbamonte, 'The Unfair Commercial Practices Directive and Its General Prohibition', in S Weatherill and U Bernitz (eds), *The Regulation of Unfair Commercial Practices Under EC Directive 2005/29: New Rules and New Techniques* (Hart Publishing, 2007) 22.

52 *Bolam v Friern Hospital Management Committee* [1957] 1 WLR 582.

53 M Griffiths, 'Unfair Commercial Practices. A New Regime' (2007) 12(6) *Communications Law* 198.

54 Twigg-Flesner et al. (n 19) 6.

55 Government Response to the Consultation on an EC Directive on Unfair Business-to-Consumer Commercial Practices in the Internal Market (March 2004) 3.

56 OFT, 'Policy Statement on the Role of Self-Regulation in the OFT's Consumer Protection Work' (September 2009) s. 2.8, http://80.86.35.165/shared_oft/reports/consumer-policy/oft1115.pdf.

the first time, brought (the breach of) the professional diligence requirement in relation to (the breach of) a code of practice.[57] In this criminal case, the defendant had presumably engaged in an unfair commercial practice resulting from the sale of security systems to a 76-year-old customer described as vulnerable, thereby violating its own code of practice.

3.5 Conclusion

Self-regulation has not exerted much impact on the interpretation of the directive's general clause by public authorities. Codes of conduct barely flesh out the clauses, mainly because the professional diligence requirement is not applied very often (United Kingdom) but also because of the lack of such codes (France). Codes of conduct clearly inform the content of the professional diligence requirement in the Netherlands. As expected, codes appear more successful in providing evidence that a practice is unfair than in proving fairness. In none of the three Member States under scrutiny do codes operate as safe harbours.

Dutch public authorities have established non-compliance with the requirement of professional diligence by testing a commercial practice against self-regulatory standards. Interestingly, the CA/ACM nor the administrative court have yet explicitly tested the codes of conduct filling in the professional diligence requirement against the UCPD standards (including the black list). Professional standards that outreach the directive's level of protection can only constitute an unfair – misleading – practice if the trader has made his commitment *public* (article 6[2][b]). The risk of binding not publicly committed traders to professional standards that are too high in respect of the directive's level of protection is further increased by the consumer-friendly interpretation the administrative authority gives to the codes it holds onto. Instead of turning to the (plausible) interpretation of the code by the responsible private bodies, the CA/ACM gives private standards its own (extensive) interpretation. In the NLE case, the court blew the whistle, finding that the public authority had conferred a wrong interpretation on the Consumer and Energy Supplier Code.

Because of the use of general clauses, it may, however, prove difficult to define the directive's level of protection with exactitude and thus to determine whether the threshold in private regulation is set too high. The administrative authority and the courts do not have many other benchmarks of fairness at their disposal than the existing codes and, what is more, a less protective public standard may discourage self-regulatory initiatives. The information duties laid down in article 7 and the exhaustive black list do, however, provide some useful guidance.

57 *R. v X Ltd* [2013] EWCA Crim 818 (23 May 2013).

4. Codes of Conduct's Contribution to Consumer Protection: The Enforcement of the UCPD By Code Owners

4.1 Three Conditions

Private enforcement of the UCPD requires that codes of conduct are devised, which traders sign and live up to (section 4.2). It also demands that self-regulatory bodies ensure the fairness of their codes (section 4.3) and enforce them effectively, in conformity with the directive (section 4.4). Effective self-regulation that contains firm commitments towards consumers can reduce the need for detailed legislation and administrative and judicial enforcement action.[58] The effective enforcement of the UCPD by code owners requires codes to contain the standard set by the UCPD as a minimum[59] and the possibility for code owners to enforce their codes by means of ex-ante tools (aiming at prevention) and/or ex-post schemes (aiming at redress). To what extent has the implementation or application of the UCPD stimulated the establishment of these three conditions at the European and national level? Has the UCPD led to new codes being designed and enacted?

4.2 Devising New Codes

For a start, the UCPD has failed in fostering new initiatives at the European level. No new EU-wide codes of conduct regarding unfair B2C commercial practices have been devised since the directive was enacted.[60] Codes of conduct not being formally awarded a 'safe harbour'-status may lower the incentive for self-regulation. And the directive provision deeming a breach of a code a misleading practice (article 6[2][b]) may even act as a disincentive. The Polish advertising self-regulatory body has for example stated that some businesses have become reluctant to sign up to a code after the implementation of the UCPD.[61]

---

58 Self-regulation also reduces enforcement costs for consumers. Many consumers cannot afford the time, expense and anxiety of taking a case to court (if this is even possible under national law) and therefore fail to exercise their legal rights.

59 European Parliament, DG for Internal Policies, 'Misleading Advertising on the Internet' (July 2010) 17, http://www.europarl.europa.eu/document/activities/cont/201007/20100713ATT78790/20100713ATT78790EN.pdf.

60 Recently seven national e-commerce associations created the E-commerce Association Europe (EAE). Their mission and goals, however, do not state anything about a European code of conduct or trustmark. EASA has drafted a Best Practice Self-Regulatory Model and Charter in the build-up to the UCPD, keen to show its willingness to contribute to the harmonization process. It is, however, not a code since it does not set any rules.

61 European Parliament, DG for Internal Policies, State of Play of the Implementation of the Provisions on Advertising in the Unfair Commercial Practices Legislation (July 2010) 20, http://www.europarl.europa.eu/document/activities/cont/201007/20100713ATT78792/20100713ATT78792EN.pdf.

The rigorous public enforcement of the UCPD standards may, however, have fostered self-regulation at the national level, spurring traders to devise codes of conduct that incorporate these standards.

As far as national initiatives are concerned, the picture is mixed. The enforcement of the UCPD in France seems not to have had any stimulating effect on self-regulatory practice, for new initiatives have been rare. Recent initiatives are confined to those fields where self-regulation had already been induced by 'older' sectoral directives, such as the directives on advertising and e-commerce.[62] In the United Kingdom, but mainly in the Netherlands, new codes have been devised under pressure of the public supervisory bodies *after* the directive took effect.[63] The UCPD is, however, only one of the many regulations public bodies are responsible for enforcing. The new codes were induced by the continuous failure to live up to different legal rules.

The UCPD has not *in itself* been a great impulse towards more self-regulation of B2C practices at the national level. This may partly be imputed to the general nature of the directive, which was designed as a framework directive. Sector-specific directives have had a greater impact on self-regulation.[64] As regards advertising, national self-regulatory bodies already existed in most Member States (including France). It is, however, in this field that the UCPD has had the most noticeable impact. In the new Member States, the UCPD has largely added to the already-existing European legal incentives for self-regulation thanks to the European Advertising Standards Alliance (EASA)'s proactive role (section 5.2).[65] The emphasis put by the Dutch administrative authority on non-compliance with codes of conduct (section 3.3) has not evidently affected self-regulatory practice for the time being, either negatively – by putting off potential signatories – or positively – by reducing the free-rider problem.

62 A code of conduct pertaining to the e-sales of electrical and electronic devices was recently devised by, among other trade associations, the FEVAD (e-commerce and distant selling).

63 See the Code of Conduct of the European Union Secondary Ticketing Association (2009), the SMS Advertising Code (2009) and the Uneto-VNI Code of Conduct on Sale Guarantees (2012) in the Netherlands and the Code of Conduct of the Home Builders' Federation (2010) in the United Kingdom. There are still sectors left where a code of conduct is direly needed: the Dutch Competition Authority recently made an urgent call to comparison websites to devise a code.

64 The enforcement of the Doorstep Selling Directive has had a major influence on the Dutch Consumer and Energy Supplier Code which was devised in 2006 under pressure of public authorities.

65 PWJ Verbruggen, *Private Regulation in the European Advertising Industry: Analyzing the Emergence and Governance of the Private Regulation of Advertising* (2012) 75–77 and 80–81, http://papers.ssrn.com/sol3/papers.cfm?abstract_id=2256043.

4.3 Fair Codes

4.3.1 Bringing codes of conduct in conformity with the UCPD

Based on article 10 UCPD, Member States may, in addition to ensuring effective enforcement of the directive (as required by article 11), encourage the control exercised by code owners on unfair commercial practices. Code owners can only exercise this control as long as their codes are attuned to the directive's standards. Moreover, a code can only serve as a benchmark of fairness to courts applying the UCPD provided its content can be deemed 'fair'. The fairness of a code of conduct hinges on the extent to which national code owners have internalized the UCPD standards. The scope of the general duty applies to trade associations and other organizations that make recommendations on trading practices and draw up codes.

The UCPD has *broadened* the standards by which commercial practices are judged.[66] The UCPD obviously affects advertising rules and information duties most but all the practices that influence the consumer's ability to make an informed decision about a commercial transaction (before, during and after the conclusion of a contract) must *at least* match the UCPD standard (but may provide for a higher level of protection than the UCPD). So after-sales practices, complaint handling schemes and warranties have to fit the legal standard. This standard, however, is vaguely worded and the directive's open-textured nature makes compliance uncertain. The formulation of some of the commitments laid down in a code can be as vague as the directive itself.[67] The available guidance (including that issued by the Commission) and case law do not prevent diverging interpretations.

Most national and European codes of conduct that focus on B2C commercial practices at the national and European level have integrated the directive provisions.[68] There is considerable variation in the way and extent to which the UCPD norms have been internalized by code owners. Some codes of conduct include a general duty to trade fairly or a prohibition on misleading practices (most advertising codes). In the field of advertising, self-regulatory bodies have been keen to ensure compliance with the UCPD misleading clauses.[69] Another

---

66 Most of the behavioural norms laid down in the UCPD, however, already applied to traders or at least embrace more specific norms that could effectively be enforced (under the Doorstep Selling Directive for example) and had been processed in existing codes.

67 Art 2.1 of Seldia's code of conduct towards consumers and art 3(a) of the Code of Practice for consumers of the UK Direct Selling Association stipulate that direct sellers shall 'not use misleading, deceptive or unfair practices'. Art 1 of the Code of Practice of the British Association of Removers (BAR) for example obliges trader to act 'fairly and responsibly'.

68 Codes and recommendations pertaining to direct and distance marketing contributed to implementing the UCPD in Europe as is shown by the European Code of Conduct towards consumers drafted by Seldia (art 2.12) and the EASA Best Practice Recommendation on Online Behavioural Advertising.

69 The Dutch *Stichting Reclame Code* had implemented the UCPD long before the directive was implemented into Dutch law. In the United Kingdom, the Broadcast

way for code owners to implement the directive's standards is to lay down the obligation to interpret the code in conformity with the directive.[70] In many cases, the 'transposition' of the UCPD into codes of conduct is badly visible and does not consist of the transcription of the directive's general clauses. Some sectoral codes put down rules that (supposedly) meet the directive's standards, such as comprehensive information duties and 'fair' promotional practices.[71] Many codes do not literally transpose nor explicitly refer to the UCPD. This is a reason why enforcement agencies refrain from establishing equivalence between codes of conduct and the UCPD when it comes to defining fair behaviour.[72] In some Member States, advertising bodies still do not cover *all* commercial practices covered by the UCPD. The Austrian and German codes for instance lack a broad concept of unfair commercial practices. The Austrian code does not even include 'misleading' advertising.[73]

The directive's enactment has not led to the spontaneous adjustment of all existing codes.[74] The Dutch SMS Code of Conduct (2003) has only been updated following pressure from public authorities. In 2008 and 2010, this Code was adjusted to tackle (unfair) practices many consumers were complaining of: them not being aware of subscribing to a SMS premium service, ignoring the costs and finding it difficult to unsubscribe from the service.[75] To spur traders to integrate the UCPD standard into their codes, national regulators and enforcement bodies have different, more or less intrusive methods at their disposal. The directive leaves the choice of those methods to the Member States. In the United Kingdom code owners are often subject to scrutiny or formal supervision by a public regulatory body which for example sits on the Code of Conduct Committee.[76]

Committee of Advertising Practice (BCAP) carried out a consultation in July 2008 on proposed changes to bring the codes entirely into line with the new requirements set out in the CPR 2008. The CAP code – the non-broadcast arm of the ASA – is based on ICC codes and has been updated to reflect the requirements of the new consumer regulations. The ICC itself integrated the UCPD into its codes.

70 The Irish Commission for Communications Regulation devised a Code of Practice for Premium Rates Services stating the practices it lies down 'are to be interpreted and understood in light of the provisions of the Unfair Commercial Practices Directive'.

71 See the *Code déontologique du e-commerce et de la vente à distance* that has recently been enacted by the FEVAD.

72 BAC opinion (n 50) s. 3.5.

73 European Parliament, 'Misleading Advertising on the Internet' (n 59) 17.

74 FEDMA is currently still revising the Code of Conduct for E-Commerce and Interactive Marketing.

75 The adjustments did, however, not suffice according to the Dutch Ministry of Economic Affairs since vulnerable consumers would still not get enough protection.

76 Ch JS Hodges, I Benöhr and N Creutzfeldt-Banda, *Consumer ADR in Europe* (Hart Publishing, 2012) 264 and 329 (Trading Standards sit on the Travel Association Code Committee, which reviews the content of the Code).

4.3.2 The carrot approach

National enforcement authorities can stimulate the compliance of codes with the UCPD by providing guidance[77] or publicly endorsing fair codes. Statutory endorsement schemes do not exist in the Netherlands or in France but are common in the United Kingdom.[78] A carrot approach such as the granting of a public approval to codes of conduct is not provided for by the UCPD. One of the core criteria for consumer codes of practice to obtain OFT approval is compliance with the UCPD standards as far as the advertising and marketing rules are concerned.[79] The British system of (voluntary) approval of codes of conduct has, however, not been boosted by the CPR 2008. The expected spur to obtain OFT approval[80] did not occur.[81] Although OFT approval not conferring a shield may have decreased its appeal to traders, the very relative success of the OFT scheme may above all be explained by its long and relatively labour-intensive application process. The scheme has been criticized for being bureaucratic and inflexible, and evidence of strong consumer recognition of – and trust in – the OFT approval logo was limited.[82] Meanwhile, the Trading Standards Institute (TSI) has established a successor scheme to the Consumer Codes Approval Scheme on a self-funding basis.[83]

---

77 The OFT has for example published guidance for second-hand car dealers on compliance with the CPR 2008.

78 Alternatives to the OFT scheme are the TrustMark scheme of the Department for Business, Innovation and Skills (BIS) (building repair, maintenance and improvement sector) and the local authority assured trader schemes run by local Trading Standards services.

79 OFT, 'Consumer Codes Approval Scheme – Core Criteria and Guidance' (March 2008) 15, http://www.ftc.gov/sites/default/files/documents/public_events/enforceable-codes-conduct-protecting-consumers-across-borders/oft-code-scheme.pdf.

80 Twigg-Flesner et al. (n 19) 8.

81 To date, 10 codes of practice have been approved with a further 10 working towards approval. BIS, 'Consumer Landscape Review: Impact Assessment' (June 2011) 13, https://www.gov.uk/government/uploads/system/uploads/attachment_data/file/31395/11-981-consumer-landscape-review-impact-assessment.pdf.

82 Ibid 28.

83 http://www.tradingstandards.gov.uk/advice/ConsumerCodes.cfm. The potential costs associated with lack of consumer confidence due to removal of the OFT consumer code approval scheme are expected to be negligible: ibid 2. Under the UK Government's proposals to create a single Competition and Markets Authority (CMA), the OFT will be merged into the new body which will have a principal focus on competition and markets. For the same, debatable, reasons why the Commission is not empowered to endorse European codes of conduct, a continuing role in consumer codes approval is not deemed appropriate for the CMA: BIS, 'Empowering and Protecting Consumers: Consultation on Institutional Changes for Provision of Consumer Information, Advice, Education, Advocacy and Enforcement' (June 2011) 8, https://www.gov.uk/government/uploads/system/uploads/attachment_data/file/31394/11-970-empowering-protecting-consumers-consultation-on-institutional-changes.pdf.

4.3.3 The stick approach

If a soft approach proves ineffective, a more drastic line may be needed. One obvious strategy would be to threaten the sector failing to adjust its code with formal regulation. The Dutch SMS premium services sector has constantly been facing government's threats to legislate. The SMS Code and its adjustments have, however, not prevented the Dutch legislator to tighten the legal regulations for SMS services in 2011. A similar legislative intervention occurred in the field of predrawn sweepstakes, where a code of conduct failed to address misleading practices. Member States, though, do not dispose of a great margin of manoeuvre in view of the maximum harmonization scope of the UCPD.[84] They are not allowed to prohibit practices that are not listed in the directive's first annex.[85]

If a code offers less protection than the UCPD by *promoting* non-compliance with legal requirements, a Member State may also decide to enable a legal action against the *code owner* (article 11[1][b] UCPD). Such a legal facility was created both in the Netherlands (article 305d[2] of Book 3 of the Dutch Civil Code)[86] and in the United Kingdom (Regulation 4) – not in France – but without a potentially discouraging criminal offence being attached to it. Any enforcement action, if needed, will be taken through the civil route. Enforcement bodies are likely to rely on this prohibition where the promotion takes the form of a statement in the code of conduct and altering the code of conduct looks like a more effective method of dealing with the unfair practice than taking action against any individual trader or traders who are engaging in the practice. No actions have been brought against unfair code owners as of today.

4.4 Enforceable Codes of Conduct

4.4.1 Private enforcement

To raise the level of consumer protection, 'fair' codes of conduct need to be compulsory for their members and to be enforceable through independent, non-legal, both preventive (guidelines, certification[87]) and oppressive instruments (redress schemes with sanctions). Code owners must oversee enforcement of codes on their members. At the European level, between the purely voluntary schemes and the genuinely compulsory schemes, there are lots of mixed schemes.[88]

---

84 Cf WH van Boom, 'Wetsvoorstel doorverkoop toegangskaarten: nuttig en nodig?' (2011) 5 *Tijdschrift voor Consumentenrecht en Handelspraktijken* 183 (n 37).

85 Joined Cases C–261/07 and C–299/07 VTB-VAB and Galatea [2009] ECR I-2949.

86 Amendments made to the enforcement mechanism for the UCPD, however, seem to prevent public authorities from getting access to this facility.

87 Since 2009, all Thuiswinkel.org members (a Dutch distance selling association) applying the Thuiswinkel Code of Conduct are obliged to get certified every year.

88 P van der Zeijden and R van der Horst, *Self-Regulation Practices in SANCO Policy Areas* (Final Report 2008), 20–21, http://ec.europa.eu/dgs/health_consumer/self_regulation/docs/self-reg-SANCO-final.pdf.

The same applies to the national level. Consumer complaint schemes coupled to sanctions for non-compliance and/or prescriptions for redress play an essential role in enforcing codes of conduct. Consumer ADR is quite effective in the three Member States under scrutiny, especially in the United Kingdom and in the Netherlands.[89]

In the United Kingdom, most codes of conduct are enforced through consumer complaint schemes (self-regulatory structures are usually based on codes of conduct[90]). The OFT-approved codes of conducts all have user-friendly and prompt procedures for dealing with customer complaints and bestow access to low-cost, independent advice to resolve disputes. Some codes even have independent redress schemes (the Travel Association ABTA for example). In the Netherlands, the two-sided GTC are systematically coupled to bilateral dispute committees, which solve individual disputes related to the compliance with the GTC. In France many sectors and major companies have mediators at their disposal who can best be compared to what is called an 'ombudsman' in many Member States.[91] Consumer ADR is less often than in the Netherlands and the United Kingdom tied to a code of conduct promoting fair commercial practices. An example of an independent complaint scheme enforcing a code of conduct is the Commission Paritaire de Médiation de la Vente Directe. Another independent board upholding breaches of a code is the Jury for Advertising Deontology (JDP), which has handled complaints regarding advertising since 2008.[92]

4.4.2 Public enforcement

The UCPD stimulates public enforcement bodies acting as the 'enforcer of last resort' (article 10).[93] There are two reasons why public enforcement is necessary and self-regulatory systems cannot substitute legal enforcement. First, codes of conduct do not always contain appropriate and effective mechanisms for monitoring and enforcing their members' compliance. Nor are codes always coupled to consumer complaint schemes.[94] A code's strongest sanction is to end membership, and few code owners have pro-active compliance monitoring schemes. The enforceability of private regulation remains its weaker component since it proves difficult for code owners to act against their own members. Enforcement possibilities that work independently of any influence from their members are often lacking.

89 Hodges et al. (n 76) passim.

90 Ibid 263.

91 Ibid 37.

92 The Mediator of the French Federation of Insurance Companies upholds the Code of Good Conduct some insurance companies have agreed upon: http://www.gema.fr/sites/all/files/pdf/Recueil.AFA_.2011.juillet.pdf. Advertising self-regulatory bodies have mainly focused on the ex-ante control of advertisements (before their publication). The Jury is meant to strengthen the ex-post control.

93 COM (2001) 531 final (n 7) 14.

94 To cite but an example the FEVAD-code of conduct (e-commerce and distant selling) in France.

Even if an independent redress mechanism is available, public authorities may have to intervene to force compliance with a code of conduct and following on from this, with the directive's standards.[95] Individual dispute resolution schemes are moreover not apt to cope with unfair practices that only marginally affect individual consumers – who will then refrain from employing those schemes. Neither are those schemes adapted to deal with large-scale infringements.

Second, the interpretation of the UCPD by self-regulatory bodies may not always be the right one. Private bodies are interpreting and enforcing the directive rules, which have been integrated into their codes.[96] The Dutch administrative court responsible for enforcing the Directive has on the one hand very clearly stressed that decisions by private enforcement bodies are not conclusive as to the fairness of a commercial practice.[97] In the United Kingdom, on the other hand, courts seem quite reluctant to interfere with decisions of specialized bodies like the Advertising Standards Authority (ASA).[98]

4.4.3 Misleading claims to abide by a code

Article 6(2)(b) UCPD is meant to strengthen self-regulatory practice by providing public authorities with a tool to enforce code compliance. In the Netherlands, this article was transposed into article 193c(2)(b) of Book 6 of the Civil Code. This article, it is fair to say, has secured the ACM's position as enforcer of last resort in the past years. The public body actively cracks down on misleading claims to abide by a code of conduct[99] or two-sided GTC (which are considered to be codes of conduct).[100] The ACM has taken a firm line on the enforcement of codes

95 The OFT for example 'worked with The Travel Association (ABTA) in 2007 on misleading pricing of holidays which resulted in ABTA requiring its members to address the issue or face action under their Code of Conduct': http://80.86.35.165/OFTwork/consultations/self-regulation#.U6HIg_mSwqQ.

96 Self-regulatory bodies may also enforce UCPD rules not laid down in a code but applying to the practice the consumer is complaining about.

97 CFI Rotterdam 19 April 2012, ECLI:NL:RBROT:2012:BW3358, s. 23.3.

98 *R (On the Application of Coys of Kensington Automobiles Ltd) v ASA* [2012] EWCH 902 (QBD).

99 *Celldorado* (case 510, 17 June 2010) and *Smart Media Services* (case 220, 26 January 2009) were fined for breaching the SMS Code of Conduct. *Garant-o-Matic* (a mail-order firm) got collared for breaching the Promotional Lottery Code (case 544, 21 September 2010). *Greenchoice* (case 661, 27 May 2011) and the *Nederlandse Energie Maatschappij* (case 527, 6 September 2010) were fined for not complying with the Consumer and Energy Supplier Code.

100 In *Keukenkampioen* and *Keukenconcurrent* (cases 426 and 427, 19 November 2009) followed by CFI Rotterdam 19 January 2010, ECLI:NL:RBROT:2010:BK9796 and ECLI:NL:RBROT:2010:BK9798 and CFI Rotterdam 14 April 2011, ECLI:NL:RBROT:2011:BQ1281 two kitchen selling companies – both members of the Living Central Trade Association (CBW) – were sentenced for infringing on the CBW's bilateral GTC. *Grando Retail* on its turn has undertaken to stop acting in breach of the CBW code (cases 317 and 318).

of conduct since the UCPD was implemented. It has imposed a €1.2 million fine on an SMS services provider who kept pushing the boundaries of the code it had signed up to.[101]

The French provision implementing the 'misleading practice' – article L 121-1 Consumer Code – does not refer to the misleading claim to live up to a code of conduct. The reason why the directive provision has been left aside is not clear as it was not explicitly motivated during the transposition process. Maybe the legislator figured article L 121-1 would cover the practice described in article 6(2)(b). The case of French price comparison website proves him correct (section 3.2). I however doubt whether those articles would achieve the clarity and precision needed to meet the requirement of legal certainty the CJEU expects implementing provisions to fulfil.[102]

Regulation 5(3)(b) transposes article 6(2)(b) in the United Kingdom. Breaching this provision does not constitute a criminal offence according to regulation 9, to not discourage self-regulation. Prior to the UCPD, the practice consisting of a misleading claim to abide by a code already fell within the ambit of the Control of Misleading Advertisements Regulations 1988 (CMAR 1988). Such practices were also caught by the Trade Description Act 1968. A motor dealer was found to have breached section 14 TDA 1968 for falsely claiming that he complied with the Motor Industry Code of Practice.[103] The new regulation has, however, not yet been applied and tested before court. The OFT will generally seek to obtain compliance by education, giving advice and guidance in the first instance.[104] A close cooperation with the public enforcement body helps traders escape administrative and judicial scrutiny.

4.4.4 Filters

The effectiveness of well-functioning private enforcement mechanisms eventually depends on official bodies handing them over some responsibility. The enforceability of codes of conduct can be enhanced by introducing filters that encourage the use of complaint schemes run by code owners. Article 11(1) UCPD enables Member States to decide whether the courts or administrative authorities are *allowed* to require prior referral to other established means of dealing with complaints (including code complaints schemes) before pursuing legal remedies.[105] There are, at the national level 'strong differences between the

101 *Celldorado* (case 510, 17 June 2010). The CA and the AFM are entitled to sanction and to fine traders breaching the UCPD rules.

102 Case C–144/99 *Commission v Netherlands* [2001] ECR I-3541.

103 *V.G. Vehicles (Telford) Ltd* [1981] 89 Monthly Review 91.

104 OFT, 'Guidance on the UK Regulations Implementing the Unfair Commercial Practices Directive' (OFT Guidance May 2008), 51, https://www.gov.uk/government/uploads/system/uploads/attachment_data/file/284442/oft1008.pdf.

105 Courts and administrative authorities cannot be forced to refer a matter to a code complaint scheme.

way [self-regulatory organizations in the field of advertising] may derive a degree of legitimacy from public law or public actors'.[106]

Public enforcers in the United Kingdom advocate compliance by the most appropriate means, in line with their enforcement policies, priorities and consistent with available resources.[107] Civil and criminal enforcement come the very last in the order of priority. Relationships have been developed with 'established means' to resolve breaches of the CPR 2008. The OFT could already require prior referral to code complaints schemes in cases of misleading advertising.[108] The CPR 2008 have extended the scope for the use of 'established means' to all behaviours covered by the directive (regulation 19[4]).[109] Public bodies and consumer organizations (Citizens Advice, for example) actively promote extra-judicial complaint handling and direct individual consumers to ADR where this is available.

In the Netherlands, referral is the expected norm too.[110] The cooperation between different established means is being formally addressed by means of so-called *samenwerkingsprotocolen*. The Dutch Consumer Protection Enforcement Act allows for such cooperation protocols to be agreed upon by the administrative authorities responsible for enforcing the UCPD and self-regulatory bodies. A protocol regulates among other things the exchange of information and the cross-referrals between the public and the private enforcement body. In the field of advertising, the ACM yields its enforcement task to the Stichting Reclame Code (SRC) according to such a protocol. A *samenwerkingsprotocol* has also been signed between the ACM and the aforementioned bilateral dispute committees. Those committees handle individual complaints arising in the many sectors making use of bipartisan GTC whilst the ACM tackles practices violating collective consumer interests.

In France, the collaboration between public and private enforcement bodies is less formal. Even if a self-regulatory compliance mechanism has been set into motion, the administrative agency may decide to simultaneously and

---

106 Verbruggen (n 65) xiii.

107 OFT Guidance May 2008 (n 104) 51.

108 The CMAR 1988 empowers the Director General of Fair Trading (now the OFT) to require that a reasonable opportunity has been allowed for self-regulatory bodies to deal with the complaint in question: regulation 4(3)(3). See Verbruggen (n 65) 128–130.

109 The OFT also held a public consultation on a draft set of principles that it proposed to apply when working with its partners to maximize compliance with the CPR: OFT, 'Compliance Partnerships. An OFT Consultation on Developing the Use of "Established Means"' (December 2008), http://80.86.35.165/shared_oft/consultations/oft1043con.pdf and 'Compliance Partnerships. Response to Consultation' (July 2009), http://80.86.35.165/shared_oft/consultations/OFT1043resp.pdf.

110 The need for administrative bodies to show some restraint while self-regulatory solutions are sought was emphasized during the directive's transposition process: Minutes of the Upper House 2008/09, No 1, 31. The CA undertook enforcement actions in the *Celldorado* case only after self-regulatory measures had failed: BAC opinion (n 50) s. 5.18.

independently undertake an action of its own.[111] The DGCCRF leaves it to the consumer where to file a complaint and does not specially recommend ADR. Independent B2C mediation and conciliation are steadily turning into established means of complaint but these forms of ADR often result from public regulation. Privately initiated mediation and conciliation are only seldom coupled to a code of conduct that contributes to enforce the UCPD. The consumer has found his way to the JDP[112] but remains free either to file his complaint at a public agency or to go to court instead.[113]

As concerns judicial recourse by (groups of) consumers or professionals, courts in all three scrutinized Member States are fully free to not demand referral and hear the matter directly. In Italy and East and Central European states collaborative arrangements do not even exist.[114]

4.5 Concluding Remarks

In Member States with a tradition of self-regulation not much has changed after the UCPD was enacted. In the United Kingdom and in the Netherlands, self-regulation assists in raising the level of consumer protection. Free complaints schemes are very effective in handling individual complaints. Responsibility is being handed over to those private bodies that have effective (fair) codes of conduct. Self-regulation is, however, not always successful and the Dutch ACM plays a substantial role in enforcing compliance with codes of conduct and two-sided GTC. Article 6(2)(b) provides a useful tool to this end. The long-term effects of the far-reaching public control on self-regulation are, however, not clear: it may either raise or lower the attractiveness of self-regulation.

The UCPD, however, did not 'lift' self-regulation and consumer organizations have little faith in the benefits of self-regulation in terms of the enforcement of the UCPD.[115] The importance of national advertising self-regulatory bodies for example still strongly differs from one Member State to another.[116] The directive also fell short of evidently increasing the number of self-regulatory initiatives in other areas than the already harmonized fields of advertising and e-commerce.[117]

---

111 Both the JDP and the DGCCRF tackled the misleading practices used by the Repertoire des sociétiés et des indépendants (RSI): CA Paris 8 November 2011, No 11/16050 and JDP decision of 8 July 2011, http://www.jdp-pub.org/RSI,230.html.

112 As appears from the report 'Un an d'activité en chiffres', http://www.jdp-pub.org/Statistiques,103.html.

113 The DGCCRF only has had the power to enforce the prohibition on misleading advertising since 2007.

114 Verbruggen (n 65) 130–131.

115 BEUC, 'Answer to the European Commission's Questionnaire on the Application of Directive 2005/29/EC', 18, http://www.beuc.eu/publications/2011-09895-01-e.pdf.

116 European Parliament, 'Misleading Advertising on the Internet' (n 59) 15.

117 See for example: V Valce, 'Codes of Conduct and Unfair Commercial Practices' (2012) 1 *Bancaria* 95–97: As regards the banking sector, 'the legislative indications in

Many existing codes have integrated the UCPD and have been geared towards addressing new developments (new media) and complaints (SMS services providers) but overall few *new* codes of conduct were devised since the directive took effect, even in those Member States where self-regulation is well-developed. The reliance on codes is still very much confined to advertising, where a positive interaction exists between the UCPD and self-regulation.

With regard to minor violations of the UCPD a report commissioned by the European Parliament concludes it could be an option to envisage a more developed cooperation between advertising self-regulatory bodies and enforcement bodies in the European Union.[118] Self-regulatory bodies could help prevent misleading commercial practices in the first place by promoting compliance with codes of conduct and by issuing guidelines.[119] They could also concern themselves with 'easier' cases, helping national enforcement authorities to save time and costs.[120] The interaction between private and public bodies is working rather well in those countries where this interaction has been institutionalized. For now, the possibility for code owners to enforce their codes by means of *ex ante* tools (aiming at prevention) and/or *ex post* schemes (aiming at redress) is not sufficiently being supported by the directive.

5. Self-Regulation's Contribution to Fulfilling the Harmonization Objective

5.1 Converging National Private Standards of Fairness

Not all codes integrate the UCPD standards or flesh them out (section 4.3.1). But if they do so, codes tend to focus on different types of commitments as practices in a same sector differ across markets and countries. Code owners are moreover not formally required to confine themselves to the legal standards set by the UCPD and may award more protection to consumers than the directive. The UCPD is a minimum harmonizing instrument with regard to codes of conduct. Codes of conduct varying from one Member State to another, therefore, contribute to differentiating the fairness appraisal – if they were to impact on this appraisal. This, however, turns out not to be the case very often (section 3).

The level of convergence between private standards can be measured by comparing codes of conduct in a same sector of activity across the European Union. In the car sector, the Dutch two-sided BOVAG terms can for instance be collated with the Vehicle Builders & Repairers Association (VBRA) Code in the United Kingdom. There are differences in the type of commitments traders reach to enable the consumer to make an informed decision. The VBRA stipulates that

---

terms of self-regulation have remained largely unheeded and typical features of the codes of conduct have not been sufficiently exploited'.

118 European Parliament, 'State of Play' (n 61) 18.

119 Ibid 21.

120 European Parliament, 'Misleading Advertising on the Internet' (n 59) 17.

the customer should be *advised* that, if required, any displaced parts can be made available for inspection or returned with the exception of those parts required for exchange or warranty. Where parts are required to be fitted, the customer should be provided with a clear explanation for the need for replacement. According to the BOVAG terms, parts that have been replaced may be reclaimed by the customer at the time the order to repair the car was placed. They do not mention any obligation to inform the consumer about his rights before the replacement takes place.

In the field of direct selling, the Consumer Code of Practice of the UK Direct Selling Association can be compared with the French Code Ethique de la Vente Directe and the two-sided GTC of the Dutch Vereniging Directe Verkoop. The trader's response to a complaint should occur within respectively 10, 21 and 14 working days. The British Code is much longer and more detailed than its French and Dutch counterparts. This code, to quote but one example, provides for concrete guidelines as to the time of day an appointment should be made (9 A.M. to 8 P.M.) and what can be regarded as a visit of reasonable length in the case of a straightforward product (maximum 30 minutes) and a party plan visit (maximum 2 hours).

Codes of conduct include many general clauses and open-textured commitments. Given the similar general wording of most advertising codes – which oblige their members to refrain from using misleading practices – interpretation differences may arise among self-regulatory bodies from different Member States.[121] What is more, a major focus of self-regulatory codes in the field of advertising seems to be on nationally tainted issues of 'taste and decency', which are not addressed by the UCPD (recital 7) but nonetheless influence the fairness assessment by private bodies. Finally, the fact that self-regulatory bodies have no access to preliminary procedures also hinders harmonization.

5.2 EU-Wide Codes of Conduct

Private regulation has contributed to European legal integration, mainly in the fields of advertising (EASA), direct marketing (FEDMA), timeshare (OTE), direct selling (FEDSA) and distance selling (EMOTA).[122] The EASA Best Practice Self-Regulation Model has driven the coordination and integration of different national self-regulatory regimes in the field of advertising. The EASA was implicitly mandated thereto by the Commission.[123] The Model has benefited the creation of self-regulatory regimes in the new Member States (section 4.2). The run-up to the UCPD has acted as a catalyst for this process for it was clear that the directive would to some extent recognize and incorporate private regulation

121 Interpretation divergences regarding the content of codes also occur between self-regulatory bodies and administrative authorities, as shows the *Celldorado* case.

122 Van der Zeijden and Van der Horst (n 88) 19–20.

123 Verbruggen (n 65) xiii and 135.

in the advertising industry and the EASA wanted to demonstrate its goodwill.[124] The move towards full harmonization has bolstered the EASA's coordinating role without, however, leading to the drafting of a European advertising code.[125]

The directive does not expressly encourage the allocation of a complementary function to code-based schemes in regulating commercial practice and it has hardly impacted on EU-wide self-regulation of other commercial practices and sectors. EU-wide codes remain scarce.[126] Unlike the Services Directive or the E-commerce Directive, the UCPD does not promote the development of EU-wide codes of conduct. It goes without saying that differences in national laws keep hampering the development of EU-wide codes of conduct.

In its Green Paper, the Commission stated the option for EU-wide self-regulation could only work if non-compliance with a voluntary code would define as either a misleading or unfair trading practice and if the general duty would apply to trade associations and other organizations that make recommendations on trading practices and draw up codes.[127] Although the reinforcement of the responsibility of code owners in developing codes was left to the Member States, the directive has made voluntary commitments legally binding. Article 6(2)(b), however, has not yet fostered self-regulation at the European level. The technique of creating 'safe harbours' might have been a greater stimulus for self-regulation at the EU level given that EU-wide codes of conduct could effectively help creating practicable and attractive 'safe harbours'.[128]

6. Amendment Proposals

6.1 Optimizing the Interplay between Codes of Conduct and the UCPD

Codes of conduct hold many (economic) advantages for traders. They are often coupled to accessible low-cost ADR schemes and constitute an effective marketing instrument. For legal-cultural reasons mainly, with the exception of the advertising sector,[129] codes of conduct, however, do not contribute much to achieving the UCPD's twofold goal of consumer protection and harmonization. The directive and its implementation do, however, not sufficiently encourage such

124 Ibid xiii and 80.

125 Ibid xxii and 144.

126 European Communities, 'Enhancing the Quality of Services in the Internal Market: The Role of European Codes of Conduct' (2007) 5: http://ec.europa.eu/internal_market/services/docs/services-dir/codeconduct/the_role_of_european_codes_of_conduct_en.pdf.

127 COM (2001) 531 final (n 7) 14.

128 Collins (n 12) 30.

129 Verbruggen (n 65) passim.

a contribution.[130] How can the directive's potentially counterproductive effect on self-regulatory initiatives be prevented?

In the United Kingdom and the Netherlands, codes of conduct – not surprisingly – effectively add to the level of consumer protection. The case of the Dutch SMS Code, however, shows the necessity for public enforcement of the UCPD. The directive has been a welcome addition to the consumer protection arsenal, filling in the gaps left by existing law and failing self-regulation. But from the way codes have been fleshing out the directive's standards in the Netherlands, it appears that the balancing of consumers' and traders' interests might need further consideration. The purpose of this chapter is to ascertain how a further integration of codes of conduct into the UCPD, its interpretation and enforcement could both serve its consumer protection and harmonization goals *and* strike the delicate balance between consumers' and traders' interests.

6.2 Codes of Conduct and the Interpretation of the UCPD Standards

The directive should stimulate self-regulation by increasing its role in the interpretation of the fairness standard.

6.2.1 The breach of a code by a signatory

An infringement on a code to which the trader has publicly undertaken and indicated to be bound constitutes an unfair commercial practice because of the breach of consumer confidence it causes. While the breach of 'firm and capable of being verified' provisions is dealt with by article 6(2)(b), the infringement on open-ended code provisions is tackled with help of the general clause (as is shown by Dutch enforcement practice). To determine the latter infringement, public agencies and courts will have to interpret the code provisions. It will not always be clear whether a specific practice violates a code and consequently breaches the legal standard. Diverging views on the exact interpretation of firm provisions may arise as well.

To establish the breach of code of conduct, the public body should take the code sponsor's interpretation as a point of reference. If this 'private' meaning is not clear and the public body has no choice but to interpret the code, the following rules should apply. An ambiguous provision would have to be construed against the professional insofar as consumer organizations have *not* been involved into its drafting.[131] Such a rule could provide an incentive for (representative) trade associations to engage in a proper mutual dialogue with (representative) consumer associations and to draft codes that are as clear and explicit as possible. 'Bilateral'

130 At the national level the UCPD has not succeeded in giving self-regulation a more prominent role in countries where there is no tradition of self-regulation. 'Those countries which lack a history of using soft law techniques are only likely to take it seriously if it forms part of the legal regime': Howells, 'Co-Regulation's Role' (n 24) 125.

131 In analogy with art 5 of Directive 93/13/EEC on unfair terms in consumer contracts (OJ 1993 L 95/29).

codes should be construed objectively by explicitly balancing the interests of both parties in the light of the directive. By relying more evidently on the private interpretation of a code to determine a breach of commitment (and consumer trust), public agencies may increase the attractiveness of self-regulation.

Such reliance would not jeopardize the enforcement duties incumbent upon the public supervisory body since it still may tackle the (unfair) practice itself, independently from whether this practice infringes on a code. The legal standard may appear to be stricter than the private standard.[132] Even if the private standard condones the practice, the public body may conclude that the code and as a matter of fact the commercial practice at issue contravenes the legal standard (as interpreted by the public body). Due to the openness of this standard, its interpretation by the public agency may more often than not be subject of debate. A decision to impose stricter standards than the self-regulatory ones should therefore be duly motivated. The public body should always thoroughly reason a decision to depart from a private standard.[133]

6.2.2 Codes setting the fairness standard: Non-compliance with the fairness standard

Due to a lack of alternative benchmarks, codes of conduct often help define the expected level of professional diligence. Here again drawing a clear distinction between the public and the private standard would benefit private rule-making without compromising public enforcement duties. When code provisions are ambiguous, the above rules should apply and public enforcers should refrain from giving a consumer-friendly interpretation to an otherwise clear code provision.[134]

The content of a code should only fill in the legal fairness clause insofar as the private standard *equals* the UCPD standard. Enforcement authorities and courts should keep in mind that the UCPD is a minimum harmonizing instrument as regards codes of conduct and should thus explicitly acknowledge whether the level of protection afforded by the code matches the UCPD standard. Binding a non-member to a code that outreaches the legal standard (entailing stricter information duties or banning practices that are not listed) is not permitted in view of the directive's full harmonization goal. Although possibly justified from the perspective of consumer protection and legal security, codes fleshing out the professional diligence clause may not become a means to bypass the maximum standards laid down in the UCPD and to falsify competition.[135]

132 The other way around is conceivable as well: a practice contravening a code may, but need not, be unfair. This depends on the interpretation of the directive standards. The code standard may appear to be stricter than the directive standard.

133 Cafaggi (n 9) 122 puts forward the 'harmonise or explain' principle according to which a national regulator has duty to explain why, in its interpretation of professional diligence, it deviates from the common interpretation by self-regulatory bodies.

134 Cf. CFI Rotterdam 13 December 2012, ECLI:NL:RBROT:2012:BY6184, s. 15.4.4.

135 Cf. Hodges et al. (n 76) 414.

In the event that private and public standards converge – in the sense that a practice both breaches a code *and* is deemed unfair – emphasis should be put on the fact that the self-regulatory rules are in line with the legal standard and that free-riding is not being tolerated. The widespread support for a code and the "representativity"[136] of its drafting organization(s) are valid reasons to put a concrete private standard on an equal footing with an open-worded legal standard. This outcome should, however, also highlight the fact that the code sponsor has been unsuccessful in tackling this very practice and would hopefully exhort this sponsor to tighten its own enforcement procedure and to increase its effectiveness (section 6.3).

6.2.3 Codes setting the fairness standard: Compliance with the fairness standard

To increase the appeal of codes of conduct, a presumption of conformity should be put into place for concrete and firm commitments. Such commitments may even form safe harbours provided *they have been endorsed by a national public enforcement authority or the European Commission* (section 6.4).[137] This endorsement should be made conditional upon consumer associations having been invited to participate into the self-regulatory process and again upon the "representativity' of the parties to the dialogue'.[138] The legitimacy of a code as a benchmark of fairness increases if factors attesting of a code's legitimacy – its endorsement, the involvement of stakeholders in their drafting or the wide support for a code – are explicitly taken into consideration by supervisory bodies and courts.

This presumption of conformity would offer determinate guidance and legal certainty to traders and foster the creation of new codes of conduct. It should, however, only be introduced insofar as the commitments are put in sufficiently clear and firm wordings. This may lead code owners to flesh out the code's open-textured provisions and to sharpen their commitments. The use of general clauses in national codes hinders harmonization as much as the use of such clauses in the UCPD itself. There will of course be a good deal of debate about just how concrete and firm a commitment is but guidance from the Commission or the CJEU may help draw the line.

6.3 Codes of Conduct and the Enforcement of the UCPD Standards

The directive should be amended to increase self-regulation's role in the enforcement of the directive standards. Code-based schemes should be more explicitly incorporated into the legal framework.

---

136 Collins (n 12) 34.

137 The prior approval by a relevant public body warrants that codes comply with legal standards: ibid 31.

138 Ibid 34.

6.3.1 'More' codes

The directive should explicitly encourage the drafting of and adherence to codes of conduct. The aforementioned interpretation 'rules' show features of a carrot approach and reduce the thwarting effect of article 6(2)(b) without putting the indispensable stick approach at risk. The devising of codes can be directly stimulated by public authorities but can at the same time be supported by national or European self-regulatory entities, whose functioning should be facilitated by the European institutions. The proposal for a directive on ADR acknowledges the need for complementary means of dispute settlement and may foster the proliferation of codes of conduct.[139] Having regard to the fact that ADR schemes 'usually do not base their decisions only on the law and case law, but [...] focus on the practical solution of the dispute [and] take into account what is reasonable and fair, good practices, term of conditions negotiated ex-ante between business associations and consumer unions, or codes of conduct and equity',[140] the proposed legislation will possibly boost self-regulation in Member States where it remains underdeveloped.

6.3.2 'Fair' codes

Having regard to the directive's full harmonization goal, codes must be tested against the UCPD standards before defining the required level of professional diligence. A fairly unlikely but yet possible outcome of this test could be that a code does not meet the legal standard. Code owners should then be held responsible and article 11(2) should not leave this for the Member States to decide. Public authorities need to play a role in the background, controlling the fairness and enforcement of the codes. The enforcement authorities' interference with the process of self-regulation should, however, depend on the private actors' readiness to cooperate and to integrate legal standards. In first instance, public bodies should confine their involvement to facilitating and rewarding initiatives. The directive should welcome approval schemes at both the national and the European level.

6.3.3 The enforcement of fair codes

The directive should lend more legitimacy to the complementary function of ADR schemes that decide not only on the basis of legal rules but also on the basis of 'fair' codes of conduct. The consumers' interests are secured by fair codes of conduct that are enforced through easy accessible dispute settlement procedures and proactive compliance mechanisms that act as a first port of call. The establishment of such procedures and mechanisms needs to be supported by formal collaborative arrangements, applicable to both agencies *and* courts and by an adequate monitoring of the ADR schemes' functioning. The UCPD does not expressly stimulate the creation of such means.

---

139 Directive 2013/11/EU of the European Parliament and of the Council of 21 May 2013 on Alternative Dispute Resolution for Consumer Disputes and Amending Regulation (EC) No 2006/2004 and Directive 2009/22/EC (OJ 2013 L 165/63).

140 SEC (2011) 1408 final.

The recently enacted ADR directive to a certain extent makes up for this omission. Article 17 of the ADR directive includes rules governing the cooperation between ADR entities and national authorities enforcing EU consumer protection law whereas Chapter IV addresses the monitoring of ADR entities. Hopefully the ADR directive will foster the creation of effective ADR schemes *based on fair codes of conduct.*[141] The cooperation between ADR and the judiciary should rely on a system of cross-referrals in which an ADR body can refer to a court for determination of the law and consumers would be incited towards opting for ADR instead of filing their complaints at a local court.[142]

Public supervisory bodies and courts should help increase the legitimacy of high-quality private enforcement decisions pertaining to the UCPD standards that have been literally transposed into codes, by expressly acknowledging those decisions. When testing a practice against the statutory general clause, public bodies should not only refer to this clause's interpretation by the field's code owner (section 6.2) but also to the review of a comparable practice by an established independent means.[143] Although this can be considered to be at odds with the principle of self-regulation, it cannot be ruled out that a private enforcement scheme will interpret a code more extensively than the code owner itself.[144] This may help the public body define where the legal standard lies.

6.4 European Codes of Conduct

Finally, the directive should explicitly encourage the drawing of EU-wide codes like the E-commerce Directive does. EU-wide codes can contribute to harmonization as long as they:

- are widely supported and preferably publicly endorsed by the Commission,

141 H-W Micklitz, 'The Expulsion of the Concept of Protection from the Consumer Law and the Return of Social Elements in the Civil Law: A Bittersweet Polemic' (2012) 35 *J Consum Policy* 292 considers the 'access to justice and the enforcement of rights' to be at stake in this proposal. The free access to justice should indeed always be warranted and the quality of the codes and associated ADR schemes ought to be controlled by public bodies. The out-of-court procedure may well be the only procedure a consumer considers to enroll. Consumers opting for out-of-court dispute settlement would otherwise often have refrained from filling their complaint at a local court. Dutch and English ADR schemes function properly. This expertise will most certainly be shared at the European level. If consumers did not feel adequately protected by the dispute settlement schemes, they would most probably turn their back on out-of-court procedures.

142 Hodges et al. (n 76) 415.

143 I do not refer to the situation where a supervisory body or court is reviewing a decision by a private body but to the situation where a commercial practice is directly placed under public scrutiny.

144 EH Hoogenraad, '"Ieder voordeel heb zijn nadeel". De andere zijde van zelfregulering' (2005) *Intellectuele Eigendom en Reclamerecht* 67.

- are rigorously enforced – both by code owners and by (closely cooperating[145]) public authorities, and
- play an important role in concretizing the directive's general clauses.

Consumer organizations should participate in the development of EU-wide codes. There is, however, a lack of institutional mechanisms that could help establish a dialogue between consumers and traders at the EU level. The consumer programme 2014–2020 projects to offer grants for action to EU-wide bodies for the development of codes of conduct but does unfortunately not intend to develop such mechanisms.[146]

In the wake of the implementation of the Services Directive the Commission suggested the following measures to stimulate the drafting of codes of conduct:[147]

- ensuring transparency of existing codes;
- ensuring that the recipients of services are informed;
- raising the profile of European codes of conduct (by granting labels – possibly a European label, professional cards, registration of members);
- heightening awareness of the importance of codes of conduct (information campaigns).

These proposals were only marginally supported by the Commission and have not had a significant impact on self-regulatory practice at the European level. The time may have come for a follow-up and a more substantial role for the Commission.

Bibliography

Abbamonte GB, 'The Unfair Commercial Practices Directive and Its General Prohibition', in S Weatherill and U Bernitz (eds), *The Regulation of Unfair Commercial Practices Under EC Directive 2005/29: New Rules and New Techniques* (Hart Publishing, 2007).

Cafaggi F, 'Private Regulation in European Private Law', in AS Hartkamp et al. (eds), *Towards a European Civil Code* (Kluwer Law International 2011).

145 When assessing whether a trader acts in breach of an EU-wide code, national enforcement bodies would need to cooperate within the Enforcement Network created by Regulation (EC) No 2006/2004. General clauses in a European Code may hamper harmonization insofar as the national authorities acting as 'last enforcers' have different interpretations of the commitments that were reached. It goes without saying that codes of conduct can only lead to harmonization provided national self-regulatory bodies, public authorities and courts cooperate closely.

146 European Commission, 'Proposal for a Regulation of the European Parliament and of the Council on a Consumer Programme 2014–2020' COM (2011) 707 final, 15.

147 European Communities (n 126) 17–19.

Collins H, 'EC Regulation of Unfair Commercial Practices', in H Collins (ed.), *The Forthcoming EC Directive on Unfair Commercial Practices* (Kluwer Law International, 2004).

Department for Business, Innovation & Skills, 'Consumer Landscape Review: Impact Assessment' (June 2011).

———, 'Empowering and Protecting Consumers: Consultation on Institutional Changes for Provision of Consumer Information, Advice, Education, Advocacy and Enforcement' (June 2011).

European Commission, 'Green Paper on EU Consumer Protection' COM (2001) 531 final.

———, 'Follow-up Communication to the Green Paper on EU Consumer Protection' (Communication) COM (2002) 289 final.

———, 'Explanatory Memorandum Proposal for a Directive Concerning Unfair Business-to-Consumer Commercial Practices in the Internal Market and Amending Directives 84/450/EEC, 97/7/EC and 98/27/EC', COM (2003) 356 final.

———, 'Guidance on the Implementation/Application of Directive 2005/29/EC on Unfair Commercial Practices' SEC (2009) 1666, 20.

———, 'Proposal for a Regulation of the European Parliament and of the Council on a Consumer Programme 2014–2020' COM (2011) 707 final, 15.

———, 'Proposal for a Directive of the European Parliament and of the Council on Alternative Dispute Resolution for Consumer Disputes and Amending Regulation (EC) No 2006/2004 and Directive 2009/22/EC (Directive on Consumer ADR) COM (2011) 793 final.

European Communities, 'Enhancing the Quality of Services in the Internal Market: The Role of European Codes of Conduct' (2007).

European Parliament, DG for Internal Policies, 'Misleading Advertising on the Internet' (July 2010).

———, 'State of Play of the Implementation of the Provisions on Advertising in the Unfair commercial Practices Legislation' (July 2010).

Griffiths M, 'Unfair Commercial Practices. A New Regime' (2007) 12(6) *Communications Law* 196–204.

Hodges Ch, I Benöhr and N Creutzfeldt-Banda, *Consumer ADR in Europe* (Hart Publishing, 2012).

Hoogenraad EH, '"Ieder voordeel heb zijn nadeel". De andere zijde van zelfregulering' (2005) *Intellectuele Eigendom en Reclamerecht* 67.

Howells G, 'Co-Regulation's Role in the Development of European Fair Trading Laws', in H Collins (ed.), *The Forthcoming EC Directive on Unfair Commercial Practices* (Kluwer Law International, 2004).

———, 'Codes of Conduct' in G Howells, H-W Micklitz and T Wilhelmsson, *European Fair Trading Law: The Unfair Commercial Practices Directive* (Aldershot: Ashgate, 2006).

Micklitz H-W, 'A General Framework Directive on Fair Trading', in H Collins (ed.), *The Forthcoming EC Directive on Unfair Commercial Practices* (Kluwer Law International, 2004).

———, 'The Expulsion of the Concept of Protection from the Consumer Law and the Return of Social Elements in the Civil Law: A Bittersweet Polemic' (2012) 35 *J Consum Policy*.

Office of Fair Trading, 'Consumer Codes Approval Scheme – Core Criteria and Guidance' (March 2008).

———, 'Guidance on the UK Regulations Implementing the Unfair Commercial Practices Directive' (May 2008).

———, 'Compliance Partnerships. An OFT Consultation on Developing the Use of "Established Means"' (December 2008).

———, 'Compliance Partnerships. Response to Consultation' (July 2009).

———, 'Policy Statement on the Role of Self-Regulation in the OFT's Consumer Protection Work' (September 2009).

Twigg-Flesner C et al., *An Analysis of the Application and Scope of the Unfair Commercial Practices Directive. A Report for the Department of Trade and Industry* (2005), http://www.dti.gov.uk/files/file32095.pdf.

Valce V, 'Codes of Conduct and Unfair Commercial Practices' (2012) 1 *Bancaria*.

van Boom WH, 'Wetsvoorstel doorverkoop toegangskaarten: nuttig en nodig?' (2011) 5 *Tijdschrift voor Consumentenrecht en Handelspraktijken*.

Van der Zeijden P and R Van der Horst, *Self-Regulation Practices in SANCO Policy Areas* (Final Report, 2008).

Verbruggen PWJ, *Private Regulation in the European Advertising Industry: Analyzing the Emergence and Governance of the Private Regulation of Advertising* (2012), http://papers.ssrn.com/sol3/papers.cfm?abstract_id=2256043.

Chapter 7
A Common Approach to the Enforcement of Unfair Commercial Practices and Unfair Contract Terms[1]

Hans-W. Micklitz

1. Breaking Boxes – A Common Approach?

On 15 March 2012 (C-453/10 *Pereničova*)[2] and 26 April 2012 (C-472/10 *Invitel*)[3] the ECJ reached two important decisions with regard not only to the relation of the law on unfair contract terms and the law on unfair commercial practices, but also to the interplay between individual and collective law enforcement. This leads to fundamental considerations about the relationship between the law on unfair contract terms, unfair commercial practices and individual/collective enforcement. The overall hypothesis I would like to defend is that we might see the emergence of a common approach to two areas of law which are normally regarded as being separate and guided by different philosophies.

I will develop my arguments in four steps. I will first explain what I mean by breaking boxes, by overcoming the invisible boundaries between unfair commercial practices and unfair terms. Therefore I will contrast the old thinking found in the old Member States with the new thinking in the new Member States. The starting point for a new approach is laid down in the two judgments of the ECJ, *Pereničova* and *Invitel*. These two judgments then serve as a starting point to look into the interplay of the two fields of law, in substance and in enforcement, individually and collectively. Here the questions are formulated which require an answer for the development of a common approach (II). The matter is complex: two fields of law, different ways of enforcement, individually and collectively and no, or a very limited link between individual and collective enforcement. Relatively easy to grasp is the approximation of the substance of unfair terms and unfair commercial practices. The two judgments are used to pave the way for a much stronger and more systematic interplay of the substance of the two fields (III). Enforcement, however,

---

1 This paper has been written in the context of the ERC grant on European Regulatory Private Law. A first version, focusing on the two judgments of the ECJ, has been published under the joint authorship of Hans-W Micklitz and Norbert Reich in *Europäische Zeitschrift für Wirtschaftsrecht*, *EuZW* 2012, 257.

2 ECJ 2012 I-nyr = *EuZW* 2012, 302 (with comments by Werkmeister).

3 ECJ 2012 I-nyr.

has to be broken down into different steps in order to be able to combine the joint substance with the paradigm of individual and collective enforcement. *Invitel* sets the tone for a new reading of collective redress under the unfair terms directive. The ECJ paves the way for linking the effects of an action for injunction to individual redress (IV). In unfair commercial practices the biggest gap is to be found in the lack of appropriate individual redress. Here combining Directive 2005/29/EC on commercial practices with the Constitutional Charter enhances the conclusion that consumers must have the opportunity to get out of a contract which is the result of unfair or misleading commercial practices (V). In a last step I will then transfer the new reading of collective redress in unfair terms to the field of commercial practices, thereby linking substance and procedure, individual and collective redress in the two fields and between the two fields (VI). The envisaged 'common approach' might still need a number of further preliminary references to the ECJ but the Court is definitely on course to introduce a new way of thinking about the relationship between unfair terms and unfair commercial practices legislation (VII).

1.1 The Rise and Decline of German Law as a Blueprint for European Action

This is not an article on German law. However, German law played a central role in the Europeanization of these two fields of law, and that is why it is necessary throughout the paper to refer to German law which is paradigmatic for the old type of thinking. The German Act on General Terms and Conditions of Trade (AGBG) of 1976 provided a model law for the adoption of Directive 93/13/EEC on Unfair Terms in Consumer Contracts. The German Unfair Competition Act (UWG) smoothed the way for the drawing up of Directive 84/450/EEC on Misleading Advertising. In the meantime, the latter has been amended by Directive 2005/29/EC concerning unfair business-to-consumer (B2C) commercial practices and Directive 2006/114/EC regarding misleading business-to-business (B2B) advertisement. Seen against the series of unfair terms legislation which were adopted in the 1970s and 1980s, Directive 93/13 did not provide many new insights, perhaps with the exception of the introduction of an action for injunction as a means of collective redress. In contrast, differences with the legal systems of the Member States' law on unfair commercial practices came to light at an early stage. Already Directive 97/55/EC, which legalized comparative advertising, did not correspond to harmony-seeking industrial operators that refrain from using comparative advertising as a means to enhance competition. Such an attitude is widespread in the legal orders of continental Member States. More than ever this holds true for Directive 2005/29/EC which contradicted established preconceptions both with regard to the differentiation of B2B and B2C situations and with a view to its substantive arrangements. It suffices to recall the information paradigm and the key role of blacklists in the UCPD in which the blanket clause plays a subsidiary role only.[4]

4 Consistent practice since *VTB*, Joined Cases C-261 + 299/07 *VTB et al. v Total et al.* Slg. 2009 , I-2949, confirmed by C-140/08 *Mediaprint v 'Österreich' Zeitungsverlag*, ECR 2010 I-nyr.

Gradually the German legal system lost its influence over EU law making, last but not least its insistence on collective private enforcement by trade and consumer associations. Entrusting enforcement to private associations might have represented an adequate response to the German economy of the late nineteenth and the first half of the twentieth century, with its huge number of small and medium-sized firms, when market transactions were bound to the national territory.[5] However, the system of private collective law enforcement does not meet the requirements of the European Internal Market. The prerogative to take action has been undertaken by others, by public enforcement bodies in particular, whose introduction has been promoted by the European Union via Regulation 2006/2004/EC and who fulfil their tasks in an innovative way. Their approach does not necessarily comply with an understanding of contract law, and unfair terms and commercial practices law premised on the notion that they are two autonomous fields of law that have to be precisely separated, not only with regard to substance – contract vs. advertising – but also with regard to the shaping of the appropriate enforcement mechanisms. Administrative enforcement is very much guided by the search for pragmatic solutions beyond the neat boundaries of substantive or procedural legal categories.[6]

The separation between contract law and unfair commercial practices is set in stone in Article 3(2) of Directive 2005/29/EC: 'This Directive is without prejudice to contract law and, in particular, to the rules on the validity, formation or effect of a contract.' However, I will argue throughout the text that exactly this distinction is gradually vanishing away. In my opinion these new tendencies should be studied carefully and welcomed as a chance to break with the error of thinking in traditional categories and to embark, without fear or prejudice, upon the feasibility of a common approach, one which unites both fields of law in substance and in their enforcement. The two judgments under discussion herein push us back to a debate which took place in the 1970s when the Nordic countries were introducing consumer protection legislation which was hard to reconcile with the tendency to think in established legal categories.

1.2 Old Thinking – Old Member States – vs. New Thinking – New Member States?

It seems somewhat ironic that crucial improvements are promoted through the Europeanization of the law on unfair contract terms, which is putatively so similar to German law. The submissions were provided by a Slovenian and a Hungarian court. AG Trstenjak comes from Slovenia and the reporting judge in both procedures at the ECJ was the former president of the Polish constitutional court,

---

5 See the doctoral thesis (PhD), often overlooked in Germany, of A Bakardjieva, 'Fair Trading in Flux', University of Stockholm 2005.

6 Ch Hodges, *The Reform of Class and Representative Actions in European Legal Systems, A New Framework for Collective Redress in Europe*, 2009.

Marek Safjan. This strong Central and Eastern European dimension has to be emphasized, though obviously not to give way to some kind of conspiracy theory. This note rather serves the purpose of making private lawyers from the old Member States realize that legal rules are not only exported, but must also be developed in the exporting country and finally may even be re-exported or re-imported to the country of origin – according to one's perspective. Beyond national private law this understanding is common knowledge, especially with regard to international commercial law.[7] The discussion on the creation of a European Civil Code, enshrined in the Draft Common Frame of Reference, subsequently condensed in the Draft Regulation on a Common European Sales Law, was again dominated by the 'old' Member States, as if legal export is the only way of communication. The DCFR proved a disappointing choice in view of all the efforts of the 'new' Member States, which joined the European Union after 2004, to include their private law systems. The rising number of submissions by Central and Eastern European civil courts reveals quite to the contrary that the new Member States are ready to play a more active role in the implementation of Directives. The two references fit very well into such an understanding. The competent institutions in the new Member States, legislatures, agencies or courts, take hold of EU rules and interpret them according to their own comprehension, which might still be influenced by socialist reasoning. This proves to be particularly true with regard to the strong instrumentalization of private law,[8] in which European private law and socialist civil law find harmony in a strange and remarkable way. Thus there is an undercurrent in the idea of a common approach which deserves further scrutiny. However, such investigation is beyond the scope of this chapter.

2. The Legal Questions in *Pereničova* and *Invitel*

2.1 Impact on Misleading Unfair Commercial Practices (Incorrect Statement on the Annual Percentage Rate) and of a Collective Action on Unilateral Price Amendment Terms on Individual Contracts

The *Pereničova* case dealt with the control of unfair commercial practices required in Directive 2005/29/EC and its impact on the validity of an incorrect statement on the annual percentage rate (58,76 per cent instead of the indicated 48,63 per cent) in the context of an *individual* dispute relating to a B2C credit agreement under

7 R Knieper, 'Möglichkeiten und Grenzen der Verpflanzbarkeit von Recht. Juristische Zusammenarbeit aus der Sicht eines Beraters' (2008) 72 *RabelsZ* 88–113.

8 Ch Schmid, 'The Instrumentalist Conception of the Acquis Communautaire in Consumer Law and its Implications on a European Contract Law Code' (2005) 1 *European Review of Contract Law* 211–227; updated in: Stephan Grundmann and Martin Schauer (eds), *The Architecture of European Codes and Contract Law* (Kluwer Law International, 2006) 255–267; in a more developed version in *Die Instrumentalisierung des Privatrechts durch die Europäische Union*, 2010.

Slovakian law. I will come later to the differences between contract terms in individual contracts and standardized contract terms. The relevant EU law on consumer credit of the old Directive 87/102/EEC and the new Directive 2008/48/EC does not, despite its excessive information obligations, cover the essential question of the legal consequences of omitted or incorrect information.[9] In both cases before the national courts and the ECJ, the total amount of the interest rate played no role. This is even more striking with regard to the fact that the inflation rate in Slovakia amounted to 8.4 per cent in 2003, but dropped rapidly thereafter. According to a German or Austrian understanding, the legally admissible limits are exceeded to a distinctive extent here. Thus the level of the interest rate advertised for might have had an indirect influence on the court's decision to link the details of the interest rate to the question of the invalidity of the credit agreement. What is at stake is the degree to which unfair commercial practices might have an impact on the validity of individual and maybe even standardized contractual relations.

The *Invitel* case deals with a collective action of the Hungarian National Consumer Protection Office against a telecommunications services provider, which used a unilateral price amendment clause without a valid reason and without explicitly describing the method by which prices could vary. The consequences of a potential prohibition of the collective action on individual contracts with the defendant business company are of particular interest. Most contract lawyers might consider the problem as being commonly known. What is at stake? Judgments are binding *inter partes* only. In the case the parties are the consumer agency and a company, the final judgment of the competent court might bind only these two parties. But what about the potential effect of the collective action, the action for injunction, on individual contracts which contain exactly the term which has been declared void in the collective action? *Invitel* raises a number of new legal questions on the interplay between individual and collective action from an entirely European perspective, which give reason to reflect. The most recently decided *Putz/Weber* case vividly showed the considerable extent to which the ECJ is willing to break new ground in private law.[10] It will have to be shown that there is a link between *Putz/Weber* and *Invitel*.

2.2 Unfair Commercial Practices and Contract Law – Divided or United?

The first issue revolves around the dominating idea of a clear dissociation of contract law from the law on unfair commercial practices. The referring court only

9 H-W Micklitz, N Reich and P Rott, *Understanding EU Consumer Law* (2009) at 5.17.

10 ECJ, Judgment of 16.6.2011, Case C-65 + 87/09, ECJ 2011 I-nyr; see in this context Purnhagen, EuZW 2011, 626 and the subsequent decision of the BGH, NJW 2012, 1073.

indirectly made this clear in the question referred.[11] The division leads basically to a shortening of individual legal redress, since the consumer who, influenced by the advertisement, concludes a contract will have de facto no possibility to disengage himself from the contract. The de jure alternative – to complain about the defectiveness of the object purchased because it does not comply with the advertising – plays just as limited a role in practice as the right to withdraw from the contract by asserting a potential claim according to § 280 BGB in Germany;[12] to claim mistake or fraud in the common law systems[13] is hard to prove in practice.[14] For the consumer there remains the possibility of relying on those institutional players which are regarded as qualified entities under European directives on unfair terms and unfair commercial practices, be it public bodies in the vast majority of the Member States, or private trade and consumer organizations – which are the only ones that have standing in Austria, Germany and Slovenia. Partly owing to German pressure, individual legal redress to the benefit of consumers, although promoted by the European Commission,[15] was not integrated in the final text of Directive 2005/29/EC. This is left to Member States.

2.3 Collective Action and Individual Action – United or Divided?

The second issue may be of even more fundamental reach, as it is of utmost practical importance. What is the potential effect of a decision of a national court holding that this and that standard contract term used by a company or recommended by a business association is void? Does it affect individual contracts in which the very same term shows up? Is a potential effect tied to the same user or is the potential impact directed against the unfair term? This question came up in the early 1970s

---

11 '1. Is the scope of consumer protection under Article 6(1) of [...] Directive 93/13 [...] such as to make it possible, where unfair contractual clauses are found in a consumer contract, to conclude that the contract as a whole is not binding on the consumer, if that is more advantageous to the consumer?

2. Are the criteria determining what is an unfair commercial practice in accordance with [...] Directive 2005/29 [...] such as to permit the conclusion that, if a supplier quotes in the contract a lower [...] APR [...] than is in fact the case, it is possible to regard that step by the supplier towards the consumer as an unfair commercial practice? If there is a finding of an unfair commercial practice, does Directive 2005/29 [...] permit there to be any impact on the validity of a credit agreement and on the achievement of the objective in Articles 4(1) and 6(1) of Directive 93/13, if invalidity of the contract is more advantageous for the consumer?'

12 Art 280 concerns a compensation claim. The damage, however, in such a case is the contract which the consumer had been pulled into via unfair commercial practices.

13 S Whittaker, 'Form and Substance in the Reception of EC Directives into English Contract Law' (2007) *ERCL* 381.

14 Some Countries like the Netherlands are discussing to reverse the burden of proof at least in exceptional cases.

15 COM (2002) 289 final at 18.

when the German law on unfair standard terms was hotly debated in academic circles and political fora. Every German unfair contract terms enthusiast knows that § 11 UKlaG (German Injunctions Act) enables individual consumers to refer to a judgment in a collective action in order to make sure that the *same* term used by the *same* user in individual contracts cannot gain legal effect to the detriment of the consumer. The Federal Ministry of Food, Agriculture and Consumer Protection (BMELV) commissioned a study in 2010 which confirmed what insiders know all too well: that the rule in § 11 on the so-called Rechtskrafterstreckung – extension of *res judicata* – does not play a role in practice.[16] Neither Directive 93/13/EEC nor Directive 2009/22/EC on injunctions for the protection of consumers' interests give concrete indications on how to respond to the question of a possible link between individual and collective legal redress.

This lacuna led to great diversity in the Member States. Most of the Member States did not adopt particular rules,[17] unlike Poland and Hungary, from which *Invitel* originates, which granted *erga omnes* effect to injunctions. Little is known as to how the *erga omnes* effect functions and how courts and private litigants make sure that a term registered as invalid may not gain effect despite the *erga omnes* rule.[18] So how could the ECJ in *Invitel* get into an issue which EU law has not regulated and where Member States defend and uphold their 'procedural autonomy'? It should be recalled that EU law is per se more open and tries to detach itself from 'national traditional thinking', since it always pursues integration-related objectives. The Hungarian Court raised the question of whether and to what extent the *erga omnes* rule is in compliance with EU law and whether it should be applied ex officio:[19]

> May Article 6(1) of that directive be interpreted, where an order which benefits consumers who are not party to the proceedings is made, or the application of an unfair standard contract term is prohibited, in an action in the public interest, as meaning that an unfair term which has become part of a consumer contract is not binding on all consumers also as regards the future, so that the court has to apply the consequences in law thereof of its own motion?

---

16 There is no evidence – not even in the recently concluded empirical study – of the degree to which consumers are making use of the possibility in their litigation to a judgment of a court against the same supplier that has declared the incriminated term void, Höland and Meller-Hannich, *Gutachten Evaluierung der Effektivität kollektiver Rechtschutzinstrumente* (2011).

17 See U Docekal, P Kolba, H-W Micklitz and P Rott, 'Verbraucherschutz durch Unterlassungsklagen, Rechtliche und Praktische Umsetzung der Richtlinie Unterlassungsklagen 98/27/EG in den Mitgliedstaaten' (2007) *VIEW Schriftenreihe*, Band 17, with regard to Hungary see Reich, FS E Schmidt (2005) 239, [248].

18 On Poland, H-W Micklitz, 'Reforming European Union Unfair Terms Legislation in Consumer Contracts' (2010) *ECRL* 347, 352.

19 ECJ Case C-472/10 nyr.

As the efforts of the EU Commission to promote the development of collective legal redress have more or less ground to a halt,[20] debates over the potential link between the unfairness of the term and a possible compensation for the loss these consumers suffered from are compelled to shift into courtrooms.[21] This is all the more true as the European Commission never seriously considered the extension of *res judicata*, not even during the most ambitions discussions on the then envisaged revision of the consumer *acquis* which later ended up in the rather modest Directive 2011/83/EC on Consumer Rights, modest because the Directive no longer includes unfair terms and consumer sales regulation.

2.4 Injunction and Skimming Off – Divided or United?

Thirdly, the action for injunction belongs to the *acquis communautaire* of European consumer law. The action for injunction may be regarded as a kind of minimum standard all Member States have to guarantee. In the author's understanding this comprises also the duty to grant consumer organizations standing. The Hungarian national consumer protection authority, acting as a plaintiff, did not merely want to obtain a declaration that the contested term was void as being unfair with regard to all consumers that had concluded a contract with the defendant telecommunications services provider, in effect linking the collective and the individual legal effects together. The Hungarian national consumer protection authority also claimed reimbursement of the sum which the defendant business had received as a consequence 'of the illegal invoicing of money order fees'. It therefore referred the following questions to the ECJ:

> (1) May Article 6(1) of [the Directive] […] be interpreted as meaning that an unfair contract term is not binding on any consumer where a body appointed by law and competent for that purpose seeks a declaration of the invalidity of that unfair term which has become part of a consumer contract on behalf of consumers in an action in the public interest (*actio popularis*)?
>
> May Article 6(1) of that directive be interpreted, where an order which benefits consumers who are not party to the proceedings is made, or the application of an unfair standard contract term is prohibited, in an action in the public interest, as meaning that an unfair term which has become part of a consumer contract is not binding on all consumers also as regards the future, so that the court has to apply the consequences in law thereof of its own motion?
>
> (2) May Article 3(1) of [the Directive], in conjunction with points 1(j) and 2(d) of the annex applicable by virtue of Article 3(3) of that directive, be interpreted

20 Communication from the Commission 'Towards a European Horizontal Framework for collective Redress', COM (2013) 401/2, 11.6.2013.

21 ECJ Case C-92/11, RWE-Vertrieb/VZ NRW 2013 ECR I-nyr, is just another example. See for details H-W Micklitz and N Reich, 'Von der Mißbrauchs- zur Marktkontrolle' (2013) *EUZW* 457.

> as meaning that, where a seller or supplier provides for a unilateral amendment of a contract term without explicitly describing the method by which prices vary or giving valid reasons in the contract, that contract term is unfair *ipso jure*?

Germany which was at the forefront of fighting for the Europeanization of the action for injunction needed more than 25 years of discussion before a political agreement could be reached to introduce a collective remedy for confiscating or 'skimming off' unlawful profits (*Gewinnabschöpfungsanspruch*) in the law on unfair commercial practices. However, the outcome was a mere 'paper tiger', which did not even make it into the law on unfair contract terms and which has not to date produced any noteworthy results. Thus, the profit which resulted from the use of an unfair term remains with the businessman. Consumer organizations if they want to skim off illegal profits resulting from unfair terms end up in a deadlock.[22]

Hungary is not the only country with a collective redress scheme that provides for remedies beyond the stop-order mechanism enshrined in the action for injunction. Whereas the action for injunction can be found in Article 209/B of the Hungarian Civil Code, the claim for damages and of confiscating or 'skimming off' unlawful profits is regulated in Article 39(1) of the Hungarian law on consumer protection:

> (1) The consumer protection authority, the non-governmental organisation for the protection of consumers' interests or the public prosecutor may bring proceedings against any party whose illegal activities affect a wide range of consumers or cause substantial disadvantage, in order to defend a wide range of consumers or eliminate substantial disadvantage. Such an action may also be brought even if the identity of the consumers adversely affected cannot be established.

The openness of this rule corresponds to its purpose. Article 39(1) does not state that the claimant organization is allowed to take the unlawfully acquired proceeds. One could also imagine a system whereby the proceeds do not accrue to the organization but according to which it can merely order the trader to pay back to the consumer directly. To a traditional Western European private lawyer it might induce beads of sweat, since it seems to be an exercise in political goal setting rather than a right to sue based on legal criteria. This rule paradigmatically reflects the openness of many legal rules, in the new Member States, but also in the older new Member States like Greece and Portugal.[23] The ECJ did not have to deal with the precise requirements of Article 39, however. The demand submitted by the defendant obviously aims at questioning the legality of a claim of confiscating

22 Cf. for example, the attempt of the Hamburg consumer organization, http://www.vzhh.de/energie/30195/5000-euro-klage-gegen-flexstrom.aspx.

23 Cf. H-W Micklitz and A Stadler, *Verbandsklage in der Informations- und Dienstleistungsgesellschaft* (Griechenland, 2005) 169. The reason might be that private law has a lesser influence in these countries on the shaping of remedies.

unlawful profits, which goes beyond the explicitly cited requirements of Directive 93/13/EEC. The ECJ confirmed the leeway granted to the Member States in Article 8 of Directive 93/13/EEC, which codifies minimum harmonization (see recitals 39–40 of the *Invitel* case). More interesting is what AG Trstenjak says on the skimming-off procedure. I will come back to this issue later on.

3. The Family Resemblance of Unfair Terms and Unfair Commercial Practices

3.1 On the Way to an Approximation of the Control Methodology (from Blacklists to General Clauses) in Both Fields of Law via the ECJ

EU secondary law is breath-taking with regard to the field we are interested in. Both fields of law are painted with a broad brush, so to speak. Whereas the regulatory technique of Directive 93/13/EEC might still be acceptable in view of its proximity to the then already-existing national laws on unfair contract terms control, Directive 2005/29/EC does not correspond to established legal conceptions of the law on unfair commercial practices. The Directive establishes a catalogue of prohibitions (the blacklist) and makes the blacklist the starting point of the examination. The system of control according to the inverted pyramid from the blacklist down to the blanket clause, which was celebrated as a success e.g., in the German law on unfair terms (but not in the Nordic countries),[24] meets much resistance in some Member States with regard to the law on unfair commercial practices. It seems to be a strange logic to applaud blacklists in contract terms but to criticize them in unfair commercial practices, in particular if the discourse takes place in the same country.

The ECJ now seems ready to take a common approach to both directives – from the blacklist to the general clause in unfair commercial practices and from the general clause to the 'blacklist' in the law on unfair terms. Contrary to *Freiburger Kommunalbauten* and much more in line with *Océano*, in *Invitel* the ECJ granted the indicative list a rather prominent position. *Penzüghyi*[25] was the break-even point in the development of the case law. Since then the ECJ uses the indicative list as the starting point for evaluating the unfairness of contract clauses.

In a way *Invitel* could be understood as a variation of the *VTB* case law[26] on sales promotion. In this respect, it seems as if the ECJ merges the different control methods in the application of the two directives into one, although it remains to be

24 See, therefore, Sweden, which was not ready to integrate the indicative list into the law and succeeded before the ECJ Case C-478/99, *European Commission vs. Sweden*, 2002 ECR I-4172.

25 ECJ, Judgment of 9.11.2010, Case C-137/07, *VG Penzügyi Lízing*, nyr.

26 ECJ, Judgment of 23.4.2009, Joined Cases C261/07 and C299/07 2009 ECR 2949.

seen in two pending cases, in *Mohamed Aziz*[27] and in *RWE*[28] whether and to what extent the ECJ is ready to confirm the merger or whether variations are possible. The rather different conclusions of the two advocate generals Kokott (*Aziz*, rather reluctant) and Trstenjak (*RWE*, rather forceful) demonstrate an element of uncertainty in the current case law. If the ECJ would follow the line commenced in *Penzüghyi* and confirmed in *Invitel*, in the pending cases, one might very well argue that the ECJ is ready to put the blacklist test in the most prominent position.

3.2 On the Way to a Coherent Interpretation

Both catalogues, the blacklist and the indicative list, exist side by side as if one had nothing to do with the other. Therefore, it is high time to compare the two lists. In all likelihood the result would be a complex mélange of rules, which reflect the intertwining of commercial practices and contract. Neither decision gave the ECJ an opportunity to get involved. *Invitel* did not deal with the evaluation of the interaction between the advertising and contract clauses. *Pereničova* is exactly about this, but the incriminated marketing strategy does not appear in Directive 2009/29/EC's catalogue of prohibited clauses. Nor does the indicative list in Directive 93/13/EEC provide any assistance.

From this perspective, Article 3(2) of Directive 2005/29/EC, which formally confirms traditional thinking, would give way to a coherent interpretation. Such an integrated approach is favoured by AG Trstenjak, when she speaks in *Pereničova* of the need for a 'coherent interpretation' that should even extend to the blanket clauses of the two directives (recital 90). It is to be noted that this statement is preceded by the formal separation of the two fields of law, since an unfair commercial practice in terms of 'legal consequences' must be regarded as irrelevant for the evaluation of the validity of the contract (recital 85). It should be equally recalled that AG Trstenjak had only to decide on the impact of an unfair commercial practice on individual contract terms and not on standardized contract terms. We will have to come back later to the fundamental implications which result from the distinction between individual and collective contract terms.

The ECJ did not pick up the proposed terminology, but followed the AG on substance. Seen this way, it appears necessary to promote the concept of a coherent interpretation.

3.3 Doing Away with the Strict Separation

Both directives operate with large blanket clauses, which represent the heart of each directive. On the one hand, there are the non-binding terms, which contradict the principle of unfairness as laid down in Article 3 of Directive 93/13/EEC.

27 ECJ Judgment of 14 March 2013 C-415/11 *Mohamed Aziz v Caixa*, nyr.

28 C-92/11 *RWE Vertrieb AG gegen Verbraucherzentrale Nordrhein-Westfalen e.V*, nyr.

On the other hand we have the unfair commercial practices. The scope of Directive 2005/29/EC is quite wide. The interpretation of unfair commercial practices developed by the ECJ in the framework of the *VTB* case law includes contract clauses, if the unfairness of a commercial practice is caused in particular by the use of unfair terms (AG Trstenjak in *Pereničova*, recital 91).[29] The ECJ followed this argumentation without taking over the arguments. Thus Directive 2005/29/EC mutates into a catch-all element of any unfair commercial practice, be it advertising, sales promotion or standard contract terms. Nordic countries might perceive this finding as a late confirmation of their consumer protection policy applied ever since.[30] However, this wide conception does not automatically improve the situation of the consumer, since initially the AG and the ECJ soften the strict separation of law on unfair terms and the law on unfair commercial practices.

> According to Art. 3(2) of Directive 2005/29/EC is 'without prejudice to contract law and, in particular, to the rules on the validity, formation or effect of a contract' (ECJ recital 44 of *Pereničova*). But the ECJ has also emphasized that 'a finding that a commercial practice is unfair is one element among others on which the competent court may base its assessment of the unfairness of contractual terms under Article 4(1) of Directive 93/13' (recital 43).

3.4 ... Provided There Is an Unfair Commercial Practice and the Scope of Application of the Unfair Terms Directive Is Opened Up

The consequence is that the individual consumer can be helped only if the unfair commercial practice itself can be referred to, to evaluate the unfairness of a contract clause. In *Pereničova* the AG and then the ECJ worked out precisely how the interaction should appear. First of all, it has to be determined that the incorrect information on the annual percentage rate represents an unfair or misleading commercial practice in terms of Directive 2005/29/EC. The crucial question for the consumer is whether or not and if so, how the incorrect information affects the

---

29 'A number of situations will serve to illustrate the close link between the two directives: as regards the circumstances in the main proceedings, for example, it is conceivable that the unfairness of a commercial practice consists in the very use in consumer contracts of unfair terms within the meaning of Directive 93/13. (43) The trader's use of such terms is likely to be seen as a misleading act, since false information is provided or the consumer is unclear as to the actual scale of the contractual rights and obligations, especially with regard to rights and obligations arising from the clauses which are unfair and so invalid for the consumer. A similar assessment is likely to be made of a situation in which the trader words vital terms in language which is not plain or intelligible in order to withhold essential information from the consumer. Conversely, it is also conceivable, however, that false and thus misleading information in a contractual term within the meaning of Directive 2005/29 is the very reason for its unfair nature. This is also the situation which the referring court clearly suspects in the main action and which will need to be examined in the following.'

30 B Dahl, *Consumer Legislation in Denmark* (Surrey: Van Nostrand Reinhold, 1981).

review of the contract term (*Inhaltskontrolle*; substantive fairness test) required according to Directive 93/13/EEC. This depends on whether the scope of Directive 93/13/EEC is opened up for the evaluation of unfair or misleading commercial practices. A coherent interpretation of both blanket clauses would come close to an approximation of the assessment criteria. The AG and the ECJ find themselves on new legal ground.

The AG and the ECJ overcome the dividing line between the two fields of law with a simple trick. The control of unfair terms also applies where the author drafted the clause with a view to its *possible* use (AG's conclusions *Invitel* of 6.12.2011 recital 65, ECJ *Invitel* recital 37). 'It is therefore not necessary for general use to be actually or certainly planned' (AG recital 65, ECJ recital 37 with reference to *Commission v Italy*[31]). By this manoeuvre the control of unfair terms is shifted to an earlier stage of the examination, thus paving the way for the inclusion of commercial acts, as far as the latter meet the formal requirements of being treated as 'contract terms'.

3.5 Unfair Commercial Practices as an Indication of Unfair Contract Terms

Clauses for calculating interest rates are to be measured against the principle of transparency, laid down in Article 5 of Directive 93/13/EC.[32] Whereas the AG finds herself constrained to a strict analysis in her conclusions concerning the *Pereničova* case (recital 117), the ECJ does not even dedicate a single line to this question. It focuses exclusively on Article 4(1) of Directive 93/13/EEC, according to which it is possible to include a commercial practice deemed to be unfair in the assessment of the unfairness of the contract terms as 'one element among others' (ECJ, *Pereničova*, recital 43). The AG emphasizes (recital 124) that 'Article 4(1) of Directive 93/13/EEC can be regarded as something of a gateway for assessments under the legislation on fair trading practices.' In contrast to the ECJ, she wants to pay particular attention to legislative assessments by the legislature (recital 123).

What are the consequences? Is it possible to transfer the decision's evaluation to other cases of a similar nature? Can contract clauses be effective, even if they have to be classified as unfair or misleading commercial practices? An important distinction has to be drawn between the potential impact of unfair commercial practices on *individual* contracts, in which the validity of one term might depend on a coherent interpretation of the two areas of the law and the potential impact of unfair commercial practices on *collective* actions. Article 4(1) of Directive 93/13/EEC seems to be the dominant understanding, concerning the control of unfair terms in individual litigation only. The ECJ had not yet to decide on the applicability

31 ECJ, Judgment of 24.1.2002, Case C-372/99, ECR 2002, I-819 recital 14.

32 I will refrain from discussing whether and to what extent interest rates form an integral part of the price and are therefore exempted from any form of control, at least in countries like Germany and the United Kingdom where courts have not been given the power to exercise control over so-called core terms.

of Article 4(1) to collective actions. However, it insisted on restricting the scope of the *contra proferentem* rule to individual litigation,[33] without, however, seeing and discussing the problem of a consistent interpretation in individual and collective litigation. In light of the recognized tendency of the ECJ to develop a common approach on the two different fields of law, it might not be farfetched to assume that the ECJ might be ready to strive for consistency also in the rules governing the control of contract terms by individual or via collective actions, meaning in particular the reach and application of Article 4 of Directive 93/13/EEC. I have proposed to overcome the antinomies between individual concrete and collective abstract terms in merging the two into a concept of a general-concrete fairness test.[34]

4. A New Reading of Collective Actions against Unfair Terms

4.1 The Action for an Injunction as a European Remedy

The *Invitel* case allowed the ECJ to comment for the first time on the principles of the system of legal redress with regard to Directive 93/13/EEC. A central question is the Europeanization of the action for injunction which in EU law belongs to the *acquis communautaire*, enshrined in the substance-related directives on unfair terms and commercial practices but also in the so-called "Injunctions Directive", Directive 2009/22, which puts emphasis on the procedural side of the remedy. Whatever the collective legal redress might look like, the action for injunction represents the benchmark according to which national collective remedies have to be evaluated. Despite this being widely known, and although the action for injunction is well recognized as an instrument of collective legal redress in the Member States, beyond this diffused consensus disagreement prevails.

The parameters in the relevant directives remain vague. Each directive features a slightly different formulation.[35] Neither of them includes a definition of the distinctive elements of an action for injunction nor of the parties who have the right to file a suit and under what conditions. There is also a lack of information on what the action for injunction aims at and on which role it plays with regard to the substantive law to which it is assigned. Readers are furthermore left in the dark as to the relationship between the action for injunction and individual remedies. In brief, the action for injunction represents a marvellous field for debates about legal theory and dogmatism, not only within the Member States but also for comparisons of European or international legislation.[36]

33 ECJ, 9 September 2004, C-70/03, *Commission/Spain* [2004] ECR I-7999.

34 H-W Micklitz, N Reich and P Rott, *Understanding EU Consumer Law*, recital 3.20.

35 Art 7 Directive 93/13, art 11 Directive 2005/29, art 4 Directive 2009/22.

36 The list of open questions is long: Is the claim of substantive or procedural nature, a question which leads to a lot of difficulties in a cross-border context, cf. A Stadler, *Juristenzeitung* (2009) 121.

In *Invitel* AG Trstenjak took advantage of the opportunity to establish a basic EU position on the action for injunction, which will engage the case law of the Member States into the future. This applies all the more as the ECJ has not only followed the AG on the result, but refers to the statements of the AG (in recital 38 the ECJ refers to recital 51, in recital 39 to recitals 57–61 of the AG). The reasoning of the AG promotes a clear distinction between the three categories of supra-individual legal redress:

> (1) the procedure for a finding of the *unfairness of a term* (recital 64),
>
> (2) the *action for injunction aiming at the protection of the collective interest of consumers* (recital 67) – all means deemed by the Member States to be 'appropriate and effective to prevent the use of such terms' in terms of Art 7 of Directive 93/13/EEC (recital 75) – and
>
> (3) the *refund of costs and expenses charged* (recital 73), in the form of the so-called claim of skimming-off procedure to recover unlawful profits – *Gwinnabschöpfungsanspruch* and/or via an order to refund the individual consumers.

The ECJ followed this differentiation in the way it built its argument.

4.2 Interlocking of Individual and Collective Redress via Article 7 Para 2 of Directive 93/13/EEC

The differentiation is important, since there are connections between the finding of unfairness and the action for injunction for the protection of consumers' interests. For the first category Article 6(1) of Directive 93/13/EEC plays a decisive role. According to its wording, this rule is *not* restricted to individual procedures but, due to Article 7(2) of Directive 93/13/EEC, it is deeply linked to *collective* legal redress (AG recital 50). In this significant section the ECJ adapts the argumentation of the AG's recital 51 (ECJ recital 38). In view of its crucial importance it deserves to be quoted in full:

> AG (recital 51) However, in order effectively to achieve the objective of consumer protection in proceedings for collective judicial protection, the legal consequence of the non-binding nature of the term laid down in Article 6(1) of Directive 93/13 must also apply if the persons or organisations named in Article 7(2) of Directive 93/13 have brought proceedings in the interest of the consumers concerned, because otherwise a collective action would be of little benefit to consumers. It must not be forgotten that *in abstracto* verification, as an instrument of collective judicial protection, was designed to eliminate unfair terms 'drawn up for general use'. These terms are therefore intended for use in a large number of consumer contracts. They can therefore be combated effectively only if the decision of the national court finding a particular term to be unfair is *accorded fairly wide applicability*. [emphasis H-W M]

> ECJ (recital 38) The effective implementation of that objective requires, as the AG essentially noted in point 51 of her Opinion, that terms of the GBC of consumer contracts which are declared to be unfair in an action for injunction brought against the seller or supplier concerned, such as the term here at issue in the main proceedings, *are not binding on either the consumers who are parties to the actions for an injunction or on those who have concluded with that seller or supplier a contract to which the same GBC apply.* [emphasis H-W M]

4.3 Extension of Res Judicata *to Third Parties and/or to the Term?*

It does not take much imagination to picture that the aforementioned section played a crucial role in the deliberations of the court. The AG focuses on the *effet utile* of the directive which requires an extension of *res judicata* (*Rechtskrafterstreckung*). Whereas the AG explicitly excludes third parties not involved in the proceedings, since their right to be heard has not been respected, the ECJ does not comment on this question despite referring directly to the AG (recital 39), although it limits the effects 'on those who have concluded with that seller or supplier a contract'.

The submission of the Hungarian court does not require that a distinction be drawn between the two forms of extension of *res judicata*, as the relevant Hungarian law does not include third parties. The addressee of the extension of *res judicata* is the same user of the term, not the term itself declared as illegal, even if the incriminated contract is applied literally identical by another businessman.

However, the ECJ's formulation in recital 40 leaves more leeway (open wording) and would make it theoretically possible to extend the *effet utile* to the term, regardless of the original user, e.g., if a Member State wants to use some sort of system of *ex parte* court order by which each and every trader has to abstain from using the banned terms on penalty of fines or other sanctions, that seems to be up to that Member State. It is hardly comprehensible why a user, who applies the same incriminated term, should be allowed to refer to a 'legitimate interest'. The reading of the AG might be in line with the Member States' laws where every extension of *res judicata* is met with suspicion. It has to be made equally clear that the distinction which the AG so forcefully underlines stands in the way of the overall development of a common approach to the two fields of law. It still reflects elements of traditional private law thinking, where not the practice but the contract is regarded as the key element in deciding on the potential effects of an unfair term.

The argument could be made that context matters and that a term may be valid under certain circumstances and invalid under others. This argument goes to the heart of the distinction between blacklisted terms and those whose validity has to be assessed under the general fairness test. I would argue that blacklisted terms serve to clean the market and that there is no room for taking particular circumstances into account, similar to the interpretation of the black list in the Unfair Commercial Practices directive.

4.4 The Extension of Res Judicata *as a Minimum Requirement for Member States*

Are Member States now *obliged* to introduce *erga omnes* effect to actions for injunctions declaring a contract term to be unfair or are they only *entitled* to do so as the Directive lays down minimum requirements only? Let us recall what AG Trstenjak said:

> They [these unfair terms] can therefore be combated effectively only if the decision of the national court finding a particular term to be unfair is accorded fairly wide applicability (51).
>
> Consequently, the national provision in question meets the requirement of 'effectiveness' set out in Article 7(2) of Directive 93/13(58).

The ECJ argues in a similar direction (recitals 37, 39, 38 reprinted above):

> In this respect, it should be added that the deterrent nature and dissuasive purpose of the measures to be adopted, together with their independence of any particular dispute, mean that such actions may be brought even though the terms which it is sought to have prohibited have not been used in specific contracts (see *Commission v Italy*, paragraph 15) (37).
>
> [...] It should be noted that, as the Advocate General pointed out in points 57 to 61 of her Opinion, national legislation such as that referred to in the present paragraph satisfies the requirements of Article 6(1), read in conjunction with Article 7(1) and (2), of the Directive (39).

The opinion of the AG and the ECJ judgment read together suggest that the Member States are under an obligation to extend *res judicata* beyond the contracting parties. Both seem to start from the premise that adequate and effective protection under Article 7 cannot be limited to the parties to the dispute but must include all those who have concluded a consumer contract with the same supplier. A certain uncertainty results from the operative provisions of the judgment. Both the AG and the ECJ formulate: 'Article 6(1) of Directive 93/13, read in conjunction with Article 7(1) and (2) thereof, must be interpreted as meaning that: – it does not preclude the declaration of invalidity of an unfair term included in the standard terms of consumer contracts in an action for an injunction.' This formula does not find any equivalent in the judgment, where the minimum character of the Directive and the potential link to the extension of *res judicata* is not discussed. One might therefore wonder whether further clarification is needed in order to decide the mandatory character of the extension to third parties. Even if the Member States are obliged to introduce an extension of *res judicata*, they have substantial leeway in how to shape the extension. This goes together with the principle of procedural autonomy as stressed by the AG (recital 38).

4.5 Ex officio

Whereas the discussion of the reach of the extension of *res judicata* remains bound to a distinction between contract law and commercial practices, the drumbeat gives rise to immediate consequences. In full agreement with the AG, the ECJ transfers the ex officio jurisdiction in individual proceedings developed with regard to Article 6 of Directive 93/13/EEC to the extension of the *res judicata* rule in collective proceedings under Article 7 of Directive 93/13/EEC. Recital 43 reads (open wording):

> It follows that, where the unfair nature of a term included in the GBC of consumer contracts has been recognised in an action for injunction, such as that here at issue in the main proceedings, the national courts are required, of their own motion, and also as regards the future, to draw all the consequences provided for by national law in order to ensure that consumers who have concluded a contract to which those GBC apply will not be bound by that term. [emphasis H-W M]

'Drawing the necessary consequences' in combination with 'of their own motion' must be read as an obligation imposed on national judges to investigate the potential extension of *res judicata*. Hence § 11 UKlaG, which requires the consumer to refer to a decision of a German court in an action for injunction where the identical contract term has been declared unfair, is destined for the wastepaper basket.[37] Therefore after *Invitel* a consumer does not have to examine and judge whether the incriminated term is already the subject of a procedure concerning an action for injunction or of an identical individual procedure. It is not for the consumer to raise this objection, but for the responsible court to gain an overview ex officio. Neither the ECJ nor the AG distinguishes with regard to the extension of *res judicata* between decisions of lower courts or high courts. Even the consumer as a third-party beneficiary can expect the higher court to re-visit a decision of a favourable lower court decision. Therefore, an extension of binding legal force would be sensible for final judgments only.

National legislators are not only required to introduce the ex officio requirement, but also to reflect on how the court can manage the ex officio duty imposed by EU law. De facto the ECJ obliges the Member States to provide a list, which has to name the term as well as the user. Otherwise the responsible court cannot meet the parameters. Should the user of unfair terms remain hidden, as it is the case in a number of national procedural laws, the responsible court can only revert to the term, which raises complex questions about the extension of *res judicata* to third parties. The original proposal of Directive 2011/83/EC on the rights of consumers contained exactly such a mechanism.[38] The suggested extension of

37 Comment on the ECJ judgment by Ebers LMK 2012, 333520 beck online EuGH: Missbräuchlichkeit einer Preisanpassungsklausel und Wirkung von Unterlassungsurteilen, Klocke, Rechtsfortbildung im und am Unterlassungsklagegesetz, VuR.2013, 203.

38 COM (2008) 614 final art 39.

res judicata raises complicated issues on European standards of accessibility of national judgments. There will certainly be follow-up references.

4.6 Beyond the Action for Injunction – Skimming-Off Procedures

Far less spectacular are the statements in the judgments concerning collective remedies to skim off unlawful profits. The AG and the ECJ agree that Article 7(2) of Directive 93/13/EEC does not require an elimination of the consequential effects. Conversely, the Member States are free to take this step at national level, since the Directive only provides minimum requirements for legal redress. Neither the AG nor the ECJ dealt with the meaning of the word 'prevent'. The AG restricts the sense to mean the transfer from the individual to the collective level (recital 37). The term 'prevent' could also be interpreted in a way that it is incumbent on the Member States not only to ensure the protection of third consumers, who are faced with the identical terms of the same businessman, but also to prevent once and for all further debates on the consequential effects. Such a reading would also cover the skimming off of unlawful profits. An additional support is provided by Article 47 of the EU Charter of Fundamental Rights (in the following: Charter).

5. Striving for *Individual* Rights against Unfair Commercial Practices

5.1 Gaps in the Enforcement of Unfair Commercial Practices

When it comes to remedies in contract law, the reach and content of individual remedies are at the forefront of the analysis. This is different in the field of unfair commercial practices due to the traditional understanding of unfair commercial practices as public law meant to regulate the behaviour of market participants. It is then for public authorities or associations with a quasi-public mandate to survey the market.

If any, an independent legal remedy could be deduced from Article 5(1) of Directive 2005/29/EC, maybe in conjunction with Article 7(4) which in my understanding grants the consumer an individual right.[39] The potential effects of such a right would be rather limited, though, as they remain bound to the requirements of Article 7(4) – the so-called existence of an invitation to purchase.[40]

The remedial gap in the protection of *individual* rights existing between Directive 2005/29/EC on unfair B2C commercial practice and Directive 93/13/EEC on unfair terms in consumer contracts can be closed by reverting to the European Union's fundamental rights. Let us recall where the problem lies: under EU law the consumer who is a victim of an unfair commercial practices has no

39 See Münchener Kommentar zum UWG-Micklitz (2nd edition to be published 2013), art 11 Rndr. 18 under reference to Apostolopoulos WRP 2004, 841.

40 The ECJ has already provided its understanding of art 7(4) in Case C-122/10 – *Konsumentombudsmannen* nnr.

European remedy to get out of a contract in which he or she was drawn into. The common understanding is that it is for the Member States to designate the appropriate remedies to the consumer. In practice this may lead to a situation where the consumer has difficulties applying national contractual remedies to constellations in which the true problem results from misleading or unfair commercial practices. Collective redress via an action of injunction does not help him or her as the consumer does not benefit from a court decision which declares a particular commercial act as misleading or unfair. He or she remains largely dependent on the national laws and the degree to which they allow the recovery of the ill-gotten gains which result from unfair terms or unfair commercial practices.

I will first embark on individual rights of a consumer affected by a misleading and unfair commercial practice in this contractual commitment before I will address the much more complicated issue of if and how an action for injunction against unfair and misleading advertising might affect the contractual rights of individual consumers – the transfer of *Invitel* to the field of unfair commercial practices.

5.2 Constitutionalization of Remedies

Constitutionalization concerns the concretization of the European Union's principle of effectiveness with a view to EU consumer law remedies. In Article 47 of the Charter, which since 1.12.2009 has the same legal value as the EU treaties (Article 6(1) TEU), it is formulated as follows:[41]

> (1) Everyone whose rights and freedoms guaranteed by the law of the Union are violated has the right to an effective remedy before a tribunal in compliance with the conditions laid down in this Article.

This is completed by Article 19(1) 2 TEU:

> Member States shall provide remedies sufficient to ensure effective legal protection in the fields covered by Union law.

According to Article 51 of the Charter, fundamental rights apply with respect to all measures of the European Union and Member States when they are implementing EU law. In case of the interpretation of EU law by the Member States' courts, they have to be taken into consideration.[42]

The principle of effectiveness of Article 47 of the Charter has already found its concretization in more recent decisions of the ECJ. It applies in all fields where EU

41 As to the general meaning cf. N Reich, *Individueller und kollektiver Rechtsschutz im EU-Verbraucherrecht*, Schriften der Juristischen Studiengesellschaft Hannover Nr. 51, Baden-Baden: Nomos 2012, 19 et seq.

42 ECJ, Judgment of 27.6.2006, Case C-540/03 *EP v Rat*, ECR 2006 I-5769 recital 105 concerning the Directive 2003/86/EC of 22.9.2003 on the right to family reunification.

law creates individual rights. The principle *ibi ius ibi remedium*[43] was confirmed, but what it means *in concerto* depends on a whole variety of factors. Hence it was of consequence when the ECJ invoked Article 47 to develop legal remedies at the EU level even before the EU Charter on Fundamental Rights became formally valid.[44] This was, for example, the case with regard to the *Unibet* decision concerning legal standing in 2007[45] and the 2008 *Kadi* decision concerning the legal redress of so-called terrorists incriminated by the UN Security Council.[46] The subsequent decisions in *Alassini* of 2010[47] concerning the shaping of out-of-court settlements to enforce consumer rights in the field of telecommunications, *Mono-Car-Styling*[48] regarding the enforcement of the employees' right to information in case of collective redundancy and *DEB*[49] relating to legal aid already show a tendency towards a 'constitutionalization of legal remedies'. EU consumer law benefits from this too: According to Article 24(1) of Directive 2011/83/EC on consumer rights[50] and in terms of the positively interpreted principle of effectiveness, '(t) he penalties provided for must be effective, proportionate and dissuasive'. This wording belongs to the standard repertoire of the EU legislative authority.

The application of these principles to the interplay between the law on unfair commercial practices and law on unfair contract terms results in the claim that a consumer, who has been the victim of an unfair commercial practice, has to have the right to free himself from any *disadvantageous contractual consequences*. Otherwise there would be no 'effective legal redress' in terms of Article 19(1) 2 TFEU. Thus it concerns a kind of claim of confiscating unlawful profits,[51] though in the form of individual redress. Within the limits of the promoted coherent interpretation the distinction between contract law and unfair commercial practices

---

43 In this context the fundamental essay of V Gerven, 'Of Rights, Remedies, and Procedures' (2000) *CMLRev* 501, who requires 'adequate remedies'; also V Trstenjak and E Beysen, 'European Consumer Protection Law: *Curia semper dabit remedium?*' (2011) *CMLRev* 95, 119.

44 The EU Charter on Fundamental Rights became formally valid with the coming into force of the Lisbon Treaty on 1.12.2009.

45 ECJ, Judgment of 13.3.2007, Case C-432/05 Unibet v Justiekansleren, ECR 2007, I-2271 recital 37.

46 ECJ, Judgment of 3.9.2008, Case C-402 + 415/05P, Kadi et al v Rat der EU, ECR 2008, I-6351 recital 335.

47 ECJ, Judgment of 18.3.2010, Case C-317–320/08 Rosalba Alassini et al. v. Telecom Italia, ECR 2010, I-2213 recital 61.

48 ECJ, Judgment of 16.7.2009, Case C-12/08, ECR 2009 I-6653, para 47.

49 ECJ, Judgment of 22.12.2010, Case C-279/09 *DEB Deutsche Energiehandels- und Beratungsgesellschaft mbH v Bundesrepublik Deutschland* [2010] ECR I-nyr recital 31.

50 Official Journal of the EU, No L 304/64 of 22.11.2011.

51 In this context see H-W Micklitz, before § 1 UKlG recital 43, § 1 UKlaG recital 5/6 with reference to the '*effet utile*' of Directive 93/13/EEC and Klocke, loc. cit.

can be overcome. In *Invitel* in recitals 42–43 the ECJ focuses on the principle of effectiveness:

> 42 National courts which find that a term included in [the] GBC is unfair are required under Article 6(1) of the Directive to draw all the consequences that follow under national law, so that the consumer is not bound by that term (see *Pereničová and Perenič*, paragraph 30 and case law cited).
>
> 43 It follows that, where the unfair nature of a term included in the GBC of consumer contracts has been recognised in an action for an injunction, such as that here at issue in the main proceedings, the national courts are required, of their own motion, and also as regards the future, to draw all the consequences provided for by national law in order to ensure that consumers who have concluded a contract to which those GBC apply will not be bound by that term.

The broad wording could be considered as an implicit claim for remedial action that allows for eliminating the potential effects of the unlawful commercial act. However, eliminating the effects relate to the 'non-binding' part – so payments made on the basis of an invalid term must be paid back. Such restitutionary remedies do not constitute necessarily actions for skimming off similar to skimming off in e.g., competition law. The ECJ is not advocating the introduction of a fully-fledged skimming off of profits derived from partially invalid contracts, all that can be deduced from the relevant ECJ judgments is that the Member States must introduce some sort of payback system. Such a remedy has to be arranged by national law, but it cannot be completely rejected. This is the logical and binding consequence of the invalidity of the incriminated term and thus a concretization of Article 47 of the Charter in conjunction with Article 19(1)2 TEU.

6. Towards a Common Approach to Unfair Terms and Unfair Commercial Practices

In all likelihood Member States will try to restrict the effects of both decisions on the law of unfair terms, that is to say how the legal position of the consumer with regard to unfair terms is affected by unfair commercial practices. However, there is good reason to reflect in light of *Pereničova* and *Invitel* more systematically on the degree to which a common approach can be developed with regard to the effects of the two areas of law. *Pereničova* cuts across the boundaries of contract law and commercial practices law. However, its impact is yet limited. Unfair commercial practices are just one factor among others to decide over the unfairness of contract terms. The more far-reaching question is what are the potential effects of unfair commercial practices, which are 'prohibited, on contract terms'? Is it possible to give a verdict on a prohibited commercial practice a more general meaning? In that it affects the assessment of unfairness in contract law? Can there be deviating standards on unfairness in the law on unfair commercial practices and the law on unfair terms? If the answer is no – what the ECJ seems to argue – is there a 'general' effect on commercial practices which are 'prohibited' on contract terms?

Does the assessment of unfairness in the law on commercial practices 'infect' the fairness of contract terms, generally? Does this extend beyond all boundaries of individual litigation and individual circumstances?

This is the first issue I would like to analyse in more detail. The second concerns whether and to what extent it is possible to use *Invitel* as an argument to discuss an extension of *res judicata* for actions of injunctions on unfair commercial practices to unfair contract terms. By now *Invitel* remains within the boundaries of Directive 93/13/EEC. It concerns the extension of *res judicata* of contract terms which have been declared unfair in an action for injunction to individual litigation. Then pushing the issue further ahead, the question arises whether the action for injunction in the field of unfair commercial advertising produces some sort of a 'general effect' which reaches beyond the 'prohibited' unfair commercial practices and covers contract terms which are infected by the commercial practices.

Both proceedings might give important thought-provoking impulses.[52] Before delving deeper into the questions, however, it has to be recalled that there are important conceptual differences between the two Directives, respectively the two fields of law. The law on unfair commercial practices differs from that of Directive 93/13/EEC, since Directive 2005/29/EC is not addressing the individual consumer. The individual dimension can only be read into the law on unfair commercial practices by using fundamental rights rhetoric. Its focus lies rather on the collective level, on regulating the market behaviour of the participants. So it seems as if the law on unfair commercial practices is perhaps not only, but mainly to be regarded as collective regulation. The law on unfair terms starts exactly from the opposite premise. The focus lies on individual litigation where the contracting parties enjoy contractual remedies to challenge unfair terms. The collective litigation was added later and took shape only in the last 25 years of the last millennium. At the collective level the parallel between the two fields seems more obvious. A certain bias remains – the law on unfair commercial practices is going to be individualized, this means its effects on contractual relations are becoming ever clearer; the law on unfair terms is already collectivized, a development which has gone on for a couple decades now, but which never triggered a systematic analysis and the linkage between the collective and the individual dimension.

A common approach to the two fields first and foremost requires us to compare the respective rules in the two Directives regulating the effect of 'unfairness'. Article 6 of Directive 93/13/EEC does not have a direct counterpart in Directive 2005/29/EC, at least not explicitly. But there is more. What is equally needed is to take a hard look at the distinction between the individual versus the collective dimension of unfair commercial practices and unfair terms, a distinction which concerns rights, remedies and effects.

Translated into a table, the solved and the unsolved issues are more easily captured.

52 As to the relation of the law on unfair commercial terms and contract law for example with regard to misleading vs. malice, see S Whittaker, 'Form and Substance in the Reception of EC Directives into English Contract Law' 381.

Table 7.1 A Table of Problems

	UCTD (Unfair Contract Terms Directive)	Common Approach (*Pereničova/Invitel*)	UCPD (Unfair Commercial Practices Directive)
Substance individualized	Unfair Good faith Significant imbalance	*Pereničova* Coherent interpretation Art 4(1) 'gateway'	Unfair/misleading/ aggressive Problem: no such thing as 'individual commercial advertising', but what about 'sales promotion'?*
Substance standardized	Unfair Good faith Significant imbalance	Coherent interpretation Art 4(1) and (2) applicable to standard terms? Commission v Sweden?	Unfair/misleading/ aggressive commercial practices Collective regulation *per definitionem*
Procedure/ effects Individual relations	Contractual remedies Term is 'not binding' Art 6	Towards a common approach via constitutionalization Art 47 Charter	Individual rights to stop unfair commercial practices? Effects on individual contract? Right to withdrawal? Contrary to Art 3(2) and Art 11 UCPD
Procedure/ effects Extension of res judicata Ex officio	Action for injunction Art 6(1) 'not binding' applicable to Art 7(2) *Invitel* Minimum standard? Mandatory	UCTD extension from collective to individual (*Invitel*) UCPD extension to UCTD (across subjects)	Action for injunction Art 5 'shall be prohibited' Problem: what does this imply?

Note: *There is a case pending exactly on this issue, Case C-388/13 – U*PC Magyarország Kft. v Nemzeti Fogyasztóvédelmi Hatóság*.

6.1 Effects of Collectively Prohibited Unfair Commercial Practices on Standardized Contractual Relations?

The question is whether and to what extent unfair commercial practices, which are judicially prohibited, may have an impact on contracts. So what is at stake is the supra-individual variant of the constellation in the *Pereničova* case. Do unfair commercial practices affect consumer contracts per se? But there is more. It is not only the effect of unfair commercial practices which has to be discussed but also the potential remedies for consumers who have suffered from the conclusion of undesirable contracts, individually and collectively. Here we face a kind of claim to remedial action *sui generis*. In *Putz/Weber* the ECJ embarked exactly upon this path.

The first issue is the determination of the potential effects. We would again encounter the *Pereničova* decision, but with the particularity that the illegality of the incriminated commercial practice has already been determined. Let us presume that the factual circumstances underlying the *Pereničova* case are not an isolated case, but a strategy on a massive scale. The competent bodies which enjoy standing launch an action for injunction. The court finds the commercial practice to be unfair. Can the assessment of the illegality of an incorrect interest rate have a positive impact on all consumers who concluded a contract with the same bank due to the same advertising?

Article 5(1) of Directive 2005/29/EC formulates in an apodictic way: 'Unfair commercial practices shall be prohibited.' The parallel to Article 101 TFEU immediately springs to mind: 'Any agreements or decisions prohibited pursuant to this Article shall be automatically void.' 'Shall be prohibited' refers to the illegality of the incriminated commercial practice. Seen through the lens of a collective regulation, commercial practices can only be illegal if they cannot be void. The picture looks different if we change perspective and look for the potential effects of an unfair commercial practice. It seems as if the verdict of illegality is inherently bound to the question of a possible extension. This means the effects only become clear when one does not look at the unfair commercial practice itself but at the effects it produces on consumer contracts. We will come back in regards to the analysis of Article 11 of Directive 2005/29/EC.

The second issue concerns the links between the potential effect and the existence of remedies. The wording of Article 101 TFEU served the ECJ in *Courage*[53] to establish an independent claim for damages in favour not only of business but also of the individual consumer. Does it make sense to reflect on a remedy as a logical consequence of the effects of 'shall be prohibited'? With regard to individual remedies Article 47 of the Constitutional Charter seems to be a more promising avenue. But what about collective rights? Here the remedy

---

53 ECJ, Judgment of 20.9.2001, C-453/99 *Courage Ltd v Crehan*, ECR 2001, I-6297 recital 26.

that would make sense is a skimming-off action to recover the ill-gotten gains or a court-ordered restitution to individual consumers.

6.2 Extension of Res Judicata *through Reference to Article 11 of Directive 2005/29/EC?*

Already the question is bold: extension of *res judicata* not only from the collective to the individual action in unfair terms, but from collective actions for injunction in unfair commercial practices to collective action for injunction in unfair contract terms – and from there via *Invitel* to individual actions in unfair contract terms? The justification for such an attempt should be found in the idea of a common approach, an approach which joins the two areas of the law together and which starts from the premise that the statement of unfairness cannot so easily be broken down into boxes, in order to deprive it from its beneficial effects to consumers.

A certain support for a grand solution, a collective expansion of binding legal force could be provided by Article 11(1), which reads as follows:

> Member States shall ensure that adequate and effective means exist to combat unfair commercial practices in order to enforce compliance with the provisions of this Directive in the interest of consumers.

Article 11 is about the action for injunction. In light of *Invitel*, an appropriate and efficient means with regard to the law on unfair commercial practices can include at least two levels: a finding of the unfairness and the future elimination of the unlawful state of affairs. These two forms can also be found in the law on unfair commercial practices.

Article 11(2) contrasts

> cessation of unfair commercial practices' in paragraph (a) with the preventive prohibition in paragraph (b), as long as 'the unfair commercial practice has not yet been carried out.

In comparison to Article 7 of Directive 93/13/EEC, this formulation is weak. Nevertheless, it is worthwhile to think about the possible implications of the distinction in the light of both ECJ decisions.

7. Conclusion

The analysis of the two recent judgments demonstrates a certain inclination to a common approach of the two fields of law; an approach which can be characterized by the regulatory technique of an inverted pyramid, where the blacklists serve to clear markets, where a common approach is defined by setting differences between standardized and non-standardized practices aside, where individual redress stands side by side with the collective action for injunction, where *res judicata* is extended in unfair terms, where a minimum of standards in unfair commercial practices can be recognised; last but not least where courts are ex officio requested to test the possible extension of *res judicata*.

It will still require a series of further preliminary references before the importance of *Invitel* and *Pereničova* for the interplay of the law on unfair terms and the law on unfair commercial practices becomes tangible. Both decisions open a new chapter in the discussion about the arrangement of the individual-collective legal redress in the interplay of the law on unfair terms and the law on unfair commercial practices. It is to be hoped that consumer agencies and consumer associations will participate actively in the process of Europeanization instead of restricting themselves to free-riding or mere defensive strategies.

Bibliography

Bakardjieva A, *Fair Trading in Flux: National Legacies, Institutional Choice and the Process of Europeanisation* (Stockholm: Stockholms Universitet, 2005).

Beysen E and V Trstenjak, 'European Consumer Protection Law: Curia semper dabit remedium?' (2011) 9 *CMLRev*, 95.

Commission Communication, *Towards a European Horizontal Framework for Collective Redress* COM (2013) 401/2.

Dahl B, *Consumer Legislation in Denmark* (New York and London: Van Nostrand Reinhold, 1981).

Docekal P, P Kolba, H-W Micklitz and P Rott, 'Verbraucherschutz durch Unterlassungsklagen, Rechtliche und Praktische Umsetzung der Richtlinie Unterlassungsklagen 98/27/EG in den Mitgliedstaaten' (2007) *VIEW Schriftenreihe*, Band 17.

Gerven WV, 'Of Rights, Remedies, and Procedures' (2000) 37 *CMLRev* 501–536.

Grundmann S and M Schauer, *The Architecture of European Codes and Contract Law* (Alphen aan den Rijn: Kluwer Law International, 2006).

Hodges C, *The Reform of Class and Representative Actions in European Legal Systems, A New Framework for Collective Redress in Europe* (Oxford: Hart Publishing, 2009).

Höland A and C Meller-Hannich, *Gutachten Evaluierung der Effektivität kollektiver Rechtsschutzinstrumente* (Bonn: Bundesministerium für Ernährung, Landwirtschaft und Verbraucherschutz (BMELV), 2011).

Knieper R, 'Möglichkeiten und Grenzen der Verpflanzbarkeit von Recht. Juristische Zusammenarbeit aus der Sicht eines Beraters' (2008) 72 *RabelsZ* 88–113.

Micklitz H-W, 'Reforming European Union Unfair Terms Legislation in Consumer Contracts' (2010) *ECRL* 347.

———, *Münchener Kommentar zum UWG-Micklitz* (2nd edition, C.H. Beck, 2013).

Micklitz H-W and N Reich, 'AGB-Recht und UWG :: (endlich) ein Ende des Kästchendenkens nach EuGH Perenieova und Invitel?' (2012) 23(7) *EuZW* 257–264.

———, 'Von der Mißbrauchs- zur Marktkontrolle' (2013) *EuZW* 457.

Micklitz H-W, N Reich and P Rott, *Understanding EU Consumer Law* (Antwerp: Intersentia, 2009).

Reich N, *Individueller und kollektiver Rechtsschutz im EU-Verbraucherrecht* (Schriften der Juristischen Studiengesellschaft Hannover, Nr. 51. Baden-Baden: Nomos, 2012).

Schmid C, 'The Instrumentalist Conception of the Acquis Communautaire in Consumer Law and Its Implications on a European Contract Law Code' (2005) *European Review of Contract Law* 211–227.

Schmid C-U, *Die Instrumentalisierung des Privatrechts durch die Europäische Union: Privatrecht und Privatrechtskonzeptionen in der Entwicklung der Europäischen Integrationsverfassung* (Baden-Baden: Nomos, 2010).

Stadler A, 'Grenzüberschreitender kollektiver Rechtsschutz in Europa Zuerst ersch' (2009) 64(3) *Juristenzeitung* 121–133.

Stadler A and H-W Micklitz, *Verbandsklage in der Informations- und Dienstleistungsgesellschaft* (Münster-Hiltrup: Landwirtschaftsverl, 2005).

Whittaker S, 'Form and Substance in the Reception of EC Directives into English Contract Law' (2007) 3 *European Review of Contract Law* 381.

PART IV
Enforcement

Chapter 8
Law and Economics of Enforcing Misleading Advertising Laws: Incentives of Bona and Mala Fide Traders Assessed[1]

Franziska Weber

1. Introduction

Misleading advertisements, such as for ring tones, being a typical example of an unfair commercial practice have over the past years caused substantial harm to European consumers, and to society. This is particularly so because in many cases the enforcement response given a legal breach is slow or does not happen at all. The harm is typically trifling for the individual, but widespread.[2] A discrepancy can be observed between mala fide and bona fide traders. While the latter inadvertently breaches the law, rogue traders' interests lie in the short-term profit generated by illegal activity. They do not mind changing sectors and try to hide, abusing current loopholes in the legal system. The gap between both types of traders is arguably increasing and so are the profits of the mala fide traders, not least due to new technologies that facilitate their operations; most prominently the internet. There

---

1 This chapter strongly builds upon F Weber, 'Abusing Loopholes in the Legal System – Efficiency Considerations of Differentiated Law Enforcement Approaches in Misleading Advertising' (2012) 5(4) *Erasmus Law Review*, and is partly extracted from F Weber, *The Law and Economics of Enforcing European Consumer Law. A Comparative Analysis of Package Travel and Misleading Advertising* (Markets and the Law Series, Ashgate, 2014). The latter contains an even more in depth study of enforcement of misleading advertisement, including a comparative legal assessment.

I wish to thank the participants of the workshop 'Experiencing the Unfair Commercial Practices Directive' (Durham, December 2012), of the German Association of Law and Economics Annual Meeting (Magdeburg, October 2012) and of my seminar: 'Abusing Loopholes in the Legal System – Efficiency Considerations of Differentiated Law Enforcement Approaches in Misleading Advertising, Amsterdam Centre for the Study of European Contract Law – Consumer Law Series' (Amsterdam, March 2013) for their valuable comments.

2 In contrast, see F Weber, 'Assessing Existing Enforcement Mechanisms in Consumer Law – The Unavailability of an Allrounder' (2011) 3 *Swedish Journal of European Law (Europarättslig tidskrift)* 536–554. It illustrates the considerations for a high damage case.

is a high potential for keeping one's anonymity when operating via the internet – it renders it difficult to verify the seat of the traders' business premises.[3]

This chapter deals with the efficient design of enforcement mechanisms addressing misleading advertising laws. Enforcement is crucial to induce individuals to law-abiding behaviour. The goal is to add to the knowledge on design requirements for optimal enforcement solutions, particularly in terms of players that need to be involved. The Unfair Commercial Practices (UCP) Directive leaves national legislators with considerable discretion regarding the enforcement and the provisions, and institutions involved in the countries thus vary and not in all countries the optimal balance might have been struck yet.[4]

In line with the law and economics approach, enforcement shall be discussed from the point of view of deterrence theory. According to this theory, the incentives of a (potential) wrongdoer to break the law can be eliminated if the sanction for her wrongdoing multiplied by the probability of detection and the dependent probabilities of apprehension and conviction are at least equal to her benefits from a violation.[5] The prevention perspective can furthermore add to deterrence.[6] The aim of this chapter is not to advocate perfect, but rather optimal, enforcement. The

3 A recent National Audit Office report has identified the costs to consumers, and hence the economy, of sharp practices as £6.6 billion in the United Kingdom. As reasons for Consumer Protection Cooperation (CPC) regulation facilitating cross-border cooperation in certain consumer law violations: (at that time) Health and Consumer Protection Commissioner David Byrne said: 'Catching rogue traders is hard enough in a single Member State but it becomes almost impossible when they relocate to another country', Press releases RAPID, 'No Hiding Place for Rogue Traders: Commission Proposes EU-wide Network of National Watchdogs' (22 July 2003) http://europa.eu/rapid/press-release_IP-03–1067_en.htm?locale=en. Cross-border problems are growing as rogue traders adapt to new technologies and opportunities. For example, the European Advertising Standards Alliance (EASA) estimates that around 63% of the cross-border complaints received between 1992 and 2002 concerned rogue or peripheral traders, and this rises to about 86% for direct mail. As will be set out, this research is restricted to case studies on traders that hide within the countries while traders hiding behind country borders are likewise increasingly a problem.

4 See art 10 on enforcement of the Directive 2005/29/EC of the European Parliament and of the Council of 11 May 2005 concerning unfair business-to-consumer commercial practices in the internal market and amending Council Directive 84/450/EEC, Directives 97/7/EC, 98/27/EC and 2002/65/EC of the European Parliament and of the Council and Regulation (EC) No 2006/2004 of the European Parliament and of the Council ('Unfair Commercial Practices Directive'). See also the contribution in this volume of Marios Koutsias and Christopher Willett ('UK Implementation of the Unfair Commercial Practices Directive'). Also in this volume, Dörte Poelzig, 'Private or Public Enforcement of the UCP Directive? Sanctions and Remedies to Prevent Unfair Commercial Practices', refers more specifically to the requirements that the UCP Directive stipulates in terms of enforcement.

5 See GS Becker, 'Crime and Punishment: An Economic Approach' (1986) 76 *Journal of Political Economy* 169–217.

6 See S Shavell 'The Optimal Structure of Law Enforcement' (1993) 36 *Journal of Law and Economics* 255–288; T Friehe and A Tabbach, 'Preventive Enforcement' (2013) 35 *International Review of Law and Economics*.

cost perspective is considered and the level of enforcement that society considers desirable shall be found. Different institutions have different sanctions at their availability and their respective powers influence the probabilities of detecting a wrong and apprehending and convicting someone. Common European definitions of the following enforcement solutions shall be discussed: private – via the civil court or Consumer Alternative Dispute Resolution (CADR) – and public law enforcement – via an administrative agency or a criminal court, same as self-regulatory systems. Aside from individual litigation, the costs and benefits of various types of group litigation as a procedural tool will be assessed.[7] In order to come to conclusions on the enforcement mechanisms, the efficiency of substantive law need not be evaluated.

The two mentioned types of traders calculate with differently high benefits. Consequently they are to be deterred by different means that call for a differentiated approach in legal responses and institutions involved. Throughout the chapter, two hypothetical case studies – a bona fide and a mala fide trader case scenario (to be set out) – within misleading advertisement shall illustrate what is needed from the enforcement side. Path dependency explains why no one-size-fits-all solutions are available in the European Union, and the chapter aims at providing a set of design requirements that can be adapted to the respective legal system, particularly in terms of the players that need to be involved.[8]

After this introduction, an analytical framework is set out (Section 2) whose parameters are applied when assessing the value of different enforcement mechanisms, specifically in the case of misleading advertising (Section 3). This application leads to design suggestions for optimally mixing the enforcement mechanisms (Section 4). The chapter ends with some conclusions (Section 5).

2. The Framework

In order to evaluate existing enforcement mechanisms and their value in relation to misleading advertising, a framework is needed. The analysis follows three stages. The first stage of the analysis aims to verify that victims are put into a situation to potentially initiate lawsuits, which are desirable from a social welfare point of view.[9] The initiation of enforcement processes (in many instances) is dependent on private parties' actions. In order for this to happen, the risk involved in litigation has to be spread in an efficient way. In other words, risk allocation has to be optimized.

---

7 For the remainder of the chapter these different enforcement solutions shall be labelled 'enforcement mechanisms'.

8 See P Legrand, 'European Legal Systems Are Not Converging' (1996) 45 *International and Comparative Law Quarterly* 52–81; K Heine and W Kerber, 'European Corporate Laws, Regulatory Competition and Path Dependence' (2002) 13 *European Journal of Law and Economics* 47–71; AI Ogus, 'The Economic Basis of Legal Culture: Networks and Monopolization' (2002) 22(3) *Oxford Journal of Legal Studies* 419–434.

9 The upcoming analysis shall embark from the standard assumption of risk-aversion.

Three factors will be assessed at this stage: The first factor is the 'rational apathy' problem. The rational individual, in some situation, will not sue, as the costs outbalance the benefits for her.[10] As there is a divergence between the individual and social incentive to sue, this might happen despite a lawsuit being in society's interest.[11] The 'free-riding' problem can occur if, in certain situations in which many victims suffer from a law infringement but all gain as soon as one of them sues, it is efficient for everybody to wait for someone else to sue and then profit from the result.[12] A third factor concerns 'funding' options. The amount of the monetary investment that someone has to make when it comes to litigation obviously influences the degree of risks that one feels when involving in litigation and the amount of money needed or available – funding – will be decisive for the risks that one will bear (this can, for example, be influenced by legal aid or insurances[13]).

The second stage concerns the incentives. Optimal deterrence induces the efficient amount of wrongdoers not to violate the law. To achieve this level of deterrence any actor involved in the enforcement process (individuals, enforcers such as judges or public agencies) has to be induced with incentives to guarantee this enforcement process. Here information asymmetries are assessed that have implications on the incentives for the behaviour of the better- and worse-informed parties which can lead to inefficiencies in that the desirable enforcement level is not achieved. In turn, a potential wrongdoer is not induced to welfare-enhancing behaviour. This factor primarily refers to characteristics of the products or services, but then also to the characteristics of the parties. It can result in low probabilities of detecting legal violations or convicting wrongdoers. Capture is another incentive problem, meaning the exertion of influence on, for instance, the public administration that can lead to public officials pursuing industry interests.[14]

---

10 See R Van den Bergh, 'Should Consumer Protection Law Be Publicly Enforced?', in WH van Boom and MBM Loos (eds), *Collective Enforcement of Consumer Law* (2007) 184.

11 See WM Landes and RA Posner, 'The Private Enforcement of Law' (1975) 4(1) *Journal of Legal Studies* 33; H-B Schäfer, 'The Bundling of Similar Interests in Litigation. The Incentives for Class Action and Legal Actions Taken by Associations' (2000) 9(3) *European Journal of Law and Economics* 195; G Howells and S Weatherill, *Consumer Protection Law* (2nd edn, 2005) 604; N Garoupa, 'Optimal Law Enforcement When Victims Are Rational Players' (2001) 2 *Economics of Governance* 233, as to the factors that motivate individuals. Please note that this category also fits under the first stage. F Cafaggi and H-W Micklitz, *New Frontiers of Consumer Protection – The Interplay Between Private and Public Enforcement* (2009).

12 See R Van den Bergh and LT Visscher, 'The Preventive Function of Collective Actions for Damages in Consumer Law' (2008) 1 *Erasmus Law Review* 14; Landes and Posner (1975) 29.

13 See WH van Boom, *Efficacious Enforcement in Contract and Tort* (2006) 48.

14 See AI Ogus, *Regulation: Legal Form and Economic Theory* (1994) 57. In particular attention has to be paid to the life cycles of agencies; C Hood, H Rothstein and R Baldwin, *The Government of Risk: Understanding Risk Regulation Regimes* (1st edn, 2001)

People's incentives might be diluted by other personal interests. There are cases in which instead of the suing party the defendant turns out to be the victim – the victim of a 'frivolous lawsuit' that is not based on merits and socially not desirable.[15] The reason is a misallocation of incentives. Error costs refer to, for example, courts arriving at mistaken decisions.[16] They can generally be divided in two groups: Error I costs are those that occur when an individual who is guilty might mistakenly not be found liable ('mistaken acquittal').[17] Error II costs on the other hand occur if an innocent individual might mistakenly be found liable ('mistaken conviction'). Both cases dilute deterrence and consequently reduce efficiency. A weakness inherent to, for example, the client and lawyer relation is that agency problems can occur between them.[18] The client (principal) cannot fully control the quality of the performance of the lawyer (agent).[19] The basis for any principal agent problem is an information asymmetry between two parties.[20] This can lead to issues such as moral hazard.[21] The agent basically makes use of the inability of the other party to assess the value of the steps she takes and acts according to her personal interests. The problem is common to the relationship between the representing and the represented party in the enforcement process, and it gets a greater dimension if one considers 'society' to be the principal of

---

112; N Garoupa and F Gomez-Pomar, 'Punish Once or Punish Twice: A Theory of the Use of Criminal Sanctions in Addition to Regulatory Penalties' (2000) *Harvard Law School John M. Olin Center for Law, Economics and Business Discussion Paper Series*. Paper 308, 5, 17, also deals with the aspect of collusion as to administrative agencies. See also JQ Wilson, *Bureaucracy – What Government Agencies Do and Why They Do It* (1989) 433.

15 See A Renda et al., *Making Antitrust Damages Actions More Effective in the EU: Welfare Impact and Potential Scenarios* (2007) 562.

16 See RA Posner, 'An Economic Approach to Legal Procedure and Judicial Administration', in A Posner and F Parisi (eds), *The Economic Structure of the Law: The Collected Economic Essays of Richard A. Posner* (2000) 291. He refers to system costs as 'direct costs' of operating the legal dispute-resolution machinery.

17 See AM Polinsky and S Shavell, 'The Theory of Public Enforcement of Law' (2005) *NBER Working Paper 11780*, 36.

18 See S Shavell, 'The Fundamental Divergence between the Private and the Social Motive to Use the Legal System' (1997) 16 *Journal of Legal Studies* 599.

19 See S Shavell, 'Risk Sharing and Incentives in the Principal and Agent Relationship' (1979) 10(1) *Bell Journal of Economics, The RAND Corporation* 55–73; H Collins, *Regulating Contracts* (1999) 236.

20 See K-G Löfgren, T Persson and JW Weibull, 'Markets with Asymmetric Information: The Contributions of George Akerlof, Michael Spence and Joseph Stiglitz' (2002) 104(2) *Scandinavian Journal of Economics* 195–211.

21 See C Keser and M Willinger, 'Experiments on Moral Hazard and Incentives: Reciprocity and Surplus-Sharing', in E Brousseau and J-M Glachant (eds), *The Economics of Contracts Theories and Applications* (2002) 293–312. They devote a whole section to the principal agent problem and moral hazard. Moral hazard arises because an individual does not internalize the full consequences of her actions, and therefore has a tendency to act less carefully than she otherwise would.

the players in the enforcement process. An enforcer, like a lawyer or a judge, for example, can be considered the agent of the society at large which leads to overall costs and benefits of their intervention being discussed.

As the previous points suggest the whole analysis revolves around balancing costs and benefits. At the third stage, administrative costs shall be considered as a separate category because they can be a substantial social cost. Those costs relate, broadly speaking, to costs incurred throughout the enforcement process by the enforcers. Emphasis in this chapter is put on design suggestions; therefore, rather than systematically elaborating every step of the framework, it focuses on the key costs and benefits identified.

3. Developing Efficient Enforcement Designs in Misleading Advertising

3.1 Preliminary Considerations

In this section, different existing enforcement mechanisms as applied to two hypothetical case studies – a bona fide and a mala fide trader case scenario – shall be assessed in a model world based on the European context along the previously explained framework.[22] Misleading advertising, typically, has a small effect on each individual but is widespread.[23] The individual damage incurred in our case scenarios is assumed to be EUR 15.[24] The bona fide trader inadvertently breaks the law (Case Scenario 1).[25] An example of misleading advertising that is illustrative by a mala fide trader (Case Scenario 2) can occur with ring tone advertisement. This has been prominent in the headlines over the last few years, and consumers have been misled into concluding a contract instead of a one-time download. The profit-maximizing mala fide trader calculates her profits up to the moment when she will incur a fine, then hides (within the country)[26] and/or changes the sectors in

22 The generic term 'trader' shall be used. The company and the advertiser shall be assumed to be the same, and no additional questions on liability shall be discussed, as it is not relevant to the general argument.

23 See ER Jordan and PH Rubin, 'An Economic Analysis of the Law of False Advertising' (1979) 8(3) *Journal of Legal Studies* 530: 'no one consumer has an interest to sue'.

24 Jordan and Rubin (1979) 529: the role of advertising differs depending on which type of good is involved. In relation to experience goods (determine the quality only by purchasing and using the goods), advertisers might have an incentive to mislead and make false claims.

25 See MG Faure, AI Ogus and NJ Philipsen, 'Curbing Consumer Financial Losses: The Economics of Regulatory Enforcement' (2009) 31(2) *Law & Policy* 169.

26 In fact, the trader can also hide abroad and there are various pieces of European legislation available in this regard: Regulation (EC) No 2006/2004 of the European Parliament and of the Council of 27 October 2004 on Cooperation Between National Authorities Responsible for the Enforcement of Consumer Protection Laws (the Regulation on Consumer Protection Cooperation [CPC]), and the European Small Claims Procedure,

which she conducts business. She is assumed to primarily operate via the internet. We will refer to both situations in which the competitor incurs a damage of – let's say – EUR 100,000 and those where she has no interest in the case.[27]

Applying the common core of European procedural law[28] the 'loser-pays' rule is assumed for the model world as to the private law proceedings.[29] When it comes to the payment of lawyers, contingency fees shall be excluded, as is currently widely the case in Europe.[30] In terms of group litigation due to the overall strong resistance in Europe to class actions, reference shall only be made to representative actions.[31] The definitions of the mechanisms analysed (civil court, CADR, administrative agency, criminal court, self-regulatory systems and group litigation) will be set out at the beginning of the respective Subsections 3.2.–3.6.[32] In terms of available remedies, three main categories are chosen: compensation,

---

same as the Order for Payment Procedure (Regulation [EC] No 1896/2006 of the European Parliament and of the Council of 12 December 2006 Creating a European Order for Payment Procedure) and Proposal for a Directive of the European Parliament and of the Council on Alternative Dispute Resolution for Consumer Disputes and Amending Regulation (EC) No 2006/2004 and Directive 2009/22/EC (Directive on Consumer ADR) Brussels, 29.11.2011 COM (2011) 793 final. Legislation is upcoming, and possibilities to tackle traders that hide behind borders are on the rise. Concerning cross-border enforcement see also the contribution 'Private or Public Enforcement of the UCP Directive? Sanctions and Remedies to Prevent Unfair Commercial Practices' by Dörte Poelzig in this volume.

27 See Jordan and Rubin (1979) 535: competitors are harmed because sales that they would have made have been diverted to the other firm. They can be expected to lose substantially more than consumers.

28 Apart from a thorough study of three countries – the Netherlands, Sweden and England – in the ambit of the PhD dissertation (see fn 1), a variety of interviews was carried out with a number of different institutions in different Member States and large amounts of information were generated in this way.

29 See C Hodges, S Vogenauer and M Tulibacka (eds), *The Costs and Funding of Civil Litigation – A Comparative Perspective* (2010) 28: in almost all jurisdictions the general position is that the loser pays the costs of the court, evidence and lawyer (in civil litigation). Some exceptions are possible. In fact, often not the full amount of costs can be shifted.

30 Hourly fees are the rule. There is a strong cultural resistance in many states, see Hodges, Vogenauer and Tulibacka (2010) 25. Such arrangements are banned, e.g., in the Netherlands; see for an overview on rules in various countries, MG Faure, FJ Fernhout and NJ Philipsen, *Resultaatgerelateerde beloningssystemen voor advocaten – Een vergelijkende beschrijving van beloningssystemen voor advocaten in een aantal landen van de Europese Unie en Hong Kong* (2009).

31 See C Hodges, 'Collective Actions', in P Cane and HM Kritzer (eds) (2010) 707. See the contribution by Hans-W Micklitz ('A Common Approach to the Enforcement of Unfair Commercial Practices and Unfair Contract Terms') in this volume.

32 See also the analysis of the advantages and disadvantages of private and public enforcement by Dörte Poelzig in this volume.

injunctions and 'fining'.[33] The latter is chosen artificially, and would cover any financial sanction that is not compensation (such as fines, profit disgorgement and the like). Any group litigation is assumed to be able to seek all types of remedies. The same is true for individual actions. Unless indicated otherwise, the available courts and agencies are theoretically empowered to issue any of the remedies.[34] Prima facie all cross-uses of facts and findings in one proceeding of the same claimant are possible.

3.2 Litigation before a Civil Court

Enforcement via a civil court is defined as a system where the principle of party presentation is prevalent rather than judicial investigation. Litigation can be initiated by individuals themselves (under special circumstances), lawyers and representatives. Judges are assumed to be impartial, and an appeal system is in place. The state subsidizes the procedure.[35]

In terms of assessing its value in the context of misleading advertising as long as the advertisement continues to be made public, the harm to society is on-going, and there will be benefits in interrupting the emission of the advertisement or changing it. In an individual lawsuit before the civil court, the 'rational apathy' is pre-existing with EUR 15 of damage.[36] Even the costs involved for the individual in a small claims case can be regarded as too high – even in the light of a loser-pays rule.[37] In some countries civil procedural rules require a minimum threshold. From a social welfare point of view, litigation costs in the civil court would, for instance, only justify legal aid being made available for this amount of damage for individual damage cases if stopping the advertisement was a side effect of a procedure and thus a remedy for the widespread harm that was caused.[38] Per definition, everyone profits from an injunction. Particularly because free-riding

33 In line with the deterrence theory, costly sanctions (like fines) can outweigh low probabilities of detection and uphold the deterrent effects of a legal response in these cases.

34 Imprisonment is considered as an additional sanction in the subsection on criminal law enforcement.

35 See Landes and Posner (1975) 31.

36 See Landes and Posner (1975) 33; Schäfer (2000) 195; Howells and Weatherill (2005) 604; Garoupa (2001) 233 as to the factors that motivate individuals. Cafaggi and Micklitz (2009). According to a recent European Union study, 5% would take a business to court for EUR 20 or less, 4% for EUR 21–50 and 6% for EUR 51–100; see European Commission, Special Eurobarometer n 342 Consumer Empowerment (requested by Eurostat and DG SANCO 2011), 218. This is the average data for Europe. The percentage for taking a business to court in case of a damage of EUR 20 or less is 9%.

37 This is particularly related to the preparation of such a formal procedure, expressed in contrast to an ADR procedure, see interview with Alicia Menéndez González, Spanish ADR board (Madrid 16 November 2011).

38 It might indeed be worthwhile from a social welfare perspective to make available some form of funding if the harm is widespread.

to injunctions is widespread and no individual profit for whomever has already incurred damage is available, the individual would be reluctant to bring forward such an action.[39] The same is true for any form of 'fining'. If a consumer has suffered only minor harm, any litigation only results in further net costs for her. The cost-benefit analysis looks different for competitors if they have an interest in the case. They profit from any remedy that will harm their competitor's business or stop the considerable harm caused to them (e.g., by way of an injunction combined with a claim for the lost profits). If she were given standing to sue for various remedies from the category 'fining', this could be highly beneficial for her and her business; even if the proceeds do not go to her, the competitor's business would be damaged. Hence, there are various possibilities to upholding a deterring effect.

From a rational point of view, the case scenarios at hand would not induce an individual consumer to sue; however, the 'optimal provision of incentives' category shall be analysed, as the competitor is an efficient risk-taker. A competitor may have an interest in using the law strategically – even potentially for cases where she has suffered no harm (thus, frivolous lawsuits).[40] In particular, this might be the case if she has easy access to remedies from the 'fining' category. This must be kept in mind when designing legal provisions and procedural safeguards. Frivolous lawsuits, for example, can be deterred by sanctioning those who bring them forward. Generally in a civil court, trivial issues such as a claimant's lack of information as to the identity and location of the wrongdoer can hinder litigation.[41] The problem persists if lawyers and the civil judges are also unable to generate this information.[42] This can in practice be an issue as regards the mala fide trader that hides. The competitor might have information advantage over a consumer as regards her competitor's business, and therefore suffer less from the inability of her lawyer or the civil judge to generate crucial information.[43]

The competitor's intervention could come in handy for the individual consumer, as it deters the wrongdoer's action. In a proceeding involving a connected damage claim, she might use findings from, for instance, an injunctions case, and free-ride. However, if damage is very small from the consumer's perspective, not even this effort for the connected damage claim might seem justified. While an intervention, as regards the competitor, can be efficient, it is not certain, particularly in situations

---

39 See Van den Bergh and Visscher (2008) 14; Landes and Posner (1975) 29.

40 Regarding the situation of competitors in antitrust cases, see Renda (2007) 563. It can effectively become a medium used to restrict entry to new competitors and create a net loss in social welfare, see Jordan and Rubin (1979) 540.

41 See Van den Bergh (2007) 180, 201.

42 Special regimes apply for instance to websites, such as http://cqcounter.com/siteinfo/, that allow to track IP addresses.

43 See Renda (2007) 77, who sets this out for antitrust cases; CBP Mahé (2009), 'De concurrent als "handhaver" van consumentenbescherming', in E Engelhardt et al. (eds), *Handhaving van en door het privaatrecht*, 174: there are little or no information asymmetries as they know the market segment.

where one industry creates a cartel-like situation in one advertising sector, and there would be no deterrence because no competitor would intervene.[44]

Consequently, when creating incentives for the consumer side to oppose wide societal harm by misleading advertisements, the possibility of 'group litigation' comes to mind. The applied definition captures any representative action before a court or agency that is primarily carried out by an association or a state authority. These representatives typically have some advanced possibilities of collecting information.[45] Individual interests are bundled in the procedure.[46] It is essential to note that group litigation can be carried out before any enforcement body, and will hence be discussed in every subsection as an alternative to individual litigation. It might serve as an efficient allocation of risks for actions initiated by the consumers' side. While it might not be worthwhile to make available a funding possibility if only one individual suffers minor harm, the situation is different if a group of individuals suffer minor harm and societal harm is extensive. Regarding the design of the representative group action that is being discussed here, an optimal design for any representative body is assumed to be possible.[47] Ingredients like the opt-in or opt-out nature of the action or mandatory procedures have to be taken into account.[48]

'Group litigation' has a potential to remedy an individual's 'rational apathy'. This is regarded as a main advantage over individual litigation. Free-riding problems can be mitigated. If well-designed, group litigation serves as a funding

44 Another aspect is the question when the competitor realizes a loss of profit and if she, for example, invests in regularly checking advertising measures of her competitors. Note that Jordan and Rubin (1979) 531, argue that in a competitive industry no firm would lose from false advertising by competitors; neither would any competitor sue in a monopolist situation, only in cases of oligopolies. There would indeed again be no lawsuit if all the oligopolists engaged in the false advertising.

45 See for the characteristics of an administrative agency (such as powers to monitor, investigate, carry out market surveys) also the respective Subsection 3.4.

46 See for the various forms that group litigation can take: for instance, S Keske, *Group Litigation in European Competition Law: A Law and Economics Perspective* (2010).

47 Regarding the question of which form of group litigation can more successfully be designed in an optimal way, there is currently no consensus, although many suggestions for a design have been made that remedy certain weaknesses of other enforcement mechanisms. Cf. R Van den Bergh, 'Enforcement of Consumer Law by Consumer Associations', in MG Faure and FH Stephen (eds), *Essays in the Law and Economics of Regulation – In Honour of Anthony Ogus* (2008) 279–306, who is critical about optimizing group litigation involving consumer associations; R Van den Bergh and S Keske, 'Rechtsökonomische Aspekte der Sammelklage', in M Casper et al. (eds), *Auf dem Weg zu einer europäischen Sammelklage?* (2009) 40; as to favouring an adequate design of representative actions over class actions instigated by lawyers: van Boom (2006) 40; Keske (2010) 246: substantial changes are needed to both collective and representative actions. See generally the suggestions for a workable design in G Howells and H-W Micklitz (eds), CLEF, *Guidelines for Consumer Associations on Enforcement and Collective Redress* (2009) 14.

48 See Van den Bergh and Visscher (2008) 9.

mechanism. However, the representative will also weigh carefully before which body of law an action is feasible from a financial point of view, which is why its rationale for intervention will consequently be outlined regarding the various law enforcement bodies involved.

In the case of an injunction, everybody can profit, independently of whether they contributed. For instance, enabling the carrying out of injunctions by way of group litigation can enhance welfare. However, the deterrent effect of an injunction for a mala fide trader might be low, since the extent of a company's profits up until the moment of the injunctions might lessen deterrence. A speedy proceeding involving interim measures to stop the advertisement immediately can be crucial, particularly in relation to Case Scenario 2 – the mala fide trader who counts on a fine in the best case scenario after she has made considerable profits.

Group litigation has the potential to remedy funding issues for individuals by reducing the individual's financial burden: for instance, when costs are split or taken over by a funder. It depends, however, on the individual amount of damage at stake if this calculation works. As to direct damage claims, in cases of very small claims for damages, where the consumer's decision is led by the 'rational apathy', the option of collective action for damages might also fail.[49] It is highly likely that the EUR 15 scenario will fall below this threshold. To guarantee deterrence in this type of situation, other ways of forcing the company to face a sanction need to be found, even if the individual does not directly profit from it. Group actions can aim at various remedies from within the 'fining' category, and then everyone profits as well. An action for an injunction to side-line this action can be imagined. Not only the bringing of the action, depending on the body before which it is brought, but also the various remedies, in their preparation and realization, entail varying costs for the representatives. Injunctions are less costly to prepare and to litigate than are mass-damage cases.[50] 'Fining' triggers another set of incentives. Whereas Europe currently still has a severe funding problem in this regard,[51] one possible reason being that contingency fees are in general not accepted, new forms of financing processes are developing.[52]

---

49 See RA Posner (ed.), *Economic Analysis of Law* (8th edn, 2011) 785, regarding class actions.

50 This was confirmed in an interview with the Spanish consumer association Organización de Consumidores y Usuarios (OCU) (Madrid 16 November 2011) as regards requiring less preparation and accuracy as to the exact amount of damage that was suffered.

51 See GP Miller, 'Compensation and Deterrence in Consumer Class Actions in the US and Europe', in F Cafaggi and H-W Micklitz (eds), *New Frontiers of Consumer Protection – The Interplay between Private and Public Enforcement* (2009) 282.

52 See F Cafaggi and H-W Micklitz, 'Administrative and Judicial Enforcement in Consumer Protection', F Cafaggi and H-W Micklitz (eds), *New Frontiers of Consumer Protection – The Interplay between Private and Public Enforcement* (2009) 418. In Austria, a system of pre-financing was developed where the Verein für Konsumenteninformation (Association of Consumer Information – VKI) concludes an agreement with a finance company that refinances the costs of the procedure. If the case is successful, they retain

A crucial point is the different degrees of information asymmetries. A hiding trader cannot be traced in a scenario before a civil court. Case Scenario 2 involving the mala fide trader will fail *prima facie*. Investigative powers at the civil court are limited. Group litigation can, however, be a partial remedy, and in cases where harm is difficult to detect, for instance, it has a potential to outweigh to some extent the missing investigative powers in private law enforcement. The representatives may be able to add to locating wrongdoers. While consumer associations are able to generate some additional information,[53] this is particularly true if it is a public agency that has certain investigative powers and can engage in monitoring that will become the representative. As regards online trade and advertising, they have tools to track traders in hiding by digital investigation. Hence, there is a potential to outweigh information asymmetries, and the strengths of this depend on the combination of bodies bringing actions and adjudicating actions. The most crucial point from a welfare perspective, apart from improving the risk ratio for the individual, is the assessment as to which body can generate the desired information for Case Scenario 2 in the least costly way, up to the limit where society would no longer approve of generating this information. The optimal combination of entities could guarantee an efficient 'information finding'. Importantly, a public law element would have to be involved in one way or another when it comes to mala fide traders. Within a criminal law setting, police involvement has a high potential to generate information, whereas less information can be generated within a procedure involving a consumer association acting in the civil court, for instance.[54] Moreover, both, agencies and associations have more detailed knowledge about consumer protection laws, and can therefore easier identify law infringements.[55]

Capture of associations or public agencies is an issue that leads to severe problems regarding principal agent situations, aggravated the greater the number of players involved. This is generally all the more likely, the higher the issues that are at stake. While the danger of frivolous lawsuits as to individual consumer

---

one-third of the proceeds. This system has certain similarities with contingency fees. An advantage with several insurers would be that they could then compete, see H-W Micklitz, 'Collective Private Enforcement of Consumer Law: The Key Questions', in WH van Boom and MBM Loos (eds), *Collective Enforcement of Consumer Law – Securing Compliance in Europe through Private Group Action and Public Authority Intervention* (2007) 22.

53 A network or resources from membership, for instance. Then again, problems are reported, for example, from Germany where consumer associations lack the possibility to generate the information on the profits of the company that they would need to generate in line with the skimming-off procedures. This was discussed at the conference, Borderless Consumer Protection!? Effective Enforcement, Powerful Consumers (Berlin, 7 November 2011).

54 See Van den Bergh (2008) 284.

55 See Van den Bergh and Visscher (2008) 17.

cases is regarded as minor, in group litigation this is a given.[56] In this regard, particularly remedies that can have an immediate effect need to be carefully designed. The same is true for cases in which competitors can profit considerably from potentially frivolous damage to their rival's business.

In misleading advertising cases, a competitor or a trader association may be a candidate to step in, and the rest of the society can free-ride on its efforts. Whereas it is costly to design an efficient form of group litigation, the benefits in the category risk allocation are very high. Societal benefits may justify this effort. The big advantage emerging is that the case is brought at all, and is not left unenforced in cases where the competitor does not step in. Furthermore, as regards other administrative costs, it is true that they vary with the remedy and with which body is carrying out the information search. Group litigation entails fewer costs per individual, but the procedure as such is more costly.[57] The question is whether one wants to set these total administrative costs in relation to the situation in which all cases have been brought in an individual proceeding, or exclude the number of cases that might not have been brought because the individual cost-benefit analysis would not have justified it.

While Case Scenario 1 can be dealt with, for example, by consumer associations as a representative at the civil court, in Case Scenario 2, investigative powers of some kind would be needed. Pure private law enforcement will fail, but it could be outweighed by another entity involved as a representative, for instance, to generate this information (for instance a public agency).

3.3 Litigation before a CADR

'CADR' refers to adjudication by a body, unrelated to a publicly financed court, where the procedure is considerably less formalized. Typically, industry and the state are responsible for the financing of the institution.[58] The body is composed of consumer and business representatives. The involvement of a legal representative is generally not required, and the awards are prima facie of a lower value in terms of enforceability.[59] Systems to strengthen these awards are imaginable.[60] Another

---

56 A formal model on incentives for frivolous suits was developed by D Rosenberg and S Shavell, 'A Model in Which Suits Are Brought for Their Nuisance Value' (1985) 5 *International Review of Law and Economics* 3–13. For Europe see Schäfer (2000) 183–213.

57 See van den Bergh and Keske (2009) 26.

58 See N Creutzfeldt-Banda, 'Empirical Findings,' in C Hodges, I Benöhr and N Creutzfeldt-Banda (eds), *Consumer ADR in Europe – Civil Justice Systems* (2012) 382.

59 See C Hodges, I Benöhr and N Creutzfeldt-Banda, 'Findings and Conclusions', in C Hodges, I Benöhr and N Creutzfeldt-Banda (eds), *Consumer ADR in Europe – Civil Justice Systems* (2012) 390, 420.

60 A prime example is the system of 'underlying business guarantees' available in the Netherlands: see F Weber and C Hodges, 'Netherlands', in C Hodges, I Benöhr and N Creutzfeldt-Banda (eds), *Consumer ADR in Europe* (2012) 160. See for instance,

typical characteristic is that the procedure involves little costs for the consumer if she acts as a claimant.[61] The most typical remedy is compensation.

It derives from the foregoing that the smaller the individually suffered harm, the lower the procedural costs for the individual consumer actually have to be in order to induce her to take up the investment in litigation. The CADR body can capture low-value claims to some degree, more than the civil court, but from a rational point of view, even for the CADR body, damage in some cases might be too small to make a claim. Procedural rules reflect this in claims below certain thresholds not being admitted (even if an optimistic individual might be inclined to bring such a case given the loser-pays rule applies). This is likely to be the case for EUR 15. Whereas a single consumer's action before this body is consequently very unlikely in the case scenarios discussed, a competitor might bring a case if she was granted standing. A procedure can be set in relation to findings of unlawfulness, for instance, by way of an injunction by a public entity or a court, which might reduce the costs of the individual case for the claimant but also for society. Wrongdoers that cannot be tracked down cannot be complained against. In this sense the situation is comparable to the civil court. In general, the voluntary element on the trader's side is crucial. In various countries, the will to participate in the system is ensured by the trader being registered with the body.[62] In a way, only clear-cut cases are dealt with, and against a pre-defined set of defendants – those that volunteer to it. This distinguishes its value for cases of bona and mala fide traders generally.[63] Depending on whether systems to strengthen the CADR awards are available or not in the event of resistance on the part of the wrongdoer, the CADR procedure may only be the first step and an ordinary proceeding has to be initiated in any case. The concerns about the value of a CADR decision make an injunction assuming it can be achieved less valuable. In the context of advertising changes or interruptions of advertisement are dealt with rather by a self-regulatory entity (to be discussed) that is highly interlinked with the market. Due to concerns as to capture[64] and error costs, allowing remedies from the category 'fining' at an CADR body has to be carefully considered.

Directive 2008/52/EC of the European Parliament and of the Council of 21 May 2008 on Certain Aspects of Mediation in Civil and Commercial Matters, art 6.

61 See N Creutzfeldt-Banda (2012) 380.

62 In Spain, ADR could take place involving non-registered traders but she needs to agree, art 24(4) Real Decreto 231/2008, de 15 de febrero, por el que se regula el Sistema Arbitral de Consumo (Royal Decree That Establishes the Consumer Arbitration System). In the Dutch system registration, individually or via the sector organization, is required.

63 While in the case scenarios at hand the value of EUR 15 seems to exclude the value of a CADR body in cases of considerable damage for individual consumers, it is clearly given as illustrated in Weber (2011) 536–554.

64 See Thomas O Main, 'ADR: The New Equity' (2005) 74 *University of Cincinnati Law Review* 30, 'a certain vulnerability to capture by special interests'; 'some consumer ADR schemes are currently not satisfactory concerning independence': C Hodges, I Benöhr and N Creutzfeldt-Banda (2012) 444.

As to group litigation, the analysis can be kept short: firstly a CADR body has basically no investigative powers. And as stated, representatives have a potential to outweigh this lack of power to generate information that the individual or this body's enforcer cannot. Depending on who the representative is – namely, rather a public agency than a consumer association – the missing investigative powers can be compensated for in case of a mala fide trader. As to group litigation, capture is regarded as a big issue in terms of the various representatives: that is, associations[65] or public agencies. Likewise, it is serious as regards employees of the CADR body.[66] Consequently, in the main, there are many players involved about whom it can be assumed that they would pursue their own interests rather than the ones they should be focused on; hence, results become very uncertain. This situation speaks in favour of involving a court element – an independent decision-maker with a strict procedural law. Frivolous lawsuits can be an issue here when group litigation is allowed, and is a further argument in favour of introducing procedural safeguards. Indeed, error costs are intuitively more likely with an CADR body than in a court regarding questions of law. There is more expertise often concerning questions of fact.[67] Error costs would potentially be spread across all members of the group if mass cases were decided. These arguments speak in favour of disabling mass cases involving a CADR body. The last argument against allowing mass cases that involve a CADR body is the lack of a further development of case law which is a general effect if decisions are taken outside of the courts. A mass issue may indeed be a case where clarifications on the law are desirable. As to mala fide traders, their participation in a group procedure before a CADR body cannot be counted on, anyway, as was outlined before.

Thus, overall there seems to be no role really for the ADR body in the case scenarios. A competitor – if granted standing – might make use of it. The assumed competitor's damage is, however, high enough to also induce her to take up action before a different kind of body with a more costly procedure.

3.4 Intervention of an Administrative Agency

'Administrative enforcement' shall be defined as being performed by an agency that can carry out monitoring and has some investigative powers.[68] It can decide by itself, refer cases to a court, or even defend them in a court. Actions can be triggered by low-cost reporting or carried out on its own motion. Appeal along

---

65 See Van den Bergh (2008) 294; Schäfer (2000) 199.

66 See Thomas O Main, 'ADR: The New Equity' (2005) 330: 'a certain vulnerability to capture by special interests'; 'some consumer ADR schemes are currently not satisfactory concerning independence': C Hodges, I Benöhr and N Creutzfeldt-Banda (2012) 444.

67 See C. Hodges, I Benöhr and N Creutzfeldt-Banda (2012) 415.

68 Note that in practice, investigative powers given to public authorities vary between countries and between legal fields within these countries. Therefore, a potential in investigative powers generally is given.

the lines of the administrative law branch is possible.[69] Those authorities can grant various remedies but usually not compensation.

The efficient handling of both scenarios might be found in public law enforcement: this means any action taking place by and before a public authority, and triggered in various ways, whether by an own motion, by an individual or by a representative. It is ultimately the agency that decides when to act. Hence, the role of the lawsuit initiator is diminished. A public agency has the advantage of providing for high investigative powers (including digital investigations). In other words, after a 'low-cost' report or on an own motion, the public entity acts and thereby remedies for instance an individual's 'rational apathy' and free-riding problems as in the cases at hand.

If societal harm is extensive, with harm being less serious to the individual but widespread, it must be guaranteed that the authority obtains this information to take enforcement action. If private information – in the hands of individual consumers or competitors – needs to be transmitted, incentives have to be provided in order for this to be guaranteed.[70] Remedies can play a crucial role in this regard. Not being able to obtain compensation may be a disincentive for consumers. Having suffered only minor harm, the consumer may not be inclined to take any further action at all. Reporting strategies can be envisaged: for instance, cooperation with consumer advice centres and so on, where consumers have complained. Taking over the costs from the individual might be justified in this setting, because each individual has experienced only a minor damage for which she would not be willing to finance an entire procedure.

The entity's available investigative powers can come in handy, particularly for Case Scenario 2.[71] This factor, however, has to be set in relation to the societal harm. Monitoring and own investigations can lead to the agency becoming aware of infringements, which puts them in the position to take action on an own motion. The speed of a reaction will be another factor in the efficiency. Hence, monitoring or *ex ante* clearing might be an effective tool, particularly to protect bona fide

69 Similarly characterised in F Cafaggi and H-W Micklitz, 'Administrative and Judicial Enforcement in Consumer Protection: The Way Forward' (2008) 29 *EUI Working Papers LAW* 4.

70 See WH van Boom and MBM Loos, 'Effective Enforcement of Consumer Law in Europe: Synchronizing Private, Public, and Collective Mechanisms', in *Working Paper Series* (2008) 16; In competition law: leniency programmes are for instance regarded as providing private information within public law enforcement structures, see Keske (2010) 20; Shavell (1993) 259, 267. See on self-reporting: L Kaplow and S Shavell, 'Optimal Law Enforcement with Self-Reporting of Behavior' (1994) 102(3) *Journal of Political Economy* 583–606.

71 It is not excluded that future technological developments will render it indeed worthwhile to equip individuals or their lawyers with wider investigative powers. Low administrative (and other societal) costs might justify this at some point. For the time being, societal costs are assumed not to outweigh the benefits of equipping every individual with wide investigative powers.

traders and to single out mala fide traders; however, it is very costly in terms of administrative costs and leads to a danger of societal losses due to censorship. A public agency has deterrent sanctions at its availability, like fines, that can outweigh low probabilities of detection and conviction. Compared to criminal law the procedure is said to be less accurate which leads to a higher susceptibility to error costs.[72] Public authorities are privileged compared with pure private litigation when it comes to investigating facts about a case (e.g., powers to access business premises).

The distinction between individual and group cases becomes blurred in relation to a public authority, since it will ultimately decide whether a case is to be taken regardless of who triggers it. When purely assessing group litigation – for instance, a representative bringing a case to the authority – the individual is relieved of the reporting activity but may have to show her affiliation with the group litigation. In terms of the agency acting as a representative, certain findings as to a public agency coming before a civil court, for instance, have already been discussed in Subsection 3.2. If representative actions are brought to a public authority, advantages in risk-sharing that are given to the individual are present also for the representative. The interaction here is that monitoring or investigation could be carried out either by the representative or by the agency (the adjudicating body). The fact that the public body can generate a great deal of information is a new aspect compared with the private law branch, and it might be decisive for the cost-benefit analysis of the body carrying out a lawsuit. From the perspective of the association, it could be advantageous that there are enhanced investigative powers in comparison to a civil court (and certainly a CADR). This can be a decisive issue when assessing risks of a proceeding, and may induce the representative body to favour a public body. In this sense, the procedure is superior in terms of generating more information if it includes a public authority, which is necessary for scenarios like Case Scenario 2. The main drawback might be the lack of compensation as a remedy.

Capture is possible of the agency bringing the case or deciding a case, and within associations. The more powers that are in the hands of the same entity, the greater the danger: for example, bringing a case, and then investigating and adjudicating it, which is the situation if everything is being handled by the same body. A separation of these powers can be considered, or rules that public bodies can bring actions, for instance, only to the civil court, to a CADR body, or to specialized courts. Other reasons underlying this are the costs of spreading error cost across all members of the group, or the occurrence of frivolous lawsuits.

---

72 See Garoupa (2000) 5. The reason is the difference in sophistication that stands behind these sanctioning mechanisms – see also AI Ogus, MG Faure, and NJ Philipsen, 'Best Practices for Consumer Policy: Report on the Effectiveness of Enforcement Regimes' ,Report prepared for the UK Department of Trade and Industry and OECD (2006) 47 and MG Faure, AI Ogus, and NJ Philipsen (2009) 176.

Likewise, these are arguments in favour of introducing a court element into the procedure – as it is given in criminal law.

Administrative costs depend on the remedy involved, the amount of investigative powers used, and on whether it concerns individual or group litigation. The number of administrative bodies to be set up to reduce the risk of capture is also decisive. Lower administrative costs would depend on whether information raised could be transferred without doubling.

In total, and in particular for Case Scenario 2, the investigative powers are crucial. For Case Scenario 1, they might not be necessary. Issues of capture, frivolous lawsuits and error costs speak in favour of involving a court element in the procedure.

Competitors can have high damages at stake and therefore incentives to sue in the civil court. Due to them being from within the market, it is less likely that they need additional investigative powers.[73] It is certainly beneficial to motivate representatives to seek remedies like injunctions, where individuals would not take this step but where societal harm is extensive.

3.5 Criminal Law Enforcement

The public prosecutor is central to the functioning of the criminal process.[74] Once an investigation is initiated, for instance because a crime has been reported, the matter is investigated with the help of the police. The judgment is given by a criminal court where the prosecution brings the case as the plaintiff. A wide variety of sanctions exist, judges are impartial[75] and an elaborate appeal system is in place. The procedure entails very little administrative costs for the individual who only reported the crime. The most typical sanctions are fines and imprisonment. There is generally a way for the victim to join the procedure and to sue for damages.

Using criminal law in these case scenarios would guarantee, in particular for Case Scenario 2, that wide investigative powers could be made use of (tracking down individuals is a typical feature of this type of legal branch), irrespective of the representative involved (individual or others). The criminal procedure has the potential to outweigh any lack of investigative powers present with the players (as to the nature of the trader as crucial in Case Scenario 2 or other characteristics of the case). Where the threat to pay compensation is not, or not sufficiently, credible, an important advantage of criminal law enforcement is that there are

---

73 Here few or no information asymmetries are present as they know the market segment, see Mahé (2009) 174.

74 See J Hodgson and A Roberts, 'Criminal Process and Prosecution', in P Cane and HM Kritzer (eds), *The Oxford Handbook of Empirical Legal Research* (2010) 80: who provide an overview of empirical work carried out as to the public prosecutor's role, in particular, as to their independence.

75 See R Bowles, MG Faure and N Garoupa, 'The Scope of Criminal Law and Criminal Sanctions: An Economic View and Policy Implications' (2008) 35(3) *Journal of Law and Society* 392, as to imposing criminal sanctions.

other costly sanctions available to uphold the deterrent effect of legal responses. The costly sanctions outweigh low probabilities of detection or conviction as present in Case Scenario 2. Then again, the available investigative powers also increase the probability of being detected and convicted. The issue with regard to a 'judgment-proof defendant' – an insolvent accused – can be resolved very well by the different sanctions that are available – the prime example of a non-monetary sanction being imprisonment.[76] It is imaginable that cases that could not be tried because of missing information as to necessities to start a lawsuit at all can be tried under this branch of law, because there are possibilities of gathering information prior to the trial – for example, regarding the location of the trader. This represents the highest likelihood of Case Scenario 2 being dealt with successfully.

Courts are arguably less susceptible to capture, but prosecutors might be. The occurrence of error costs can be resolved to a certain extent by the accuracy of criminal procedural law, which, in turn, leads to high administrative costs.[77] Criminal law leaves little scope for frivolous lawsuits. It is evident that, for a representative body as well, preparing litigation could be very costly: for instance, satisfying the high burden of proof.[78]

An existing variant of this are some public agencies that can act as prosecutor (with possible police involvement).[79] In other instances, however, the procedure will be carried out by the public prosecutor, and the role of individuals or associations limited, and hence their costs as well. It is obvious that for Case Scenario 2, the use of criminal law can be warranted for certain types of traders. The procedure could be used as an underlying threat to enable exploiting less costly mechanisms and provide for non-monetary sanctions where necessary.

Should an error ever occur in a collective criminal proceeding, costs on the side of the mistakenly convicted would be very high (pay for all), as would costs for the victims if someone wrongfully walked free (no money for anyone and potentially a repeat offence). A high degree of accuracy, typically attributed tocriminal law procedures, can be of considerable value in mass cases, as they reduce the occurrence and spreading of error costs.

---

76 See R Bowles, MG Faure and N Garoupa (2008) 402.

77 See GS Becker and GJ Stigler, 'Law Enforcement, Malfeasance, and Compensation of Enforcers' (1974) 3 *Journal of Legal Studies* 3: Becker argues that with an 'increasingly thorough and expensive investigation, one can determine with increasing precision the probable behavior of a given person'.

78 See Interview with Gunnar Larsson, Swedish Consumer Ombudsman and Head of Consumer Authority (Stockholm, 25 August 2009) who reported this for the Swedish legal system.

79 The Swedish Consumer Ombudsman can act as a prosecutor in certain scenarios. In England the use of criminal prosecution is an important part of enforcement of the public regulators. In their formal enforcement role officers are required to operate to the same rules and standards as police officers and have to comply with the provisions of the Police & Criminal Evidence Act 1984, the Criminal Procedure & Investigations Act 1996 and the Regulation of Investigatory Powers Act 2000.

Criminal law is intended mainly to be a fallback option – an underlying threat – for consumer law cases such as the ones at hand.

3.6 Self-Regulation

Self-regulation shall be considered in the narrow sense, namely, as limited regulatory powers over a certain industry. As regards advertising, a code of conduct must be observed. The self-regulation system is financed entirely by the industry. Complaints can be brought, generally free of charge, in the event of breaches of the code. This procedure does not reflect an equal representation of consumers and traders. Such type of body typically offers some *ex ante* advice. Changes are made to the advertisement (in the event of a successful case and a compliant trader), and consequently everyone profits from this. All other remedies are excluded at this self-regulatory body. In fact the result of the described process is similar to an injunction. In practice this system plays a larger role than CADR bodies.

Again, the 'rational apathy' can be an issue in reporting, and individuals (consumers, traders) or representatives need to be motivated to act. Costs are borne by the market in which the self-regulation is applied.[80] In contrast to public regulation, one advantage lies in the fact that self-regulatory authorities have better information about the market to be controlled, which includes tracing wrongdoers.[81] Also, individuals just need information about the ad and not about the wrongdoer in order to file a complaint. Some traders, intuitively particularly Case Scenario 2 traders, will not participate in this type of system.[82]

The advantage in terms of information has to be contrasted with the risk of capture, which is by definition given with self-regulation. The involvement of the consumer side in the proceedings can potentially mitigate this effect. There are other potential benefits with self-regulation: for instance, it does not pose a problem under the agency issue, as no representative is needed.

Despite being limited in scope, the regulating body can create considerable benefits for case scenarios where traders are compliant. In Case Scenario 2, in the case of a trader who is not willing to comply and is potentially reluctant to become a member of the sector organization, this enforcement mechanism will be unable to force the trader to comply with its decision. However, Case Scenario 1 could be dealt with successfully. It is suggested that the cooperation with media owners is weak when it comes to internet media owners, not least because there

---

80 See JC Miller, 'The FTC and Voluntary Standards: Maximizing the Net Benefits of Self-Regulation' (1985) 4(3) *Cato Journal* 898. Industry bears the costs of self-regulation: I Ayres and J Braithwaite, 'Responsive Regulation: Transcending the Deregulation Debate' (1992) 114; Ogus (1994) 107; see RH Coase, 'Advertising and Free Speech' (1977) 6(1) *Journal of Legal Studies* 6, but it has to be looked at with suspicion.

81 See Van den Bergh (2007) 202; Miller (1985) 897.

82 See F Alleweldt et al. (Civic Consulting on behalf of IMCO), *State of Play of the Implementation of the Provisions on Advertising in the Unfair Commercial Practices Legislation* (2010) 22.

are no legal obligations for them to cooperate.[83] An advantage in particular for the Case Scenario 1 type of trader can be seen in the offer/possibilities to check the advertisement before it is put on the market: for instance, on a voluntary basis. The voluntary aspect can lead to signalling as to which trader represents which type, and would allow for some targeted monitoring: for example, in cooperation with other enforcers. Furthermore, efficiency might speak in favour of setting up ways according to which findings by this body can be used as indications in other judicial proceedings: for example, damage cases.

While generally one single complaint is sufficient, collective actions can contribute in the event that an exertion of pressure is needed. It can be desirable where individuals feel disinclined to complain due to low damages and to having little interest in preventing the trader from acting in the future. In some cases, the competitor might also have no monetary interest in intervening: for instance, as soon as a sector is organized in a cartel-like fashion. Here, the body will also not act on an own motion. For a representative's cost-benefit analysis as well, the low procedural costs will encourage them to actually complain here first. An intervention by a representative with investigative powers can enhance efficiency by generating more comprehensive information within the system. As stated previously, self-regulators generally have considerable information about their own sector and its participants. Depending upon who brings the case, there might be issues as to various entities that can be captured and agency issues. As already mentioned, the underlying threat of other enforcement systems is crucial.

From an administrative costs point of view, self-regulation costs are regarded as low compared with, for instance, public enforcement.[84] Because no damages are granted, administrative costs are presumably even lower than those involving a CADR body. However, the prevention of other societal costs has to be assured in the self-regulatory body's design. Then again, if a pre-clearance system is in place, its financing must be envisaged. Nevertheless, the way this mechanism can be used in this case scenario is not in the way of assessing damage, deciding on injunctions or fining, but is a preliminary step to changing a misleading advertisement, a less binding 'injunction'. Thus, while it might often be only a first step, the lower administrative costs could justify implementing this mechanism despite the few cases that double. The exact extent of the administrative costs depends on what the self-regulatory entity precisely looks like, and in how far it is coordinated with other entities in the enforcement mix. It does not provide a solution for every case, and it cannot exist as the only enforcement mechanism. Efficiency considerations might support that within the mechanism the funding is distributed to these established

---

83 See P Verbruggen 'Transnational Private Regulation in the Advertising Industry – Case Study Report for the Research Project Constitutional Foundations of Transnational Private Regulation (March 31, 2011)' (2011) 125, http://ssrn.com/abstract=2256043.

84 See Faure, Ogus and Philipsen (2009) 171. 'If such a system is able to achieve compliance, it will typically do so at a significantly lower administrative cost than if public enforcement processes are invoked.'

tasks, and that self-regulatory bodies do not engage in preparing collective actions. Some monitoring effort might be imaginable, however, but only as regards the code of conduct.

The value of self-regulation is in being a potential low-cost cross-financer for more costly procedures and in providing for some *ex ante* action. The results of the self-regulatory body have to be monitored carefully with regard to pursuing social welfare interests, as it is self-evident that it is more inclined to pursue industry's interests.

4. Design Suggestions

In terms of design suggestions, a first set of considerations revolves around the position of the competitor. When it comes to a competitor who has suffered substantial individual damages, her interests at stake are assumed to be high, and her business can profit from remedies such as injunctions or from the 'fining' category. Apart from the civil court, business-to-business arbitration options might also be available in a particular country that might then follow different procedural rules than the CADR procedure. They are, however, outside the scope of this contribution. Furthermore, self-regulatory solutions exist. Notably, in relation to a trader, a competitor generally suffers from a lower information asymmetry than does a consumer.[85] Therefore, in terms of optimizing responses, it seems useful if she presents the evidence without the intervention of a costly investigation. The cases are to be channelled to private law bodies rather than to a public authority or the criminal court, except in exceptional circumstances where the information asymmetry is high. The potential interest in damaging the competitor's business frivolously has to be considered. While the competitor's intervention can be beneficial for social welfare, she might not have an incentive to sue in every situation in which it would be desirable from a social point of view: for instance, the 'cartel situation'.

When it comes to trifling but widespread harm, a crucial first consideration when talking about optimal mixes is that there will be cases where it is no longer worthwhile from an economic point of view to calculate and distribute compensation for a group of individuals. In order to prevent a loss of the deterrent effect, other possible remedies are included in this assessment. Injunction or remedies in the 'fining' category are other forms that the sanction can take and that can deter the wrongdoer. It is essential to realize that mala fide traders count on the fact that the individual will not sue due to the minor harm suffered, and that the challenge consequently is to design an optimal response involving various types of remedies and players. Hence, to uphold the deterrent effect, in addition to alternative remedies, alternative initiators of an action also need to be discussed – notably, forms of grouping claims. This is particularly crucial in situations where no free-riding on the competitor's efforts is possible because she

85 See Mahé (2009) 174.

has no incentive to sue. The initiation of lawsuits via other players, like consumers or their representatives, must be guaranteed. Likewise, there can be competition between the consumer and the trader side taking action.

The conclusion regarding an optimal design can centre on certain main questions. It can be discussed which bodies should play a role in the mix, considering in particular the need to generate information and the danger of diluted incentives: for example, by capture or principal agent problems. On the basis of the previous analysis, there are good reasons why in the possible interactions a public law element for the investigation is necessary for preparing an enforcement system for type 2 case scenarios. The way in which this information enters the enforcement response is less decisive.

Solutions can involve any strategy that makes use of the threat of a sanction by a public authority, and that induces traders to find a solution for the consumer; likewise, it can be a deal resulting from informal negotiations: for instance, in which the trader commits to compensating the consumers. By the same token, enabling follow-on damage claims might be efficient as long as it does not lead to over-deterrence.[86] Rather than severely restructuring existing bodies (e.g., to enable them to grant remedies they normally do not), coordinating them more closely is desirable. Restructuring a public authority might, for instance, have an impact on the involvement of lawyers – currently not required – and procedural costs – currently low for the individual, and consequently reduce its positive effects, in particular on the cost-benefit analysis of the individual. Abstaining from restructuring enforcement bodies avoids a spill-over of weaknesses.

Only for type 1 case scenarios can a response without a 'public law element' be effective: for instance, by relying purely on a consumer association acting before a civil court. It can also be considered that associations engage in monitoring for certain types of case scenarios. A consumer association is assumed to have less investigative powers than a public authority. Generally, to maintain deterrence in the least costly way, it is necessary to fine-tune methods geared to produce necessary information. One way or the other, if there is a high information asymmetry, such as in Case Scenario 2, the information must be introduced into the enforcement response. This is true for information concerning the nature of the trader as displayed in the hypothetical scenarios but also for information deficiencies concerning other characteristics of a case.

Apart from aligning the combinations according to how the least-cost remedy for the information asymmetry – particularly in Case Scenario 2 – can be accomplished, apparently the representatives carry out their individual cost-benefit analysis as well to decide where they can afford to bring a claim. Self-regulation can be a first step involving low costs, and will be discussed below.

---

86 In reality, this type of coordination does not exist as a general policy in Europe; see F Cafaggi, 'The Great Transformation. Administrative and Judicial Enforcement in Consumer Protection: A Remedial Perspective' (2009) 21 *Loyola Consumer Law Review*, 519. The experimental character of this article justifies exploring these possibilities.

Regarding the design of the representative group action that is being discussed, an optimal design for any representative body is assumed to be possible. People may want to free-ride in these cases but this can largely be remedied by the design and the choice of remedy. Furthermore, in terms of an association's accountability, regulation can be considered. To a large extent, how serious the three issues – capture, frivolous lawsuits, and principal agent problems – become depends on the remedy; how much there is at stake. The same is true for administrative costs: for example, proving the exact harm in a damages case and then distributing it is more costly than proving that some harm could occur in an injunctions case where no distribution is necessary afterwards; 'fining' usually also excludes distribution of proceeds. Opt-in or opt-out and so on can be decisive. In relation to the different remedies, different amounts and types of information have to be generated. In practice, the financing issue of these representative entities – particularly as regards mass damage cases more than the other remedies – still needs to be improved in Europe.

As established previously, the social costs of mass cases being dealt with by a CADR body exceed the benefits, which is why this option shall be excluded. Capture, frivolous lawsuits and error costs on the part of public authorities are the main reasons to favour involving a court element in such mass procedures, too. The problem with error costs in mass proceedings is that they are spread over a group of individuals. Whereas it is suggested in the design to disable mass cases involving CADR bodies in terms of public agencies, the 'public law element' needs to be exploited, and some cases and thus some type of involvement in mass cases guaranteed. The mentioned dangers have to be considered when designing this.

Benefits can be seen in mass cases being decided on the part of an entity independent of the one that initiates the lawsuit and carries out the investigation. This is in line with the principles of separation of powers and prevention of capture. Adjudication could be undertaken by a court or by a different, independent public entity. In terms of triggering a case at the public agency independently of whether it is done by one individual or a group or on an own motion, this entity is to filter cases according to social welfare criteria. This means that capture and any pursuing of individual interest different to that of society must be prevented.

While not recommended for mass cases, CADR can likewise not be suggested for EUR 15 individual damage cases. In practice in advertising the involvement of what was defined as a 'self-regulatory' entity is more prominent than CADR solutions.

The criminal court can only be an underlying threat of the enforcement system and not a regular addressee of mass claims.[87] A case could be transferred to the

87 It would only be applicable in very exceptional cases (e.g., severe widespread harm in product safety cases). Expertentagung (2011): 'Wilhelminenberg Gespräche', Sozialministerium Österreich (Austrian Ministry of Social Affairs), Catch Me If You Can/ Geschäfte an der Grenze des Erlaubten', as reported in 'Die Presse', Internet-Abzocke: Ruf

criminal court if the investigative powers of the public agency do not suffice to adjudicate and hence to deter. Or, depending on the approach, the public agency could involve the police when acting as the prosecution. Mainly in cases where a wrongdoer does not comply with a private or administrative order, criminal law should enter the picture. In terms of providing the necessary information, any case brought to the criminal court is beneficial because, independently of many or few possibilities of the 'claimant' herself to generate information, it can be generated within the criminal process. Likewise, there is an advantage in that the accuracy of the procedure would keep error costs – which in mass scenarios are spread across everyone – low. In addition, any case involving a public authority as adjudicator or claimant has a high potential of generating information, although not as high as in a criminal investigation. Therefore, a consumer association could report a crime and the public prosecutor would take it from there at society's cost.

A very high potential of generating information *prima facie* can be guaranteed by a procedure involving both a public authority and a criminal court. Criminal law is meant to be only an underlying threat in optimal mixes for the mala fide trader. For a representative empowered to act as a prosecutor, the preparation of a case in the criminal court could be costly, due primarily to the high burden of proof that has to be satisfied.

When differentiating more specifically between the two case scenarios, it shall be set out how the optimal responses need to differ as to bona fide and mala fide traders. They are arguably often difficult to distinguish, and signalling strategies would have to be employed, which in practice do not work perfectly. While repeat offences are a comparatively clear sign that the company at stake is a mala fide trader, the company could also find ways of avoiding this signalling effect: for instance, by changing its name. The mala fide trader, the repeat offender, the one that already calculates a possible sanction in the fee for providing her service, needs to be deterred by enforcement going as far as criminal enforcement, possibly personal liability. The bona fide trader, however, must be treated differently. She is the one who places the inadvertently misleading advertisement, and does not intend any harm.

The pivotal question becomes: how high can a sanction be in order to deter a profit-maximizer from abusing the slow response – or the fact of no response – of the legal system and calculating with the existing sanctions? One is confronted with an on-going violation, and a benefit can consequently be found in terms of speed. A speedy proceeding such as an interim measure to stop something can be crucial, particularly in relation to Scenario 2, in which the trader allows for a fine that she hopes will be charged after she has made considerable profit. This is why in a legal system particular attention has to be paid to injunctions and to allowing

nach kollektiver Rechtsdurchsetzung (9 October 2011), http://diepresse.com/home/recht/rechtallgemein/699564/InternetAbzocke_Ruf-nach-kollektiver-Rechtsdurchsetzung?_vl_backlink=/home/recht/index.do. Collective actions at a criminal court are discussed in particular because they reduce the individual's cost risks.

interim measures. Encouragement can be undertaken by providing for any type of subsidies for injunction procedures, for example, in the form of a relief of court fees and the like. As regards frivolous lawsuits, there is also a particular danger in fast remedies being abused for anticompetitive purposes, resulting in a social loss. Particular attention therefore has to be given to the incentives of competitors, as with any other remedy that has a high potential of harming a competitor's business. Taken together, these are further reasons in favour of adding a court element to the procedure, meaning more accurate procedural safeguards. Likewise, some strategic use by consumers or consumer associations is possible, and these incentives need to be monitored.

When thinking along these lines, it becomes evident that the 'fastest reaction' – such as the one that possibly leads to an advertisement never appearing on the market – is some kind of *ex ante* action. Therefore, the consideration is valid – if not in both cases, viz., bona and mala fide trader – that *ex ante* control can be of added value despite very high administrative costs: in the case of the mala fide trader, to protect the consumer, and in the case of the bona fide trader, to protect the trader herself from legal consequences. One wonders whether the only possibility to protect society from the violations of the mala fide traders is to bar their access to the advertising market altogether. The prevention argument can be put forward if societal harm is extensive and should be prevented from occurring in the first place.[88] In relation to certain products that can cause considerable societal harm, obligatory pre-clearance can be discussed. One might want to argue that this can be differentiated in terms of various sectors in advertising: for instance, those that have the potential to cause substantial harm and those that do not.[89] This can potentially reduce administrative costs.

The first addressee to do this from an efficiency perspective seems to be a public agency that not only has wide monitoring powers but also fines at its disposal in cases of non-compliance. Moreover, self-regulation can provide ways of clearing advertisements before they become public. In the real world, a differentiation can be suggested as to countries where self-regulation is successful and to others where it is not.[90] While this can work for the bona fide traders in countries where self-regulation is strong, the mala fide traders will not respond to this system. Very harsh sanctions would lead to over-deterrence for even the bona fide traders. In general, cooperation between self-regulation and a public authority can be envisaged, and – apart from legal considerations against censorship and the freedom of speech – from an administrative costs point of view in terms of overall social welfare it is impossible to justify every advertisement being checked. Note

88 See Friehe and Tabbach (2013); e.g., terrorism.

89 If all advertising is scrutinized, even accurate advertising must run the risk of a charge of being misleading. High burden on advertisers, see Jordan and Rubin (1979) 552.

90 Classical examples would be the Netherlands as a successful example; see MG Faure, AI Ogus and NJ Philipsen, 'Enforcement Practices for Breaches of Consumer Protection Legislation' (2008) 20(4) *Loyola Consumer Law Review* 374.

that an indiscriminate application of preventive enforcement entails a danger of wasting society's resources in preventing inefficient and efficient violations.[91] The voluntary aspect can lead to some signalling as to which trader represents which type, keep administrative costs low and would allow for a degree of targeted monitoring: for instance, in cooperation with other enforcers. This could contribute to social welfare.

Rather than a pure deterrence approach, there is a strong prevention aspect in the design suggestions. Furthermore, the self-regulatory body is the cross-financing mechanism for other strong information asymmetry cases that need a more costly enforcement response. While self-regulation places some emphasis on *ex ante* action, the other bodies primarily work *ex post*. As to self-regulation, a sound connection with court proceedings, providing for ways to use the findings in courts, can be beneficial. It is a low-cost step for any claimant, consumers or traders, and can lead to a change in an advertisement.

If traders do not comply with enforcement actions undertaken by a public agency, the route to criminal law should be open. Cooperation between the police and public agencies as prosecutors can be warranted.

5. Conclusion

The goal of this chapter was to illustrate design suggestions for efficient enforcement mixes for two hypothetical cases within misleading advertisement, namely a bona fide and a mala fide trader case scenario. Particular attention was paid to online trade/advertising gaining in importance and potential current loopholes in the enforcement responses depending on the mechanism employed. The design suggestions were developed in enforcement models developed in a model world reflecting the common core of European procedural law.

As a first result, the competitor's natural incentives lead to a role for her. A competitor taking action allows to some degree for a consumer to free-ride and thus profit from the action – likewise for a societal benefit. There would be fewer information asymmetries due to the fact that competitors work in the same sector and there would presumably be less need of a 'public law element' to generate information.

Secondly, however, as a competitor's intervention is not certain, for instance in cartel-like situations, an enforcement response triggered by the consumer side is also needed. Individuals will not sue individually for their small harm. The topic of mass litigation is important and different representatives come into play.

Thirdly and importantly, a differentiation between responses for bona and mala fide traders is crucial due to the different amount of benefits they calculate with – they need to be deterred by different means. As to the mala fide traders, the 'public law element' is essential. Depending on the nature of the trader, those enforcers who generate more information have to be favoured whenever it is in the social

91 See Friehe and Tabbach (2013) 4.

interest. It was set out how in particular a lack of information on the side of the consumer as regards the location of the trader (potentially aggravated by the rise of internet trade that facilitates the possibility of traders hiding) is the reason for current failures in enforcement. Overall the factor 'information generator' (how, by whom, by which combination of actors) is a crucial topic especially for the mala fide trader case scenario where high information asymmetries are present. They have the potential to cause substantial societal harm. It was analysed which enforcement body can cure which information asymmetry and how mechanisms can be combined to cure each other's weaknesses while paying attention to overall social welfare considerations. Aside from different potentials to create information concerning the nature of a trader, different enforcement mechanisms also vary concerning the amount of information they can generate as to other characteristics of the case.

The intervention of mass litigation has to be optimally coordinated in terms of incentives via remedies. A definition must exist as to which players are empowered to bring lawsuits where, mitigating the problem of, for instance, frivolous lawsuits and aggravated agency and capture problems. In terms of where these actions are to be brought, a court element is favoured – mass CADR is considered not optimal from the overall welfare perspective. Individual CADR cases do not seem to be worthwhile either.

Self-regulatory solutions, if supported by the underlying threat of stronger enforcement responses, can be welfare enhancing and allow for some cross-financing. The information that is available within the market can be absorbed in this way. In relation to mala fide traders the 'speed' factor is crucial and *ex ante* actions are discussed in detail. On a voluntary basis pre-clearance can protect the bona fide trader and to some extent identify mala fide traders. In relation to some products that can cause very high societal harm, obligatory pre-clearance can potentially be effective.

In terms of policy advice, it was evidently not expected that the solution would be as easy as suggesting one optimal mix of public and private enforcement in consumer law which would then be a one-size-fits-all solution that only would have to be transplanted into the countries that one desired. Apparently countries are no dark horses. Optimality is related to institutional settings. Countries have different attributes: for instance, some have strong private consumer associations while others rely on a public authority for law enforcement purposes. The powers of these authorities can vary. Self-regulation is also not effective in every context. Some jurisdictions are more ready than others to assess damages within criminal law proceedings, and to rely on criminal law in general. A crucial factor in a country's potential to change in a 'low-cost way', a welfare enhancing way, to an optimal solution is to consider the importance of path dependency. Path dependency positively explains why countries' legal enforcement systems are shaped the way they are. While it is not argued that a country can only change along the lines of the path that it has taken, it certainly has to be considered when suggesting changes that the more they are innovative and alien to the system, the more costs of change they potentially incur which has to be weighed against societal (long-term) benefits that can be derived from this. Therefore, the design suggestions are kept sufficiently broad and can be adapted specifically to countries. In that sense, it can be welcomed that national legislators are left with discretion as to the enforcement side of the UCP Directive.

Note lastly that from the misleading advertising cases, some broader conclusions with minor variations are possible for other types of unfair commercial practices.

Bibliography

Alleweldt F et al. (Civic Consulting on behalf of IMCO), *State of Play of the Implementation of the Provisions on Advertising in the Unfair Commercial Practices Legislation* (2010).

Ayres I and J Braithwaite, *Responsive Regulation: Transcending the Deregulation Debate* (Oxford: Oxford University Press, 1992).

Becker GS, 'Crime and Punishment: An Economic Approach' (1968) 76 *Journal of Political Economy* 169–217.

Becker GS and GJ Stigler, 'Law Enforcement, Malfeasance, and Compensation of Enforcers'(1974) 3 *Journal of Legal Studies* 1–18.

Bowles R, MG Faure and N Garoupa, 'The Scope of Criminal Law and Criminal Sanctions: An Economic View and Policy Implications' (2008) 35(3) *Journal of Law and Society* 389–416.

Cafaggi F, 'The Great Transformation. Administrative and Judicial Enforcement in Consumer Protection: A Remedial Perspective' (2009) 21 *Loyola Consumer Law Review* 496–539.

Cafaggi F and H-W Micklitz, 'Administrative and Judicial Enforcement in Consumer Protection: The Way Forward' (2008) 29 *EUI Working Papers LAW*.

———, 'Administrative and Judicial Enforcement in Consumer Protection', In F Cafaggi and H-W Micklitz (eds), *New Frontiers of Consumer Protection – The Interplay between Private and Public Enforcement* (Mortsel: Intersentia, 2009) 401–445.

———, *New Frontiers of Consumer Protection – The Interplay between Private and Public Enforcement* (Mortsel: Intersentia, 2009).

CLEF, prepared by Howells, G and H-W Micklitz, *Guidelines for Consumer Associations on Enforcement and Collective Redress* (2009).

Coase RH, 'Advertising and Free Speech' (1977) 6(1) *Journal of Legal Studies* 1–34.

Collins H, *Regulating Contracts* (New York: Oxford University Press, 1999).

Creutzfeldt-Banda N, 'Empirical Findings', in C Hodges, I Benöhr and N Creutzfeldt-Banda (eds), *Consumer ADR in Europe – Civil Justice Systems* (Oxford and Portland, OR: Hart Publishing, 2012) 367–388.

Faure MG, FJ Fernhout and NJ Philipsen, *Resultaatgerelateerde Beloningssystemen Voor Advocaten – Een Vergelijkende Beschrijving Van Beloningssystemen Voor*

Advocaten in Een Aantal Landen Van De Europese Unie En Hong Kong (Den Haag: Boom Juridische Uitgevers, 2009).

Faure MG, AI Ogus and NJ Philipsen, 'Enforcement Practices for Breaches of Consumer Protection Legislation' (2008) 20(4) *Loyola Consumer Law Review* 361–401.

———, 'Curbing Consumer Financial Losses: The Economics of Regulatory Enforcement' (2009) 31(2) *Law & Policy* 161–191.

Friehe T and A Tabbach, 'Preventive Enforcement' (2013) *International Review of Law and Economics* 35.

Garoupa N, 'Optimal Law Enforcement When Victims Are Rational Players' (2001) 2 *Economics of Governance* 231–242.

Garoupa N and F Gomez-Pomar, 'Punish Once or Punish Twice: A Theory of the Use of Criminal Sanctions in Addition to Regulatory Penalties' (2000) *Harvard Law School John M. Olin Center for Law, Economics and Business Discussion Paper Series*, Paper 308, 1–30.

Heine K and W Kerber, 'European Corporate Laws, Regulatory Competition and Path Dependence' (2002) 13 *European Journal of Law and Economics* 47–71.

Hodges C, 'Collective Actions', in P Cane and HM Kritzer (eds), *The Oxford Handbook of Empirical Legal Research* (Oxford: Oxford University Press, 2010) 705–728.

Hodges C, I Benöhr and N Creutzfeldt-Banda, 'Findings and Conclusions', in C Hodges, I Benöhr and N Creutzfeldt-Banda (eds), *Consumer ADR in Europe – Civil Justice Systems* (Oxford and Portland, OR: Hart Publishing, 2012) 389–435.

Hodges C, S Vogenauer and M Tulibacka (eds), *The Costs and Funding of Civil Litigation – A Comparative Perspective* (Oxford and Portland, OR: Hart Publishing, 2010).

Hodgson J and A Roberts, 'Criminal Process and Prosecution', in P Cane and HM Kritzer (eds), *The Oxford Handbook of Empirical Legal Research* (Oxford: Oxford University Press, 2010) 64–93.

Hondius EH, 'Public and Private Enforcement in Consumer Protection – A Dutch Perspective', in F Cafaggi and H-W Micklitz (eds), *New Frontiers of Consumer Protection – The Interplay between Private and Public Enforcement* (Mortsel: Intersentia, 2009) 235–259.

Hood C, H Rothstein and R Baldwin, *The Government of Risk: Understanding Risk Regulation Regimes* (1st edn, New York: Oxford University Press, 2001).

Howells G and S Weatherill, *Consumer Protection Law* (2nd edn, Aldershot, UK, and Burlington, VT: Ashgate, 2005).

Jordan ER and PH Rubin, 'An Economic Analysis of the Law of False Advertising' (1979) 8(3) *Journal of Legal Studies* 527–553.

Kaplow L and S Shavell, 'Optimal Law Enforcement with Self-Reporting of Behavior' (1994) 102(3) *Journal of Political Economy* 583–606.

Keser C and M Willinger, 'Experiments on Moral Hazard and Incentives: Reciprocity and Surplus-Sharing', in E Brousseau and J-M Glachant (eds), *The*

Economics of Contracts Theories and Applications (Cambridge: Cambridge University Press, 2002) 293–312.

Keske S, *Group Litigation in European Competition Law: A Law and Economics Perspective* (Antwerp: Intersentia, 2010).

Landes WM and RA Posner, 'The Private Enforcement of Law' (1975) 4(1) *Journal of Legal Studies* 1–46.

Legrand P, 'European Legal Systems are Not Converging' (1996) 45 *International and Comparative Law Quarterly* 52–81.

Löfgren K-G, T Persson and JW Weibull, 'Markets with Asymmetric Information: The Contributions of George Akerlof, Michael Spence and Joseph Stiglitz' (2002) 104(2) *Scandinavian Journal of Economics* 195–211.

Mahé CBP, 'De Concurrent Als "Handhaver" Van Consumentenbescherming', in E Engelhardt et al. (eds), *Handhaving Van En Door'Het Privaatrecht* (Den Haag: Boom Juridische Uitgevers, 2009) 173–189.

Main TO, 'ADR: The New Equity' (2005) 74 *University of Cincinnati Law Review* 329–404.

Micklitz H-W, 'Collective Private Enforcement of Consumer Law: The Key Questions', in WH van Boom and MBM Loos (eds), *Collective Enforcement of Consumer Law – Securing Compliance in Europe through Private Group Action and Public Authority Intervention* (Groningen: Europa Law Publishing, 2007) 13–33.

Miller GP, 'Compensation and Deterrence in Consumer Class Actions in the US and Europe', in F Cafaggi and H-W Micklitz (eds), *New Frontiers of Consumer Protection – The Interplay between Private and Public Enforcement* (Mortsel: Intersentia, 2009) 263–282.

Miller JC, 'The FTC and Voluntary Standards: Maximizing the Net Benefits of Self-Regulation' (1985) 4(3) *Cato Journal* 897–903.

Ogus AI, *Regulation: Legal Form and Economic Theory* (Oxford: Clarendon Press, 1994).

———, 'The Economic Basis of Legal Culture: Networks and Monopolization' (2002) 22(3) *Oxford Journal of Legal Studies* 419–434.

Ogus AI, MG Faure and NJ Philipsen, 'Best Practices for Consumer Policy: Report on the Effectiveness of Enforcement Regimes' (2006) *Report prepared for the UK Department of Trade and Industry and OECD.*

Polinsky AM and S Shavell, 'The Theory of Public Enforcement of Law' (2005) *NBER Working Paper* 11780.

Posner RA, 'An Economic Approach to Legal Procedure and Judicial Administration', in F Parisi (ed.), *The Economic Structure of the Law: The Collected Economic Essays of Richard A. Posner* (Cheltenham, UK: Edward Elgar, 2000) 290–349.

——— (ed), *Economic Analysis of Law* (8th edn, New York: Aspen Publishers, 2011).

Renda A. et al., *Making Antitrust Damages Actions More Effective in the EU: Welfare Impact and Potential Scenarios*, Report for the European Commission (2007).

Rosenberg D and S Shavell, 'A Model in Which Suits are Brought for their Nuisance Value' (1985) 5 *International Review of Law and Economics* 3–13.

Schäfer H-B, 'The Bundling of Similar Interests in Litigation. The Incentives for Class Action and Legal Actions Taken by Associations' (2000) 9(3) *European Journal of Law and Economics* 183–213.

Shavell S, 'Risk Sharing and Incentives in the Principal and Agent Relationship' (1979) 10(1) *Bell Journal of Economics, The RAND Corporation* 55–73.

———, 'The Optimal Structure of Law Enforcement' (1993) 36 *Journal of Law and Economics* 255–288.

———, 'The Fundamental Divergence between the Private and the Social Motive to Use the Legal System' (1997) 16 *Journal of Legal Studies* 575–612.

van Boom WH, *Efficacious Enforcement in Contract and Tort* (Den Haag: Boom Juridische Uitgevers, 2006).

van Boom WH and MBM Loos, 'Effective Enforcement of Consumer Law in Europe: Synchronizing Private, Public, and Collective Mechanisms' (2008) *Working Paper Series*.

Van den Bergh R, 'Should Consumer Protection Law be Publicly Enforced?', in WH van Boom and MBM Loos (eds), *Collective Enforcement of Consumer Law* (Groningen: Europa Law Publishing, 2007) 179–203.

———, 'Enforcement of Consumer Law by Consumer Associations', in MG Faure and FH Stephen (eds), *Essays in the Law and Economics of Regulation – In Honour of Anthony Ogus* (Antwerp, Oxford, Portland: Intersentia, 2008) 279–306.

Van den Bergh R and S Keske, 'Rechtsökonomische Aspekte Der Sammelklage', in M Casper et al. (eds), *Auf Dem Weg Zu Einer Europäischen Sammelklage?* (München: Sellier, European Law Publishers, 2009) 17–40.

Van den Bergh R and LT Visscher, 'The Preventive Function of Collective Actions for Damages in Consumer Law' (2008) 1 *Erasmus Law Review* 5–30.

Verbruggen P, 'Transnational Private Regulation in the Advertising Industry – Case Study Report for the Research Project Constitutional Foundations of Transnational Private Regulation (March 31, 2011)', http://ssrn.com/abstract=2256043.

Weber F, 'Assessing Existing Enforcement Mechanisms in Consumer Law – The Unavailability of an Allrounder' (2011) 3 *Swedish Journal of European Law (Europarättslig tidskrift)* 536–554.

Weber F and C Hodges, 'Netherlands', in C Hodges, I Benöhr and N Creutzfeldt-Banda (eds), *Consumer ADR in Europe* (Oxford: Hart Publishing, 2012) 129–165.

Wilson JQ, *Bureaucracy – What Government Agencies Do and Why They Do It* (New York: Basic Books, 1989).

Chapter 9
Private or Public Enforcement of the UCP Directive? Sanctions and Remedies to Prevent Unfair Commercial Practices[1]

Dörte Poelzig

1. Introduction

According to the principle of national procedural autonomy, in the absence of any relevant Union rules, enforcement of EU law is a matter for the Member States.[2] But how does this comply with the full harmonization approach of Directive 2005/29/EC on unfair commercial practices in the Internal Market (hereinafter: UCP Directive)? The UCP Directive is intended to fully harmonize the rules for the fight against unfair commercial practices in order to contribute to the proper functioning of the internal market and to achieve a high level of consumer protection.[3] To ensure full effectiveness of the UCP Directive it is essential to establish a level playing field of effective enforcement in the European Union by discouraging unfair commercial practices. Uneven or incomplete enforcement of the national provisions adopted in application of the UCP Directive would not only reduce the overall benefits of the harmonized substantive law and affect the interests of the citizens or enterprises concerned but also jeopardize the mutual confidence which underlies the whole internal market structure.[4]

---

1 I would like to thank Orkun Akseli, Willem van Boom, Antonina Engelbrekt, Marine Friant-Perrot, Amandine Garde, Geraint Howells, Bert Keirsbilck, Hans Micklitz, Charlotte Pavillon, Franziska Weber, Chris Willet and the other participants of the workshop 'Experiencing the Unfair Commercial Practices Directive' and Werner F. Ebke for valuable comments. The usual disclaimers apply.

2 Case 33/76 *Rewe v Landwirtschaftskammer Saarland* [1976] ECR 1989, para 5; Case 45/76 *Comet v Produktschap voor Siergewassen* [1976] ECR 2043, para 11; Case 158/80 *Rewe v Hauptzollamt Kiel* [1981] ECR 1805, para 44.

3 See recitals 5 and 6 in the preamble and art 1 of the UCP Directive. Joined Cases C-261 & 299/07 *VTB-VAB* [2009] ECR I-2949, para 52.

4 Commission (EC), 'Communication from the Commission to the Council and the European Parliament on the Role of Penalties in Implementing Community Internal Market Legislation' (Communication) COM (95) 162 final, 3 May 1995, 6.

The debate over the most effective way to enforce the UCP Directive often reveals a division into private versus public enforcement.[5] This concerns first and foremost the question who should be the actor initiating enforcement of the UCP Directive.[6] Public enforcement in this context means enforcement by national authorities or the European Commission on their own motion or based on complaints of citizens or businesses. Public authorities can impose administrative or criminal sanctions. Private enforcement means application of the law based on the UCP Directive in civil disputes before national courts, for example in actions for injunctive relief or for damages to those who have suffered a loss caused by an infringement of the rules based on the UCP Directive. Private enforcement can be pursued by way of individual or collective redress: natural or legal persons initiate distinct legal proceedings to enforce their rights or a group of persons respectively a private entity may claim damages.

With regard to unfair commercial practices there is no centralized enforcement at the EU level as, for instance, in competition law under Regulation 1/2003. The different Member States have employed various strategies in their enforcement policies.[7] Some Member States – including Germany and Austria – essentially rely on private enforcement or partially complement it – as is the case in Sweden and Denmark – with administrative enforcement. On the other hand, Great Britain relies mainly on enforcement through administrative authorities which are able to implement administrative sanctions.[8] Administrative enforcement is complemented by self-regulation.[9] There is no private right of action against traders by businesses or consumers. Lastly, France is operating a third model which is based on a combined system: rules regarding fair commercial practices are enforced mainly by public authorities using administrative and criminal sanctions. Moreover consumers may bring a case before a civil or criminal court to claim damages, including through collective redress. In EU law, due to limited resources

5 From an economic point of view Franziska Weber, 'Law and Economics of Enforcing Misleading Advertising Laws – Incentives of Bona and Mala Fide Traders Assessed', in this volume.

6 For more details on this see Dörte Poelzig, *Normdurchsetzung durch Privatrecht* (Tübingena: Mohr Siebeck, 2012) 286 et seq.

7 Willem H van Boom and Marco Loos (eds), *Collective Enforcement of Consumer Law* (Groningen: Europa Law Publishing, 2007); Hans-W Micklitz, 'Legal Redress', in Geraint Howells, Hans-W Micklitz and Thomas Wilhelmsson (eds), *European Fair Trading Law* (Aldershot: Ashgate, 2006) 217 et seq.

8 The Consumer Protection from Unfair Trading Regulations 2008, part 4. On the implementation of the UCP Directive in the United Kingdom see Geraint Howells, 'The End of an Era – Implementing the Unfair Commercial Practices Directive in the United Kingdom: Punctual Criminal Law Gives Way to a General Criminal/Civil Law Standard' (2009) 2 *JBL* 183 et seq.

9 Willem H van Boom, *Efficacious Enforcement in Contract and Tort* (Den Haag: Boom Juridische uitgevers, 2006) 37 et seq.; Geraint Howells and Stephen Weatherill, *Consumer Protection Law* (2nd edn, Aldershot: Ashgate, 2005) 586 et seq.

of public authorities, the issue of strengthening private enforcement mechanisms has been increasingly brought on the agenda. Since the seminal decision of the ECJ in *Courage* there has been a comprehensive discussion on the merits and risks of private enforcement of European competition law. Moreover, private enforcement has traditionally been a mainstay in the US enforcement system.[10]

This paper will discern which role private and public enforcement should play in regard to the UCP Directive. The first part deals with the requirements of EU law. In the second part, the implementations and open issues in the Member States are scrutinized.

2. Requirements of EU law

According to the general principle of national procedural autonomy, in the absence of harmonized Union law governing the matter, it is for each Member State to lay down the detailed procedural rules governing actions to ensure the compliance of Union law.[11] However, in regard to the UCP Directive the general principle of national procedural autonomy is limited by some requirements.

2.1 Public and/or Private Enforcement: Articles 11–13 of the UCP Directive

Articles 11–13 of the UCP Directive provide for different rules in regard to remedies of unfair commercial practices. Article 11 provides which instruments of enforcement shall be available in national law. Article 12 regulates the competences of national courts and administrative authorities in regard to the substantiation of claims. Article 13 of the UCP Directive specifies which penalties for infringements of national provisions adopted in application of the UCP Directive Member States should lay down. Articles 11 and 13 of the Directive are interesting in this context.

2.1.1 Enforcement

Article 11(1)(3) of the UCP Directive stipulates that it shall be for each Member State to decide which of the enforcement instruments named in Article 11(1)(2) shall be available in national law.[12] According to Article 11(1)(2) of the UCP

10 As to the enforcement of the rules on unfair and deceptive acts and practices in US state law see Henry N Butler and Joshua D Wright, 'Are State Consumer Protection Acts Really Little-FTC Acts?' (2011) 62 *Florida Law Review* 163. As to rule 10b-5 in securities laws see Werner F Ebke, *Wirtschaftsprüfer und Dritthaftung* (Bielefeld: Verlag Ernst und Werner Gieseking, 1983) 187 et seq.

11 Case C-126/97 *Eco Swiss China Time Ltd v Benetton International NV* [1999] ECR I-3055, Opinion of Advocate General Saggio, para 48.

12 For detail on this see Christian Alexander, 'Die Sanktions- und Verfahrensvorschriften der Richtlinie 2005/29/EG über unlautere Geschäftspraktiken im Binnenmarkt – Umsetzungsbedarf in Deutschland?' (2005) *Gewerblicher Rechtsschutz und Urheberrecht, Internationaler Teil* 809 et seq.

Directive, persons or organizations regarded under national law as having a legitimate interest in combating unfair commercial practices need to be able to take legal action and/or to bring unfair commercial practices before an administrative authority. The first alternative stands for private enforcement, whereas the second alternative illustrates public enforcement. Similar demands were formulated in Article 4(1)(2) of Directive 84/450/EEC of 10 September 1984: Member States are to ensure that those affected could combat misleading or inadmissible comparative advertising by taking legal action or bringing such advertising before a competent administrative authority. The UCP Directive extended this rule to all cases of unfair commercial practices.

The wording 'and/or' in Article 11(1) (2) of the Directive makes it clear that both an exclusively private or public enforcement as well as a combination of the two are permissible. Member States can also require recourse to an obligatory mechanism of self-regulation prior to civil or administrative proceedings (Article 11 [1] [3] of the UCP Directive). In this case civil courts and public authorities respectively act as 'enforcers of last resort'.[13] Thus Article 11 of the UCP Directive declares civil proceedings initiated by competitors, consumers or private associations as essentially equivalent to public enforcement and permissible when used alone or in combination with the latter.[14] With this, the Directive leaves it up to Member States whether to provide public or private instruments to enforce unfair commercial practices law.[15] That coincides with the general principle of national procedural autonomy.[16] So far the UCP Directive does not go beyond the Council Directive 84/450/EEC concerning misleading and comparative advertising.

2.1.2 Penalties

Article 13 of the UCP Directive stipulates that Member States shall lay down penalties for infringements of national provisions adopted in application of this Directive and shall take all necessary measures to ensure that these are enforced. These penalties must be effective, proportionate and dissuasive. This wording goes

13 Commission, 'European Union Consumer Protection' (Green Paper) COM (17) 531 final COM 17, 2 October 2001.

14 Similarly Susanne Augenhofer, 'Individualrechtliche Ansprüche des Verbrauchers bei unlauterem Wettbewerbsverhalten des Unternehmers' (2006) *Wettbewerb in Recht und Praxis* 169, 170.

15 Helmut Gamerith, 'Der Richtlinienvorschlag über unlautere Geschäftspraktiken – Möglichkeiten einer harmonischen Umsetzung' (2005) *Wettbewerb in Recht und Praxis* 391, 403; Alexander, 'Die Sanktions- und Verfahrensvorschriften der Richtlinie 2005/29/EG' (n 12) 813.

16 Case C-126/97 *Eco Swiss China Time Ltd v Benetton International NV* [1999] ECR I-3055, Opinion of Advocate General Saggio, para 48.

back to ECJ judgements[17] and other directives.[18] As a consequence of the procedural autonomy of the Member States, Article 13 does not require Member States to provide for specific penalties. However, the UCP Directive essentially leaves the national procedural autonomy and the current diversity of sanctioning systems among Member States intact only provided that effectiveness, proportionality and dissuasiveness are guaranteed. If this is not the case by applying an existent national system, Member States concerned must either choose another system of penalties that satisfies those criteria, adapt its existing system or introduce a special system in order to meet the requirements.[19]

a) Meaning of penalty

In contrast to other directives, the UCP Directive in its English version uses the word 'penalty' instead of 'sanction'.[20] The use of different words appears to indicate a different meaning. But the wording of the UCP Directive in other languages is the same as in other directives: In German it is 'Sanktionen', in French it is 'sanctions'. Moreover, the ECJ often uses these terms as synonyms.[21] To that extent, there is no difference in the meaning of Article 13 of the UCP Directive to the wording used by the ECJ in its decisions and of that in other directives. Accordingly, the wording 'penalty' or 'sanction', respectively, is not restricted to criminal sanctions or administrative fines but also covers civil liability.[22] According to Article 13 of the UCP Directive, Member States are basically free to choose between criminal, administrative or purely civil penalties as long as they are effective, dissuasive and proportionate.

17 Case C-382/92 *Commission v United Kingdom* [1994] ECR I-2435, para 55; see Case C-7/90 *Criminal Proceedings against Paul Vandevenne* [1991] ECR I-4371, para 11; Case C-326/88 *Anklagemyndigheden* [1990] ECR I-2911, para 17; Case 68/88 *Commission v Hellenic Republic* [1989] ECR 2965, para 24.

18 See Council Directive (EC) 2000/43 Implementing the Principle of Equal Treatment between Persons Irrespective of Racial or Ethnic Origin [2000] OJ L180/22 art 15; Directive (EC) 2000/31 of the European Parliament and of the Council on Certain legal Aspects of Information Society Services, in Particular Electronic Commerce, in the Internal Market [2000] OJ L178/1 ('Directive on Electronic Commerce') art 20.

19 Commission, 'Communication from the Commission to the Council and the European Parliament' (n 4) 3.

20 See Council Directive (EC) 2000/43 implementing the principle of equal treatment (n 18) art 15; Directive on Electronic Commerce Art 20.

21 See for example Case C-387/02 *Berlusconi* [2005] ECR I-3565.

22 See for example Case 50/76 *Amsterdam Bulb BV v Produktschap voor Siergewassen* [1977] ECR 137, paras 32 et seq.; Case C-7/90 *Vandevenne and others* [1991] ECR I-4371, Opinion of Advocate General van Gerven, para 8; also Case 14/83 *Sabine von Colson and Elisabeth Kamann v Land Nordrhein-Westfalen* [1984] ECR 1891, para 23 et seq.; Case C-177/88 *Elisabeth Johanna Pacifica Dekker v Stichting Vormingscentrum voor Jong Volwassenen Plus* [1990] ECR I-03941, paras 23 et seq. In favour of a broader meaning also Hans-W Micklitz 'Legal Redress', in Howells, Micklitz and Wilhelmsson, *European Fair Trading Law* (n 7) 217, 230.

b) Effectiveness, dissuasiveness and proportionality

Whether a penalty is effective, proportionate and dissuasive within the meaning defined by Article 13 of the UCP Directive 'must be analysed by reference to the role of that provision in the legislation as a whole, including the progress and special features of the procedure before the various national authorities, in each case in which that question arises'.[23] Accordingly, the peculiarities of the national system of each Member State have to be taken into account. Moreover, the fact that the UCP Directive is a measure of full harmonization has to be taken into account.

aa) Effectiveness

The need for effective sanctions follows from the fundamental principle of effectiveness based on Article 4(3) TEU.[24] According to Advocate General Kokott 'rules laying down penalties are effective where they are framed in such a way that they do not make it practically impossible or excessively difficult to impose the penalty provided for.'[25] Advocate General van Gerven emphasized 'that the Member States must endeavour to attain and implement the objectives of the relevant provisions of Community law'.[26] According to either definition, sanctions are ineffective if they provide for conditions that are either unrealizable or incapable of proof.[27] For competitors for example it might be difficult to prove their actual loss caused or the profit of the trader generated by an unfair commercial practice. If due to the principle that the party bringing the action must provide evidence for its claim it is practically impossible or excessively difficult to claim damages, the Member States have to implement law providing for a lighter burden of proof or easier access to information and evidence held by the defendant. Moreover, the German skimming-off procedure is a 'good' example of an ineffective sanction because currently there is almost no incentive for the entitled organization to initiate a skimming-off procedure (see III. 2. c). Lastly, individual rights to claim damages might be also ineffective in the field of unfair commercial practices if

23 Case C-387/02 *Berlusconi* [2005] ECR I-3565, Opinion of Advocate General Kokott, para 91.

24 Case C-201/02 *Delena Wells* [2004] ECR I-723, para 67, with further references, and Case C-312/93 *Peterbroeck* [1995] ECR I-4599, para 12.

25 Case C-387/02 *Berlusconi* [2005] ECR I-3565, Opinion of Advocate General Kokott, para 88. On the principle of effectiveness in general, see Case 45/76 *Comet* [1976] ECR 2043, paras 11 and 18; Case C-312/93 *Peterbroek* [1995] ECR I-4599, para 12; Case C-261/95 *Palmisani* [1997] ECR I-4025, para 27; Case C-90/94 *Haahr Petroleum* [1997] ECR I-4085, para 46; Case C-231/96 *Edis* [1998] ECR I-4951, para 19; Case C-260/96 *Spac* [1998] ECR I-4997, para 18; Case C-88/99 *Roquette Frères* [2000] ECR I-10465, para 21; Case C-126/97 *Eco Swiss* [1999] ECR I-3055, Opinion of Advocate General Saggio, para 48.

26 Case C-326/88 *Hansen* [1990] ECR I-2911, 2923, Opinion of Advocate General van Gerven, para 8.

27 Alexander, 'Die Sanktions- und Verfahrensvorschriften der Richtlinie 2005/29/EG' (n 12) 811.

individuals have suffered dispersed and relatively low-value damage because they are often deterred from bringing individual actions for damages.

bb) Dissuasiveness

A penalty is dissuasive if it prevents an individual from infringing the rules laid down by Union law, here namely the national provisions adopted in application of this Directive. Therefore, the penalty must be sufficiently strict, regard being had to the objectives pursued by the UCP Directive.[28] Since compliance with the law on unfair commercial practices imposes direct or indirect costs on businesses, the potential benefits of unfair commercial practices should not outweigh the penalties incurred.[29] A penalty has a preventive effect especially if it makes it economically unattractive to infringe the law.[30] The dissuasive effect depends firstly on the nature and the level of the penalty.[31] Private enforcement mechanisms can deter unfair commercial practices forbidden by the UCP Directive. Especially private claims for damages may serve as dissuasive sanctions. Secondly, the dissuasive effect depends also on 'the likelihood of its being imposed'.[32] Anyone who commits an infringement must fear that the penalty will in fact be imposed on him. Insignificant or hypothetical penalties are not dissuasive.[33] There is an overlap here between the criterion of dissuasiveness and that of effectiveness.

cc) Proportionality

Effectiveness and dissuasiveness require a certain minimum standard of sanctioning, whereas the latter requirement, that is proportionality, places limits on the extent of penalties. The principle of proportionality is a fundamental principle of European Union law (Article 5(4) TEU).[34] It is to ensure that penalties are not so disproportionately heavy as to disrupt the market. A penalty is proportionate if it

---

28 See Case C-387/02 *Berlusconi* [2005] ECR I-3565, Opinion of Advocate General Kokott, para 89; Case C-326/88 *Hansen* [1990] ECR I-2911, Opinion of Advocate General van Gerven.

29 Commission, 'Communication from the Commission to the Council and the European Parliament' (n 4) 2.

30 For art 228(2) EC (now: art 260(2) TFEU), Case C-304/02 *Commission v French Republic* [2005] I-6263, Opinion of Advocate General Geelhoed, para 10.

31 Case C-354/99 *Commission v Ireland* [2001] ECR I-7657, para 47; Opinion of Advocate General Geelhoed (ECR I-7660), para 27. See also Case C-382/92 *Commission v United Kingdom* [1994] ECR I-2435, paras 56–58 and Case C-383/92 *Commission v United Kingdom* [1994] ECR I-2479, paras 41 and 42.

32 Case C-387/02 *Berlusconi* [2005] ECR I-3565, Opinion of Advocate General Kokott, para 88.

33 Commission, 'Communication from the Commission to the Council and the European Parliament' (n 4) 2.

34 Christian Calliess, in Christian Calliess and Matthias Ruffert (eds), *EUV/AEUV, Kommentar* (Munich: C.H. Beck, 2011) art 5 EUV, paras 44 et seq.

is effective and dissuasive and also necessary.[35] The level of sanctioning has to be ascertained on a case-by-case basis regarding the severity of the infringement. It would be disproportionate for example to sanction for infringement of a procedural requirement as severely as if, in addition to this procedural failure, substantive conditions had also been breached.[36] Moreover, the effects of the penalty on the person sanctioned must be proportionate to the aims pursued. If there a choice between several equally effective and dissuasive penalties, recourse must be had to the least burdensome.[37] Therefore, criminal penalties shall only serve as *ultima ratio* sanctions, provided that there is a particularly severe infringement. To avoid disproportionate sanctioning Member States must be able to decide not to impose penalties under certain circumstances.[38]

In the context of proportionality, a specific aspect in regard to the UCP Directive has to be taken into account: the intention of full harmonization. Whereas too strict sanctions do not impede the attainment of minimum harmonization, they might be problematic for the full harmonization approach of the UCP Directive. According to this, Member States are not allowed to impose requirements which are more restrictive or prescriptive than the UCP Directive in the field which it approximates. Bearing in mind that the level of sanctioning may also influence the standard of compliance with the prohibition of unfair commercial practices, disproportionately heavy sanctions might impede the achievement of full harmonization. If for example every unfair commercial practice is sanctioned by criminal penalties traders might forego even legal commercial practices only because there may be a risk to be liable to a criminal sanction.

2.1.3 Relationship between enforcement and penalties

Although the UCP Directive distinguishes clearly between enforcement and penalties there is still a close relationship between Article 11 and Article 13 of the UCP Directive: Enforcement and penalties are inseparably linked to each other. Administrative fines as a possible penalty under Article 13 of the UCP Directive can only be imposed in a proceeding before an administrative authority (see Article 11 [1] [2b] of the UCP Directive). In contrast, civil liability as an alternative penalty within the framework of Article 13 of the UCP Directive requires legal action initiated by persons or organizations regarded under national law as having a legitimate interest in combating unfair commercial practices (see Article 11 [1] [2a] of the UCP Directive). Even the UCP Directive itself does not

35 Case C-253/00 *Munoz* [2002] ECR I-7289, Opinion of Advocate General Geelhoed, para 54; Alexander, 'Die Sanktions- und Verfahrensvorschriften der Richtlinie 2005/29/EG' (n 12) 811.

36 See Case C-348/04 *Boehringer Ingelheim* [2007] ECR I-3391, Opinion of Advocate General Sharpston, para 76.

37 Case C-387/02 *Berlusconi* [2005] ECR I-3565, Opinion of Advocate General Kokott, para 90.

38 Case C-253/00 *Munoz* [2002] ECR I-7289, Opinion of Advocate General Geelhoed, para 54.

sharply distinguish between enforcement and penalties. Therefore the question of enforcement cannot be answered without recourse to penalties and vice versa.

2.1.4 Implications for Member States

The UCP Directive leaves it to Member States whether they rely primarily on public or private enforcement or a combination of them. According to the principle of subsidiarity and the principle of national procedural autonomy, Member States are free to choose sanctions which appear to them to be appropriate.[39] Full implementation of the UCP Directive does not require any specific form of sanction for unfair commercial practices. The Member States may basically decide whether they provide for administrative fines, criminal sanctions or civil liability. First and foremost in pursuance of the general principle of effectiveness, Member States are obliged to guarantee an effective enforcement system and to implement effective, dissuasive and proportionate sanctions. Compared to directives with a minimum harmonization approach the full harmonization approach influences especially the requirement of proportionality. In so far the national procedural autonomy is more restricted. But whether public authorities or private persons or associations should have the competence to enforce legislation based on the UCP Directive should basically be decided by each Member State itself. Nevertheless, the principle of national procedural autonomy is also restricted to that extent by some minimum standards to be complied with.

2.2 Private and Public Enforcement in Cross-Border Cases

Some cases initiated by German and French consumers' associations have revealed the difficulties which arise in cross-border enforcement. The question in these cases was mainly whether a German consumer association is entitled to make use of its right to take action in Germany in order to protect French consumers.[40] This experience triggered the adoption of the Consumer Injunctions Directive and later the Regulation (EC) 2006/2004 on consumer protection cooperation.

2.2.1 Directive 2009/22/EC on Injunctions for the Protection of Consumers' Interests

The Directive 2009/22/EC on Injunctions for the Protection of Consumers' Interests ('Consumer Injunctions Directive') obliges Member States to allow proceedings commenced by qualified entities seeking injunctions. The Consumer Injunctions Directive establishes minimum standards in regard to the entitlement of foreign-registered associations to take legal actions and the procedure. Qualified entities include private consumer protection bodies within the meaning of Article 3(b) and/

39 Case 50/76 *Amsterdam Bulb BV v Produktschap voor Siergewassen* [1977] ECR 137, para 33.

40 See in detail Hans-W Micklitz, 'Cross-Border Consumer Conflicts – A French German Experience' (1993) 16 *Journal of Consumer Policy* 411 et seq.

or public bodies responsible for consumer protection. They are entitled to seek an injunction, *inter alia*, in case of a breach of the UCP Directive in order to 'protect the collective interests of consumers'.[41] Courts or administrative authorities shall be competent especially to rule an order requiring the cessation or prohibition of any infringement or in so far as the legal system of the Member State concerned so permits, an order against the losing defendant for payments into the public purse or to any beneficiary designated in or under national legislation.

2.2.2 Regulation on Consumer Protection Cooperation

While the Consumer Injunctions Directive is intended to strengthen enforcement mainly through private consumer associations, the Regulation (EC) 2006/2004 on consumer protection cooperation promotes cooperation between competent national authorities. This regulation has brought a substantial change in the national enforcement of unfair commercial practices – at least for those Member States which, like Germany, relied exclusively on private enforcement.[42] The vital importance of undistorted competition for the general public and the considerable damage to the confidence of consumers caused by unfair commercial practices have given rise to the consideration of introducing regulatory supervision in addition to private enforcement.[43] Accordingly, by adopting Regulation (EC) 2006/2004, the European Commission considerably strengthened the public enforcement of unfair commercial practices. The Regulation applies to intra-Union infringements of the directives listed in the Annex – including the UCP Directive (see Article 3[a] Regulation on Consumer Protection Cooperation) – if the collective interests of several consumers are harmed (Article 3[k] Regulation on Consumer Protection Cooperation).[44] The Regulation on Consumer Protection Cooperation is aimed at improving the cooperation of national competent authorities with each other and with the Commission. The Regulation emphasizes the ability of competent authorities to cooperate by exchanging information, detecting and investigating

---

41 Directive (EC) 98/27 of the European Parliament and of the Council on Injunctions for the Protection of Consumers' Interests [1998] OJ L 166/51.

42 Cf. Hans-W Micklitz, 'Transborder Law Enforcement – Does It Exist?', in Stephen Weatherill and Ulf Bernitz (eds), *The Regulation of Unfair Commercial Practices under EC Directive 2005/29* (Oxford: Hart Publishing, 2007) 235 et seq.

43 Recital no 2 of the Regulation (EC) 2006/2004 on Cooperation between National Authorities Responsible for the Enforcement of Consumer Protection laws (the Regulation on Consumer Protection Cooperation) [2004] OJ L364/1. Already discussed by Carl Baudenbacher, 'Die Revision des schweizerischen UWG – Bemerkungen zum Entwurf der Expertenkommission' (1981) *Gewerblicher Rechtsschutz und Urheberrecht, Internationaler Teil* 162, 168; followed by Jochen Glöckner, *Europäisches Lauterkeitsrecht* (Munich: C.H. Beck, 2006) 611.

44 Mainly civil law regulatory areas are covered: competition law, contracts negotiated away from business premises, package travel law, distance contracts, the law of standard terms and conditions of business, distance marketing of consumer financial services, consumer credits.

intra-Union infringements of provisions protecting consumer interests in order to promote the smooth functioning of the internal market and enhance the protection of consumers (see Article 1 and recital No. 7). According to Article 4(1) of the Regulation, Member States shall designate the competent authority and a single liaison office responsible for the investigation and enforcement. The adoption of the Regulation on consumer protection cooperation was induced, *inter alia*, by the apparent lack of effective enforcement of consumer protection provisions when it came to cross-border infringements.[45] Neither private nor public enforcement mechanisms were sufficiently adapted to the challenges of the internal market. According to the European Commission, even though consumers and consumer associations will continue to have an essential enforcement role to play, a fully functioning consumer internal market can only be guaranteed if public consumer enforcement authorities act as enforcers of last resort to supplement private enforcement.[46] This is said to be the only possibility of preventing infringements before they occur, without being dependent on time-consuming legal procedures. Moreover, the enforcement authorities of Member States are said to enable decentralized but coordinated market surveillance.[47] Linked to this is the expectation that, compared to civil courts, special public authorities would be better equipped for the cross-border enforcement of provisions with more expertise as well as with instruments suitable and necessary. Centralized public enforcement at the Union level – as it is being operated in competition law – was, however, refused by the European Commission. The Commission explained that it lacked the necessary resources in this respect and that there was no corresponding competence in the EC Treaty.[48]

The enforcement model of the Regulation on Consumer Protection Cooperation is based on the cooperation of the Member States' consumer protection authorities, which entails that each public authority from one Member State provides mutual assistance on request of and for authorities of other Member States. Yet the opening clause contained in Article 4(2) (2) and Article 8(3) of the Regulation still allows Member States to designate bodies that have a legitimate interest in the cessation or prohibition of infringements to take all necessary enforcement measures available according to national law. In particular, Article 8(3) of the Regulation enables designated private consumer protection associations to act if they are instructed by public authorities. However, this possibility does not

45 Recital no 2 of the Regulation (EC) 2006/2004 on Consumer Protection Cooperation. Cf. on this BGH, Case I ZR 148/95, GRUR 1998, 419 et seq. – Werbegewinnspiel im Ausland.

46 Commission, 'European Union Consumer Protection' (n 13) 17: 'enforcers of last resort'.

47 Commission, 'European Union Consumer Protection' (n 13) 17.

48 Commission, MEMO/01/307 'Questions and Answers on the Green Paper on Consumer Protection', 2 October 2001: 'The Commission has neither the resources, inclination or Treaty mandate to assume the Fair Trade Commission role as a public enforcement body in this area.'

exonerate Member States from the duty of designating a competent administrative authority. Member States – like Germany – that operate an exclusively private law enforcement model have been required by the Regulation to set up special administrative authorities that are responsible for enforcement in cross-border cases albeit they may fulfil their obligations by instructing a private body. With this, EU law has been becoming more inclined to enforce unfair commercial practices law using public (in addition to private) means.[49]

The German Consumer Protection Enforcement Act (EG-Verbraucherschutz durchsetzungsgesetz, acronym: 'VSchDG') which implements the Regulation in German law makes use of Article 4(2) and gives precedence to private enforcement by qualified entities which can initiate legal proceedings. In German law the public authority is ultimately responsible for the combat of cross-border infringements covered by the Regulation. Hereby, the 'public authority model' complements and is subsidiary to the private enforcement system. After more than five years, the experience in Germany with the Regulation on Consumer Protection Cooperation has been generally positive. In particular, maintaining the private enforcement mechanisms has made it possible to utilize long-standing and well-founded experience and knowledge of the private entities. However, there are also some practical problems with the cooperation between public authorities and private associations: First of all, the time-consuming process of coordination is an issue. Communications between public authorities and the designated association take time and may delay the enforcement procedure. Another issue is the difficulty to deal with different languages and policies in different Member States.[50]

2.3 Private Enforcement: Stipulations of the Principle of Effectiveness

Beyond the Consumer Injunctions Directive an obligation on Member States to provide further mechanisms of private enforcement to prevent unfair commercial practices can result from the Union law principle of effectiveness: According

49 Before implementing the Regulation on Consumer Protection Cooperation, some scholars already inferred such a Union law obligation requiring Member States to create a special public authority in charge of enforcing the Directive from art 11 of the UCP Directive, which states that 'Member States shall ensure that adequate and effective means exist to combat unfair commercial practices in order to enforce compliance with the provisions of this Directive in the interest of consumers' (Frauke Henning-Bodewig, 'Richtlinienvorschlag über unlautere Geschäftspraktiken und UWG-Reform' (2004) *Gewerblicher Rechtsschutz und Urheberrecht, Internationaler Teil* 183, 193). It is argued that since the term 'means' covers individual possibilities of those affected to bring legal proceedings, the additional mentioning of 'compliance with the provisions of this Directive' could thereby only be understood as imposing an additional obligation on Member States to create a public body or organization responsible for combating unfair commercial practices (Henning-Bodewig, 'Richtlinienvorschlag' [see above] 193).

50 Report by the German Federal Government on the effectiveness of § 7 of the German Consumer Protection Enforcement Act ('VSchDG'), BT-Drs. 17/8982, 6.

to Article 13 of the UCP Directive, Member States shall lay down penalties for infringement which must be, *inter alia*, effective.

2.3.1 The case for more private enforcement

In 2003 in *Munoz*, the ECJ required Member States to grant individual rights in case of infringement of unfair commercial practices law provisions based on the principle of effectiveness.[51] In this case a trader brought a claim against a competitor for failure to comply with EU labelling requirements. The ECJ held that traders must be able to enforce the adherence to Community law quality standards by competitors in civil proceedings because this is the only way of ensuring the full effectiveness of EC law.[52] Enabling third-party claims to intervene in the relationship between competitors was intended to strengthen the 'practical working of the Community rules on quality standards' and, thereby, to contribute 'substantially to ensuring fair trading and transparency of markets in the Community'.[53] Similarly, in regard to competition law, it is necessary, according to the ECJ in *Courage* and *Manfredi*, as 'the full effectiveness of Article 85 of the Treaty and, in particular, the practical effect of the prohibition laid down in Article 85 [1] would be put at risk if it were not open to any individual to claim damages for loss caused to him by a contract or by conduct liable to restrict or distort competition.'[54] In light of this observation, EU law, in particular the principle of effectiveness, demands private enforcement if this is the only way to ensure full effectiveness.[55] Individuals affected by unfair commercial practices can help to detect those practices which would otherwise be very difficult to detect in the first place. Ultimately this safeguards fair trading and market transparency in the European Union.[56] According to the ECJ, private enforcement is not automatically rendered unnecessary if compliance with the law is already subject to exclusively public enforcement.[57] However, regulations (*Munoz*) and Article 101 TFEU (*Courage* and *Manfredi*) are directly applicable and can be relied upon by and against private individuals in actions in national courts. In contrast, the provisions of the UCP Directive are not directly applicable and do not have horizontal direct

---

51 Case C-253/00 *Munoz* [2002] ECR I-7289, para 30.

52 Case C-253/00 *Munoz* [2002] ECR I-7289, para 30.

53 Case C-253/00 *Munoz* [2002] ECR I-7289, para 31.

54 Case C-453/99 *Courage Ltd v Bernard Crehan* [2001] ECR I- 6297, para 26; Case C-295/04 *Vincenzo Manfredi v Lloyd Adriatico Assicurazioni SpA, Antonio Cannito v Fondiaria Sai SpA, Nicolò Tricarico and Pasqualina Murgolo v Assitalia SpA* [2006] ECR I-6619, para 31.

55 See the Proposal for a Directive of the European Parliament and the Council on Certain Rules Governing Actions for Damages under National Law for Infringements of the Competition Law Provisions of the Member States and of the European Union, COM (2013) 404 final, 11. June 2013.

56 Case C-253/00 *Munoz* [2002] ECR I-7289, para 31.

57 Case C-253/00 *Munoz* [2002] ECR I-7289, para 17.

effect. Directives cannot as such impose obligations on individuals and therefore cannot by themselves create rights in favour of private parties.[58]

However, the case law in *Munoz*, *Courage* and *Manfredi* is based on a general idea of Union law which facilitates the establishment of private enforcement.[59] In each of these cases, the primary reason for granting a right to claim within the relation of individuals is the effective enforcement of Union law obligations of market participants.[60] The ECJ thus acknowledged that private claims between individuals under civil law complement public enforcement by authorities. Because the UCP Directive requires Member States to implement effective sanctions, the seminal decisions of the ECJ in *Munoz*, *Courage* and *Manfredi* have to be considered. That does not mean, however, that the UCP Directive itself grants a cause of action and imposes obligations on the wrongdoer in absence of proper implementation in national law. The direct effect of a directive cannot be pleaded against an individual. However, there is one lesson to be learned from the mentioned case law: this is that Member States are obliged to implement a cause of action in national law, if otherwise the effectiveness of the UCP Directive would be put at risk.

2.3.2 Individual redress

The UCP Directive deals only marginally with rights to claim for individuals: In Article 11(2) the Directive requires Member States to implement legal provisions under which, *inter alia*, competitors may take legal action and/or bring such unfair commercial practices before an administrative authority. Consumers are only indirectly mentioned in Article 11(1) of the Directive according to which enforcement is necessary in the interest of consumers. However, individual legal redress on behalf of consumers is not mentioned at all in the UCP Directive.

a) Individual legal redress of competitors

On the basis of the straightforward wording in Article 11 of the UCP Directive, individual legal redress for competitors is beyond any reasonable doubt and is accepted among Member States. That proposition is confirmed by the judgement of the ECJ in *Munoz*: In this decision, the ECJ did not consider whether the rule infringed is intended to serve the interests of the claiming competitor. In contrast, Advocate General Geelhoed had stipulated a condition for the establishment of private law claims of third parties against private individuals: He demanded that the person concerned should 'demonstrate an actual economic interest which

---

58 Case 152/84 *Marshall v Southampton and South-West Hampshire Health Authority* [1986] ECR 723, para 48.

59 For more details on this see Poelzig, *Normdurchsetzung durch Privatrecht* (n 6) 286 et seq.

60 Andrea Biondi, 'Comment, Case C-253/00, *Antonio Munoz y Cia, Superior Fruiticola SA v. Frumar Ltd, Redbridge Produce Marketing Ltd*, Judgment of the Full Court of 17 September 2002 [ECR] 2002 I-7289' (2003) 40 *Common Market Law Review* 1241, 1250.

is protected by a regulation and differentiates that person from other economic operators'.[61] Advocate General Geelhoed did not, however, impose particularly strict requirements regarding the substance of the protected economic interest. In his eyes, it suffices that fair trade promoted by the applicable Regulation includes, *inter alia,* the protection of 'the rights of competing undertakings if they suffer loss as a result of an infringement of the regulation'.[62] The ECJ did not express an opinion on this. Yet, in the rather brief reasons given by the Court in the judgement, the ECJ also failed to deal with the claimant's submission that the direct application of a Community provision in relations between individuals does not depend on 'the intent of the Community legislature [...] to benefit any particular class of the public or to confer subjective rights'.[63] The ECJ did, however, seem to assume that individual competitors, who were entitled to bring an action, are not covered by the protective purpose of the infringed EU labelling rule. Thus, it gave the protective purpose an abstract definition with reference to the fourth recital in the Preamble to Regulation (EEC) 1035/72: 'to keep products of unsatisfactory quality off the market, to guide production to meet consumers' requirements and to facilitate trade relations based on fair competition'.[64] The individual competitors were, however, not mentioned by the ECJ. Nevertheless, it did consider a corresponding claim in civil proceedings between trader and competitor necessary in order to promote the full effectiveness of Community law.[65]

b) Individual redress for consumers

The UCP Directive in general and especially the obligation on Member States to ensure adequate and effective means of enforcement are also intended to meet consumer interests. Therefore, a more generalized right of access to the Court – whether consumers should have a right to take action against unfair commercial practices – is worth some consideration. Although the Commission initially considered an individual right for the consumer to be compensated, Article 11 of the UCP Directive does not require Member States to introduce a compensation

---

61 Case C-253/00 *Munoz* [2002] ECR I-7289, Opinion of Advocate General Geelhoed, para 76.

62 Case C-253/00 *Munoz* [2002] ECR I-7289, Opinion of Advocate General Geelhoed, para 49.

63 Case C-253/00 *Munoz* [2002] ECR I-7289, para 25.

64 Case C-253/00 *Munoz* [2002] ECR I-7289, para 29.

65 Cf. Case C-253/00 *Munoz* [2002] ECR I-7289, para 30. See also Case C-453/99 *Courage Ltd v Bernard Crehan* [2001] ECR I-6297, para 26; Case C-295/04 *Vincenzo Manfredi v Lloyd Adriatico Assicurazioni SpA, Antonio Cannito v Fondiaria Sai SpA, Nicolò Tricarico and Pasqualina Murgolo v Assitalia SpA* [2006] ECR I-6619, para 31. Similarly Gerhard Wagner, 'Prävention und Verhaltenssteuerung durch Privatrecht – Anmaßung oder legitime Aufgabe?' (2006) 206 *Archiv für die civilistische Praxis* 352, 415; Assimakis Komninos, 'New Prospects for Private Enforcement of EC Competition Law: *Courage v. Crehan* and the Community Right to Damages' (2002) 39 *Common Market Law Review* 484.

claim for the benefit of individual consumers.[66] Nonetheless, the UCP Directive requires Member States to ensure that adequate and effective means to combat unfair commercial practices are introduced 'in the interest of consumers'. These means shall – the Directive continues – be available to persons or organizations regarded under national law who have 'a legitimate interest' in combating unfair commercial practices. Principally it is national law which decides who has a legitimate interest in bringing legal action. In this respect Article11(1) (2) of the UCP Directive essentially echoes Article 4(1) (2) of the Directive 84/450/EEC concerning misleading and comparative advertising. The prevailing opinion there was that private claims for injured consumers are not compulsory, even though the recitals of Directive 84/450/EEC expressly declare protection of the economic interests of consumers to be one of the Directive's aims. To this extent the Union legislators did not intend the UCP Directive to deviate from the pre-existing legal framework. Additionally, according to its recital No. 9, the UCP Directive 'is without prejudice to individual actions brought by those who have been harmed by an unfair commercial practice'. Therefore Member States are free to determine whether and to what extent they grant individual consumers the right to claim traders. Some Member States grant a right to claim damages to each consumer who suffered loss due to unfair commercial practices. This is the case, for example, in Greece, Poland and Portugal. Ireland even grants exemplary damages for consumers. In other Member States – such as Austria, Denmark, the Netherlands, Spain, Sweden or Germany – claims for damages on consumers follow from general rules of private law. In the third group of Member States – including Great Britain – adopting a general private right of action for the Regulation as a whole was rejected.[67]

---

66 Gamerith, 'Der Richtlinienvorschlag über unlautere Geschäftspraktiken' (n 15) 403; Helmut Köhler and Tobias Lettl, 'Das geltende europäische Lauterkeitsrecht, der Vorschlag für eine EG-Richtlinie über unlautere Geschäftspraktiken und die UWG-Reform' (2003) *Wettbewerb in Recht und Praxis* 1019, 1047.

67 See the report of the UK Law Commission from 28 March 2012 which recommends limited reform in regard to liability and remedies (http://lawcommission.justice.gov.uk/areas/misrepresentation-and-unfair-commercial-practices.htm). Accordingly, consumers should have the right to unwind the transaction (get a refund), or receive a discount on the price. Additional damages shall be recoverable to compensate for additional loss. See also the Government Response to the Consultation on Draft Consumer Protection from Unfair Trading Regulations by Department for Business Enterprise & Regulatory Reform (http://www.berr.gov.uk/files/file44300.pdf): 'Consumer organizations argued that unless there is provision for traders to compensate consumers who suffer detriment as a direct result of an unfair commercial practice the CPRs will only ever have the potential to be partially effective. This is because traders may remain undeterred from breaching the Regulations taking the view that profits made far exceed enforcement costs. However, the Government remains concerned that adopting a general private right of action for the Regulations as a whole might have unintended consequences. It considers that further analysis is needed in order to determine the basis on which any private right of action was justified, and in what

But is individual redress of consumers necessary to enhance effective enforcement by discouraging unfair commercial practices? Is individual redress an effective, dissuasive and proportionate penalty under Article 13 of the UCP Directive? If the Member State legislator opts for the private enforcement of unfair commercial practices law, the private enforcement mechanisms have to comply with Article 13 of the UCP Directive either alone or in combination with public enforcement. However, an outstanding challenge for private enforcement is the so-called rational disinterest: Although unfair commercial practices often harm many individuals and private entities and thereby cause significant aggregate loss to society as a whole, individual consumers normally incur only small losses or damages. As a result, individuals are often reluctant to initiate private lawsuits against unlawful practices, in particular if the individual loss is deemed to be small in comparison to the costs of litigation. In these cases, individual lawsuits of consumers are not effective to stop unlawful practices or to obtain compensation for the harm caused by these practices.

c) Collective redress

For these reasons mechanisms of collective redress are considered to remedy the current shortcomings in private enforcement of EU law. At the EU level there are no harmonized procedures for the collective claim of compensatory relief. In June 2013 the Commission published a non-binding Recommendation on common principles for injunctive and compensatory collective redress mechanisms in the Member States concerning violations of rights granted under Union Law. The Recommendation shall ensure a coherent horizontal approach to collective redress without harmonizing Member States' systems.[68] The existing mechanisms to compensate a group of victims harmed by unfair commercial practices vary widely throughout the European Union.[69] Differences regard, for example, the standing to sue: In some Member States public authorities are entitled to initiate proceedings in certain areas (for example, the Ombudsman in Finland) whereas in other Member States private organizations such as consumer associations (for example, Bulgaria) or individuals are entitled to act on behalf of a group (for example, Portugal). And in many Member States, such as Germany, there is a

specific circumstances consumers might be able to bring proceedings for breaches of the Consumer Protection from Unfair Trading Regulations'.

68 Commission Recommendation of 11 June 2013 on Common Principles for Injunctive and Compensatory Collective Redress Mechanisms in the Member States Concerning Violations of Rights Granted under Union Law [2013] OJ L201/60. Commission, 'Commission Staff Working Document, Public Consultation: Towards a Coherent European Approach to Collective Redress' SEC 173 final, 4 February 2011, http://ec.europa.eu/dgs/health_consumer/dgs_consultations/ca/docs/cr_consultation_paper_en.pdf.

69 Cf. the 2008 study 'Evaluation of the Effectiveness and Efficiency of Collective Redress Mechanisms in the European Union' commissioned by the European Commission, http://ec.europa.eu/consumers/redress_cons/collective_redress_en.htm#Studies.

combination of several rules on standing. There are also differences in regard to the binding effect of judgements on unfair commercial practices: In most Member States decisions only bind those who have expressly consented to the proceedings according to the opt-in model. Only a few Member States provide for the so-called opt-out model according to which the decision becomes binding for all parties unless they expressly opted out. Further differences concern, *inter alia*, the scopes of application, the funding of collective redress actions or the beneficiary parties.[70]

The central issue of the aforementioned Commission's Recommendation is that all Member States should provide collective redress mechanisms for injunctive and compensatory relief in mass harm situations (No. 2). The Recommendation hereinafter states several basic principles to be implemented by the Member States. These principles concern *inter alia* the standing to bring a representative action, the information on a collective redress action and the funding of proceedings. With regard to the standing to bring a representative action, the Member States should designate non-profit-making representative entities fulfilling certain requirements laid down in the recommendation (No. 4). Whether collective redress is needed to achieve effective enforcement can only be answered, however, in due consideration of effectiveness of public enforcement instruments. If public enforcement functions effectively – as it appears to in some Member States – strengthening of private enforcement mechanisms – especially by implementing collective redress – is not necessary. Consequently, the Commission's Recommendation states that Member States can additionally or alternatively empower public authorities to bring representative actions (No. 7). From an enforcement perspective, collective redress is only necessary in jurisdictions lacking an effective public enforcement system. In German law, for example, the relatively novel skimming-off claim by private entities is a legal instrument in areas where – such as in unfair commercial practices law – no public authority exists or – such as in competition law – resources of public authorities do not suffice for effective enforcement. In these cases the collective redress serves as a subsidiary catch-all function.[71] However, the German skimming-off procedure itself in its current shape does not work effectively. Accordingly, private bodies such as consumer associations are entitled to claim skimming off ill-gotten profits by unfair commercial practices from wrongdoers. The crucial issue here is that entities with legal standing lack a true incentive to initiate proceedings because the substantial part of the profit is skimmed off in favour of the German State. The most favourable outcome for the claimant is to obtain recovery of her costs of enforcement. On the one hand the skimming-off procedure imposes stringent requirements; on the other, however,

70 In detail see Commission, 'Commission Staff Working Document – Public Consultation' (n 68) 173, final para 9.

71 See the explanatory memorandum to the Unfair Competition Act (UWG), BT-Drucks. 15/1487 p 23. Astrid Stadler, 'Der Gewinnabschöpfungsanspruch: eine Variante des *private enforcement*? ', in Susanne Augenhofer (ed.), *Europäisierung des Kartell- und Lauterkeitsrechts* (Tübingen: Mohr Siebeck, 2009) 117, 137.

private entities can only claim the profit gained by the infringing party on behalf of the state. Consequently, from a rational point of view, there is no reason to initiate a skimming-off procedure. It is hardly surprising that the skimming-off procedure is only rarely invoked. Some call it a 'toothless paper tiger'.[72]

3. Implications for Member States

As was shown, EU law leaves it essentially to the Member States whether they rely primarily on public or private enforcement or a combination of them. The UCP Directive only requires that Member States ensure that adequate and effective means to combat unfair commercial practices and effective, dissuasive and proportionate penalties exist. However, based on the rulings of the ECJ in *Munoz*, *Courage* and *Manfredi*, under certain circumstances the full effectiveness of the UCP Directive would be put at risk if Member States do not grant individuals a right to claim. Furthermore, in cross-border cases injunction procedures according to the Consumer Injunctions Directive and cooperation between national authorities responsible for enforcement under the Regulation on consumer protection cooperation are required.

3.1 Private and Public Enforcement

The effectiveness of enforcement depends firstly and foremost on the specific nature of the area of law. While in some cases public enforcement by means of administrative or criminal sanctions may be necessary (for example, in the financial market regulation), in other instances private enforcement and civil liability may be appropriate (for example, for the non-fulfilment of contractual obligations).[73] Whether private or public law instruments are appropriate to enforce national provisions adopted in connection with the application of the UCP Directive will depend on the specific advantages and disadvantages of private and public enforcement.[74]

72 Jürgen Keßler, 'UWG und Verbraucherschutz – Wege und Umwege zum Recht der Marktkommunikation' (2005) *Wettbewerb in Recht und Praxis* 264, 273.

73 Commission, 'Communication from the Commission to the Council and the European Parliament' (n 1) 6.

74 From an economic point of view see William M Landes and Richard A Posner, 'The Private Enforcement of Law' (1975) 4 *Journal of Legal Studies* 1, 14; A Mitchell Polinsky, 'Private versus Public Enforcement of Fines' (1980) 9 *Journal of Legal Studies* 105, 107; Richard A Posner, *Economic Analysis of Law* (8th edn, New York: Aspen Publishing, 2010) 659 et seq.; Steven Shavell, 'The Optimal Structure of Law Enforcement' (1993) 36 *Journal of Law & Economics* 255, 272. As to the efficient design of enforcement of misleading advertising laws see Weber, 'Law and Economics of Enforcing Misleading Advertising Laws' (n 5), in this volume.

3.1.1 Advantages of private enforcement

Firstly, private enforcement mechanisms make it possible to generate private information and to detect unfair commercial practices which would have otherwise remained undetected. Public authorities are not able to investigate and prosecute all unfair commercial practices.[75] In contrast, private parties might be directly involved in unfair commercial practices and, therefore, acquire immediately knowledge of an infringement of the law. Secondly, private enforcement enables exploitation of private incentives and motivation to enforce the rules. Injured private persons are often better motivated and possibly more tenacious in enforcing their rights than employees of public authorities, in particular if their own interests are at stake. Thirdly, some scholars argue that private enforcement allows adjustment to new policies and altered circumstances because judges have more room to refine vague and general standards contained in law, and private parties are more likely than public authorities to develop and pursue novel legal theories and new techniques of investigation and proof.[76] Finally, private enforcement is able to handle cross-border infringements by applying international private law. In contrast, administrative competences are regularly restricted to national borders according to the principle of territoriality. That renders cross-border public enforcement more difficult in practice.

3.1.2 Advantages of public enforcement

Compared hereto, the advantages of public enforcement are the following: Firstly, European and national public authorities must ensure that not only individual, but also public interests and, more broadly, the Union interest are taken into account whilst private parties have no such duty when taking steps to enforce their rights. They may initiate proceedings if they have an individual interest to enforce their rights irrespective of whether or not the public interest would require such action.[77] Private interest may coincide with the public interest but it might also diverge. Due to administrative discretion, public authorities may take targeted actions.[78] If it is in the public interest not to enforce the law in a particular case, public authorities may exercise discretion not to enforce the law, if the law permits it. However, a

---

75 Christoph Kern, 'Private Law Enforcement versus Public Law Enforcement' (2007) 12 *Zeitschrift für Zivilprozeß International* 351, 360.

76 Lars Klöhn, 'Private versus Public Enforcement of Laws – A Law and Economic Perspective', in Reiner Schulze (ed.), *Compensation of Private Losses: The Evolution of Torts in European Business Law* (Munich: Sellier, 2011) 195.

77 See also Weber, 'Law and Economics of Enforcing Misleading Advertising Laws' (n 5), in this volume.

78 See for Competition Law Wernhard Möschel, 'Behördliche oder privatrechtliche Durchsetzung des Kartellrechts?'(2007) *Wirtschaft und Wettbewerb* 483, 487; Wernhard Möschel, 'Should Private Enforcement of Competition Law Be Strengthened?', in Dieter Schmidtchen, Max Albert and Stefan Voigt (eds), *The More Economic Approach to European Competition Law, Conferences on New Political Economy* (Tübingen: Mohr Siebeck, 2007) 101, 106.

private person may still file a claim even though enforcement in the particular case would not be beneficial to the society.[79] On the other hand, private enforcement mechanisms may also result in under-enforcement if there is no private interest at stake but public interest in enforcing the law. Overall, it is difficult to determine the right level of deterrence by private enforcement mechanisms in practice.

Secondly, the risk of erroneous decisions in administrative proceedings might be lower than on the basis of private enforcement. As public authorities handle such cases repeatedly they have gained experience and expert knowledge.[80] Having mentioned that, this can also be true for private bodies such as consumer associations in civil courts having jurisdiction. Thirdly, in contrast to private parties, public authorities are able not only to enforce one-off but may follow a continuous and reliable strategy of enforcement.[81] But again this may also apply to private associations. Fourthly, if private enforcement mechanisms should work well it is often linked to the danger of abuse. In particular, in the United States negative effects of private enforcement are visible by means of the so-called strike suits by which the plaintiff seeks no more than a settlement offer from the defendant.[82] Against this background, the Commission warns that elements should be avoided which are said to encourage a 'litigation culture'.[83] However, the existing national private enforcement mechanisms in the European Union show that there are various effective safeguards to combat abusive or frivolous lawsuits. Those safeguards could be, for example, confining causes of action to qualified bodies or imposing sanctions for abusive claims. Admittedly, whether these safeguards are sufficient in a strong private enforcement system has not been proven and tested yet.

However, the most important argument in favour of public enforcement is the broad variation of instruments that public authorities may use for their investigation in order to detect infringements and to ascertain the facts. Enforcement authorities may have special investigation powers, such as powers to obtain information, powers of entry and to enter premises (see, for example, part 4 of the Consumer Protection from Unfair Trading Regulations 2008). Private persons might lack the necessary information on the identity of the wrongdoer or the fact of an infringement at all.[84] Compared to this, public authorities are better prepared to collect information required for proof of infringements and claims. In addition,

79 Poelzig, *Normdurchsetzung durch Privatrecht* (n 6) 380.

80 Matthew Stephenson, 'Public Regulation of Private Enforcement: The Case for Expanding the Role of Administrative Agencies' (2005) 91 *Virginia Law Review* 93, 116; Klöhn, 'Private versus Public Enforcement' (n 76) 194.

81 Harald Koch, *Prozessführung im öffentlichen Interesse* (Frankfurt am Main: Metzner, 1983) 85.

82 Kern, 'Private Law Enforcement versus Public Law Enforcement' (n 75) 366.

83 Commission, 'Green Paper on Consumer Collective Redress' COM (2008) 794 final, 27 November 2008, para 48.

84 Van den Bergh, 'Should Consumer Protection Law Be Publicly Enforced?', in van Boom and Loos (eds), *Collective Enforcement of Consumer Law* (n 7) 180, 201.

administrative and criminal sanctions fines could be better targeted at general deterrence by determining them according to the overall economic losses and the achieved benefits.[85] Thus, in the first instance of *Munoz*, Laddie J commented that public authorities were the most appropriate body to enforce the regulations' duties, being the one that possesses the necessary expertise: 'They not only know what they are doing but, importantly, they should be neutral. Their remit is not to advance one trader's interests at the expense of another's'.[86]

3.1.3 Private and public enforcement of unfair commercial practices

As has been shown both private as well as public enforcement can have benefits and drawbacks.[87] According to the UCP Directive, it should basically be up to the Member States to choose the most effective enforcement instruments for their respective jurisdiction.[88] Apart from the situation in cross-border cases there is no need to strengthen the requirements for any particular enforcement instrument in the Member States.[89] Only if public enforcement mechanisms should prove to be ineffective, individual Member States must strengthen private enforcement mechanisms, for example, by establishing a collective redress system. The same applies in reverse. The seminal decision of the ECJ in *Munoz* shows that the existence of public enforcement does not automatically render private enforcement unnecessary. The relative weight of the advantages and disadvantages of private and public enforcement depends on the situation and practice at issue in the respective Member States.[90] Due consideration should also be given to the cultural environment in the Member States as well as the efficiency of the existing public or private enforcement mechanisms.

However, in many Member States one finds a combination of public and private enforcement. Due to the Regulation on Consumer Protection Cooperation, public law enforcement is an essential element of enforcement in all Member States, at least in cross-border cases. However, private enforcement is also an effective instrument in many Member States. Correspondingly in Germany or Austria, private enforcement of unfair commercial practices by competitors and consumer associations as well as other qualified entities has proved to be effective

---

85 Glöckner, *Europäisches Lauterkeitsrecht* (n 43) 612 et seq. Alternatively Glöckner suggests public authorities be granted standing in civil proceedings (Glöckner, 614).

86 *Antonio Munoz y Cia SA v Frumar Ltd* [1999] 3 *CMLR* 684 (Ch), para 59 (*Laddie J*).

87 See Howell E Jackson and Mark J Roe, 'Public and Private Enforcement of Securities Laws: Resource-Based Evidence' (2009) 93 *Journal of Financial Economics* 207; Kern, 'Private Law Enforcement versus Public Law Enforcement' (n 75) 359 et seq.

88 On German law Poelzig, *Normdurchsetzung durch Privatrecht* (n 6) 76 et seq.

89 Illustrating design suggestions for efficient enforcement see Weber, 'Law and Economics of Enforcing Misleading Advertising Laws' (n 5), in this volume.

90 Kern, 'Private Law Enforcement versus Public Law Enforcement' (n 75) 378.

for a long time.[91] Conditions for private enforcement mechanisms in regard to unfair commercial practices are relatively good. As has been shown, private enforcement as a right of action is basically effective if concerned persons have free access to the necessary information to prove their case. Practices such as misleading advertising can typically be identified easily by individuals concerned by this unfair commercial practice. Therefore, in many cases, specific investigative measures by public authorities that are required, for example, in competition law are not necessary to detect unfair commercial practices. However, by combining public and private enforcement, deficits of one system may be compensated by the other system. Thus, the supervisory authorities' powers of investigation and coercion may contribute to the detection of unfair commercial practices which would otherwise have remained undiscovered or unascertainable. On the other hand, fostering private enforcement may help administrative authorities to focus on the functions they are best placed to carry out. Thus, a combined enforcement system would strengthen the impact of the UCP Directive.

3.2 Coordination of Private and Public Enforcement

Prima facie, the co-existence of public and private enforcement and the coexistence of administrative, criminal and civil sanctions may appear reasonable. For, the more enforcement tools there are in the 'toolbox' the higher is the probability of detecting and remedying unfair commercial practices. Equally, stringent sanctions also lead to more deterrent effects. But to avoid over-enforcement and regulation overkill by opening the flood gates to a wave of civil, administrative and penal sanctions it is necessary to coordinate private and public enforcement.[92] Without such coordination we would face the real risk that resources might be wasted and public and private enforcement might impede each other. Therefore, the interrelation of public and private enforcement mechanisms has to be clarified and coordinated in an optimum way.

3.2.1 Exchange of information

This regards notably the exchange of information: Consistency in the application of the UCP Directive requires that arrangements be established for cooperation between the Member States' courts and the public authorities. This is relevant for all courts of the Member States, irrespective of whether they are applying national law based on the UCP Directive in lawsuits between private parties, acting as public enforcers or as review courts. In particular, national courts should have the power to request information from public authorities or, to the extent relevant for their

---

91 Helmut Köhler, in Helmut Köhler and Joachim Bornkamm, *Gesetz gegen den unlauteren Wettbewerb (UWG), Kommentar* (Munich: C.H. Beck, 2013) § 8 UWG, para 3.1.

92 In detail see Poelzig, *Normdurchsetzung durch Privatrecht* (n 6) 563 et seq. See Case C-360/09 *Pfleiderer* [2011] ECR I-5161; Case C-536/11 *Donau Chemie* [2013] OJ C 252/11; [2013] 5 CMLR 19.

decision, on points concerning the application of the unfair commercial practices law. The competent public authorities of the Member States should also be able to submit written or oral observations to courts called upon to apply the UCP Directive. Steps should therefore be taken to ensure that the competent authorities of the Member States are kept sufficiently well informed of proceedings before national courts. The involvement of public authorities as *amicus curiae* could be modelled in accordance with Article 15(3) Regulation 1/2003. Competition law also provides for another means of coordination: According to Article 16 Regulation 1/2003 Member States shall not take decisions running counter to the decision adopted by the Commission in a particular case.

3.2.2 Coordination in cross-border enforcement

Specific problems in coordinating private and public enforcement mechanisms arise in cross-border cases. According to the Regulation on Consumer Protection Cooperation, Member States are required to designate special public authorities that are responsible for enforcement in cross-border cases. Coordination is necessary if Member States take advantage of the opportunity of Article 4(2) of the Regulation on Consumer Protection Cooperation to grant private bodies legal standing in cases concerning the cessation or prohibition of intra-Union infringements. The German experience shows that coordination is necessary especially in regard to limitation periods which should consider the time required for communication between public authorities and the designated private bodies.[93]

Another sore point in this procedure is the determination of the applicable substantive law. Whilst in private law disputes the applicable law is determined on the basis of Article 6 of the Rome II Regulation, public bodies must apply principles of conflicts of public laws. Application of different conflicts principles might lead to different applicable laws on unfair commercial practices in one and the same procedure, at least in cases with relevance to third countries outside the European Union.

3.3 Strengthening Private Enforcement

To improve the conditions for private enforcement some measures need to be taken by the Member States.

3.3.1 Coordination of individual and collective redress

According to the decision of the ECJ in *Munoz* full effectiveness of Union Law '(implies) that it must be possible to enforce that obligation by means of civil proceedings instituted by a trader against a competitor'.[94] On the other hand, collective redress is a much-discussed instrument to strengthen effective private

93 Report by the German Federal Government on the effectiveness of § 7 of the German Consumer Protection Enforcement Act ('VSchDG'), BT-Drs. 17/8982, 3.

94 Case C-253/00 *Munoz* [2002] ECR I-7289, para 30. See above III.

enforcement of consumer protection law, including the law on unfair commercial practices. The coexistence of collective redress and potential individual claims raises the issue of their relationship to each other.[95] The basic principle should be that individual victims are not deprived of their right to claim damages if they choose to bring their own action for damages. Likewise, they should not be deprived of their right not to bring an action at all. Finally, necessary safeguards should be put in place in order to avoid the same harm being compensated more than once through individual and collective actions.

3.3.2 Capability to be sued

Another crucial issue in modelling effective private enforcement mechanisms is the question who should be sued in the case of legal persons as wrongdoers. The UCP Directive does not expressly rule whether, for instance, in the case of companies enforcement measures may be addressed against the company as well as the directors of the company. According to Article 2 of the UCP Directive, 'trader' means any natural or legal person who, in commercial practices covered by this Directive, is acting for purposes relating to his trade, business, craft or profession and anyone acting in the name of or on behalf of a trader. It has to be scrutinized if a direct liability of directors and officers on behalf of consumers is a suitable means of effective enforcement.[96]

3.3.3 Adjusting civil procedural law

Private enforcement mechanisms are not effective if conditions of entitlement are so stringent that the respective party entitled to claim is regularly not able to successfully enforce the claim.[97] Therefore, effective private enforcement may require balanced rules in regard to civil proceedings.[98] On the one hand, an effective and efficient procedure is needed. On the other hand, one needs to avoid encouraging a litigation culture.[99]

At this point, only two of the issues to be discussed can be emphasized. Firstly, appropriate measures are necessary to effectively tackle the difficulties encountered by victims of unfair commercial practices to get access to justice. At the same time, safeguards against abusive litigation are indispensable. Secondly, the public interest in effective enforcement must be sufficiently considered in civil proceedings.

---

95 See Norbert Reich, *Individueller und kollektiver Rechtsschutz im EU-Verbraucherrecht* (Baden-Baden: Nomos, 2012) 50 et seq.; Poelzig, *Normdurchsetzung durch Privatrecht* (n 6) 497.

96 In detail see Poelzig, *Normdurchsetzung durch Privatrecht* (n 6) 461 et seq.

97 Cf. in detail van Boom, 'Efficacious Enforcement in Contract and Tort' (n 9).

98 As to the need of rethinking the role of civil courts van Boom, 'Efficacious Enforcement in Contract and Tort' (n 9) 47.

99 Commission, 'Green Paper on Consumer Collective Redress' COM (2008) 794 final, 27 November 2008, para 48.

a) Access to court and safeguards against abusive litigation

Effective private enforcement depends on free access to justice.[100] Access to justice may be enabled by minimizing the costs of litigation and by alleviating the burden of proof. In most Member States, costs are allocated according to the 'loser-pays' principle. This principle acts as a strong deterrent to unmeritorious litigation. However, another effect of the 'loser-pays' principle may be to discourage meritorious claims so far as victims are risk-adverse. Therefore, in order to alleviate the obstacle that legal costs may represent for potential claimants, specific measures are necessary. An example for alleviation of the normal cost rule in the interest of effective enforcement is included in Directive 2004/48/EC on the enforcement of intellectual property rights.[101] According to Article 14 of this Directive, the unsuccessful party shall bear reasonable and proportionate legal costs incurred by the successful party, unless equity does not allow this. Furthermore, the European Commission is contemplating further deviation from the loser-pays principle and limitation of expenses in the interest of private enforcement.[102] Especially the option to grant civil courts the power to allocate the costs by derogation from the loser-pays rule is a suitable means to foster private actions and, consequently, effective enforcement. To avoid abusive litigation, the court order should be subject to certain conditions. By requiring a court order for alleviation from the cost burden the court would be given the opportunity to filter and thus prevent abusive litigation.[103] Furthermore, certain requirements for standing to sue might diminish abusive litigation.

b) Access to evidence

Although the relevant information is more easily available in regard to unfair commercial practices than in other fields of law, access by claimants to such evidence is the key to making private enforcement effective. It should therefore be considered whether and to what extent particular rules concerning evidence or obligations to turn over documents should be introduced.[104]

---

100 See Christopher Hodges, *The Reform of Class and Representative Actions in European Legal Systems: A New Framework for Collective Redress in Europe* (Oxford: Hart Publishing, 2008) 89, 190.

101 Directive (EC) 2004/48 of the European Parliament and of the Council of 29 April 2004 on the Enforcement of Intellectual Property Rights [2004] OJ L157/45.

102 See the proposals for strengthening private enforcement in competition law, Commission, 'Commission Staff Working Paper accompanying the White Paper on Damages Actions for Breach of the EC Antitrust Rules' SEC (2008) 404, 2 April 2008, paras 73 et seq.

103 See Commission, 'Commission Staff Working Paper' (n 102), para 259: 'fairness, reasonableness or equity'.

104 See Commission, 'Damages Actions for Breach of the EC Antitrust Rules' (Green Paper) COM (2005) 672 final, 19 December 2005, 5.

c) Considering public interests in civil proceedings

Another issue is to consider public interests in civil proceedings.[105] One instrument is involvement of public authorities in civil proceedings as *amicus curiae* (see, for example, Article 15 Regulation 1/2003). In addition, courts and judges should become experts in the field of enforcement of the UCP Directive and hence public interests. Specialization can be achieved by constraining the competence to some few courts which focus only on cases dealing with unfair commercial practices. This could be possible by concentration of jurisdiction or setting up special courts.

3.4 International Cases

Finally, globalization poses specific challenges to effective enforcement of the UCP Directive. Recent technical progress has rendered international trade easier, faster and cheaper. This has led to a higher degree of international cooperation and competition in the field of production and sale in globalized markets.[106] Along with this development, unfair commercial practices go beyond the frontiers of the Member States as well as of the European Union. The financial crisis has shown that and to which extent commercial practices may negatively affect foreign markets and international economy. Especially the interests of consumers in the European Union need to be protected from rogue traders based in third countries. Therefore, globalization makes it necessary to develop international enforcement procedures to apprehend unfair commercial practices in third countries which affect interests of citizens in EU Member States.[107] The Commission itself recognizes this issue and recommends 'international agreements to be negotiated [at the Union level] with third countries regarding mutual assistance in the enforcement of the laws that protect consumers' interests' (recital No. 18). An alternative enforcement instrument might be private enforcement because by means of International Private Law the applicable law can be determined. According to Article 6 of the Rome II Regulation, the law applicable to a non-contractual obligation arising out of an unfair commercial practice shall be the law of the country where competitive relations or the collective interests of consumers are, or are likely to be, affected. However, specific problems arise because unfair commercial practices often cause harm in many different countries. In so-called multi-state infringements

105 In detail see Poelzig, *Normdurchsetzung durch Privatrecht* (n 6) 512 et seq.

106 Werner F Ebke, Global Economy – Global Law?, in J Attanasio and J Norton (eds), *Multilateralism v. Unilateralism. Policy Choices in a Global Society* (London: BIICL, 2005) 83, 95; Werner F Ebke, 'Foundations, Conflicts of Laws and the European Community', in Pieter Bekker, Rudolf Dolzer and Michael Waibel (eds), *Making Transnational Law Work in the Global Economy: Essays in Honour of Detlev F. Vagts* (New York: Cambridge University Press, 2010) 298 et seq.

107 For details see Poelzig, *Normdurchsetzung durch Privatrecht* (n 6) 542 et seq.; Dörte Poelzig, 'Privat(rechtlich)e Normdurchsetzung – Chance und Herausforderung auf globalen Märkten' (2011) *Zeitschrift für Vergleichende Rechtswissenschaft* 395 et seq.

it is difficult to determine jurisdiction as well as the applicable national law.[108] Furthermore, the European experience with cross-border infringements has shown that under certain circumstances it is appropriate and necessary to facilitate cooperation between public authorities responsible for enforcement of the laws that protect consumers' interests.[109]

4. Conclusion

European Union law leaves it essentially to the Member States whether they rely primarily on public or private enforcement or a combination of them. Private and public enforcement of the law based on the UCP Directive are basically considered to be equivalent. However, this chapter has demonstrated that the procedural autonomy of the Member States is limited. That concerns first of all cross-border cases. Secondly, under certain circumstances, the principle of effectiveness requires Member States to implement particular enforcement instruments in their domestic law. In light of the seminal case law of the ECJ in *Munoz*, *Courage* and *Manfredi*, this paper has shown that based on the principle of full effectiveness Member States must strengthen private enforcement by private actions if this is the only way to ensure effective enforcement and to impose effective, dissuasive and proportionate sanctions. That may be even the case if public enforcement mechanisms exist. Due to the full harmonization approach of the UCP Directive there is an increased need to focus on the requirement that sanctions have to be proportionate.

The issue of effective enforcement of the UCP Directive comprises manifold aspects which are still awaiting intensive research and discussion. This chapter set out three main aspects: Since in most Member States there is a combination of various private and public enforcement instruments, it is crucially necessary to coordinate optimally the available enforcement instruments with one another. That concerns – where available – public and private enforcement as well as collective and individual redress. Over-enforcement by opening the flood gates to a wave of civil, administrative and penal sanctions should be avoided. Public and private enforcement should complement each other in an optimum way. Secondly, if Member States rely on private enforcement either alone or in combination with public enforcement balanced rules exist, especially in regard to civil proceedings. And thirdly, in the light of globalization, the issue of enforcement of the UCP Directive does not stop at the borders of the European Union. Therefore, solutions which go beyond the European Union are required.

108 See Case C-68/93 *Fiona Shevillet et al. v Presse Alliance SA* [1995] ECR I-415.

109 Cf. Recital No 3 of the Regulation on Consumer Protection Cooperation.

Bibliography

Alexander C, 'Die Sanktions- und Verfahrensvorschriften der Richtlinie 2005/29/EG über unlautere Geschäftspraktiken im Binnenmarkt – Umsetzungsbedarf in Deutschland?' (2005) *Gewerblicher Rechtsschutz und Urheberrecht, Internationaler Teil* (*GRUR Int*) 809–815.

Augenhofer S, 'Individualrechtliche Ansprüche des Verbrauchers bei unlauterem Wettbewerbsverhalten des Unternehmers' (2006) *Wettbewerb in Recht und Praxis* (*WRP*) 169–178.

Baudenbacher C, 'Die Revision des schweizerischen UWG – Bemerkungen zum Entwurf der Expertenkommission' (1981) *Gewerblicher Rechtsschutz und Urheberrecht, Internationaler Teil* (*GRUR Int*) 162–169.

Biondi A, Comment, Case C-253/00, *Antonio Munoz y Cia, Superior Fruiticola SA v. Frumar Ltd, Redbridge Produce Marketing Ltd,* Judgment of the Full Court of 17 September 2002 [ECR] 2002 I-7289 (2003) 40 *Common Market Law Review* (*CMLRev*) 1241–1250.

Butler H and Wright J, 'Are State Consumer Protection Acts Really Little–FTC Acts' (2011) 62 *Fla. L. Rev.* 163–192.

Calliess C and M Ruffert (eds), *EUV/ AEUV, Kommentar* (Munich: C.H. Beck, 2011).

Ebke W, *Wirtschaftsprüfer und Dritthaftung* (Bielefeld, 1983).

———, 'Global Economy – Global Law?', in J Attanasio and J Norton (eds), *Multilateralism v. Unilateralism. Policy Choices in a Global Society* (London: BIICL, 2005) 83–97.

———, 'Foundations, Conflicts of Laws and the European Community', in P Beker, R Dolzer and M Waibel (eds), *Making Transnational Law Work in the Global Economy: Essays in Honour of Detlev F. Vagts* (New York: Cambridge University Press, 2010) 298–325.

Gamerith H, 'Der Richtlinienvorschlag über unlautere Geschäftspraktiken - Möglichkeiten einer harmonischen Umsetzung' (2005) *Wettbewerb in Recht und Praxis* (*WRP*) 391–437.

Glöckner H, *Europäisches Lauterkeitsrecht* (Munich: C.H. Beck, 2006).

Henning-Bodewig F, 'Richtlinienvorschlag über unlautere Geschäftspraktiken und UWG-Reform' (2004) *Gewerblicher Rechtsschutz und Urheberrecht, Internationaler Teil* (*GRUR Int*) 183–193.

Hodges C, *The Reform of Class and Representative Actions in European Legal Systems: A New Framework for Collective Redress in Europe* (Oxford: Hart Publishing, 2008).

Howells G, 'The End of an Era – Implementing the Unfair Commercial Practices Directive in the United Kingdom: Punctual Criminal Law Gives Way to a General Criminal/Civil Law Standard' (2009) 2 *Journal of Business Law* (*JBL*) 183–194.

Howells G and Weatherill S, *Consumer Protection Law* (Aldershot: Ashgate, 2005).

Jackson H and Roe M, 'Public and Private Enforcement of Securities Laws: Resource-Based Evidence' (2009) 93 *Journal of Financial Economics* (*JFE*) 207–238.

Keßler J, 'UWG und Verbraucherschutz – Wege und Umwege zum Recht der Marktkommunikation' (2005) *Wettbewerb in Recht und Praxis* (*WRP*) 264–274.

Kern C, 'Private Law Enforcement versus Public Law Enforcement' (2007) 12 *Zeitschrift für Zivilprozess International* (*ZZPInt*) 351–378.

Klöhn L, 'Private versus Public Enforcement of Laws – A Law and Economic Perspective', in R Schulze (ed.), *Compensation of Private Losses: The Evolution of Torts in European Business Law* (Munich: Sellier, 2011) 179–198.

Köhler H and Bornkamm J, *Gesetz gegen den unlauteren Wettbewerb (UWG), Kommentar* (Munich: C.H. Beck, 2013).

Köhler H and Lettl T, 'Das geltende europäische Lauterkeitsrecht, der Vorschlag für eine EG-Richtlinie über unlautere Geschäftspraktiken und die UWG-Reform' (2003) *Wettbewerb in Recht und Praxis* (*WRP*) 1019–1057.

Komninos A, 'New Prospects for Private Enforcement of EC Competition Law: *Courage v. Crehan* and the Community Right to Damages' (2002) 39 *Common Market Law Review* (*CMLRev*) 447–487.

Landes W and Posner R, 'The Private Enforcement of Law' (1975) 4 *Journal of Legal Studies* (*J.Leg.Stud.*) 1–46.

Micklitz H-W, 'Cross-Border Consumer Conflicts – A French German Experience' (1993) 16 *Journal of Consumer Policy* 411–434.

———, 'Legal Redress', in G Howells, H-W Micklitz and T Wilhelmsson (eds), *European Fair Trading Law* (2006), 217 et seq.

———, 'Transborder Law Enforcement – Does It Exist?', in S Weatherill and U Bernitz (eds), *The Regulation of Unfair Commercial Practices under EC Directive 2005/29* (Oxford: Hart Publishing, 2007), 235 et seq.

Möschel W, 'Behördliche oder privatrechtliche Durchsetzung des Kartellrechts?' (2007) *Wirtschaft und Wettbewerb* (*WuW*) 483–492.

———, 'Should Private Enforcement of Competition Law Be Strengthened?', in D Schmidtchen, M Albert and S Voigt (eds), *The More Economic Approach to European Competition Law, Conferences on New Political Economy* (Tübingen: Mohr Siebeck, 2007) 101, 106.

Poelzig D, 'Privat(rechtlich)e Normdurchsetzung – Chance und Herausforderung auf globalen Märkten' (2011) 110 *Zeitschrift für vergleichende Rechtswissenschaft einschließlich des Rechts der Entwicklungsländer und der ethnologischen Rechtsforschung* (*ZVglRWiss*) 395–407.

———, *Normdurchsetzung durch Privatrecht* (Tübingen: Mohr Siebeck, 2012).

Polinsky M, 'Private versus Public Enforcement of Fines' (1980) 9 *Journal of Legal Studies* (*J.Leg.Stud.*) 105–127.

Posner R A, *Economic Analysis of Law* (New York: Aspen Publishing, 2010).

Reich N, *Individueller und kollektiver Rechtsschutz im EU-Verbraucherrecht – Von der ‚Nationalisierung' zur ‚Konstitutionalisierung' von Rechtsbehelfen* (Baden-Baden: Nomos, 2012).

Shavell S, 'The Optimal Structure of Law Enforcement' (1993) 36 *Journal of Law & Economics* (*J.L. & Econ.*) 255–287.

Stadler A, 'Der Gewinnabschöpfungsanspruch: eine Variante des *private enforcement*?', in S Augenhofer (ed.), *Europäisierung des Kartell- und Lauterkeitsrechts* (Tübingen: Mohr Siebeck, 2009) 117–140.

Stephenson M, 'Public Regulation of Private Enforcement: The Case for Expanding the Role of Administrative Agencies' (2005) 91 *Virginia Law Review* (*Va.L.Rev.*) 93–173.

van Boom WH, *Efficacious Enforcement in Contract and Tort* (Den Haag: Boom Juridische uitgevers, 2006).

van Boom WH and M Loos (eds), *Collective Enforcement of Consumer Law* (Groningen: Europa Law Publishing, 2007).

Van den Bergh R, 'Should Consumer Protection Law be Publicly Enforced?', in WH van Boom and M Loos (eds), *Collective Enforcement of Consumer Law* (Groningen: Europa Law Publishing, 2007) 179–203.

Wagner G, 'Prävention und Verhaltenssteuerung durch Privatrecht - Anmaßung oder legitime Aufgabe?' (2006) 206 *Archiv für die civilistische Praxis* (*AcP*) 352–476.

Index

abusive litigation 259–260
safeguards against 260
access to justice 169, 259–260
free 169, 260
Administration of Justice Act (AJA) 24
administrative costs 208, 215, 219–221, 223, 226, 228–229
high 221, 228
administrative fines 239, 242–243
administrative law enforcement 12
ADR directive 169
advertising 2, 10, 25, 46, 52, 54, 101, 127, 147, 153, 162, 164, 178, 183–184, 195, 222, 228, 238
Advertising Standards Authority 158
agencies 29
bait 59, 122
codes 163
and e-commerce 152, 161
and online trade 214
comparative 1, 174
contract vs. 175
European Advertising Code 164
European Advertising Standards Alliance 152, 204
false 212
food 101
Jury for Advertising Deontology 157
law 203
and marketing rules 155
misleading 1, 16, 91, 132, 134, 154, 160, 174, 192, 208, 210, 215, 231, 257
advertising laws 203–204
Misleading and Comparative Advertising Directive 1, 82, 132, 238, 250
Professional Regulation Authority of Advertising 147
surreptitious 129
television 127, 132
amicus curiae 258, 261
average consumer 2–4, 6, 30, 34–35, 37, 39, 68, 89–91, 93, 100, 114, 119, 139, 141
concept 37–38
economic behaviour of 112, 116, 129, 140, 147
test 71, 95

blacklist 59, 66–70, 174, 182–183, 188, 198
for B2B relations 82–83
commercial practices 67, 70–71
European 66, 72–73, 75, 84
formal concept of 68
future of 82
German 73
national blacklists 71–72, 77, 81, 84
Polish 75, 84
practices 3
of unfair B2C commercial practices 68
of unfair commercial practices 14, 65, 83
uniform application of 84
burden of proof 116, 178, 260
high 221, 227
lighter 240

CADR (Consumer Alternative Dispute Resolution) 205, 209, 219, 222–223, 226
individual 230
litigation before 215–217
mass 230
procedure 224
capture 206, 214, 217, 219–222, 225–226, 230
low-value claims 216
by special interests 217
civil liability 239, 242, 243, 253

codes of conduct 2, 4, 16, 131, 140, 143–144, 150, 155, 162–163, 165, 166–168
as benchmark of fairness 141, 146–147
conclusive evidence 149
contribution to consumer protection 151–152
development of 170
drafting of 170
enforceable 156, 159
enforcement 167
EU wide 163–164
European 139, 169, 170
fair 142, 156, 161, 168–169
in France 138
honest use of 140
interplay between the UCPD and 138, 144–145, 164
conformity with the UCPD 153
interpretation of 165
transposition of the UCPD into 154
national and European 153
in Netherlands 147
OFT-approved 157
responsible use of 139, 141
United Kingdom 157
voluntary 15
collective redress 104, 174, 187, 192, 236, 251–252, 256, 258–259
Hungary 181
Commission Guidance 143
common law 24, 25, 26, 32, 103, 149, 178
community infringements 24, 25
competitors 5, 9, 10, 56, 57, 59, 69, 72, 74, 83, 103, 211, 215, 218, 220, 228, 229, 238, 240, 247, 248, 249, 256
consumer/s
associations 103, 123, 127, 147, 165, 167, 175, 199, 212, 214, 215, 228, 245, 251, 252, 255, 256
private 230, 244
average 100
collective interest of 103, 244, 261
credit rating agencies 39
economic interests of 131, 133, 250
exemplary damages for 250
financial issues 97
indebted 98
individual 158, 160, 179, 192, 198, 218, 250, 251
individual redress for 249, 251
injured 250
judicial recourse by 161
low-income 99
protection 103, 104, 109, 110, 111, 121, 133, 162, 179, 187, 191, 245, 261
rational choice actors 6
traders 138, 165, 170, 222, 229
transactional decision of 1, 2, 5, 36
vulnerable 15, 89, 90–94, 97, 98, 100, 101, 102, 104, 119, 154, 155
young 14, 94
Consumer Injunctions Directive 243, 244, 246, 253
Consumer Protection Act 1987 Part III 27
Consumer Protection from Unfair Trading Regulations (CPUTR) 2008 22, 23, 25, 27, 29, 30, 31, 32, 34, 37, 38, 39
coordination 163, 225, 246, 257, 258
costs of litigation 251, 260
Courage 197, 237, 247, 248, 249, 253, 262
credit 97
B2C 52–55, 65, 68–70, 73, 76, 77, 83, 84, 138, 151, 152, 153, 161, 174, 176, 191
consumer 97, 177
micro 97
reference agency 39
revolving 97
secured 33, 36,
unsecured 33
criminal law enforcement 210, 220
criminal sanctions 26–27, 29, 103, 220, 236, 239, 243, 253, 256
cross-border enforcement 243, 245, 258
cross-border infringements 245–246, 254, 262

deterrence 26, 204, 206, 207, 210, 212, 213, 225, 228, 229, 255, 256
domestic infringement 24

electricity 23, 95, 99
energy policy 94
enforcement 5, 11, 16, 25–26, 29–31, 76, 78, 79, 82, 83, 138, 140, 144, 146–147, 151, 154, 160, 168, 201, 225–226
administrative 175, 217, 236

aggressive 35
authorities 17, 155, 162, 166
centralized 236
collective 173, 174, 175
criminal law 220, 227
cross-border 243, 258
design of mechanisms 204–208
effective 14, 62, 151, 153, 243, 245, 251, 252, 259, 260, 261
efficient 229
of EU law 235
of fair codes 168
framework 13
individual 173, 174
judicial 151
order 23–24, 38
administrative 12
preventive control measures 38
preventive 229
private 151, 156, 169, 214, 215, 230, 237–238, 241, 243–248, 251, 253, 256–257, 262
advantages 254
strengthening 258–259
public 17, 152, 157, 159, 165, 167, 175, 218, 236–238, 243–245, 251, 253, 256–257, 262
advantages 254–255
relationship between penalties and 242
techniques 21, 40
of unfair commercial practices 191
of unfair commercial practices and unfair contract terms 173
via a civil court 210
Enterprise Act (EA) 2002 11, 12, 23, 24
error costs 207, 216, 217, 219, 220, 221, 226, 227
essential goods and services 93, 99
European Court of Justice 25, 46, 52, 91, 117
Europeanization 13, 21, 22, 24, 25, 29, 31, 32, 33, 36, 37, 40, 174 175, 181, 186, 199
of private law 30

fairness 13, 35, 36, 38, 39, 114, 149–150
assessment by public authorities 138
benchmark of 141, 144, 146, 150, 153, 167
of a code 153
of a commercial practice 158
of commercial transactions 89
compliance with 167
of contract terms 16, 195
ethic of 40
European concepts of 21, 30, 37, 40
European standards of 29, 31
FCA concepts of 36
FCA principles of 34
general fairness clause 15
interpretation of 165
non-compliance with 166
private standards of 162–163
standard 139, 143, 165, 166–167
European 22
unfairness 110
in the United Kingdom 22
substantive test 185
test 186, 188
UCPD concepts of 31, 34, 40
unfairness 3, 15, 21, 22–25, 31, 35, 36, 40, 58, 67–70, 91, 110, 112, 120, 129, 133, 180, 183, 195
assessment of 185
of a commercial practice 74, 104, 184
of contract clauses 182
of contract terms 194
general clauses of 111, 114
general test of 41
presumption of 116
FCA Handbook 33, 34
Financial Conduct Authority vii, 7, 23, 33, 41
financial services vii, 5, 8, 11, 13, 14, 21, 23, 32, 33, 36, 37, 40, 41, 98, 111, 149, 244
Financial Services Authority (FSA) 23, 33, 34, 35, 36
food 27, 94, 95, 99, 101, 122, 123, 124, 125, 128, 131, 132
advertising 101
policy 94
free-riding 167, 199, 206, 210, 212, 218, 224
frivolous lawsuits 211, 214, 217, 219, 220, 221, 226, 228, 230, 255
funding 155, 206, 210, 212, 213, 223
of collective redress actions 252

gas 23, 95, 99
natural 95
general clause 15, 24, 25, 29, 38, 74, 82, 83, 115, 116, 117, 120, 129, 134, 140, 141, 146, 148, 150, 154, 163, 165, 167, 170
aggressive practices 37, 41
big 68
European 30
grand 53
harmonization by means of 5
interpretation of 115
on misleading, aggressive and unfair commercial practices 11
on misleading practices 22
open textured 25
prohibiting unfair commercial practices 2
purpose of 70
small 68
statutory 169
UCPD 31–32
in Unfair Commercial Practices 182
unfairness 3, 111, 114
globalization 261, 262

incentive 16, 126, 144, 203, 207, 211, 212, 213, 218, 220, 229, 230, 240, 252, 254
of competitors 228
disincentive 140, 144, 151, 218
misallocation of 207
for self-regulation 151, 152
to sue 206, 224, 225
for trade associations 165
of a wrongdoer 204
individual legal redress for competitors 248
individual redress for consumers 249
information asymmetry 207, 224, 225, 229, 230

law enforcement 213, 230
administrative 12
criminal 210, 220
individual and collective 173
private 17, 21, 214, 215, 246
private collective 175
public 205, 218, 256
soft 12
legal certainty 8, 11, 14, 63, 67, 73, 83, 109, 118, 119, 121, 122, 125, 126, 129, 131, 133, 134, 159, 167
beyond the UCP Directive 120
components of 116
strengthened 82
through market integration 110
within the UCP directive 110
litigation 46, 206, 216, 221, 251
abusive 259–260
before a CADR 215
before a civil court 210–211
civil 12
collective 186, 195
culture 255, 259
group 205, 209–210, 212–215, 217, 219, 220
individual 185–186, 195, 205, 212
mass 229, 230
pure private 219
local trading standards authorities 11, 23

Manfredi 247, 248, 249, 253, 262
maximum harmonization 1, 4, 5, 8, 10, 11, 13–15, 52, 59, 109, 111, 114, 115, 116, 125, 130, 132
scope of the UCPD 156
mens rea 27, 38
minimum harmonization 5, 8, 10, 32, 33, 36, 109, 110, 115, 131, 182, 242, 243
misleading claims 95, 126, 158
misleading practice 3, 22, 30, 36, 74, 102, 113, 116, 129, 139, 140, 141, 145, 151, 153, 156, 159, 161, 163
mobility 93, 96, 97, 99
Munoz 242, 247–249, 253, 256, 258, 262

Office of Fair Trading (OFT) vii, 23, 39, 41, 61, 118, 143, 149
old consumers 94
optimal enforcement 204
opt-in model 252
opt-out model 252

path dependency 205, 231
penalty 188, 251
civil 18
dissuasiveness 241

effectiveness 240
meaning of 239
proportionality 241–242
relationship between enforcement and 242
preventive enforcement 24, 30, 229
principal-agent 207, 214, 225, 226
private associations 175, 238, 246, 255
private enforcement *see* enforcement
private law enforcement *see* law enforcement
procedural autonomy 179, 189, 235, 239, 262
national 13, 237, 238, 239, 243
professional diligence 2, 4, 22, 25, 27, 30, 38, 41, 67, 68, 112, 114, 116, 144, 166, 168
meaning of 2
requirement of 141–143
test 146–150
violation of 27, 32
public enforcement *see* enforcement
Purely Creative 3, 38, 40, 41, 66, 70, 73, 74, 80, 81, 101, 117

rational apathy 206, 210, 212, 213, 218, 222
rational disinterest 251
regulation on consumer protection cooperation 23, 208, 244–246, 253, 256, 258, 262

sanctions 13, 17, 102–104, 156, 157, 188, 205, 219, 227, 228, 235, 243, 255, 262
administrative 236
dissuasive 241–242
effective 240, 248
civil 257
criminal *see* criminal sanctions
criminal law 12, 220–221
stringent 257
self-interest 21, 40
self-reliance 21, 40
self-regulation 5, 12, 15, 137, 138, 141, 144, 145, 149, 150, 151, 152, 159, 161–168, 222, 228, 229, 230, 236, 238
in advertising 147
of B2C practices 152
of commercial practices directed to consumers 139
costs 223
definition of 137
value of 224
skimming off procedure 180–182, 187, 191, 194, 198, 214, 240, 252, 253
Supreme Court 7, 22, 40, 41
Dutch 7
French 147
German 67, 74

trade associations 142, 145, 152, 153, 164, 165
Trade Descriptions Act (TDA) 1968 27, 29, 159
transport policy 94
Treating Customers Fairly (TCF) 34

vulnerable consumers *see* consumer/s

young consumers *see* consumer/s